"This volume is an essential handbook for everyone from the lay reader to public leaders. It brings together an incredible group of talent to break down this highly complex and misunderstood area. This is precisely the type of thoughtful engagement and research needed right now on this critical topic."

Kathleen Claussen, *Associate Professor at the University of Miami School of Law, USA*

"Seventeen experts of the mechanisms and political motives behind the Chinese Communist Party's legal, illegal and grayzone technology transfer efforts present a profound analysis of the system's structure, mode of operation, scale, and its consequences for liberal, open societies worldwide. Forcefully and convincingly, the book makes a strong argument that confronted with this particular challenge for global leadership, ignorance is harmful and remedying the situation is urgent."

Volker Stanzel, *scholar at the German Institute for International and Security Affairs, former German ambassador to China and Japan*

"The intentions and practices of the Chinese Communist Party are perhaps the most important things for policymakers and the general public to understand in today's world. 'Beyond Espionage' provides excellent insight into these issues and should be required reading for anyone involved with technology policy, economic policy or national security."

Matthew Turpin, *former Director for China, U.S. National Security Council*

"In today's contested world, it is vitally important for decision makers and researchers to have access to unfettered, apolitical analyses of otherwise highly politicized subjects. This book does that. It provides an insightful description of the nexus between technology and sovereignty, and undistorted analytical advice on issues that will reshape the global order in years to come."

Daniel P. Bagge, *Cyber Attaché of the Czech Republic to the United States*

"China is engaged in the most systematic, well-funded and comprehensive technology transfer strategy in history. There is no more important topic with implications for U.S. national security. This collection of expert perspectives is a must-read to place the current technology race with China in context."

Michael Brown, *Co-Author of the DIUx Report and former Presidential Innovation Fellow*

CHINA'S QUEST FOR FOREIGN TECHNOLOGY

This book analyzes China's foreign technology acquisition activity and how this has helped its rapid rise to superpower status.

Since 1949, China has operated a vast and unique system of foreign technology spotting and transfer aimed at accelerating civilian and military development, reducing the cost of basic research, and shoring up its power domestically and abroad—without running the political risks borne by liberal societies as a basis for their creative developments. While discounted in some circles as derivative and consigned to perpetual catch-up mode, China's "hybrid" system of legal, illegal, and extralegal import of foreign technology, combined with its indigenous efforts, is, the authors believe, enormously effective and must be taken seriously. Accordingly, in this volume, 17 international specialists combine their scholarship to portray the system's structure and functioning in heretofore unseen detail, using primary Chinese sources to demonstrate the perniciousness of the problem in a manner not likely to be controverted. The book concludes with a series of recommendations culled from the authors' interactions with experts worldwide.

This book will be of much interest to students of Chinese politics, US foreign policy, intelligence studies, science and technology studies, and International Relations in general.

William C. Hannas is Professor and Lead Analyst at the Center for Security and Emerging Technology (CSET), Georgetown University, Washington, DC, USA. Prior to this he was a member of the Central Intelligence Agency's leadership cadre and a three-time recipient of its McCone Award.

Didi Kirsten Tatlow is Senior Fellow at the German Council on Foreign Relations in Berlin, Germany, and Senior Non-Resident Fellow at Project Sinopsis in Prague, Czech Republic.

Asian Security Studies

Series Editors: Sumit Ganguly,
Indiana University, USA,
Andrew Scobell,
Research and Development (RAND) Corporation, USA, and
Alice Ba,
University of Delaware, USA

Few regions of the world are fraught with as many security questions as Asia. Within this region it is possible to study great power rivalries, irredentist conflicts, nuclear and ballistic missile proliferation, secessionist movements, ethnoreligious conflicts and inter-state wars. This book series publishes the best possible scholarship on the security issues affecting the region, and includes detailed empirical studies, theoretically oriented case studies and policy-relevant analyses as well as more general works.

China and International Nuclear Weapons Proliferation
Strategic Assistance
Henrik Stålhane Hiim

Reshaping the Chinese Military
The PLA's Roles and Missions in the Xi Jinping Era
Edited by Richard A. Bitzinger and James Char

India's Nuclear Proliferation Policy
The Impact of Secrecy on Decision Making, 1980–2010
Gaurav Kampani

China's Quest for Foreign Technology
Beyond Espionage
Edited by William C. Hannas and Didi Kirsten Tatlow

For more information about this series, please visit: www.routledge.com/
Asian-Security-Studies/book-series/ASS

CHINA'S QUEST FOR FOREIGN TECHNOLOGY

Beyond Espionage

Edited by William C. Hannas and Didi Kirsten Tatlow

Routledge
Taylor & Francis Group

LONDON AND NEW YORK

First published 2021
by Routledge
2 Park Square, Milton Park, Abingdon, Oxon OX14 4RN

and by Routledge
52 Vanderbilt Avenue, New York, NY 10017

Routledge is an imprint of the Taylor & Francis Group, an informa business

British Library Cataloguing-in-Publication Data
A catalogue record for this book is available from the British Library

Library of Congress Cataloging-in-Publication Data
Names: Hannas, Wm. C., 1946– editor. | Tatlow, Didi Kirsten, 1967– editor.
Title: China's quest for foreign technology : beyond espionage / edited by William C. Hannas and Didi Kirsten Tatlow.
Description: Milton Park, Abingdon, Oxon ; New York, NY: Routledge, 2021. |
Series: Asian security studies | Includes bibliographical references and index.
Identifiers: LCCN 2020017064 (print) | LCCN 2020017065 (ebook) | ISBN 9780367473594 (hbk) | ISBN 9780367473570 (pbk) | ISBN 9781003035084 (ebk)
Subjects: LCSH: Technology and state–China. | Technology transfer–China. | Business intelligence–China.
Classification: LCC T27.C5 C552175 2021 (print) | LCC T27.C5 (ebook) | DDC 338.951/06–dc23
LC record available at https://lccn.loc.gov/2020017064
LC ebook record available at https://lccn.loc.gov/2020017065

ISBN: 978-0-367-47359-4 (hbk)
ISBN: 978-0-367-47357-0 (pbk)
ISBN: 978-1-003-03508-4 (ebk)

Typeset in Bembo
by Wearset Ltd, Boldon, Tyne and Wear

CONTENTS

FIGURES

TABLES

CONTRIBUTORS

Huey-Meei Chang is a Research Analyst at Georgetown University's Center for Security and Emerging Technology (CSET). Huey began her career as a data analyst at Taiwan's Academia Sinica, Institute of Biomedical Sciences, before emigrating to the United States. She is currently writing on China's plan to "merge" AI and human intelligence.

Ryan Fedasiuk is a Research Analyst at Georgetown's Center for Security and Emerging Technology (CSET). His work focuses on the intersection of artificial intelligence and strategic stability. He holds a BA in International Studies from American University, and studies Russian language and literature.

Hinnerk Feldwisch-Drentrup is a Berlin-based journalist writing for Spiegel Online, Zeit Online, Stern, the German Press Agency (dpa) and more. Hinnerk studied neuroinformatics and physics. He received a "Science Journalist of the Year" prize in 2018 for co-founding the online magazine "MedWatch," and has also received a "Netzwende-Award."

William C. Hannas is Professor and Lead Analyst at Georgetown's Center for Security and Emerging Technology. Prior to joining CSET in 2019, Bill was part of the Central Intelligence Agency's leadership cadre and a three-time recipient of its McCone Award. He has written several books on East Asia and was primary author of *Chinese Industrial Espionage* (2013).

Alex Joske is an analyst at the Australian Strategic Policy Institute's International Cyber Policy Centre. His research focuses on China's political influence and technology transfer efforts. He holds a BA in Chinese language from the

Australian National University, and has studied at National Taiwan Normal University.

Elsa Kania is a PhD student in Harvard University's Department of Government. Elsa is an Adjunct Senior Fellow with the Technology and National Security Program at the Center for a New American Security, a 2018 Fulbright Specialist, and Non-Resident Fellow with the Australian Strategic Policy Institute's International Cyber Policy Centre.

James Mulvenon is Director for Intelligence Integration of SOS International's Intelligence Solutions Group, where he recruited and trained a team of nearly 50 linguists. James has a BA in China Studies from the University of Michigan, a Ph.D. in political science from UCLA, and studied CPC history at Fudan University in Shanghai. In 2013, he co-authored *Chinese Industrial Espionage*.

Dahlia Peterson is a Research Analyst at Georgetown's Center for Security and Emerging Technology (CSET). Prior that she researched how China harnesses predictive policing algorithms and facial, voice, and gait recognition technologies for AI-powered surveillance programs. She has presented at the Internet Freedom Festival and at the Electronic Frontier Foundation.

Anna B. Puglisi was the US government's National Counterintelligence Officer for East Asia until 2020, now Senior Fellow at Georgetown University's CSET. She has an MPA and MS in Environmental Science from Indiana University, studied at Princeton in Beijing Chinese language school, and was visiting scholar in Nankai University's Department of Economics. She is the third co-author of *Chinese Industrial Espionage*.

Andrew Spear leads the Intelligence team at Strider Technologies. He was an analyst in the Office of the US Trade Representative where he worked on the Section 301 Investigation into IPR appropriation. He lived and worked in China for eight years. He has an MBA from the University of Hong Kong, an MA from Johns Hopkins SAIS, and was a Boren Fellow at the Hopkins-Nanjing Center.

Jeffrey Stoff is a linguist and analyst in the Department of Defense specializing in technology transfer. He has advised the National Security Council, Office of Science and Technology Policy, and multiple government departments. Jeffrey has received several ODNI awards, including the National Counterintelligence and Security Center Director's Award for Excellence.

Karen M. Sutter is a specialist in Asian Trade and Finance at the Congressional Research Service. She served as a special advisor at the US Department of Treasury and senior analyst at the CIA and led China research at the US–China

Business Council and the Atlantic Council. She worked and studied in Beijing and Taipei and received an MA from the University of Washington.

Didi Kirsten Tatlow is Senior Fellow at the German Council on Foreign Relations in Berlin, and Senior Non-Resident Fellow at Sinopsis research and media project in Prague. A graduate of the Beijing Language Institute and SOAS in London, she has been a journalist in Asia and Europe, most recently with the *New York Times* in Beijing. A Hong Konger, Didi speaks English, Chinese, and German and has received multiple journalism awards.

Greg Walton is an IT specialist who has investigated complex adaptive threats targeting civil society networks. Greg coordinated the primary field-based research for the GhostNet and the ShadowNet investigations with a team that uncovered global cyberespionage botnets operating out of China. Greg is currently a Fellow at the SecDev Foundation.

Peter Wood is a Defense Analyst at a Virginia-based defense contractor. Peter previously served as Editor of *China Brief* at the Jamestown Foundation between June 2015 and February 2018. He has an MA from the Johns Hopkins–Nanjing University Center and a BA from Texas Tech University.

Chenny Zhang is China Portfolio Lead for the Defense Innovation Board in the Office of the Secretary of Defense, where she supports initiatives to counter Chinese economic espionage in the US technology sector. Chenny has a BA from Boston College and MA from the Johns Hopkins School of Advanced International Studies, and lived in China for over seven years.

PREFACE

This book is about China's rise as a neo-totalitarian technological power, made possible through access to science and technology created by countries it now challenges for global leadership. Our aims are to describe this astonishing, yet poorly understood, phenomenon in an accurate and convincing manner for policymakers and the general public, and to propose solutions to protect, and improve, the open societies of the liberal world order.

Technology challenges all of us. Its power must be shaped toward the human good, defined by the people themselves. Where its power is shaped only by government or corporations lies great room for abuse. The present authors are concerned that this is the direction technology is going in China under conditions of political opacity, social management by the Communist Party of China (CPC), and a tightening concentration of power that enables party leadership to skew technology to support its survival, with few checks on technology's creation or consequences.

How did we get here? In short: decades of technology transfer followed by prompt and wide application, and growing indigenous innovation resulting from that transfer. Since 1949, a vast, deliberate, and unique system of foreign technology spotting and transfer has operated in China and overseas. Very little of it is secret. The projects are described in party and state documents, announced in the media, and executed in venues that are, broadly speaking, not hidden from the outside world.

"Make the West serve China," Mao's well-known dictum, illustrates the goal well. The phrase grew out of an older question: how to manage the impact of the West and Japan upon imperial China, which sought to exclude outside forces? And the dictum mimics a solution proposed one and a half centuries ago by Chinese reformers: combine "Chinese substance and Western form" (中体西用).

In other words, remain Chinese in essence (as defined now by the CPC), but "use" the West for practical matters.

This is where things stand today. China's leaders not only have achieved an historic goal of co-opting foreign technology to preserve (and extend) the autocratic state, they are also addressing a millennia-old contradiction between innovation in practical areas, where China excels, and an historical aversion to theoretical science. They are doing this by relying on foreign sources to supplement homegrown creativity, which is challenged by social and political norms that discourage innovation in other life domains.

The result is a distortion of global technology flows induced by China's manipulation of access venues. If this were not troubling enough, the Party's vision of technology as a device for social control is increasingly shaping the outside world through the export of "safe cities," telecommunications, language processing, security and transportation "solutions," and more. Western countries support this authoritarian makeover of civilization by transferring enabling technologies to China wittingly (through business interests or development), or negligently (through ignorance or a lack of due diligence).

Accordingly, this book focuses on various aspects of the China technology transfer issue, especially its extralegal and "informal" practices that fall between open purchases on the one hand and clandestine operations on the other hand. Until recently these practices eluded the attention of everyone, even though they account for many, perhaps most, of China's foreign technology acquisitions. We hope to clarify how these composite systems work in practice and foster appropriate responses.

The following chapters provide a foundation for thinking about these problems. They are arranged in six parts to showcase (I) the transfer system's structure, (II) its function in commerce and defense, and (III) its global scale of operation, followed by (IV) illustrative case studies, and (V) an exposé of foreign technology's role in China's military, surveillance, and United Front enterprises. Part VI looks at student transfer issues and espionage, as a lead-up to mitigation efforts.

A compendium of remedies is given in the volume's conclusion. These recommendations are made by the editors, exclusive of our co-authors employed by the US government, whose bylaws prohibit such statements. There is also a multilingual glossary of organizations and terms. We have sought to minimize duplication. In those cases where we failed, we endeavor to provide a consistent nomenclature to facilitate continuity between chapters.

Some readers may be familiar with an earlier book (2013) on the subject by three of this volume's authors.[1] Differences, besides the seven-year update, are an expansion of topics, a larger and more diverse authorship, greater use of primary sources (particularly in Europe where this field of study is new), more latitude of expression (some of us are no longer in government service), and the benefit of feedback from former readers. The earlier work has value as a primer and for its coverage of a few areas we did not feel the need to replicate here.

The editors wish to thank our contributors, who labored under short deadlines balancing full-time jobs, family, and other writing commitments. Their dedication was extraordinary. We are particularly indebted to our colleague Huey-Meei Chang, who besides her own chapters supported the entire volume with research, critiques, and tireless editing. Thanks also are due James Mulvenon, Anna Puglisi, Andrew Spear, Jeffrey Stoff, Remco Zwetsloot and, especially, Scott Livingston, who read parts of the manuscript and offered helpful suggestions.

We thank the German Council on Foreign Relations (DGAP) in Berlin, Germany, for their support and understanding of the time demands imposed by the project, and Sinopsis, the research institute and website in Prague, Czech Republic, for editing and other support. We also thank the directors of Georgetown University's Center for Security and Emerging Technology for their review of chapters and forbearance in allowing several of CSET's staff the latitude to contribute. Opinions expressed in the book are the editors' and co-authors' alone, and do not necessarily reflect the views of organizations with which any of us are now affiliated or have been in the past.

A word on motivation. None of us holds extreme positions. Our politics are moderate and sample both sides of the spectrum. That 17 of us[2] with mixed demographics, geographical origins, diverse academic backgrounds, and age gaps that span a half century could come together to produce this study suggests the problem we articulate is real and abiding. That being so, we offer two thoughts, one hopeful, the other cautionary.

No one here harbors animus toward China. On the contrary, most of us are Chinese linguists, whose backgrounds, circumstances, and ethnicity dispose us favorably to China, its culture, and people, wherever they reside. This is not an apology but a statement of fact. We believe the camaraderie we share in our microcosm will someday characterize the world we live in.

Rather, our pique is with the practices of a sovereign state and its political decision-makers, who skew what could be beneficial exchanges among the world's scientific talent for singular gain, and also with the foreign enablers of these practices, without whom China's lopsided programs would not succeed. We focus on this matter with the aim of restoring normalcy to international S&T, and other, relations. Ignoring it is no longer possible.

William C. Hannas
Didi Kirsten Tatlow

Notes

1 Hannas, Mulvenon, Puglisi. *Chinese Industrial Espionage*, Routledge, 2013.
2 For those counting, please note that one of our contributors cannot be acknowledged publicly.

ABBREVIATIONS

111 Project	Project of Introducing Talents of Academic Disciplines to Universities
863 Program	National High Technology Research and Development Plan
973 Program	National Basic Research Program
ACFROC	All-Chinese Federation of Returned Overseas Chinese
ACSE	Association of Chinese-American Scientists and Engineers
ACSEJ	Association of Chinese Scientists and Engineers in Japan
AECA	Arms Export Control Act
AECC	Aero Engine Corporation of China
AI	artificial intelligence
APT	advanced persistent threat
ASEAN	Association of Southeast Asian Nations
ASEM	Asia–Europe Meeting
ASPI	Australian Strategic Policy Institute
AVIC	China Aviation Industry Corporation
BAFA	Economy Affairs and Export Control (Germany)
BfV	Bundesamt für Verfassungsschutz
BIT	Beijing Institute of Technology
BMBF	Federal Ministry of Education and Research (Germany)
BRI	Belt and Road Initiative
BUAA	Beijing University of Aeronautics and Astronautics
CAAGC	Chinese American Association of Greater Chicago Area
CAE	Chinese Academy of Engineering
CAEP	China Academy of Engineering Physics
CAIEP	China International Talent Exchange Association
CALT	China Academy of Launch Vehicle Technology

CAPST	Chinese Association of Professionals in Science and Technology
CAS	Chinese Academy of Sciences
CASC	China Aerospace Science and Technology Corporation
CASD	Federation of Chinese Student and Scholar Societies in Germany
CASIA	CAS's Institute of Automation
CASIC	China Aerospace Science and Industry Corporation
CAST	China Association for Science and Technology
CBRC	China Banking Regulatory Commission
CCL	Commerce Control List
CCP	Chinese Communist Party (see "Communist Party of China")
CCSTI	Cooperation Centre for Science, Technology and Innovation
CDB	China Development Bank
CDHT	Chengdu High-Tech Industrial Development Zone
CDSTIC	China Defense Science and Technology Information Center
CEC	China Electronics Corporation
CETC	China Electronics Technology Group Corporation
CETCA	CETC Avionics Company
CFIUS	Committee for Foreign Investment in the United States
CIC	China Investment Corporation
CICC	China Institute for Command and Control
CICIIF	China Integrated Circuit Industry Investment Fund
CITTC	China International Technology Transfer Center
CITTC	China–Italy Technology Transfer Center
CMI	civil–military integration
CNKI	China National Knowledge Infrastructure
CNNC	China National Nuclear Corporation
CNRS	Centre National De La Recherche Rcientifique
COMAC	Commercial Aircraft Corporation of China
COSTIND	Commission for Science, Technology and Industry for National Defense
CPC	Communist Party of China
CPPCC	Chinese People's Political Consultative Conference
CSIRO	Commonwealth Scientific and Industrial Research Organisation (Australia)
CSIS	Canadian Security Intelligence Service
CSITTC	China–Switzerland International Technology Transfer Center
CSRC	China Securities Regulatory Commission
CSSA	Chinese Student and Scholar Association
DARPA	Department of Defense Advanced Research Projects Agency (US)
DDTC	Directorate of Defense Trade Controls (US)
DNI	Director of National Intelligence

DOD	Department of Defense (US)
DOE	Department of Energy (US)
DOJ	Department of Justice (US)
E2C2	Export Enforcement Coordination Center
EAR	export administration regulations
ECRI	Export Control Reform Initiative
EEA	Economic Espionage Act (US)
EFI	espionage and foreign interference
EO	executive order
FBI	Federal Bureau of Investigation (US)
FCPA	Foreign Corrupt Practices Act
FCPAE	Federation of Chinese Professional Associations in Europe
FFRDC	federally funded research and development center (US)
FIRRMA	Foreign Investment Risk Review Modernization Act
FYP	five-year plan
FZJ	Forschungszentrum Jülich
GAD	General Armament Department
GCAAI	German–Chinese Association of Artificial Intelligence
GCCCD	Association of Chinese Chemists and Chemical Engineers in Germany
GCI	Gesellschaft Chinesischer Informatiker in Deutschland
GDNT	Guangdong–Nortel Telecommunication Equipment Co.
GDPCH	Society for German Professors of Chinese Origin
HIT	Harbin Institute of Technology
HOME	Help Our Motherland through Elite Intellectual Resources from Overseas
HZDR	Helmholtz–Zentrum Dresden–Rossendorf
IDDS	National Innovation-Driven Development Strategy
IJOP	integrated joint operations platform
IP	intellectual property
IPR	intellectual property rights
IRS	Internal Revenue Service (US)
ISTIC	Institute of Scientific and Technical Information of China
IT	information technology
ITAR	International Trafficking in Arms Regulation
JCSAE	Japan Chinese Society of Automotive Engineers
JICA	Japanese International Cooperation Agency
JST	Japan Science and Technology Agency
JV	joint venture
KAIST	Korea Advanced Institute of Science and Technology
KIC	Korea Innovation Center in China
LBNL	Lawrence Berkeley National Laboratory
LERU	League of European Research Universities

LfV	Landesamt für Verfassungsschutz
MBI	Max-Born-Institut
MCF	military–civil fusion
MIC 2025	Made in China 2025
MIIT	Ministry of Industry and Information Technology
MLAA	Mutual Legal Assistance Agreement
MLP	Medium- and Long-Term Plan for S&T Development
MNC	multinational corporation
MOE	Ministry of Education
MOF	Ministry of Finance
MOFCOM	Ministry of Commerce
MOHRSS	Ministry of Human Resources and Social Security
MOP	Ministry of Personnel
MOST	Ministry of Science and Technology
MPS	Ministry of Public Security
MSIRC	Military Science Information Research Center
MSRA	Microsoft Research Asia
MSS	Ministry of State Security
MTCR	Missile Technology Control Regime
NATO	North Atlantic Treaty Organization
NDAA	National Defense Authorization Act
NDRC	National Development and Reform Commission
NGO	non-governmental organization
NIH	National Institutes of Health (US)
NNSF	National Natural Science Foundation
NNUT	National University of Defense Technology
NOAA	National Oceanic and Atmospheric Administration (US)
NORINCO	China Ordnance Industries Group Corporation
NSDD	National Security Decision Directive
NSF	National Science Foundation (US)
NSFC	Natural Science Foundation of China
NTTC	National Technology Transfer Center
NUAA	Nanjing University of Aeronautics and Astronautics
NWPU	Northwest Polytechnical University
OCAO	Overseas Chinese Affairs Office
OCS	overseas Chinese scholars
OCSTOF	Overseas Chinese Science and Technology Organization Federation
ODA	Official Development Assistance (Japan)
ODI	overseas direct investment
OECD	Organization of Economic Cooperation and Development
OECGIW	Austria–China International Economic and Trade Promotion Association

PACER	Public Access to Court Electronic Records System
PAP	People's Armed Police
PBOC	People's Bank of China
PLA	People's Liberation Army
PLAAF	PLA Air Forice
PLAN	People's Liberation Army Navy
PRC	People's Republic of China
R&D	research and development
RAND	Research and Development Corporation
REEs	rare earth elements
RMB	renminbi
ROK	Republic of Korea
S&T	science and technology
SABPA	Sino-America Biotechnology and Pharmaceutical Professional Association
SAFE	State Administration of Foreign Exchange
SAFEA	State Administration of Foreign Expert Affairs
SASAC	State-owned Assets Supervision and Administration Commission
SASTIND	State Administration of Science & Technology Industry for National Defense
SC	State Council
SCBA	Seattle Chinese Biomedical Association
SCEA	Silicon Valley Chinese Engineers Association
SIPRI	Stockholm International Peace Research Institute
SME	small-and-medium enterprise
SOE	state-owned enterprise
STEM	science, technology, engineering and mathematics
TTP	Thousand Talents Plan
UCAHP	US–China Association of High-Level Professionals
UF	United Front
UFWD	United Front Work Department
USML	United States Munitions List
USTR	United States Trade Representative
USW	Service Workers International Union
VC	venture capital
WFOE	wholly foreign-owned enterprise
WRSA	Western Returned Scholars Association
WTO	World Trade Organization
ZGC	Zhongguancun
ZIB	Zuse Institute Berlin

PART I
China's transfer venues

1

CHINESE TECHNOLOGY TRANSFER

An introduction

William C. Hannas and Huey-Meei Chang

China's reputation for innovative technology, exemplified in popular lore by its "four great inventions"[1] and chronicled in Joseph Needham's encyclopedic account,[2] has lost its luster in recent decades as reports of industrial espionage swamp mainstream media, and accounts of systematic intellectual property rights (IPR) abuse emerge into public view.

Evidence for this behavior is pervasive.[3] Less well known perhaps is that China's appetite for foreign technology is not a new phenomenon, and not an aberration in historical terms. That is, these practices did not begin with the founding of the People's Republic in 1949. Indeed, as will be shown below, China has struggled with a "creativity problem" for much of its history. The implications of this dependency are two-fold:

- On the one hand, attempts by foreign governments to manage China's licit and illicit transfers have had little effect, since they are rooted in habits that date back more than a century—longer if one considers cognitive preferences—and cannot be changed easily.
- On the other hand, China's ability to compete internationally despite this apparent handicap suggests that its *composite innovation system*[4]—whatever one thinks of it—has merit, and must be confronted on its own terms as a viable developmental model.

In part a product of conscious design, in part a consequence of a mindset that accords priority to practical achievement, China has built a hybrid structure that is able to exploit foreign successes, while drawing on indigenous resources as needed. Western hopes notwithstanding, there is little prospect it will transition to a "normal" (Western) model on its own.

This chapter begins with an overview of the mechanisms supporting China's drive to acquire foreign technology "by various means" (以多种方式),[5] as a foundation for exploring its causes and as an introduction to later chapters that discuss its workings and consequences.

Our immediate goal is to trace the system's development, catalog its enablers, discuss venues through which foreign technology acquires "Chinese characteristics" (i.e., is commercialized), and lay out the statutory record that ties this activity to the state. A final section addresses the myths that inhibit effective countermeasures.

Changing the soup without changing the medicine

China's quest for the world's technology began in the mid-nineteenth century in reaction to foreign threats. As always, the motivation was practical necessity. China had lost a series of wars to imperialist powers and was forced to cede territory and sovereignty. Encumbered by a moribund education system, by a social structure that rewarded the least adaptive elements of society,[6] and by its own history of success, the country was ill-prepared to counter the spectrum of challenges that industrialized nations posed.

Sweeping changes needed to effect meaningful reforms, such as those made in Japan during the Meiji era (1868–1911), were not possible in China given its size, past, and the hubris of its ruling class. What followed were efforts to patch the system without changing its nature—changing the soup without changing the medicine (换汤不换药).[7] These efforts include, notably, China's self-strengthening movement (自强运动, 1861–1895)[8] and, especially, Zhang Zhidong's (张之洞, 1837–1909) famous proposal to take "Chinese learning as substance, Western learning for application" (中学为体，西学为用).[9] Forced to choose between loss of autonomy and forfeiting its cultural identity, China sought the middle ground of acquiring abroad what was needed—but only what was needed—to preserve its traditional way of life.[10]

Unsurprisingly, the "ti-yong" (体用) proposition has been criticized universally for ignoring the social milieu of which technology is a part. Importation begs the question of how a technology can be replicated and sustained, absent the conditions that brought it to life. Yet it is impossible to look at China's subsequent history and fail to appreciate that this same formula, though not explicitly stated, has guided China's post-1949 industrial development—not unsuccessfully.[11]

Today China prospers in many technological fields through indigenous and foreign-inspired efforts, while maintaining a political structure not far removed from traditional norms. The country continues to exercise its remarkable ability to adapt, apply, and improve technology, while compensating for a lack of "Western" style creativity by reaching abroad.

If *ti-yong* is a failure, it is a remarkably persistent one.

In the same vein, China has sent hundreds of thousands of students abroad to enrich its technological base without impacting China's survival as an authoritarian dictatorship. The practice began in 1872, when China sent 120 students to the United States, and has grown to where some 25 percent of science, technology, engineering, and mathematics (STEM) graduates in the US are Chinese nationals.[12] What is notable—beyond the dependency itself—is that the West's dream of returnees transforming China into a liberal replica of the West is no closer to reality than a century and a half ago, when the first batch of students returned to find that their cultural makeover was unwelcome.[13]

Has the situation changed? Here is an excerpt from Chinese President Xi Jinping's speech in 2013 to an overseas student organization,[14] in which Xi doubles down on a statement made by one of his predecessors:

> As Comrade Deng Xiaoping profoundly pointed out, "We are carrying out socialist modernization to catch up with the developed capitalist countries economically and, politically, *create a higher and more effective democracy than the capitalist countries*. Moreover, we will train more and better skilled persons than in those countries."[15]

The message is clear: the goal of foreign study is, as before, a stronger China; "Western" democracy is not part of the agenda. Bring back the technology, leave the baggage where you found it —the very essence of *ti-yong*.

Between then and now China has steadily grown its state-supported apparatus for transferring foreign technology, from its early "lean to one side" (一边倒) reliance on Soviet Russia (1950s); through the establishment of a world-class open-source document procurement system in 1956; joint R&D ventures and more overseas study after China's "opening" in 1978; mobilization of diaspora networks and proliferation of foreign-based S&T support associations from the late 1980s; multiple foreign "talent" (人才) outreach programs beginning in 1994; the creation of Overseas Chinese Scholar (OCS) returnee parks also in 1994, where ideas (and IPR) accessed abroad are commercialized in safe and subsidized enclaves; the National Technology Transfer Centers, which link Chinese developers to the latest foreign technologies (2001); and more recently, leveraged buyouts of technology-rich companies, state-funded "angel" investments, and sponsorship of international start-up competitions—not to mention direct purchases, trade-for-technology clauses, overseas subsidiaries (tech spotting and talent acquisition), state-hosted technology exchange forums (physical and virtual), patent mining, "dual-base" labs, short-term consultative visits, appointments of foreigners to advisory staffs, and a host of illicit activities (a fraction of which are discussed in Chapter 17).

These venues will be discussed in detail later in subsequent chapters. Meanwhile, the authors, with the benefit of age and hindsight, wish to temper earlier statements disparaging of China's derivative approach to national development[16] by acknowledging that China has succeeded in achieving what more than a century ago seemed impossible: modernization and near-parity in the technology needed to preserve the autocratic Chinese state, with little change in its essential characteristics.

How long the foreign enablers of technology transfer—nations victimized by these "exchanges" with China—will endure this state of affairs is another matter entirely.

China's foreign tech transfer infrastructure

Several years ago, three of the present book's authors surveyed the venues and access points used by China to transfer foreign technology. Our findings were incorporated in a study released in 2013.[17] At that time, we identified fewer than 300 state-run technology conversion enclaves—the returnee "parks" and "technology transfer centers" that cover China's landscape, converting knowhow acquired abroad into durable artifacts. We also had data on some 60 Sino-foreign science and technology (S&T) professional organizations globally—ethnic guilds of technical experts abroad responsive to Beijing's transfer incentives—along with information on China's outreach organizations, transfer programs, and foreign facilitators.

A few years later in 2017, we revisited the issue in an unpublished whitepaper. Using the same publicly available information (i.e., "open sources"), we determined that the same government offices in China and their affiliated support groups abroad were still actively transferring foreign technology, but the number of conversion facilities, under whatever name, had risen to 900 and our count of Sino-foreign professional associations exceeded 100. In mid-2019, these latter two figures were hovering at 2,000 and 200, respectively, according to independent counts,[18] with no decline in the activity observed across other access venues—i.e., the same organizations were still engaging in the usual transfer practices. We had no difficulty in 2019 finding examples of every type of transfer delineated in the 2013 and 2017 studies.[19]

The increase in the number of conversion facilities—and in overseas support groups feeding them—might be attributed to better search methodology, were it not for the fact that the growth coincided with new government transfer programs (see below), an expansion in foreign "talent" recruitment,[20] a rescoping of targeted co-optees,[21] and the introduction of new forms of transfer, such as state "angel investments" and start-up competitions in advanced countries.

This applies to legal and "extralegal" channels. Meanwhile, data compiled by the Center for Strategic and International Studies of "publicly reported instances of Chinese espionage directed at the United States" shows 27 percent of the cases occurring in 2000–2009 and the remaining 73 percent in the following decade 2010–2019.[22] Economically motivated cybercrime—the third pillar of Chinese technology transfer—may also be rising. According to CrowdStrike:

> Driven by requirements laid out under the government's Made in China 2025 Plan, Chinese threat actors have been observed targeting

technology, energy, and healthcare sectors. During the past year, CrowdStrike has identified an uptick in China-based adversaries, due in part to the souring U.S.-Sino relations.[23]

Our point here, buttressed in the section below on statutory indicators, is that there is little ground to support a belief that growth in China's indigenous innovation—if it is happening at all—is accompanied by a decline in China's predatory transfer behavior.

To put things in perspective, here is an outline of the major technology transfer venues and practices used by China over the decades and validated as recently as 2019.[24] These transfer vectors are categories, each with several to several thousand examples.

"Extralegal" indicates that the types of transfer these organizations sponsor typically are not subject to outside scrutiny, hence the legality of the transactions is unknowable. Examples of document acquisition facilities are the Institute of Scientific and Technical Information of China (中国科学技术信息研究所) and its military analog the China Defense Science and Technology Information Center (中国国防科技信息中心). The two are components of

TABLE 1.1 Legal transfers[25]

China-based foreign subsidiaries	Joint research agreements
Conferences and colloquia	Patent mining and exploitation
Direct technology purchases	PRC-backed venture capital funds
Enrollments at US universities	Startup competitions
Foreign-based labs, representative offices	State-backed investments in foreign research
Investments/acquisition of companies	Tech exchanges, trade-for-tech agreements

TABLE 1.2 Illegal transfers

Breach of contract	Reverse engineering
Copyright infringement	Traditional espionage
Computer network exploitation	Violation of NDAs
Insider operations	Willful patent infringement

TABLE 1.3 Extralegal transfers (organizations)

Document acquisition facilities	Recruiting and brokerage websites
Foreign-based alumni associations	Sino-foreign professional associations
Foreign-based facilitation companies	Technology transfer centers
Front organizations for PRC offices	Technology transfer forums
Overseas scholar returnee facilities	Transfer incentive programs
PRC ministry offices (national, local)	University-linked 'innovation' parks

China's foreign S&T literature acquisition network, arguably the world's finest. Returnee parks, "pioneering" parks, tech transfer centers and technology "incubators"—large physical complexes storeys high and acres wide—share the common mission of commercializing foreign technology and are mostly opaque to outside observers. Their distinctions, an artifact of sponsorship, are evaporating.

Extralegal conduits supporting technology transfer also include the Sino-foreign professional associations discussed above, with memberships that can exceed 10,000. "Talent" recruitment programs spot overseas scientists and engineers with skills needed for PRC technical projects. These programs offer incentives for support that range from a year or more onsite to a "two-bases" (两个基地) schema whereby a candidate remains abroad and sends information to China. "Thousand Talents Plan" (千人计划) is commonly cited, but there are hundreds of such programs.

Although aspects of these networks are highly systematized (patent and standards exploitation, civilian and military open-source procurement, "talent" spotting and recruitment), much of it is decentralized. New initiatives are piled on and programs adapt as needed. At its root, we view this behavior less as the output of a system and more as the product of a particular mindset that has evolved over decades—probably centuries—to regard practical achievement as primary and the theory supporting these accomplishments of less relevance.

Whatever the motivation, it is clear that China more than any other country[26] devotes extraordinary efforts to reduce the risk and cost of innovation by accessing research done elsewhere. We do not see this pattern changing soon or ever.

TABLE 1.4 Extralegal transfers (personnel)

- Professional facilitators
  ◦ administrators of returnee parks and tech transfer centers
  ◦ diplomats at embassies and consulates (S&T consuls)
  ◦ employees of NGOs that front for declared transfer facilities
  ◦ managers of 'talent' recruitment and other incentive programs

- Scientists, overseas scholars and entrepreneurs
  ◦ attendees at overseas exchange forums
  ◦ awardees of sponsored transfer incentive programs
  ◦ members of overseas Chinese professional associations
  ◦ organized alumni of Chinese technical universities
  ◦ PRC post-docs at foreign research facilities

- S&T intelligence workers (科技情报工作人员)
  ◦ talent spotters attached to factories and labs
  ◦ members of S&T 'business intelligence' groups
  ◦ staffers of China's open source S&T collection network

The statutory record

China's foreign technology transfer practices are not part of a diabolical master plan hatched in secret to defeat the West. By the same token, they did not arise spontaneously from the action of independent opportunists. Rather, the Chinese state over the course of decades has enacted hundreds[27] of statutory provisions to promote foreign transfers in an overlapping mosaic that is more ad hoc than the product of premeditated design.

While we do not deny the existence of state-supported industrial espionage, many—perhaps most—of these transactions stem from measures announced openly: indeed, they must be to reach their intended audiences. We list ten such programs to provide a sense of how the system developed over its formative decade, just before and after the turn of the millennium, and to illustrate the program's links to the Chinese state.

1994: "*MOP Notice on 'Implementing Temporary Measures to Subsidize Overseas Chinese Scholars who Return to China for Short Periods to Work in Areas Outside the Educational System.*'"[28] Share while continuing to access foreign technology abroad.

1996: *Ministry of Personnel,* "*Plan for Working with Overseas Scholars in the Personnel System during the Ninth 5-Year Plan.*"[29] Details state plans to encourage technology transfer from ethnic Chinese scholars overseas.

1999: "*Decision of the Chinese Communist Party Central Committee and the State Council on Strengthening Technical Innovation, Developing High Technology and Realizing Industrialization.*"[30] Rules on building enclaves to commercialize foreign IPR.

2000: "*Notice on Trial Work to Organize and Develop the Model Construction of National OCS Pioneering Parks.*"[31] Core document establishing safe haven development zones in China for returnees bearing foreign technology.

2001: "*Circular on the Release of Opinions on Encouraging Overseas Chinese Scholars to Serve the Country by Multiple Means.*"[32] Five ministries endorse the "multiple means" formula—a carte blanche to provide whatever is useful, wherever it is found.

2003: "*Notice on Joint Working Committee for Overseas Chinese Scholars to Return and Serve the Country.*"[33] Joint statement by 12 ministries—one of China's periodic efforts to rationalize foreign technology acquisition and stop working at cross purposes.

2005: "*Guiding Opinions for Defining High-level Talent in Our Work to Bring in Overseas-educated Talent.*"[34] Four ministries lay out guidelines for China's ubiquitous foreign "talent" recruitment programs.

2006: "*Means for Accrediting and Managing S&T Commercial Incubators (Innovation Service Centers for New and High Technology).*"[35] China's Ministry of Science and Technology consolidates, rebrands its foreign technology commercialization enclaves.

2006: "*Project of Introducing Talents of Academic Disciplines to Universities*."[36] Plan to populate 100 "innovation centers" at Chinese universities with "first-class minds from around the world." Also called the "111 Project."

2007: "*Opinions on Building a Green Channel for the Return to China of High-level Overseas-educated Talent Abroad*."[37] A plan to facilitate recruitment, immigration of foreign S&T talent. Ethnic Chinese born abroad are considered "returnees."

These earlier efforts by China to transfer foreign technology went mostly unnoticed by the countries providing the accesses because China— "the world's factory"—had not risen to a technologically advanced nation and was not seen as a threat, although the signs were there to see. There was also a widely shared belief that China's habit of "standing on the shoulders of giants" (站在巨人肩上) would give way to genuinely collaborative exchanges as China's own technology and confidence matured.

Fast forward to the next decade of state-directed transfer programs, and it becomes evident that these hopes were misplaced. It's still the same old "medicine" (药).

2008: "*Overseas High-level Talent Introduction Program*" (*Thousand Talents Plan*).[38] AKA "Global Experts Recruitment Program." Landmark initiative to accelerate priority (重点) S&T projects by recruiting foreign experts.[39]

2010: "*Homeland-Serving Action Plan for Overseas Chinese*."[40] Enables ethnic Chinese abroad "temporarily unable to return" to "serve the country by multiple means." A 2018 wrap up claims 18,000 persons participated in more than 7,000 cooperative projects.[41]

2011: "*Opinions on Supporting Overseas Scholars Who Return to Start a Company*."[42] A comprehensive framework for financial support to overseas Chinese with "patents, scientific research results, or proprietary technology" to commercialize them in China.

2014: "*Plan to Deepen Central Fiscal S&T Planning (Special Projects, Funds, Etc.) Management Reform*."[43] Consolidates government funding for conversion enclaves and "talent" programs.

2016: "*Planning Guide for Manufacturing Talent Development*."[44] Joint plan to import (another) "1,000" foreign experts able to make "breakthrough" improvements, via talent programs and other venues. Emphasizes recruiting from "famous overseas companies."

2016: "*Strengthening the Administration of Permanent Residency Services for Foreigners*."[45] Clears the path for foreigners with critical technical skills recruited through the Thousand Talents Plan and other venues to obtain permanent residency.

2016: "*Notice on Promulgating the 13th Five-year National Development Program for the Development of Strategic Emerging Industries.*"[46] Article 9 is a blueprint for building a one-sided "global innovation and development network."

2017: "*Plan to Build a National Technology Transfer System.*"[47] A comprehensive articulation of China's tech transfer system. The acquisition of "high-level overseas talent" is emphasized throughout.

2017: "*National S&T Innovation Base Optimization Plan.*"[48] Ensures China's tech commercialization enclaves, many of which are dual-hatted as "Overseas High-Level Talent Innovation Bases," are aligned with the state's strategic developmental goals.

2017: "*13th Five-year Plan for S&T Military and Civil Fusion.*"[49] Cross-pollination of military and civilian tech, e.g., quantum telecommunication and computing, neuroscience and brain-inspired research, will be supported by a range of foreign outreach initiatives.

This last program, an effort to boost China's strategic edge, is particularly ambitious in calling for:

> cooperation with internationally renowned research institutions, establishing R&D institutions overseas, co-establishing a number of international cooperation platforms—such as joint research centers, technology transfer centers, model technology promotion bases, and S&T parks—with countries that have innovative advantages in related fields, creating a development model for S&T military–civil fusion.
>
> *(section 11)*

To be clear, China is courting foreign support to upgrade its military. Besides these overarching projects, there are programs to develop specific high-tech areas such as biotechnology,[50] integrated circuits,[51] and "next-generation" artificial intelligence.[52] Each such program highlights the role foreign technology and "talent" are expected to play. Also omitted from our account are sundry programs that, though not statutory, are state-sponsored, such as:

> The China Association for Science and Technology's (CAST,[53] 中国科学技术协会) "HOME Program" (or Haizhi Plan, 海智计划; see Chapter 2)," instituted in 2004 to "Help Our Motherland through Elite Intellectual Resources from Overseas," and supported by China's central and local governments.[54] Its 2019 slate includes 29 projects, the first three of which call for new or deeper ties with its overseas "bases" in Europe and Japan.[55]

A June 2017 publicly available CAST document lists by name 96 "overseas S&T organizations" from 17 countries and areas providing "experts and scholars" to the

HOME Program. Some 47 of these organizations are in the United States and another 29 are in Europe.[56]

Concrete examples are provided in later chapters. Our purpose, however, is not to belabor what is already known about China's foreign technology transfer practices, but to emphasize that:

- The programs continue to this day.
- They are spread throughout the industrialized world.
- They have not been supplanted by indigenous innovation.
- They are unquestionably state-sponsored.
- There is no indication they will disappear of their own accord.

Selling the program—appeals to the heart

China's technology transfer projects succeed because of their design, state backing, financial incentives, scale of implementation, the persistence with which they are carried out, and—in large part—thanks to an unending stream of propaganda meant to encourage China's diaspora population to participate. People are made to believe that what they are doing benefits not only one's "small self" (小我) but a "larger self" (大我), namely, one's homeland and kin.[57] These united front (统战) appeals are emotionally powerful and must be understood and countered if host countries are to survive the challenge.

We offer a few examples of high-level endorsements of the transfer program to demonstrate its continuity through different eras, and some contemporary sayings used in its implementation that portray the psychological dimension.

Mao Zedong, April 1956:[58]

> "We are willing to learn from all countries in the world. If the American people are willing, we will learn from them, too."

Deng Xiaoping, July 1983:"[59]

> "Leverage foreign intellect, and invite foreigners to participate in our key and all other aspects of construction." Deng linked the 1978 "opening of China to the outside world" (对外开放) with the opportunity to transfer foreign technology.

Jiang Zemin, October 1998:[60]

> "Actively introduce foreign intellectual resources (智力). Absorb and learn from the advanced technologies and management experience of all countries."

BOX 1.1 SLOGANS USED TO SUPPORT TECH TRANSFER

为国服务	Serve the country (China)
报效祖国	Repay the ancestral country (also translated "motherland")
牵线搭桥	Match the "talent" to the need. ("be a matchmaker")
海外赤子智力报国	Loyal overseas Chinese repay the country with intellect.
聚天下英才而用之	Gather talent from all over the world and use it (for China).
落地生根、开花结果	Put down roots (in China) and let your fruit blossom.
不忘初心、牢记使命	Don't forget your beginning, keep the mission in mind.
异国采花、中华酿蜜	Pick flowers in foreign lands to make honey in China.

"China needs batch after batch and generation after generation of outstanding people with independent spirit, who are good at learning from others (善于向别人学习)."

Hu Jintao, December 2003:[61]

"We must be good at using both international and domestic talent resources (人力资源), paying equal attention to the independent cultivation and development of talent and to the introduction of overseas talent."

Xi Jinping, October 2013:[62]

Promote the "Thousand Talents Plan" and "Ten Thousand Talents Plan" with greater efforts, and do everything possible to create the conditions for overseas scholars who return to China to have ample scope to exercise their abilities and for overseas scholars who remain overseas to have *a gateway to serve their country.* (留在国外有报国之门)

Why does it happen? Myth and reality

Meanwhile, outside the Sino-centric universe, where these clichés are less appealing, the dialog on Chinese technology transfer has moved in recent years from gross naiveté and even abetting on the part of donor nations to growing awareness of a problem that needs to be managed. Some of this volume's authors have been privileged to brief US government executive offices and congressional committees and support mitigation in other capacities. We have found our US government counterparts to be well informed and eager to ameliorate the excesses described here. That said, many corporations—multinationals especially— universities, and other national governments are less ready to scrutinize critically their China engagement, so progress here is by no means assured, although we are more optimistic now than a few years ago.

As countermeasures are considered, and as efforts continue to communicate the downside of China's technology transfers, it will be helpful to dispel some misconceptions about the problem that inhibit a full understanding. Of particular concern is the common dismissal of China's so-called "copycat culture," which conveys a false sense of security to China's competitors—while ignoring that country's ability to *innovate on a practical level*, with or without foreign models. The nuances here are important and worth a moment's reflection.

We alluded earlier to a creativity problem attributed to East Asia, and China in particular, by Westerners and by the principals themselves.[63] Scholars with backgrounds as varied as Joseph Needham[64] and Charles Murray[65] have documented China's achievements in the arts and in practical technology on the one hand, coexisting on the other hand with a conspicuous lack of scientific progress of the Western sort, as characterized by a quest for abstract causes and theory-driven experimentation.[66] The same preference for concrete results over theory is noted even today,[67] most recently by Silicon Valley entrepreneur Kai-Fu Lee, who cannot be accused of a pro-Western bias.[68]

While the origin of these preferences is unclear, what cannot be denied is the dichotomy itself, which has existed for centuries and will continue to color the types of research done inside and outside China.[69] How does this impact competing nations? Quite simply: (1) China focuses on what China has always done best— improving ideas and bringing them to market—often before the originators, while (2) using its worldwide venues to tap into more radical innovations with no risk, little investment in basic research, and without jeopardizing its ages-old authoritarian polity with a creativity-friendly culture. It is hard to imagine a more one-sided arrangement.

Meanwhile, mired in hubris and self-adulation, the West fails to appreciate that its storied penchant for breakthrough science matters little without the will, skills, and infrastructure to commercialize its abstract discoveries. Accordingly, we believe the West's so-called creative advantage relative to China is overstated for the following reasons:

- China can innovate in areas it believes are important. If this reality contradicts one's worldview, it is the latter that needs to be adjusted.

- How the innovation occurs—through co-opted principals, international collaboration, espionage, or in the minds of Chinese citizens working independently—is irrelevant.
- The scale of China's S&T investment, whatever its orientation, is more than sufficient to compensate for any relative lack of creativity.
- Abstract innovations in basic science matter less in the real world than one's ability to commercialize or weaponize the innovations.
- The internationalization of science, catalyzed by the Chinese diaspora, has made debate over what China can and cannot do a sterile exercise.

In short, China's system works. It is competitive, and for cultural and political reasons will continue following its own dynamic. Weaning China away from these predatory practices with platitudes about fairness and the respect of the world community, while hoping for the best, is more pipedream than solution, although the process needs to start somewhere.

Notes

1 The compass, gunpowder, papermaking, and printing.
2 Joseph Needham, *Science and Civilisation in China: History of Scientific Thought*, New York: Cambridge University Press, 1956–2016.
3 E.g., "The IP Commission Report." The Commission on the Theft of American Intellectual Property (May 2013). William C. Hannas, James Mulvenon and Anna Puglisi, *Chinese Industrial Espionage*, London and New York: Routledge, 2013) hereafter "*CIE*." Michael Brown and Pavneet Singh, "China's Technology Transfer Strategy" (DIUX, February 2017). Office of the United States Trade Representative, *Section 301 Report into China's Acts, Policies, and Practices Related to Technology Transfer, Intellectual Property, and Innovation* (27 March 2018). US–China Economic and Security Review Commission, "2019 Annual Report to Congress" (November 2019).
4 "Composite" in the sense of relying on both foreign and indigenous elements. The former tends to account for innovation at the foundational or abstract end of the spectrum, while indigenous innovation is generally—but not always—of a more practical nature. Needless to say, exceptions abound.
5 Also, 以多种形式.
6 Advancement in pre-Republican China was achieved by demonstrating a mastery of classical texts; by merchant activity tolerated as necessary but unbecoming a gentleman (君子); and by insurrection against the state. Artisans, whose achievements kept China a step ahead of its neighbors, were disparaged as people of "small skills" (小技). Their status was famously depicted by Tang Dynasty literatus and official Han Yu (韩愈): "Shamans, physicians, musicians, and craftsmen are not to be ranked with gentlemen" (巫医乐师百工之人, 君子不齿).
7 Chinese aphorism meaning to change the form and leave the substance.
8 As represented by early efforts at military modernization, which ended badly. John Rawlinson, *China's Struggle for Naval Development, 1839–1895*, Cambridge, Harvard University Press, 1967.
9 The juxtaposition of *ti* (体) and *yong* (用) is a key tenet of Chinese philosophy dating back two millennia. The formula's application was captured in a late-Qing slogan (attributed to Wei Yuan 魏源) "Learn foreign advanced technology to control the foreigners" (师夷长技以制夷).

10 Zhang Zhidong, "Exhortation to Study" (劝学篇). 1898.

11 Anna Puglisi, *CIE*, pp. 5–6.

12 Stats attributed to Michael Brown. David Vergun, "Chinese Set Sights on High-Tech Production," October 29, 2019. www.defense.gov/explore/story/Article/2002618/chinese-set-sights-on-high-tech-production.

13 Described in "Chinese Education Mission Connections 1872–1881." www.cemconnections.org.

14 The Western Returned Scholars Association (欧美同学会). The WRSA's charter focuses entirely on benefits the party and state expect to gain by sending students abroad, and on students' obligation to provide those benefits. (www.wrsa.net/content_39103492.htm).

15 Xi Jinping, "使留学人员回国有用武之地, 留在国外有报国之门." *Xinhua*, October 21, 2013. Our italics. www.xinhuanet.com//politics/2013-10/21/c_117808372.htm.

16 William C. Hannas, *The Writing on the Wall*, Philadelphia, University of Pennsylvania Press, 2003 and Hannas, Mulvenon, Puglisi., *CIE*, 2013.

17 Hannas, Mulvenon, Puglisi, *CIE*, 2013.

18 Conducted by the authors of Chapters 2 and 3, and by a research fellow at Georgetown University's Center for Security and Emerging Technology (CSET) with no access to our prior data.

19 William C. Hannas and Huey-Meei Chang, "China's Access to Foreign AI Technology—an Assessment," Georgetown University/Center for Security and Emerging Technology, September 2019.

20 The Thousand Talents Plan included eight separate plans as of 2018, each targeting a different "talent" demographic. www.jmsdj.gov.cn/uploadfiles/GongZuoJianBao/2018-6/2018060209160662988.pdf.

21 4,000 non-ethnic Chinese foreign scientists (外国人) were recently given permanent residency status in Beijing. We have no figures for the rest of China. www.boxun.com/news/gb/china/2019/09/201909132305.shtml.

22 Center for Strategic and International Studies, "Survey of Chinese-linked Espionage in the United States Since 2000," September 20, 2019.

23 www.crowdstrike.com/blog/meet-the-adversaries/.

24 Based on sources in endnotes 5–8, and primary Chinese sources listed in *CIE*, pp. 274–276.

25 Adapted with permission from Hannas and Chang. Op. cit., September 2019.

26 Unclassified annual reports by the National Counterintelligence Executive (NCIX) and its successor, the DNI's National Counterintelligence and Security Center invariably rank China first among "informal" collectors of US proprietary technology. The office at one time considered issuing separate China reports.

27 Plans, proclamations, and implementation notices issued at state, provincial, and municipal levels.

28 人事部关于下发《资助留学人员短期回国到非教育系统工作暂行办法》的通知, MOP (10), October 14, 1994.

29 关于印发《"九五"期间人事系统留学人员工作规划》的通知, MOP, August 21, 1996.

30 中共中央, 国务院关于加强技术创新, 发展高科技, 实现产业化的决定, SC (14), August 20, 1999.

31 科学技术部, 人事部, 教育部关于组织开展国家留学人员创业园示范建设试点工作的通知, MOST, MOP, MOE (257), June 21, 2000.

32 关于印发＜关于鼓励海外留学人员以多种形式为国服务的若干意见＞的通知, MOP (49), MOE, MOST, MOF, and Ministry of Public Security, 2001.

33 留学人员回国服务工作部际联席会议制度的通知, SC (11), February 27, 2003.

34 人事部, 教育部, 科技部, 财政部关于印发《关于在留学人才引进工作中界定海外高层次留学人才的指导意见》的通知, MOP (25), MOE, MOST, MOF, April 14, 2005.

35 关于印发《科技企业孵化器 (高新技术创业服务中心) 认定和管理办法》的通知, MOST (498), December 7, 2006.

36 高等学校学科创新引智计划, MOE and SAFEA, 2006. Formal PRC translation is "Project of Introducing Talents of Academic Disciplines to Universities."

37 关于建立海外高层次留学人才回国工作绿色通道的意见, MOP (26), February 15, 2007.

38 海外高层次人才引进计划 (千人计划). CPC Central Committee, 2008.

39 In 2019, the "Thousand Talents Plan" was merged with similar programs and reintroduced as the "High-end Foreign Experts Recruitment Plan" (高端外国专家引进计划). See "Ministry of Science and Technology Notification on the 2019 High-end Foreign Experts Recruitment Plan" (科技部办公厅关于申报2019年度高端外国专家引进计划的通知), MOST (6) 2019.

40 海外赤子为国服务行动计划, MOHRSS, 2010.

41 MOHRSS statistics for ten years of operation. www.gov.cn/xinwen/2019-01/30/content_5362232.htm.

42 关于支持留学人员回国创业意见, Joint declaration by 20 ministries, government offices, and semi-private organizations, MOHRSS (23), February 23, 2011.

43 深化中央财政科技计划 （专项、基金等）管理改革方案, SC (64), December 3, 2014.

44 制造业人才发展规划指南, MOE, MOHRSS, MIIT (9), December 27, 2016.

45 关于加强外国人永久居留服务管理的意见, CPC General Office and State Council, February 18, 2016.

46 国务院关于印发"十三五"国家战略性新兴产业发展规划的通知, SC (67), November 29, 2016.

47 国家技术转移体系建设方案, SC (44), September 15, 2017.

48 国家科技创新基地优化整合案, MOST (250), MOF, National Development and Reform Commission, August 18, 2017.

49 十三五" 科技军民融合发展专项规划, MOST (85), CMC, April 12, 2017.

50 十三五" 生物技术创新专项规划 (*13th Five-year Plan for Biotechnology Innovation*), MOST (103), April 24, 2017.

51 国家集成电路产业发展推进纲要 (National Integrated Circuit Industry Development Plan), State Council, June 24, 2014.

52 新一代人工智能发展规划. (Next-Generation Artificial Intelligence Development Plan), State Council (35), July 8, 2017.

53 CAST (中国科学技术协会) claims to be China's "largest non-governmental organization of scientific and technological professionals in China" and in the same sentence goes on to state that it "serves as a bridge that links the Communist Party of China and the Chinese government to the country's science and technology community." http://cast.org.cn/col/col471/index.html.

54 CAST, 海智计划概论, http://210.14.113.47:7001/n17040442/n17134804/n17135856/n17137769/17200205.html.

55 www.cast.org.cn/art/2019/9/24/art_464_102068.html.

56 http://hzb.cast.org.cn/art/2019/1/7/art_265_9870.html.

57 China New York Consul-General Zhang Qiyue's (章启月) address to overseas students, September 12, 2016. The article claims that "more than 100,000 overseas Chinese students reside within the New York consulate's jurisdiction alone." http://world.people.com.cn/n1/2016/0912/c1002-28708212.html.

58 毛泽东年谱 (Mao Zedong Chronology) 1949–1976 (Vol. 2), Beijing: Central Party Literature Press, 2013, p. 559.

59 http://politics.people.com.cn/n/2013/0711/c1001-22159742.html.

60 http://people.com.cn/item/ldhd/Jiangzm/1998/huijian/hj0016.html.

61 www.people.com.cn/GB/shizheng/1024/2256582.html.

62 Our emphasis. www.xinhuanet.com//politics/2013-10/21/c_117808372.htm.

63 See Hannas, *The Writing on the Wall*, 2003, pp. 88–112.
64 Joseph Needham, *Science and Civilisation in China: History of Scientific Thought*, New York: Cambridge University Press, 1956–2016.
65 Charles Murray, *Human Accomplishment: The Pursuit of Excellence in the Arts and Sciences, 800 B.C. to 1950*, New York: Harper, 2003, pp. 515–573.
66 Joseph Needham, *The Grand Titration: Science and Society in East and West*, London: George Allen & Unwin, 1969, p. 15.
67 Baum (1980), Herbig (1995), Logan (1986), Nakamura (1964), Nakayama (1973), Nisbett (2001), Nisbett et al. (2003), Suttmeir (1986).
68 Kai-Fu Lee, *AI Superpowers: China, Silicon Valley and the New World Order*, Boston: Houghton Mifflin Harcourt, 2018.
69 For a detailed psychological account, see Richard E. Nisbett, Kaiping Peng, Incheol Choi, and Ara Norenzayan. "Culture and Systems of Thought: Holistic Versus Analytic Cognition." *Psychological Review* 108, no. 2 (April 2001), pp. 291–310, pp. 193–194 and Richard E. Nisbett, *The Geography of Thought: How Asians and Westerners Think Differently … and Why*, New York: The Free Press, 2003, pp. 56, 88.

Bibliography

Baum, Richard. *China's Four Modernizations: The New Technological Revolution*. Boulder, CO: Westview Press, 1980.

Brown, Michael and Pavneet Singh. "China's Technology Transfer Strategy," Defense Innovation Unit Experimental (DIUX), February 2017.

Center for Strategic and International Studies. "Survey of Chinese-linked Espionage in the United States Since 2000," September 20, 2019.

Communist Party of China Central Committee. 海外高层次人才引进计划 (千人计划). ("Recruitment Program for Global Experts (Thousand Talents Plan)"), 2008.

Communist Party of China General Office. 关于加强外国人永久居留服务管理的意见 ("Strengthening the Administration of Permanent Residency Services for Foreigners"), CPC GO and SC, February 18, 2016.

Hannas, William C. *The Writing on the Wall*, Philadelphia, PA: University of Pennsylvania Press, 2003.

Hannas, William C., James Mulvenon and Anna Puglisi. *Chinese Industrial Espionage*, London and New York: Routledge, 2013.

Hannas, William C. and Huey-Meei Chang. "China's Access to Foreign AI Technology—an Assessment," Georgetown University/Center for Security and Emerging Technology, September 2019.

Herbig, Paul. *Innovation Japanese Style*, Westport, CT: Praeger, 1995.

Lee, Kai-Fu. *AI Superpowers: China, Silicon Valley and the New World Order*, Boston, MA: Houghton Mifflin Harcourt, 2018.

Logan, Robert K. *The Alphabet Effect*, New York: Morrow, 1986.

Mao, Zedong (毛泽东). 毛泽东年谱 (*Mao Zedong Chronology*) 1949–1976 (Vol. 2), Beijing: Central Party Literature Press, 2013.

Murray, Charles. *Human Accomplishment: The Pursuit of Excellence in the Arts and Sciences, 800 B.C. to 1950*, New York: Harper, 2003.

Nakamura, Hajime. *Ways of Thinking of Eastern Peoples: India, China, Tibet, Japan*, Honolulu: University of Hawaii Press, 1964.

Nakayama, Shigeru and Nathan Sivin. *Chinese Science: Explorations of an Ancient Tradition*, Cambridge, MA: MIT Press, 1973.

Needham, Joseph. *Science and Civilisation in China: History of Scientific Thought*, New York: Cambridge University Press, 1956–2016.

Needham, Joseph. *The Grand Titration: Science and Society in East and West*, London: George Allen & Unwin, 1969.

Nisbett, Richard E., Kaiping Peng, Incheol Choi, and Ara Norenzayan. "Culture and Systems of Thought: Holistic Versus Analytic Cognition," *Psychological Review* 108, no. 2 April, 2001.

Nisbett, Richard E. *The Geography of Thought: How Asians and Westerners Think Differently … and Why*, New York: The Free Press, 2003.

Office of the United States Trade Representative. *Section 301 Report into China's Acts, Policies, and Practices Related to Technology Transfer, Intellectual Property, and Innovation*, March 27, 2018.

PRC Ministry of Education. 高等学校学科创新引智计划 ("Project of Introducing Talents of Academic Disciplines to Universities"), MOE and SAFEA, 2006.

PRC Ministry of Education. 制造业人才发展规划指南 ("Planning Guide for Manufacturing Talent Development"), MOE, MOHRSS, MIIT (9), December 27, 2016.

PRC Ministry of Human Resources and Social Security. 海外赤子为国服务行动计划, ("Homeland-Serving Action Plan for Overseas Chinese"), 2010.

PRC Ministry of Human Resources and Social Security. 关于支持留学人员回国创业意见 ("Opinions on Supporting Overseas Scholars Who Return to Start a Company"), MOHRSS (23), February 23, 2011.

PRC Ministry of Personnel. 人事部关于下发《资助留学人员短期回国到非教育系统工作暂行办法》的通知 ("MOP Notice on 'Implementing Temporary Measures to Subsidize Overseas Chinese Scholars who Return to China for Short Periods to Work in Areas Outside the Educational System'"), MOP (10), October 14, 1994.

PRC Ministry of Personnel. 关于印发《"九五"期间人事系统留学人员工作规划》的通知 (*Nr. 75, Plan for Working with Overseas Scholars in the Personnel System during the Ninth 5-Year Plan*), August 21, 1996.

PRC Ministry of Personnel. 关于印发＜关于鼓励海外留学人员以多种形式为国服务的若干意见＞的通知 ("Circular on the Release of Opinions on Encouraging Overseas Chinese Scholars to Serve the Country by Multiple Means"), MOP (49), MOE, MOST, MOF, and MPS, 2001.

PRC Ministry of Personnel. 人事部、教育部、科技部、财政部关于印发《关于在留学人才引进工作中界定海外高层次留学人才的指导意见》的通知 ("Guiding Opinions for Defining High-level Talent in Our Work to Bring in Overseas-educated Talent"), MOP (25), MOE, MOST, MOF, April 14, 2005.

PRC Ministry of Personnel. 关于建立海外高层次留学人才回国工作绿色通道的意见 ("Opinions on Building a Green Channel for the Return to China of High-level Overseas-educated Talent Abroad"), MOP (26), February 15, 2007.

PRC Ministry of Science and Technology. 科学技术部、人事部、教育部关于组织开展国家留学人员创业园示范建设试点工作的通知 ("Notice on Trial Work to Organize and Develop the Model Construction of National OCS Pioneering Parks"), MOST, MOP, MOE (257), June 21, 2000.

PRC Ministry of Science and Technology. 关于印发《科技企业孵化器（高新技术创业服务中心）认定和管理办法》的通知 ("Means for Accrediting and Managing S&T Commercial Incubators (Innovation Service Centers for New and High Technology)"), MOST (498), December 7, 2006.

PRC Ministry of Science and Technology. "十三五" 科技军民融合发展专项规划 ("13th Five-year Plan for S&T Military and Civil Fusion"), MOST (85) and Central Military Commission, April 12, 2017.

PRC Ministry of Science and Technology. 国家科技创新基地优化整合案 ("National S&T Innovation Base Optimization Plan"), MOST (250), MOF, National Development and Reform Commission, August 18, 2017.

PRC Ministry of Science and Technology. 科技部办公厅关于申报2019年度高端外国专家引进计划的通知 ("Ministry of Science and Technology Notification on the 2019 High-end Foreign Experts Recruitment Plan"), MOST (6), 2019.

PRC State Council. 中共中央、国务院关于加强技术创新、发展高科技、实现产业化的决定 ("Decision of the Chinese Communist Party Central Committee and the State Council on Strengthening Technical Innovation, Developing High Technology and Realizing Industrialization"), SC (14), August 20, 1999.

PRC State Council. 留学人员回国服务工作部际联席会议制度的通知 ("Notice on Joint Working Committee for Overseas Chinese Scholars to Return and Serve the Country"), SC (11), February 27, 2003.

PRC State Council. 国家集成电路产业发展推进纲要 ("National Integrated Circuit Industry Development Plan"), June 24, 2014.

PRC State Council. 深化中央财政科技计划 （专项、基金等）管理改革方案, ("Plan to Deepen Central Fiscal S&T Planning (Special Projects, Funds, Etc.) Management Reform"), SC (64), December 3, 2014.

PRC State Council. 国务院关于印发"十三五"国家战略性新兴产业发展规划的通知 ("Notice on Promulgating the 13th Five-year National Development Program for the Development of Strategic Emerging Industries"), SC (67), November 29, 2016.

PRC State Council. 国家技术转移体系建设方案 ("Plan to Build a National Technology Transfer System"), SC (44), September 15, 2017.

Rawlinson, John. *China's Struggle for Naval Development, 1839–1895*, Cambridge, MA: Harvard University Press, 1967.

Suttmeier, Richard P. "New Directions in Chinese Science and Technology," in John Major, ed., *China Briefing*, Boulder, CO: Westview Press, 1986.

The Commission on the Theft of American Intellectual Property. "The IP Commission Report," May 2013.

US–China Economic and Security Review Commission. "2019 Annual Report to Congress," November 2019.

Vergun, David. "Chinese Set Sights on High-Tech Production," October 29, 2019. www.defense.gov/explore/story/Article/2002618/chinese-set-sights-on-high-tech-production.

Xi, Jinping (习近平). "使留学人员回国有用武之地，留在国外有报国之门," *Xinhua*, October 21, 2013. www.xinhuanet.com//politics/2013-10/21/c_117808372.htm.

Zhang, Zhidong (张之洞). 劝学篇 ("Exhortation to Study"), 1898.

2

SERVE THE MOTHERLAND WHILE WORKING OVERSEAS

Andrew Spear

In the modern era, China's drive to acquire foreign technology began in earnest on June 23, 1978 when Deng Xiaoping declared, "Thousands, or even tens of thousands, should be sent abroad rather than only a handful.... We should make every effort to speed it up and increasingly widen our path."[1] According to China's Ministry of Human Resources and Social Security (MOHRSS), in the 40 years since (1978–2018), 5.86 million Chinese scholars went abroad to study, 4.32 million have finished their study, and 3.65 million (or 84.46 percent of all who have finished their study) have returned to China.

The focus of this chapter, however, is China's efforts to utilize the 2.21 million Overseas Chinese Scholars (留学人员, OCS) that remain abroad to generate large-scale technology transfer.[2] English-language sources often frame the issue as "brain drain" from China, and suggest that the physical location of talent determines which country benefits.[3] The Chinese government's so-called "overseas scholar work" (留学人员工作), however, is not fixated on recruiting talent physically back to China (though talent recruitment programs, discussed in Chapter 3, are a key part of the effort). Supporting scholars to go abroad, welcoming those that return, but also utilizing those that remain abroad, are mutually reinforcing features of China's composite innovation system (see Chapter 1). As CPC general secretary Xi Jinping made clear in a speech to overseas Chinese scholars given at a United Front organization in 2013,

> The Party and state respect the choice of overseas scholars. If they return to China to work, we will warmly welcome them with open arms. If they stay overseas, we support them in serving the country through various forms (通过多种形式为国服务). Everyone must keep in mind that no matter where you are, you are all sons and daughters of China. The

motherland and the people will always remember you. The motherland will forever be your warm spiritual homeland.[4]

Chinese scholars working overseas face entreaties from the PRC government, backed by financial incentives, to "serve their country" by means of the "advanced science and technology within their grasp."[5] The "service" the Chinese government obtains is integrated into a government-coordinated, whole-of-society approach to international technology transfer, with flexible and evolving techniques. This chapter is an overview of the palette of techniques that China employs in the US and elsewhere—they are similar around the world—to generate this large-scale technology transfer.

The chapter begins with a summary of some key concepts that animate China's "overseas scholar work." The next section surveys the policy system that operationalizes these concepts. The final section examines four specific PRC government programs. These programs emotionally entreat and financially incentivize overseas scholars to "serve the motherland" while working overseas. Special attention will be given to the role of so-called "societal organizations" (often tax-exempt 501(c)(3) organizations in the US) that play a central role in implementing these programs in the US and other foreign countries. For examples, and figures, of similar systems at work in Europe, another major high-tech hub, see Chapters 7 and 8.

Key concepts

In 1993, the *Decision of the CPC Central Committee Regarding a Number of Issues Concerning the Establishment of a Socialist Market Economy*, a seminal document in the development of China's economic system, set the overall policy direction of China's "overseas scholar work" as "support overseas study, encourage returning to China, freely come and go" (支持留学、鼓励回国、来去自由),[6] a call that has been reiterated in many policy documents since.[7] In 2013, Xi updated this long-standing policy direction toward overseas scholars by adding a phrase to the end—"support overseas study, encourage returning to China, freely come and go, *play a useful role* (支持留学、鼓励回国、来去自由、发挥作用)" (bold italics added). According to Xi, "playing a useful role" means serving China's national strategies whether one returns to China or remains overseas.[8] Therefore, China must "do everything possible to create the conditions for overseas scholars that return to China to have ample scope to exercise their abilities *and* for overseas scholars that remain overseas to have a gateway to serve their country."[9]

The notion of "playing a useful role" in China's national strategies, regardless of country of residence, is consistent with Xi's call in 2018 for a "flexible concept of talent recruitment" (柔性引才理念) that "does not seek everything, only what is *useful*; does not seek that they are here, only that they act" (不求所有、但求所用，不求所在、但求所为).[10] With this flexible concept, it is possible to "mobilize talents to engage in offshore innovation in foreign countries" (在国外调动人才离岸搞创新) or "attract 'migratory bird talent' to engage in part-time innovation" (吸引"候鸟型人才"兼职搞创新) in China, while employed overseas.[11]

In China's composite innovation system, a flexible approach to talent acquisition facilitates the exploitation of two types of human resources—domestic and international—to, paradoxically, realize the goal of "indigenous innovation." China aims to "fully develop and *use* both domestic and *international talent resources*, actively bring in and *use overseas talent* (充分开发利用国内国际人才资源，积极引进和用好海外人才)."[12] The concept of two types of resources—both domestic and international—is not limited to talent. In order to realize "indigenous innovation … [China] must deepen international exchange and cooperation, fully *use global innovation resources* (充分利用全球创新资源), [and thereby] advance indigenous innovation from a higher starting point."[13] Similarly,

> it is necessary to deepen international science and technology exchanges and cooperation, advance indigenous innovation from a higher starting point, actively deploy and proactively *use international innovation resources* (主动布局和积极利用国际创新资源).[14]

Finally, according to Xi,

> only if the core technology is grasped in our own hands can we then really seize the initiative in competition and development … of course, we can't lock ourselves up from the world, we need to proactively develop technology exchanges with the outside, strive to *use* well the two kinds of *science and technology resources*—international and domestic (努力用好国际国内两种科技资源).[15]

Policy system

For decades, these concepts have been codified and operationalized in an evolving policy system. The long-standing goal of China's overseas scholar work is to entice overseas scholars to (1) return to China to work (回国工作), (2) return to China to start a company (回国创业), and/or (3) serve China (为国服务) whether one returns or not.[16] As early as 2011, policy documents began calling for the construction of a "three-in-one" (三位一体) system that integrates these three objectives.[17] Notably, the vision in 2011 was to "create new talent recruitment methods" (创新引才方式) by integrating the three objectives and thereby form a "talent recruitment mechanism whereby full-time return and short-term cooperation are mutually advanced by each other."[18] By mid-2019, China had issued over 30 policy documents forming the "three-in-one" policy system, which it still describes as "preliminary."[19]

China's overseas scholar work is supported by, and integrated into, a government-guided whole-of-society approach to technology transfer. The government's vision was articulated in the State Council's 2017 *Plan to Build a National Technology Transfer System*, which calls for "strengthened technology transfer talent cultivation" where "enterprises, universities, and scientific research institutes play their role in acquiring high-level overseas talent through various vehicles and forms such as projects, bases, and educational cooperation."[20] Another key policy document similarly calls for "giving play to the government's guiding role in encouraging enterprises, universities, scientific research organizations, *societal organizations* (社会组织), and individuals, [etc.] to participate in an orderly manner in human talent resource development and talent recruitment."[21]

As the next section will show, PRC enterprises, universities, research institutes, societal organizations, and individuals do indeed play a key role in implementing PRC government programs in foreign countries. Of special note are so-called "societal organizations" (a broad concept including student groups, professional groups, and other non-government organizations) established in the US and other countries that greatly facilitate PRC government programs in those countries. This facilitation, which will be detailed throughout this chapter, is guided by PRC government documents including the MOHRSS's *Opinions on Strengthening Construction of the Overseas Scholar Returnee Service System* (hereafter *Construction of the Overseas Scholar System*), issued in 2011, which calls for "giving full play to relevant overseas group organizations" (海外有关团体组织) in a layered and indirect manner.[22]

Pursuant to the *Construction of the Overseas Scholar System*, in 2011 the MOHRSS established the Overseas Scholar Returnee Service Alliance (留学人员回国服务联盟, hereafter "Alliance") as a joint initiative of 92 China-based "overseas scholar service organizations (留学人员服务机构) and "overseas scholar organizations" (留学人员组织).[23] The China-based Alliance members are directed to extend their work into foreign countries by "adopting *flexible and diverse methods*" (灵活多样的方式) to strengthen connections and communication with overseas-based Chinese student, scholar, and professional groups in order to provide them information, consultation, and "matchmaking" (牵线搭桥) services (i.e., recruitment of talent and/or their projects).[24] Furthermore, "in countries and regions where overseas scholars are relatively concentrated," Alliance members are directed to establish "Overseas Scholar Returnee Service Workstations" (海外留学人员回国服务工作站).[25] According to a speech by a MOHRSS official in August 2019, the Alliance has grown to 117 China-based "overseas scholar service organizations" (留学人员服务机构) and going forward will be key to furthering the PRC government's objective of "recruiting more high-level overseas talents to return to China to work, start companies, and/or serve the country, thereby injecting great momentum into the Chinese Dream of the Great Rejuvenation of the Chinese Nation."[26]

Specific programs

Backed by this policy system, a series of PRC government programs emotionally entreat and financially incentivize overseas Chinese to "serve the motherland" while working overseas. The remainder of this chapter examines four such programs.

Homeland-serving action plan for overseas Chinese

In 1979, the year after Deng initiated the modern wave of Chinese scholars going abroad to study, a state-owned movie company released *A Loyal Overseas Chinese Family* (海外赤子, also translated as *Hearts for the Motherland*),[27] a movie that propagated the more open "overseas Chinese policy" (华侨政策) the CPC adopted in 1978. The movie depicts how the restrictive overseas Chinese policy of the Cultural Revolution era prevented patriotic Chinese "with overseas connections" (海外关系) from serving their country. In doing so, it repudiated the view predominate during the Cultural Revolution (1966–1976) that overseas Chinese were politically unreliable and that "overseas relationships" (海外关系) were tantamount to "reactionary relationships" (反动关系), and popularized an emotionally charged term—"overseas Chinese" (海外赤子)—that connotes loyalty to China's ruler.[28]

In 2009, the MOHRSS leveraged the emotional content of the term by launching the *Homeland-Serving Action Plan for Overseas Chinese* (hereafter *Serve the Homeland Action Plan*) (海外赤子为国服务行动计划), which is a rebranded implementation of a policy,[29] in place since 2001, that outlines "funding support" (经费支持) and "remuneration" (报酬) for foreign-based talent in order to "fully exploit overseas talent resources and encourage overseas scholars to serve the motherland through various methods while they are studying or working overseas" (为充分开发海外留学人才资源，鼓励在海外学习和工作的留学人员以多种方式为祖国服务).[30] The 2001 policy document specifies the following methods of service to be incentivized:[31]

1   Accept concurrent part-time technical work positions in China.
2   Coordinate research cooperation between overseas and Chinese entities.
3   Conduct research overseas that is commercialized by Chinese entities.
4   Commercialize patents and technology by establishing enterprises in China.
5   Leverage overseas institutes to help Chinese employers train their talent.
6   Introduce foreign technology into Western China.
7   Establish "intermediary organizations" to facilitate the introduction of foreign technology to China and create more methods to serve the country in addition to those listed above.

The rebranded *Serve the Homeland Action Plan* aims to "facilitate coordinated and standardized management of the various activities whereby overseas scholars serve the country, form a combined force, and thereby recruit more overseas scholars to serve the country with their brainpower through various forms,"[32] presumably means like the incentivized ones listed above. It is an extremely flexible format. Each year PRC government entities and, notably, foreign-based overseas scholar groups (海外留学人员团体)[33] submit proposals for various *Serve the Homeland Action Plan* activities and 30 to 50 are selected by MOHRSS to receive "policy support" and "funding support," among other types of support.[34] Recently, *Serve the Homeland Action Plan* activities have focused on providing direct benefit to domestic commercial enterprises that "break the foreign technology monopoly"[35] in *Made in China 2025* sectors including automotive, AI, new materials, and biomedicine.[36]

Serve the Homeland Action Plan activities can take many forms, but a recently publicized case demonstrates how they can serve as a platform for the transfer of foreign technology to China. On November 13, 2019, Huzhou city in Zhejiang province held a *Serve the Homeland Action Plan* event that attracted teams representing 36 projects (i.e., research projects and/or start-ups) from six countries (US, Canada, Japan, Germany, UK, and Italy) that covered Huzhou's key industrial areas, including high-end equipment, information economy, new energy vehicles and components.[37] After the event, representatives from regional enterprises, entrepreneurship platforms, industrial parks, and government departments engaged in one-on-one "docking negotiations" (对接洽谈)[38] with the "overseas Chinese" (海外赤子) on "project introduction needs, technology cooperation, and service needs."[39] In all, 130 people participated in the event, including venture capitalists, headhunters, and representatives from other types of "intermediary organizations" (中介机构).

The Chinese government-reported scale of the *Serve the Homeland Action Plan* is remarkable.

- In 2017, MOHRSS funded 31 *Serve the Homeland Action Plan* activities that yielded over 2,000 incidents of overseas scholars serving the country, which resulted in over 2,000 projects that signed Cooperation Agreements or reached an Intent to Cooperate. In addition, over 300 lecture events were held that trained over 10,000 personnel.[40]
- In 2018, MOHRSS funded 30 *Serve the Homeland Action Plan* activities that yielded over 10,000 incidents of overseas scholars serving the country, over 18,000 individual technology cooperation projects that participated in "docking" (对接) (i.e., negotiations), which resulted in over 7,000 projects that signed Cooperation Agreements or reached an Intent to Cooperate. In addition, over 500 lecture events were held that trained over 10,000 personnel.[41]

HOME Program

The *Help Our Motherland through Elite Intellectual Resources from Overseas Program*
(HOME Program, also known as "Haizhi," 海外智力为国服务行动计划)[42] was
jointly established by the China Association for Science and Technology (CAST)
and no less than 35 overseas-based science and technology groups (海外科技团体)
in December 2003, with the support of the CCP Central Committee Organization
Department and the MOHRSS. The aim: to build a platform to recruit overseas
talent to "serve the country" (为国服务) in the spirit of "united struggle and
patriotic dedication" ("团结奋斗，爱国奉献"的精神).[43] CAST is a massive
"people's organization under the leadership of the Chinese Communist Party" (中
国共产党领导下的人民团体) that claims more than 4.3 million members across
various subsidiary organizations and serves as a "bridge and link between China's
science and technology workers and the [Chinese] government and Party."[44]

As of June 2017, 47 US-based science and technology organizations were listed
as "overseas S&T groups liaising with the HOME Program" (海智计划联系的海
外科技团体), out of a worldwide total of 96.[45] Though it describes itself as a "non-
profit and non-political organization" and is registered as a tax-exempt 501(c)(3)
non-profit organization with the IRS,[46] the China Association for Science and
Technology, USA (CAST–USA) is one of the US-based S&T organizations listed
as an overseas S&T group liaising with the HOME Program. CAST–USA is
organized into 16 chapters and claims more than 10,000 members[47] in the US
"working in universities, industries, government agencies and other sectors, many
in the world's top 500 multinational corporations, or prestigious universities or
research institutions."[48]

The first incarnation of the HOME Program leveraged overseas S&T
groups, like CAST–USA, to employ "various forms" (多种形式) of activity, such
as academic exchanges, project cooperation, technical consulting, technology
introduction, and special investigations, to contribute to the economic
construction of China.[49]

As with the *Serve the Homeland Action Plan*, the PRC government-reported
scale of the HOME Program is stunning. In 2017, it had cumulatively achieved
the following results:[50]

- Held 1,012 "intellect recruitment docking activities" (引智对接活动) that
  yielded 1,099 signed cooperation agreements (合作协议) and negotiations
  on 5,928 start-up projects (洽谈项目), of which 1,267 have relocated (落地)
  to China.
- Recruited 796 teams (引进团队) and 2,880 individual talents (引进人才),
  145 of which became "Thousand Talents Plan" selectees (see Chapter 3 on
  talent recruitment).
- Organized 232 groups that have traveled overseas to hold "intellect
  recruitment activities" (引智活动) in other countries.

Since 2014, CAST Party Secretary Shang Yong (尚勇) has called for a "HOME Program 2.0" that was "more flexible" (更加灵活) and "more in accordance with the efficiency of overseas talent [conducting] offshore innovation and entrepreneurship."[51] Accordingly, the HOME Program began establishing Offshore Innovation and Entrepreneurial Bases for Overseas Professionals (国家海外人才离岸创新创业基地, hereafter Offshore Entrepreneurial Bases). Offshore Entrepreneurial Bases enable a method of talent recruitment whereby recruited overseas talents "do not necessarily directly come to China to work" (不一定直接到国内工作). Instead, overseas talents monetize research conducted in their host country via a stake in a commercial enterprise in China by, for example, a "technology for equity" (技术入股) exchange.[52] This model connects "overseas innovation resources" (海外创新资源) with "incubation teams" (孵化团队) in China that commercialize their innovative ideas.[53]

Offshore Entrepreneurial Bases utilize a hub-and-spoke model where a base in China incubates and commercializes innovative ideas sourced from a network of offshore innovation centers in foreign countries. For example, the Chengdu High-Tech Industrial Development Zone (CDHT) launched an Offshore Entrepreneurial Base in 2016 along with a network of affiliated offshore innovation centers. According to Wang Lei, Deputy Director of the Zone's MOHRSS Office, "the overseas talents will not have to stay in the Chengdu high-tech zone. They can just do research overseas and achieve their scientific research at the high-tech zone's overseas centers."[54] By July 2019, it boasted 31 overseas centers spread across Japan, Korea, Europe, and the US.[55]

One of the CDHT Offshore Entrepreneurial Base's first tributary offshore innovations centers—the San Diego Center—was established in 2017.[56] An article in the *Sichuan Daily* announcing its opening stated that "compared to the traditional concept of 'recruiting talents back to work in the locality,' overseas high-end talents do not necessarily have to leave their familiar environment but can stay abroad to innovate and relocate the achievements to China."[57] Day-to-day operations of the San Diego Center rely on two California-based organizations:[58]

- Sino-America Biotechnology and Pharmaceutical Professional Association (SABPA) (美中生物技术与制药专业协会), a 501(c)(3) nonprofit organization with more than 3,500 members that was founded in early 2002 by professionals and scholars from the Chinese community in San Diego.[59]
- GIMDZ, Inc. (吉迪思诊断有限公司), a California-based subsidiary of Guangzhou Improve Medical Instruments Co., Ltd[60] that "specializes in commercial collaborations and R&D laboratory support for IVD [in vitro diagnostics] companies with particular emphasis on addressing China's unique market needs."[61]

According to the CPC's *United Front News Network* (中国统一战线新闻网), by February 2018 China had established ten Offshore Entrepreneurial Bases in Shenzhen, Shanghai, Wuhan, Chengdu, Suzhou, Hefei, Ningbo, Qingdao, Tianjin, and Hangzhou—each with its own network of tributary offshore centers.[62]

Chunhui Cup start-up competition

In 1997, the Ministry of Education (MOE) began implementing the Chunhui Plan (春晖计划).[63] Article 1 of the policy document governing the plan sets the tone by stating that

> in order to implement the national overseas scholar work policy direction and create the necessary conditions to support China's overseas scholars in serving the motherland through various forms (以多种方式报效祖国), the Ministry of Education establishes the Chunhui Plan.[64]

The Chunhui Plan funds a number of initiatives. The focus of this section, however, is the "Chunhui Cup" (春晖杯) China Overseas Scholar Innovation and Entrepreneurship Competition (hereafter "Chunhui Cup"),[65] one of dozens of PRC government-organized global start-up competitions that aim to relocate overseas start-up projects to China.

These PRC government-sponsored start-up competitions generally leverage a network of subsidiary competitions in foreign countries, organized and/or promoted by PRC embassies and consulates alongside foreign-based nonprofit groups, that feed into China-based final competitions. The Chunhui Cup website states plainly that is uses an "overseas subsidiary competition model (海外分赛区模式) to excavate more overseas innovation resources," and then pairs them with domestic company talent and technology needs, "to create a platform that connects overseas talent, technology, and projects with domestic policy, circumstances, and capital."[66] More specifically, it "creates the conditions for competition participants to engage in project docking with OCS Pioneer Parks, university science and technology parks, and enterprises" along with "venture capital organizations and domestic entrepreneurs that review, negotiate, and select awards for projects in order to encourage overseas scholars to establish high-tech enterprises in China."[67]

The Chunhui Cup casts a very wide net. The 14th Annual Chunhui Cup in 2019 included subsidiary competitions in North America, France, Germany, Australia, UK, Spain, Japan, and Singapore.[68] In the North American New York region alone, the PRC Consulate in New York promoted the Chunhui Cup alongside ten nonprofit organizations and held training sessions in ten regional cities, including New York, Philadelphia, Pittsburgh, Cleveland, Columbus,

Buffalo, and Ithaca.[69] In California, similarly, the PRC Consulate in San Francisco promoted the competition alongside nonprofit groups like the Silicon Valley Chinese Engineers Association (硅谷华人工程师协会, SCEA), a 501(c)(3) nonprofit professional organization founded in 1989[70] with reportedly over 6,500 members.[71]

According to SCEA, applicants must be overseas Chinese scholars with a bachelor's degree or above and currently studying or working in the US Submitted projects must "conform with [China's] industrial policy" and "possess high technology" among other conditions.[72] Applications must include a "Business Plan" and "Intellectual Property Statement" and SCEA requested that its members mark SCEA as the "recommending work unit" (推荐单位). From April to mid-July 2019, the PRC Consulate in San Francisco arranged training sessions on the Business Plan and IP Statement, including an "informational meeting" at the US–Zhejiang Innovation Center (美国浙江创新中心) in Santa Clara.[73] From July to September, applications were reviewed and a shortlist of projects was published. In December 2019, the shortlisted projects were invited to go to China to participate in the awards ceremony and conduct "project docking negotiations" (项目对接 洽谈)[74] with various industrial parks, enterprises, and investors, during a roadshow across China that included stops in Ningbo, Tianjin, Wuxi, Shanghai, Xiamen, and Beijing.[75] Round-trip airfare expenses were reimbursed by the MOE's Chunhui Program.[76]

Almost half of the shortlisted overseas start-up projects relocate to China. Through the first 13 annual Chunhui Cup competitions (2006–2018), 2,528 overseas scholar's start-up projects have been shortlisted and 448 have returned to China to establish a company. Of those returnees, about half have also received national or local-level talent program awards. In addition, over 643 shortlisted

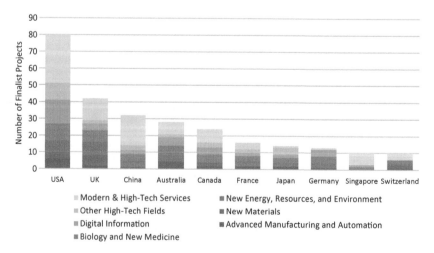

FIGURE 2.1   2019 Chunhui cup finalists by country of origin and technology area.

projects have landed in China-based enterprises (落户企业) spread among 76 cities in 25 provinces.[77]

On September 9, 2019, the MOE announced 301 shortlisted projects for the 2019 Chunhui Cup.[78] An analysis of the reported country of origin and technology area of the 301 finalists[79] reveals that only 34 finalist projects (11 percent of the total) originate from mainland China, Hong Kong, and Macao; the rest originate from other countries. Countries that contributed ten or more finalist projects to the 2019 Chunhui Cup shortlist include the US (80), UK (42), Australia (28), Canada (24), France (16), Japan (14), Germany (13), Singapore (10), and Switzerland (10). Figure 2.1 shows that the projects sourced from these countries are disproportionately in technology areas like automation, new materials, new energy, and biotech, while the China-sourced projects are disproportionally in services.

111 Project

In 2006, the PRC Ministry of Education and the State Administration of Foreign Experts Affairs (now under the Ministry of Science & Technology) established what is officially translated as the Project of Introducing Talents of Academic Disciplines to Universities (高等学校学科创新引智计划), more commonly known as the 111 Project (111计划).[80] The 111 Project aims to create 100 "world first class" (世界一流) academic discipline innovation bases (学科创新基地) in Chinese universities by recruiting 1,000 overseas experts from the top 100 research institutions in the world.[81] It aims to do this "by means of creating foreign intellect recruitment innovation bases" (以建设学科创新引智基地为手段) to act as receiving platforms within universities.[82]

Each of the 111 Project's "foreign intellect recruitment innovation bases" (创新引智基地) is required to hire at least ten foreign-based experts, including at least one "academic master" (学术大师)[83] who is renowned in their field[84] and will spend at least one month per year in China[85] and at least nine "academic backbones" (学术骨干) who are associate professors or above in their country of residence,[86] at least three of whom come to China to work at least 3 months per year[87] and the remaining six of whom come to China a total of six times in a year for short-term academic exchanges.[88] This foreign-based team is to be "equipped with" (配备) an accompanying domestic-based team in the base that consists of at least ten researchers.[89]

China has vastly exceeded the original goal of creating 100 111 Project bases. According to the official blog of the *China Science Daily*,[90] by 2017 China had already established 350 such "foreign intellect recruitment innovation bases" (创新引智基地).[91] In 2018, another 62 bases were newly established,[92] bringing the total to 412 and suggesting that since 2006 China has successfully recruited at least 4,120 foreign intellects (at least ten overseas experts per base) pursuant to the 111 Project. Furthermore, the 111 Project is an important avenue for the continuous transfer of foreign technology with military applications (see

TABLE 2.1 Examples of the 111 Project Foreign Intellect Recruitment Innovation Bases

Foreign Intellect Recruitment Innovation Base	Host Institution
Aerospace Advanced Materials Discipline Innovation and Talent Introduction Base (空天先进材料学科创新引智基地)	Beihang University (北京航空航天大学)
Aviation Propulsion Theory and Engineering Innovation and Talent Introduction Base (航空推进理论与工程创新引智基地)	Beihang University (北京航空航天大学)
Aviation Science and Technology Innovation and Talent Introduction Base (航空科学与技术创新引智基地)	Beihang University (北京航空航天大学)
Aviation Aerospace and Advanced Manufacturing Technology Innovation and Talent Introduction Base (航空宇航先进制造技术创新引智基地)	Northwest Polytechnical University (西北工业大学)
Security and Defense Disciplines Innovation and Talent Introduction Base (安全与防护学科创新引智基地)	Beijing Institute of Technology (北京理工大学)
New Radar Systems Theory and Key Technology Disciplines Talent Introduction Base (新体制雷达系统理论与关键技术学科创新引智基地)	Beijing Institute of Technology (北京理工大学)
Advanced Ceramics Composites and Coatings Innovation and Talent Introduction Base (先进陶瓷复合材料与涂层创新引智基地)	Harbin Engineering University (哈尔滨工业大学)
Deep Sea Engineering Science and Technology Innovation and Talent Introduction Base (深海工程科学与技术创新引智基地)	Harbin Engineering University (哈尔滨工业大学)
Millimeter Wave Terahertz Detection Imaging Technology Innovation and Talent Introduction Base (毫米波太赫兹成像探测技术学科创新引智基地)	Harbin Engineering University (哈尔滨工业大学)
Key Technology of High-Performance Piezoelectric Drive Systems Innovation and Talent Introduction Base (高性能压电驱动系统关键技术创新引智基地)	Nanjing University of Aeronautics & Astronautics (南京航空航天大学)
Complex Environmental Photoelectric Information Sensory S&T Innovation and Talent Introduction Base (复杂环境光电信息感知科学与技术学科创新引智基地)	Xidian University (西安电子科技大学)

Source: Chinese Ministry of Education, author calculations.

Chapter 13, Liu Ruopeng case study). Table 2.1 contains a sampling of the 111 Project's "foreign intellect recruitment innovation bases" in technology areas with defense applications that are attached to PRC institutions that directly support China's defense R&D and industrial base.

Notes

1 "June 23, a Day Worth Remembering for Chinese People" (6月23日，一个值得中国人记住的日子). http://edu.china.com.cn/2019-06/26/content_74923429.htm.

2 The term "overseas Chinese scholar" (留学人员) is frequently used in Chinese policy documents. The Shanghai municipal government defines "overseas Chinese scholars" as those who have received a bachelor's degree or above from abroad, or those who received a bachelor's or vocational degree in China and subsequently spent at least a year abroad as a visiting scholar at a university or staff at a scientific research organization. This definition excludes current undergraduate students but includes individuals with decades of overseas work experience. See 留学人员的基本定义是什么? http://rsj. sh.gov.cn/201712333/bmfw/bmwd/wgzjgz/01/201711/t20171101_1265602.shtml.

3 See, for example, MIT Technology Review, "China's path to AI domination has a problem: brain drain," August 7, 2019. www.technologyreview.com/f/614092/china-ai-domination-losing-talent-to-us/.

4 习近平在欧美同学会成立100周年庆祝大会上的讲话. www.wrsa.net/content_391 03656.htm.

5 关于鼓励海外留学人员以多种形式为国服务的若干意见, Preamble.

6 中共中央关于建立社会主义市场经济体制若干问题的决定, Article 43. Article 43 of the Decision also calls for "adopting various forms, encourage overseas talent to serve the motherland" (采取多种形式，鼓励海外人才为祖国服务) alongside the policy direction.

7 For example, "九五"期间人事系统留学人员工作规划, Section 2(3); 留学人员回国工作"十一五"规划, Section 2(1) and 留学人员回国工作"十二五"规划, Section 2(1).

8 习近平在欧美同学会成立100周年庆祝大会上的讲话 (www.wrsa.net/content_391 03656.htm).Also 留学关键词：十六字方针. www.chisa.edu.cn/rmtnews1/subject/2 01970zn/70znlxgjc/201909/t20190918_261540.html.

9 Ibid.

10 习近平在全国组织工作会议的讲话. www.12371.cn/2018/09/17/ARTI153715084 0597467.shtml.

11 Ibid.

12 See, for example, 胡锦涛在中国共产党第十八次全国代表大会上的报告 in 2012 and 习近平在欧美同学会成立100周年庆祝大会上的讲话 in 2013, which both used the quoted phrase.In addition, the 中共中央国务院关于进一步加强人才工作的决定, Section 6 (14), in 2003 called for "full exploitation of both domestic and international human talent resources."

13 在十八届中央政治局第九次集体学习时的讲话. www.gov.cn/ldhd/2013-10/01/ content_2499370.htm.

14 在中国科学院第十九次院士大会、中国工程院第十四次院士大会上的讲话. www.xinhuanet.com/politics/leaders/2018-05/28/c_1122901308.htm.

15 在参加全国政协十二届一次会议科协、科技界委员联组讨论时的讲话. http://m. news.cctv.com/2018/04/18/ARTIdwgrDYHnPrJSoFdBWLd0180418.shtml.

16 For example, "九五"期间人事系统留学人员工作规划, 留学人员回国工作"十一五"规划, 留学人员回国工作"十二五"规划, and 关于加强留学人员回国服务体系建设的意见.

17 关于加强留学人员回国服务体系建设的意见, Section 2(1). See also 留学人员回国工作"十二五"规划, Section 2(2) and Section 4(2).

18 留学人员回国工作"十二五"规划, Section 2(2).

19 人力资源社会保障部对政协十三届全国委员会第二次会议第3819号（社会管理类293号）提案的答复.

20 国务院关于印发国家技术转移体系建设方案的通知, Section 2(8). www.gov.cn/ zhengce/content/2017-09/26/content_5227667.htm.

21 科技部关于印发《"十三五"国家科技人才发展规划》的通知, Section 3(3). www. stdaily.com/kjzc/rencai/2017-04/13/content_561273.shtml.

22 关于加强留学人员回国服务体系建设的意见. www.mohrss.gov.cn/gkml/zcfg/ gfxwj/201407/t20140717_136305.html.

23 Ibid., Section 2(2).The listed organization types include "overseas scholar service centers" (留学人员服务中心), "overseas scholar work stations" (留学人员工作站), "OCS Pioneer Parks" (留学人员创业园), "overseas scholar associations" (留学人员联谊会), and other societal "intermediary service organizations" (社会中介服务机构) or "group organizations" (群团组织) that service overseas scholars.

24 Ibid.

25 Ibid.

26 人社部李金生：我国形成了史上最大规模留学人员归国潮. www.xinhuanet.com/fortune/2019-08/26/c_1210257278.htm.

27 Hong Kong Movie Database, 海外赤子. http://hkmdb.com/db/movies/view.mhtml?id=12367&complete_credits=1&display_set=eng.

28 "海外赤子"的由来 (侨史珍藏) (http://paper.people.com.cn/rmrbhwb/html/2007-06/26/content_13245156.htm). According to this *People's Daily* article on the origins of the term, which literally means "overseas red seed" or "overseas red children," ancient Chinese referred to newborn babies as "red children" (赤子) because of their red color at birth. Because newborn babies were innocent, the term was also used to refer to common people that are loyal to their rulers. "Overseas Chinese" (海外赤子) is adapted from the term "domestic Chinese" (海内赤子), which has its origins in a story about the loyalty of the common people to Emperor Taizong of the Tang Dynasty (唐太宗), who ruled from A.D.626 to 649.

29 关于实施海外赤子为国服务行动计划的通知, Section 1, cites as a "policy guarantee" the 关于鼓励海外留学人员以多种形式为国服务的若干意见. MOHRSS called the *Homeland-Serving Action Plan for Overseas Chinese* a "new brand" for overseas scholars serving the country in an article on its website titled: 赤子计划：树立留学人员为国服务新品牌.

30 关于鼓励海外留学人员以多种形式为国服务的若干意见, Preamble.

31 Ibid., Section 2(1–7).

32 关于实施海外赤子为国服务行动计划的通知, Section 1.

33 Ibid., Section 2.

34 Ibid., Section 4(1–3).

35 祖国的需要 赤子的方向. www.mohrss.gov.cn/zyjsrygls/ZYJSRYGLSgongzuodongtai/201802/t20180228_288996.html.

36 服务归国人才"赤子计划"成名片. www.mohrss.gov.cn/SYrlzyhshbzb/rencaiduiwujianshe/gzdt/201804/t20180418_292561.html.

37 2019"海外赤子为国服务行动计划"湖州行活动成功举办. http://hrss.huzhou.gov.cn/zwgk/zwxxgkml/zwdt/tpxw/20191114/i2546365.html.

38 The term "docking" [对接] is frequently used to refer to negotiations between overseas talent with start-up projects, technology, IP, and/or knowhow and domestic Chinese investors, enterprises, industrial parks, and/or government entities seeking access to the start-up projects, technology, IP, and/or knowhow.

39 Ibid.

40 服务归国人才"赤子计划"成名片. www.mohrss.gov.cn/SYrlzyhshbzb/rencaiduiwujianshe/gzdt/201804/t20180418_292561.html.

41 2018年"赤子计划"开展30项服务活动. www.gov.cn/xinwen/2019-01/30/content_5362232.htm.

42 This is the official translation of the program, see 实施"海外智力为国服务行动计划. http://scitech.people.com.cn/GB/25509/56813/63493/63494/4351330.html.

43 CAST website, 海智概览. http://hzb.cast.org.cn/col/col264/index.html.

44 China's central government website, 主要社会团体. www.gov.cn/test/2005-05/24/content_18314.htm.

45 海智计划联系的海外科技团体名单 (http://hzb.cast.org.cn/art/2019/1/7/art_265_9870.html).

46 中国旅美科技协会总会章 (www.cast-usa.net). See the CAST–USA 2017 Form 990 here: https://apps.irs.gov/pub/epostcard/cor/113659421_201712_990_20181213160 00164.pdf.

47 Invitation Letter for Yale Summit 2018 on Science and Technology Innovation and Economic Leadership and The 26th Annual Conference of Chinese Association for Science and Technology, USA (http://docs.wixstatic.com/ugd/ad4f2f_6bc56210a125 4944a88810695d15d5f5.pdf).

48 About CAST–USA. https://GNY,castgny.org/en/index.php/about-us-3/.

49 CAST website, 海智概览. http://hzb.cast.org.cn/col/col264/index.html.

50 Ibid. Also: http://before.cast.org.cn/n200685/c57776903/content.html and www.sohu.com/a/210350400_749128.

51 For example, at the 2016 中国科协海智计划基地工作会议召开. http://before.cast.org.cn/n200675/n202195/n202367/c400634/content.html. See also 海外人才离岸创新创业基地概述 (http://before.cast.org.cn/n200675/n202200/n202372/c400650/content.html), which states that in 2015, a State Council policy document (《国务院关于大力推进大众创业万众创新若干政策措施的意见》第二十四条) called for "strengthening the construction of overseas S&T talent offshore entrepreneurial bases to bring in more foreign innovation and entrepreneurial resources."

52 致公党中央：关于构建离岸创新创业新模式　吸引海外人才为国服务的提案. http://tyzx.people.cn/n1/2018/0227/c417761-29837415.html.

53 国家海外人才离岸创新创业基地花落宁波 (rencai.people.com.cn/n1/2017/1206/c364615-29689254.html). Models to be explored include: "Chinese entrepreneurs + overseas scientists," "Chinese new emerging industries + overseas advanced technologies," "Chinese startups + overseas innovation," and "Chinese financial innovation + foreign technology innovation."

54 Flexibility central to attracting international talents. www.chinadaily.com.cn/regional/2016-10/27/content_27191223.htm.

55 成都海外人才离岸创新创业基地已设立31个海外工作站. https://e.chengdu.cn/html/2019-07/02/content_653307.htm.

56 成都高新区全球揽才 已设立13个海外人才离岸基地. http://cd.newssc.org/system/20170711/002222441.html.

57 海外人才离岸创新创业服务体系初建成. https://epaper.scdaily.cn/shtml/scrb/2017 0801/169548.shtml.

58 成都高新区全球揽才 已设立13个海外人才离岸基地. http://cd.newssc.org/system/20170711/002222441.html.

59 SABPA website, About SABPA. https://member.sabpa.org/web/about.php.

60 广州阳普医疗科技股份有限公司 2016 年年度报告, p. 4. www.improve-medical.com/Uploads/attached/file/20170413/20170413100102_31998.pdf.

61 GIMDx, Inc. and IncellDx, Inc. Announce Acceleration of Chinese Commercialization of HPV OncoTect Kit. www.prnewswire.com/news-releases/gimdx-inc-and-incelldx-inc-announce-acceleration-of-chinese-commercialization-of-hpv-oncotect-kit-300617046.html.

62 致公党中央：关于构建离岸创新创业新模式　吸引海外人才为国服务的提案. http://tyzx.people.cn/n1/2018/0227/c417761-29837415.html.

63 "春晖计划"十年历程. www.chinaqw.com/lxs/rdjj/200703/21/65940.shtml. "Chunhui" (春晖) has been formally translated both as "Spring Light" and "Spring Sunshine." We use the Chinese term throughout.

64 教育部"春晖计划"专项经费管理规定, Article 1, 1996.

65 "春晖杯"中国留学人员创新创业大赛. http://cyds.cscse.edu.cn.

66 "春晖杯"中国留学人员创新创业大赛简介. http://cyds.cscse.edu.cn/cyds/index/wxtl/359300/index.html.

67 Ibid.

68 www.scea.org/post/第十四届-春晖杯-中国留学人员创新创业大赛 Applications can also be submitted virtually from anywhere in the world.
69 http://newyork.lxgz.org.cn/publish/portal119/tab6009/info140702.htm.
70 SCEA By Law. www.scea.org/bylaw.
71 www.chineseinsfbay.com/company/task_view/id_19033/硅谷中国工程师协会.html.
72 www.scea.org/post/第十四届-春晖杯-中国留学人员创新创业大赛.
73 驻旧金山总领馆举办第十四届"春晖杯"中国留学人员创新创业大赛旧金山领区说明会. http://cyds.cscse.edu.cn/cyds/cyal/394901/index.html.
74 www.scea.org/post/第十四届-春晖杯-中国留学人员创新创业大赛.
75 http://cyds.cscse.edu.cn/cyds/ycxw/index.html.
76 www.scea.org/post/第十四届-春晖杯-中国留学人员创新创业大赛.
77 "春晖杯"中国留学人员创新创业大赛简介. cyds.cscse.edu.cn/cyds/index/wxtl/359300/index.html.
78 第十四届"春晖杯"中国留学人员创新创业大赛预入围项目公示 (http://cyds.cscse.edu.cn/cyds/ycxw/399395/index.html). The announcement states that the 301 projects are "pre-shortlisted" (预入围) and if there is no objection during the 7-day public announcement period then these projects officially become finalists.
79 第十四届"春晖杯"创新创业大赛入围项目汇总. http://webcache.googleusercontent.com/search?q=cache:azeR3UPRDg0J:hrss.xm.gov.cn/xxgk/tzgg/201911/P020191125529015464919.docx.
80 Also translated as "111 Plan," "111 Program," and "Program 111."
81 高等学校学科创新引智基地管理办法 (教技〔2006〕4号), Article 3, accessible at: www.moe.gov.cn/srcsite/A16/s7062/200608/t20060830_82287.html.
82 Ibid., Article 11 (2.1). The term *yinzhi* (引智) literally means "introducing (or bringing in) intelligence," and within the context of the 111 program can be translated as "foreign intellect recruitment."
83 Ibid., Article 11 (2.1).
84 Ibid., Article 11 (3.4).
85 Ibid., Article 11 (3.6).
86 Ibid., Article 11 (3.5).
87 Ibid., Article 11 (3.6).
88 Ibid., Article 11 (3.6).
89 Ibid., Article 11 (2.1).
90 Sciencenet.cn is the website of the China Science Daily Media Group, which is co-sponsored by several PRC government organs.
91 高校入选"111计划"基地数量排行及地域分布. http://blog.sciencenet.cn/blog-2903646-1071560.html.
92 教育部　国家外国专家局关于2018年度新建高等学校学科创新引智基地立项的通知, Attachment 1.

Bibliography

PRC Ministry of Education. 高等学校学科创新引智基地管理办法 ("Administrative Measures for Bases for the Recruitment of Innovative Intellects in Academic Disciplines to Universities"), MOE (4), August 30, 2006.

PRC Ministry of Human Resources and Social Security. 关于实施海外赤子为国服务行动计划的通知 ("Homeland-Serving Action Plan for Overseas Chinese"), MOHRSS (103), August 27, 2009.

PRC Ministry of Human Resources and Social Security. 关于加强留学人员回国服务体系建设的意见 ("Opinions on Strengthening Construction of the Overseas Scholar Returnee Service System"), MOHRSS (46), April 19, 2011.

PRC Ministry of Human Resources and Social Security. 关于印发留学人员回国工作"十二五"规划的通知 ("Twelfth 5-Year Plan on Working for the Return of Overseas Scholars"), MOHRSS (80), July 22, 2011.

PRC Ministry of Personnel. 关于印发《"九五"期间人事系统留学人员工作规划》的通知 ("Plan for Working with Overseas Scholars in the Personnel System during the Ninth 5-Year Plan"), MOP (75), August 21, 1996.

PRC Ministry of Personnel. 关于印发＜关于鼓励海外留学人员以多种形式为国服务的若干意见＞的通知 ("Circular on the Release of Opinions on Encouraging Overseas Chinese Scholars to Serve the Country by Multiple Means"), MOP (49), MOE, MOST, MOF, and MPS, 2001.

PRC Ministry of Personnel. 关于印发《留学人员回国工作"十一五"规划》的通知 ("Eleventh 5-Year Plan on Working for the Return of Overseas Scholars"), MOP (123), November 15, 2006.

PRC Ministry of Science and Technology. 科技部关于印发《"十三五"国家科技人才发展规划》的通知 ("Thirteenth 5-Year Plan for National Science and Technology Talent Development"), MOST (86), April 13, 2017.

PRC State Council. 国家技术转移体系建设方案 ("Plan to Build a National Technology Transfer System"), State Council (44), September 15, 2017.

Xi, Jinping (习近平). "习近平在欧美同学会成立100周年庆祝大会上的讲话" ("Speech by Xi Jinping at the 100th Anniversary Celebration of the Establishment of the Western Returned Scholars Association"), *Xinhua*, October 21, 2013.

Xi, Jinping (习近平). "习近平：在中国科学院第十七次院士大会、中国工程院第十二次院士大会上的讲话" ("Xi Jinping: Speech at the 17th Academician Conference of the Chinese Academy of Sciences and the 12th Academician Conference of the Chinese Academy of Engineering"), *People's Daily*, June 9, 2014.

Xi, Jinping (习近平). "习近平：为建设世界科技强国而奋斗" (Xi Jinping: Struggle to Build a World Science and Technology Superpower), *Xinhua*, May 30, 2016.

Xi, Jinping (习近平). "习近平：在中国科学院第十九次院士大会、中国工程院第十四次院士大会上的讲话" ("Xi Jinping: Speech at the 19th Academician Conference of the Chinese Academy of Sciences and the 14th Academician Conference of the Chinese Academy of Engineering"), *Xinhua*, May 28, 2018.

Xi, Jinping (习近平). "习近平在全国组织工作会议的讲话" ("Speech by Xi Jinping at the National Organization Work Conference"), *Communist Party Member Network*, July 3, 2018. www.12371.cn/2018/09/17/ARTI1537150840597467.shtml.

3

CHINA'S TALENT PROGRAMS

Jeffrey Stoff

The previous chapter examined how China uses individuals overseas to serve China's technology transfer objectives through various means (以多种方式). This chapter focuses on China's state-run talent recruitment programs. These programs aim to attract experts from around the world to come work in China, on a part- or full-time basis, to facilitate the transfer of technology and knowhow.

Despite their ubiquity, there is still limited public information on the structure, scale, and scope of these programs. Nevertheless, what data is available indicates that China's state-sponsored talent programs are about more than simply increasing the hiring of global experts; they also entail a highly developed supporting ecosystem to locate and facilitate talent introduction. This includes dedicated state research funding, the support of ostensibly private venture capital funds, global recruitment and candidate evaluation networks, overseas experts' databases, information service platforms, and a plethora of other domestic and overseas supporting organizations.

This chapter offers a primer on China's talent programs and seeks to illuminate their lesser-known aspects. We start by examining the origins of these talent programs through an understanding of their doctrinal and policy components. We then turn to a discussion of some less reported features of the flagship Thousand Talents Plan. The remainder of the chapter then provides some background on the supporting infrastructure that China has built out for these programs both domestically and overseas. While our discussion focuses mainly on China and the United States, China's operations are global and most advanced nations are affected in similar ways and thus warrant similar scrutiny.

Origins of PRC talent programs

The PRC government has long understood that advancing its economy and military requires advanced human capital—that is, scientists and engineers who can help China develop critical capabilities and next-generation technologies in order to achieve its goal of becoming a technological superpower. Its leadership recognized the value and importance of transferring the intellectual capital of overseas technical experts as early as 1955, when American-trained Chinese physicist Qian Xuesen (钱学森) returned to China after working at Caltech and on the Manhattan Project in World War II. Qian went on to become the most prominent figure in China's nuclear weapons and ballistic missile programs in the 1950s and 1960s. Despite this early success, it was not until 1994 that China initiated a program to recruit experts from overseas: the Hundred Talents Plan (百人计划), the progenitor of the "talents" series, run by the Chinese Academy of Sciences (CAS) with 1,569 participants to date.[1]

Seeing the value of the Hundred Talents Plan, the PRC Ministry of Education (MOE) created the Changjiang Scholars Award Program (长江学者奖励计划) in 1998 to recruit overseas-based experts to work in academic positions in various Chinese research institutions. Ten years later, the PRC state and Communist Party of China (CPC) established what is now considered to be its flagship talent program: the "Recruitment Program for Global Experts" (海外高层次人才引进计划), or, as it is more commonly known, the "Thousand Talents Plan" (千人计划).

The Changjiang Scholars, Hundred Talents, and Thousand Talents programs have had notable success recruiting world-class experts who have made significant contributions to China's S&T development. For example, Pan Jianwei (潘建伟), one of the first selectees recruited via the Thousand Talents Plan from Austria and Germany[2] and a key figure in quantum physics and communications research, transferred research funded by foreign governments and facilitated the recruitment of a dozen or more other talent program selectees from overseas to work with him at the University of Science & Technology of China.[3] These talent programs were foundational to a monumental policy shift that recognized that human capital investment was key to China's S&T development. The number of state-run talent recruitment programs and corresponding resources and supporting infrastructure has grown exponentially over the last decade and will continue to grow, based on the goals of a major 10-year plan on talent development described later in this chapter.

Today, China's talent recruitment programs, of which there are hundreds, are run at national, provincial, municipal, and even institutional levels, and are woven into government and CPC organs, state-owned enterprises, defense research and academic institutions, national laboratories, "private" industry, domestic and overseas "NGOs," and global diaspora organizations. These programs all have a single purpose: to transfer to China intellectual capital and property from around the world by any means necessary to bolster China's economic, technological, and military competitiveness.

US government (USG) agencies have recently increased their scrutiny of China's talent programs.[4] Yet there is still little understanding of their scale, scope, and supporting infrastructures. Additionally, attention from US law enforcement or affected research institutions has primarily focused on illicit activities carried out by talent program selectees, and indeed some selectees have been convicted of economic espionage and intellectual property theft or for violating conditions of federal research grants. But this narrow focus on criminal activity does not fully address other legal or extralegal activity that may have national and economic security implications.

In this light, one significant but under-reported feature of these talent programs is their integration into China's United Front organization—a global influence apparatus (discussed in Chapter 15) through which China's overseas affiliates assist in working toward pre-defined national policy goals, in this case the recruiting, hosting, and organizing of talent programs and start-up contests, among other talent initiatives. In other words, *China's (predominantly) CPC-led influence apparatus intersects with or directly supports its global technology transfer apparatus.* US and allied nations subjected to its campaigns—when they analyze the issue at all—artificially bifurcate these two domains despite their interconnectivity.

Given the complexity and scale of these talent programs,[5] this chapter cannot adequately cover all areas that merit scrutiny. The US Senate Homeland Security and Government Affairs Committee issued a comprehensive report in November 2019 on the Thousand Talents Plan and federal agencies' responses to date, which covers many of its aspects.[6] Rather than duplicate the work done in that report, this chapter focuses on lesser-known aspects of the talent programs.

Policy and doctrine supporting the talent programs

While there are several policies and directives to attract and develop S&T talent, the one that serves as the lynchpin of China's talent recruitment programs was issued by the CPC and State Council in June 2010, officially known as the Outline for the National Medium and Long-term Talent Development Plan (2010–2020).[7]

This ten-year plan was the product of several years of party deliberations spearheaded by the CPC Central Committee Organization Department, the entity responsible for appointing leadership in the CPC, government, state-owned enterprises, and academia. It was the first policy to incorporate the "Talent Superpower Strategy" (人才强国战略), a concept added to the CPC's ideological cannon at the 17th CPC National Congress in 2007, and incorporated in the CPC Party Constitution that same year.[8] Wang Huiyao (王辉耀), an architect of the plan,[9] described its importance to PRC leadership and to China's S&T and economic development:

> It is remarkably unusual that these two leadership bodies [CPC and State Council] would jointly endorse a plan on such a high note. The announcement of this plan was also very unusual in that President Hu Jintao and all of the other eight Politburo Standing Committee Members attended its formal release ceremony, where President Hu,

Premier Wen Jiabao and Vice President Xi Jinping all delivered important speeches." ... The plan emphasizes that talent is the top priority resource for China's social and economic development. This new paradigm shift in China's model of development, led by the country's top leaders, has sent a very strong signal that unlike the past, when much importance was attached to hardware, it is now human talent that is the most valuable and important asset for China to have and cultivate.[10]

The plan was also notable for the vast amount of media attention it received on its release, with one report noting that "China's official news agency, Xinhua, and all other major Chinese media simultaneously released the 19,000-word plan nationwide and China's central TV station CCTV broadcasted a series of programs on the subject during primetime." According to this report, "[t]his media effort indicate[d] that China's top leaders have attached unprecedented importance to the Talent Development Plan and are committed to publicizing it throughout Chinese society."[11]

The Talent Development Plan calls for allocating some 15 percent of the country's gross domestic product (GDP) to human capital development by 2020. The plan does not specify which GDP figures it will base this 15 percent spending goal on, i.e., whether this target is derived from a median or average GDP over the 10-year period or based on the GDP of a particular year. Regardless, this is a staggering commitment that reflects China's transition from equipment to human-based investment and covers the full range of HR development,[12] including programs and measures to attract overseas talent *to facilitate technology transfers*. Noteworthy elements are:

- Vigorously attract foreign talent to establish businesses or conduct research in China.
- Continue existing recruitment programs and replicate them at local levels.
- Build up the network of foreign technology commercialization bases in China.
- Create databases of overseas talent for targeting and recruitment.
- Encourage PRC enterprises to set up overseas R&D institutions.
- Promote the "transformation of S&T achievements" and "technology transfer using overseas talent."[13]

In other words, the plan seeks to attract and utilize overseas talent to both acquire technology and commercialize it. A "responsible person" in the CPC Central Committee Talent Work Coordination Group, the key policy body on talent recruitment programs, summed up the critical role overseas talent plays in China's technology transfer and S&T innovation strategies as follows:

Overseas returnee scientists are the talent power behind knowledge and technology transfers, and have gradually become China's new force in academic development and S&T innovation, promoters of high and new technology applications, and frontrunners in promoting China's innovative development.[14]

Overview of major talent programs

China's state-sponsored talent recruitment programs have proliferated since the Outline for the National Medium and Long-term Talent Development Plan (2010–2020) was issued. The programs and their supporting offices are run at national, local, and institutional levels. They involve innovation bases, academic-oriented programs, and entrepreneurial contests that connect research labs, state-owned enterprises, and technology start-ups. More rigorous surveys of these programs are needed to determine their number and assess the full measure of their security implications to the US and other nations. Meanwhile, we can highlight some features common to the better-known programs.

Vetting and approval of talent candidates is overseen by the CPC Organization Department (at the central or local level), while funding and administration is done by the PRC government—typically the Ministry of Science and Technology (MOST), MOE, and the State Administration of Foreign Expert Affairs, or their local counterparts. As such, these talent program selectees are hired and compensated by the PRC government and can receive additional or matching compensation from the employing institution and their host municipality. Thus, these selectees placed in business enterprises receive de facto state subsidies that pay their salary (or match their employer's salary) and provide relocation expenses, travel reimbursements, and other benefits. This creates unfair competitive advantages for PRC businesses, regardless of whether transfers of technology take place.

In other cases, talent programs have short-term components that allow selectees to stay at their current posts overseas and simultaneously advise or lead parallel research efforts in China (see Chapter 2). This offers opportunities for the selectees to "remain in place" while contributing to China's development. Several identified programs such as Thousand Talents and Changjiang Scholars also recruit non-ethnic Chinese. An example is German physicist Ulf Leonhardt, recruited as a short-term Thousand Talents selectee. Leonhardt was unaware of conditions in the Chinese version of his contract, and later discovered China was diverting his research to military projects, while failing to provide some of the promised compensation.[15]

The Senate Homeland Security report on the Thousand Talents Plan provides examples of talent program contracts that require the transfer of intellectual property to China, specify actions that undermine research integrity, and threaten US national security.[16] In some cases the US-based selectees are made to abide by PRC law and not disclose contract conditions to their US employers. Many contracts are for short-term or visiting positions that allow recruited experts to remain in their posts abroad. Talent call announcements and the contracts themselves focus on individuals who have already developed a high level of expertise and can demonstrate access to critical research or technologies.

The case of USA v. Chunzai Wang

The contract examples in the Senate Homeland Security report were obtained through Congressional oversight requests to federal agencies. These efforts to expose details of the Thousand Talents Plan are important, as are the public records of talent plan recipients whose contracts caused them to run afoul of US law. One such person is Chunzai Wang, a federal research scientist employed by the National Oceanic and Atmospheric Administration (NOAA). Wang was convicted in 2018 of illegally supplementing his USG salary with PRC funds.

US law forbids federal employees from receiving outside compensation for work that directly pertains to one's official government duties.[17] Public court records show that Wang, as a federal employee, was simultaneously under contract with the Chinese government through Thousand Talents and Changjiang Scholars, as well as the National Basic Research Program of China (973 Program). The court records included copies of these three contracts,[18] which reveal not only criminal activity as judged by the court, but also conflicts of interest and commitment. Although these latter activities are not necessarily illegal, the case epitomizes the ambiguity in situations where US law has not kept up with what most Americans regard as unethical practice.

On the criminal side, Wang was indicted on five counts of defrauding the government through false time and attendance claims—alleging to have worked for the US government while on personal travel in China—and three counts of illegal supplementation of salary (via Thousand Talents, Changjiang Scholars, and 973 programs). Through a plea deal, Wang accepted guilt for one count of illegal supplementation of his government salary via the Changjiang program.

The Changjiang Scholars contract contained in court records indicates that Wang was expected to work a minimum of two months per year for three years as a visiting scholar at the Ocean University of China. Compensation was 15,000 RMB (approximately $2,344) per month for each month he worked in China. Wang was also provided two million RMB (about $312,500) for "scientific research and support"[19] though it is not clear whether some of that additional two million could be used for personal compensation. Based on this one-count conviction, the Committee of 100 (百人会, a group of prominent Chinese–Americans) issued a press release criticizing the federal government for prosecuting a renowned climate scientist,[20] and the Committee of Concerned Scientists urged NOAA's head to recognize the case as "prosecutorial overreach" and welcome Wang back "for the sake of scientific integrity and independence."

Both organizations argued that Wang was on annual leave from his government job and simply paid "a small per diem fee" for mentoring students.[21] The three contracts used as court exhibits tell a different story.

Besides the Changjiang Scholars contract, which was the basis of his conviction, Wang was also under contract with the 973 Program and Thousand Talents. The former provided two-year compensation totaling 200,000 RMB ($31,250); Thousand Talents provided another 15,000 RMB ($2,344) per month (for a minimum of two months per year) in wages for five years, plus an award of 500,000 RMB ($78,125) by the PRC central government, a matching 500,000 RMB from the provincial government, and 250,000 RMB ($39,062) from the employing institution.[22] It is hard to characterize these figures as a "small per diem fee." The two-month commitment also doesn't square well with the annual leave typically granted to federal employees.[23]

The stipulations in these contracts also point to potential conflicts of interest and violations of research integrity, areas that may not be illegal but nonetheless represent security concerns:

- In addition to requiring training of Ph.D. students and other "Thousand Talent Team members," the Thousand Talents contract signed by Wang detailed the type of scientific research to be carried out *in the US*.[24] In other words, the contract was tantamount to a PRC tasking to work in specific areas utilizing US research labs, capabilities, and knowhow.
- Wang's "major achievements," papers, books, or patents had to credit the Ocean University of China, and research published in scientific journals had to name the PRC institution as the primary affiliation[25] *regardless of where the research took place.*
- Wang was to "accept and train Ph.D. students, advise and train post-doctoral students, and encourage outstanding graduate students to study abroad,"[26] a provision that potentially undermines merit-based hiring decisions.
- Wang was expected to "serve an important bridging role" between Ocean University of China and NOAA.[27] While no specifics were provided on what that entails, it does highlight yet another potential for abuse inherent in these "talent" programs, if, for example, such bridging is a means by which China can utilize a US federal employee to surreptitiously advocate for Chinese interests and goals.

To what extent actions like these are, or should be, treated as criminal is a matter for legislators to decide and courts to affirm. That aside, it is hard to ignore the fact that these contracts with a sovereign foreign nation harbor significant potential for ethical abuse that, at minimum, should be addressed by the professional societies that sprang to Wang's defense. The arrest in January 2020 of Harvard University chemistry professor Charles Lieber, a self-described "pioneer in nanoscience and nanotechnology,"[28] charged with allegedly making a false statement over his involvement in a talent plan demonstrates scrutiny of these activities is not limited to persons of Chinese ethnicity.[29]

China's flagship Thousand Talents Plan: its lesser-known elements

The Recruitment Program of Global Experts[30]—commonly known as the Thousand Talents Plan—was launched in 2008 and is widely regarded as China's flagship talent program, given the prestige bestowed on selectees by the PRC government and the lucrative compensation offered. While there is substantial press coverage of the Thousand Talents Plan (TTP) partly due to recent US government actions,[31] there is little reporting on corresponding infrastructures in China and overseas. The remainder of this chapter will explore some of the TTP's partnering entities, namely, its venture capital structures, a TTP Expert Association, and the talent introduction bases that support the exploitation of foreign technology in China. Other supporting entities, such as the TTP's own think tank and service centers, are beyond the scope of this study.

TTP Venture Capital Center, entrepreneurial contests

One indicator of the importance the PRC government places on recruiting overseas talent to transfer technology and knowhow is the fact that the TTP has its own venture capital component that is part of the largest state-owned, RMB-denominated venture capital fund of funds. Thus, the TTP also uses venture capital investment to recruit talent and launch businesses.

The Thousand Talents Venture Capital Center (千人计划创投中心), established in 2011 and headquartered in the Suzhou Industrial Park, is China's "first comprehensive investment and financing platform for the TTP."[32] The center is run by Suzhou Oriza Holdings, a state-owned company managed by the Suzhou municipal government's Suzhou Industrial Park Administration Committee. Oriza Holdings is a large equity investment and financial services firm with over 50 billion RMB ($7.2B) in assets under management.[33] Besides the Thousand Talents center, the company manages China's first equity investment fund of funds and China's largest angel investment platform.[34]

In May of 2012, the TTP Venture Capital Center held its first promotional event in Silicon Valley, with a goal of "introducing the TTP and the TTP Venture Capital Center to high-level talent in Silicon Valley, and to launch the inaugural TTP Start-Up Contest." At the event, a representative of the center stated that the contest serves as a platform for talented individuals willing to launch businesses in China who have not yet been recruited through the TTP.[35]

The promotional event also announced the establishment of the TTP Venture Capital Center's first "overseas liaison office" based in Silicon Valley (硅谷建立千人计划创投中心的首个海外联络处).[36] No further information was found on the specific location or function of this Silicon Valley liaison office. However, according to the Office of the US Trade Representative, Oriza Holdings is the lead manager of Silicon Valley (Santa Clara)-based Oriza Ventures Technology

Fund, also known as Oriza Ventures.[37] Oriza Ventures has served as a TTP Start-Up Contest organizer, such as the 2017 North America round held at the Santa Clara Convention Center,[38] which suggests it may have this additional role.

After its inaugural launch in 2012, the TTP Start-Up Contest has held rounds annually in the San Francisco/Silicon Valley Area. The seventh round (2018), also organized by the TTP Venture Capital Center, was held in Santa Clara[39] in the offices of HYSTA SVC—an organization that is the result of a merger between the Hua Yuan S&T Association and the SVC Venture Club that claims to support the "largest US-China investment network."[40] HYSTA SVC's office is located in a suite next to Oriza Ventures.[41] According to an online announcement, the TTP Start-Up Contest has changed its name to the "Jinji Lake Start-Up Contest" (金鸡湖创业大赛), with no reference to "Thousand Talents."[42] The 2019 US round of the Jinji Lake Start-Up Contest was held in Silicon Valley in May 2019, though the announcement did not specify the location.[43]

TTP Expert Association

The aforementioned TTP Start-Up Contest is jointly run by the TTP Venture Capital Center and the TTP Expert Association (千人计划专家联谊会).[44] According to its website, the latter is a "non-profit social organization" (非营利性社会团体) and a branch of the Western Returned Scholars Association (WRSA) established "under the guidance" of the CPC Organization Department Talent Bureau's Overseas High-Level Talent Introduction Work Special Office. Members of the TTP Expert Association are current or former TTP selectees. The association's mission is to "unite and serve domestic and overseas scholar talents, actively implement the strategy of rejuvenating the country with science and technology and strengthening the country with talent, and strive to become a new force in national innovation and entrepreneurship."[45] WRSA itself is directly subordinate to the CPC United Front Work Department, China's key organ for global influence operations.[46]

The TTP Expert Association has eight professional committees, which support the tasks listed above, including committees for information science and technology; mathematics and physics; chemistry and chemical engineering; biology, pharmaceuticals, and life science; energy, resources, and environment; economics, finance, and management; engineering and materials; and a general committee for high-tech industry. These committees confer on technology and industry developments and probably advise or facilitate TTP recruitment activities.[47]

Supporting infrastructure: talent innovation bases in China

Similar to the 111 Plan's "foreign intellect recruitment innovation bases" discussed in Chapter 2, the TTP establishes "Overseas High-Level Talent Innovation

Bases" in China (海外高层次人才创新基地). These bases are housed in PRC enterprises, universities, research institutes, and high-technology development zones.[48] According to Li Zhiyong (李智勇), Deputy Director of the CPC Central Committee Organization Department and Deputy Chair of the CPC Central Talent Work Coordination Group, these bases serve several functions, including: to co-locate overseas talents; carry out incentives and related policies to promote innovation; establish investment, technology, information, and service platforms; and create service structures for higher educational institutions.[49] The numbers of overseas recruits brought into these innovation bases suggest they likely coordinate with other talent recruitment programs, not just the TTP. One of these bases located in the Dalian High-Technology Zone claimed that since 2009 over 3,000 overseas scholars relocated there to start-up businesses or joint ventures.[50]

In the commercial sector, Overseas Talents Innovation Bases are attached to major technology firms and state-owned enterprises. Examples of firms housing these bases include defense industry conglomerates China National Nuclear Corporation, China Electronics Corporation, China Aerospace Science & Technology Corporation, Aviation Industry Corporation of China, and China Ordnance Industries Group Corporation (aka NORINCO).[51] Other major firms such as Huawei and ZTE also house these bases.[52] Thus, the PRC government is providing resources and talent recruitment program support to facilitate technology or knowhow transfers and bolster innovation development at major defense and commercial enterprises– without the companies themselves having to bear these costs, which brings into question China's adherence to WTO agreements, and confirms that talent co-optees serve China's military establishment.

Supporting infrastructure: talent databases for targeting overseas experts

For decades, China has been developing information technology (IT) to support its "overseas scholar work" (留学人员工作) and talent recruitment programs.[53] This IT infrastructure has been integrated into a "service system" (服务体系) centered on PRC government-backed "overseas scholar service organizations" (留学人员服务机构) discussed in Chapter 2. For example, in 2006, the 11th Five-Year Plan on Working for the Return of Overseas Scholars stressed the need to "give full play to the roles of every type of overseas scholar organization and social group,"[54] build service platforms of information networks and "overseas scholar talent information databases" (留学人才信息库), and establish a "nation-wide unified overseas scholar talent information system" (全国统一的留学人才信息系统)."[55]

In 2011, the Ministry of Human Resources and Social Security (MOHRSS) issued a document entitled, "Opinions on Strengthening Construction of the Overseas Scholar Returnee Service System,"[56] which discussed building an "overseas scholar returnee service information platform" (留学人员回国服

务信息平台) composed of numerous databases including: overseas scholar information databases (留学人员信息库), overseas scholar scientific research project databases (留学人员科研项目库), databases of needed talent (人才需求库), and databases of returned experts (回国(来华)专家库)."[57] The "Opinions" further specified that this platform, along with other government-supported information networks, "rely on the China Overseas Talent Information Network (中国留学人才信息网)" to spread information on overseas talent work projects, policies, and funding.[58] These vehicles are a "window and bridge for creating connections with and services for the masses of overseas scholars, both within China and abroad."[59]

- The China Overseas Talent Information Network website links to a "Join the Overseas Talent Database" (加入留学人才库), where prospective recruits can obtain information on PRC talent programs,[60] review openings at universities,[61] research institutes[62] and enterprises[63] in China, and signal their willingness to participate.
- A China Overseas Talent Network (中国海外人才网) serves as a "search platform for overseas high-level talent to return to China to start a company or work," and obtain information on "recruitment work of each locality in China."[64] It links to the same "Join the Overseas Talent Database."[65]
- A Chinese Overseas Talent Pool (海外人才库) database[66] is managed by the China Overseas-Educated Scholars Development Foundation (中国留学人才发展基金会), an organization established with WRSA support in 2007 (both are United Front).[67] Its homepage states in English that it "empowers global talents to build a better future." The Chinese version runs: "Bring in global talent to build a better future for China."[68]

These examples of networks and databases are illustrative; many more exist. An August 2019 MOHRSS document states that the PRC government intends to build an Overseas Scholar Employment and Entrepreneurship Service Information Platform (留学人员就业创业服务信息平台), conduct research on building more high-level talent databases (高层次人才库), and use big data methods to improve services.[69]

China also engages in precise targeting of overseas talent by leveraging information networks and databases. In March 2016, the CPC published "Opinions on Deepening Reform of the Talent Development System," which called for "improving overseas talent recruitment methods" by "implementing precision recruitment" (实现精准引进).[70] The CPC Organization Department published a "National Introduction of Overseas High-Level Talent Reference Catalogue" (国家引进海外高层次人才参考目录)[71] to "raise the level of precision in overseas talent recruitment work" across PRC government entities. Contents of the catalogue include:[72]

- 2,600 "globally famous experts" working at "the frontiers of science and on key technology trends"[73] for targeting by the Central Talent Work Coordination Group Office.[74]
- 10 science and technology "national talent recruitment key areas" (国家引才重点领域) from which talent is to be targeted.[75]
- 686 "national talent recruitment receiving platforms" (国家引才承接平台).[76] These platforms probably include the Talent Innovation Bases described above.

Survey of other talent programs

The TTP's website links to 182 local talent programs. Some have their own Hundred Talents and Thousand Talents plans (e.g., Hubei Hundred Talents, Shanghai Thousand Talents, etc.).[77] The list is by no means exhaustive, as there are other national and institution-run programs not listed. Some examples are provided in Table 3.1. A comprehensive survey is needed to fully assess their scale and scope.

In sum, China's state-sponsored talent recruitment programs play a critical role in transferring intellectual capital and property to China. The USG and media's narrow focus on the Thousand Talents Plan does not support a nuanced

TABLE 3.1 Sample of talent programs not listed on TTP's website[F1]

National-Level Talent Programs	Individual Institution-Run Talent Programs
Innovative Talents Promotion Plan (创新人才推进计划)	Harbin Engineering University Longjiang Scholars (哈尔滨工程大学龙江学者)
CAS Innovation Teams International Cooperation and Partners Plan (创新团队国际合作伙伴计划)	Beijing Institute of Technology "Hundred Talents Plan" (北京理工大学 "百人计划")
MOHRSS Project for Experts' Return and Settlement in China (回国(来华)定居工作专家项目)	Beihang University "Distinguished Hundred Talents Program" (北京航空航天大学 "卓越百人计划")
Ministry of Education New Century Talents Plan (教育部新世纪优秀人才支持计划)	Xidian University Huashan Scholars Plan (西安电子科技大学华山学者计划)
Ministry of Agriculture – Chinese Academy of Agricultural Sciences Youth Talent Plan (中国农业科学院青年英才计划)	Nanjing University of Aeronautics and Astronautics Changkong Scholars Program/Changkong Star (南京航空航天大学 "长空学者"计划长空之星)

Note

1 Sources listing these talent programs include: www.mohrss.gov.cn/SYrlzyhshbzb/rencaiduiwujianshe/zcwj/zhuanyejishurenyuan/201412/t20141204_145662.html;blog.sciencenet.cn/blog-425155-1198487.html; www.gz.gov.cn/gzgov/snzc/201908/cbc404e36697440c9387245719c4b65c/files/c1e632665cf647ccade3e28e6f3505bc.pdf

understanding of these programs' scale and scope and the extent to which they represent a threat to US and global economic security.

Notes

1 baike.baidu.com/item/百人计划.

2 www.hfnl.ustc.edu.cn/detail?id=2898 and www.cas.cn/xw/cmsm/201406/t20140613_4137298.shtml. Also referred to in Chapter 7, Europe.

3 www.ustc.edu.cn/_s57/3118/list.psp. See also Strider Global Intelligence Team, "Quantum Dragon—How China Is Exploiting Western Government Funding and Research Institutes to Leapfrog in Dual-Use Quantum Technologies," Strider Technologies, November 2019 (www.strider.tech/wp-content/uploads/2019/11/Strider-Quantum-Dragon-Report.pdf). See also Chapter 7.

4 www.wsj.com/articles/energy-department-bans-personnel-from-foreign-talent-recruitment-programs-11560182546 and www.insidehighered.com/news/2019/04/16/federal-granting-agencies-and-lawmakers-step-scrutiny-foreign-research.

5 It is difficult to quantify the total number of PRC state-sponsored talent programs. The Thousand Talents Plan website lists 182 talent programs run at provincial or municipal levels (1000plan.org), but there are others not included on that list. Examples are included later in this chapter.

6 United States Senate, "Threats to the US Research Enterprise: China's Talent Recruitment Plans," *Staff Report Permanent Subcommittee on Investigations of the United States Senate Committee on Homeland Security and Governmental Affairs*, November 2019.

7 PRC State Council, "国家中长期人才发展规划纲要 (2010–2020 年)," June 6, 2010 (www.gov.cn/jrzg/2010-06/06/content_1621777.htm). This Talent Development Plan should not be confused with the more overarching National Medium and Long-term Plan for Science and Technology Development (2006–2020), a document that also targets technological development and which has received considerably more attention in the West.

8 Communist Party of China, "CPC Charter-Amendments to the 17th CPC National Congress, Passed on Oct. 21, 2007" (中国共产党章程 中国共产党第十七次全国代表大会部分修改, 2007年10月21日通过). www.gov.cn/ztzl/17da/content_786434.htm.

9 Wang Huiyao is Director General of the Center for China and Globalization, which is part of the Western Returned Scholars Association (WRSA) and serves as WRSA vice-chairman. WRSA is subordinate to the CPC United Front Work Department (profiled in Chapter 15) that conducts global influence operations.

10 Wang Huiyao, "China's National Talent Plan: Key Measures and Objectives," *Brookings*, November 2010.

11 www.brookings.edu/research/chinas-national-talent-plan-key-measures-and-objectives/.

12 www.gov.cn/jrzg/2012-05/15/content_2137899.htm.

13 "国家中长期人才发展规划纲要 (2010–2020年)," June 6, 2010. www.gov.cn/jrzg/2010-06/06/content_1621777.htm.

14 "海归梦,中国梦," November 7, 2017. www.xinhuanet.com//mrdx/2017-11/07/c_136733044.htm.

15 Mara Hvistendahl, "China's Programme for Recruiting Foreign Scientists Comes Under Scrutiny," November 3, 2014. www.scmp.com/news/china/article/1631317/chinas-programme-recruiting-foreign-scientists-comes-under-scrutiny.

16 See "Appendix A: China's Talent Recruitment Plan Contracts," *Staff Report Permanent Subcommittee on Investigations of the United States Senate Committee on Homeland Security and Governmental Affairs*, November 2019.

17 www.justice.gov/usao-sdfl/pr/former-research-oceanographer-sentenced-accepting-salary-people-s-republic-china.

18 CASE NO. 17-20449-CR-ALTONAGA, Defendant's Notice of Filing Three (3) Exhibits to Memorandum in Support of Motion in Limine (DE 28-1), United States of America v. Chunzai Wang, United States District Court, Southern District of Florida, Public Access to Court Electronic Records.

19 Ibid.

20 Committee of 100, "Committee of 100 Expresses Concern About Unfair Prosection of Chunzai Wang," March 2, 2018. www.prnewswire.com/news-releases/committee-of-100-expresses-concern-about-unfair-prosecution-of-chunzai-wang-300607546.html.

21 Committee of Concerned Scientists, "US Scientist Leaves US After Petty Felony Conviction," April 27, 2008. https://concernedscientists.org/2018/04/us-scientist-leaves-us-after-petty-felony-conviction/.

22 CASE NO. 17-20449-CR-ALTONAGA, Defendant's Notice of Filing Three (3) Exhibits to Memorandum in Support of Motion in Limine (DE 28-1), United States of America v. Chunzai Wang, United States District Court, Southern District of Florida, Public Access to Court Electronic Records.

23 Federal government employees with 15 or more years of service earn eight hours of annual leave per biweekly pay period, or 26 workdays per year. That is far short of Wang's contractual commitment of about 40 workdays per year in China.

24 CASE NO. 17-20449-CR-ALTONAGA, Defendant's Notice of Filing Three (3) Exhibits to Memorandum in Support of Motion in Limine (DE 28-1), United States of America v. Chunzai Wang, United States District Court, Southern District of Florida, Public Access to Court Electronic Records.

25 Ibid.

26 Ibid.

27 Ibid.

28 https://cml.harvard.edu/people/charles-m-lieber.

29 www.justice.gov/opa/pr/harvard-university-professor-and-two-chinese-nationals-charged-three-separate-china-related.

30 "Recruitment Program for Global Experts" is the official English name. The official Chinese name (海外高层次人才引进计划) more closely translates to "Overseas High-Level Talent Introduction Plan."

31 For example, the Lieber case.

32 www.chinanews.com/lxsh/2012/05-07/3868699.shtml.

33 www.oriza.com.cn/eAboutUs.aspx?CID=1.

34 Zhu, Xiaoshan (朱筱珊), "探究元禾控股:" 千人计划"创业大赛项目已获得超过8.5亿元融资," *Securities Times*, April 30, 2016 (news.stcn.com/2016/0430/12696511.shtml). Oriza Holdings' website has an organizational chart that lists the TTP Venture Capital Center as part of its operations (www.oriza.com.cn/about.aspx?cid=28). The English-language version of Oriza Holdings'"About Us" page removes the TTP Venture Capital Center from its chart. (www.oriza.com.cn/eAboutUs.aspx?CID=1).

35 www.chinanews.com/lxsh/2012/05-07/3868699.shtml.

36 Ibid.

37 "Update Concerning China's Acts, Policies and Practices Related to Technology Transfer, Intellectual Property, and Innovation," *Office of the United States Trade Representative*, November 20, 2018.

38 www.jiqizhixin.com/articles/2017-06-06-4.

39 www.liuxuejobs.com/m/news-show.php?id=1194.

40 www.hystasvc.com/aboutus.

41 HYSTA SVC's address is 3300 Central Expressway, Suite B, Santa Clara, CA, and Oriza Ventures address is 3300 Central Expressway, Suite A, Santa Clara, CA. www.orizaventures.com/about-us.

42 www.tyacay.com/Index/activitydetails.html?id=1233.

43 Ibid.

44 www.oriza.com.cn/news.aspx?action=details&id=261.

45 www.1000plan.org.cn/lianyihui2/intro.

46 The WRSA is profiled in Chapter 15's discussion of China's United Front apparatus.

47 www.1000plan.org.cn/lianyihui2/intro.

48 www.1000plan.org/qrjh/section/2?m=more.

49 http://politics.people.com.cn/GB/14562/12017723.html.

50 Ibid.

51 www.1000plan.org/qrjh/section/2?m=more.

52 Ibid.

53 "九五" 期间人事系统留学人员工作规划, 1996 MOHRSS, Section 5(6). www.topjob
way.com/law/law061.htm.

54 "留学人员回国工作" 十一五 "规划," November 15, 2006 MOHRSS Section 4(3).
www.mohrss.gov.cn/gkml/zcfg/gfxwj/201407/t20140717_136312.html.

55 Ibid.

56 "关于加强留学人员回国服务体系建设的意见," MOHRSS (2011 No. 46) April 29,
2011. www.mohrss.gov.cn/gkml/zcfg/gfxwj/201407/t20140717_136305.html.

57 Ibid, Section 2(3).

58 Ibid.

59 Ibid.

60 See Talent Work (人才工作) webpage accessible at: www.liuxuehr.com/news/rencai
gongzuo/.

61 See University Recruitment (高校招聘) webpage at: www.liuxuehr.com/gaoxiao/index.
html.

62 See Scientific Research Organization (科研机构招聘) webpage at: www.liuxuehr.
com/kyzp/index.html.

63 See Famous Enterprises Recruitment (名企招聘) webpage at: www.liuxuehr.com/
mingqizhaopin/index.html.

64 See About Us (关于我们-海外人才网) webpage at: www.chinahwrc.com/abouts.html.

65 Both sites link to a registration page "留学生招聘网" at: www.liuxuezp.com/
members/register/utype/2.html.

66 www.china-ossc.com/1212.html.

67 www.cosdf.org.cn/aboutus/foundation/.

68 www.china-ossc.com/1212.html.

69 PRC Ministry of Human Resources & Social Security, Reply to Proposal of Second
Session of 13th National Committee of CPPCC No. 3819 (Social Management
Category No. 293) (Ren She Ti Zi [2019] No. 30) (人力资源社会保障部对政协
十三届全国委员会第二次会议第3819号（社会管理类 293 号）提案的答复 (人
社提字〔2019〕30 号)), August 6, 2019. www.mohrss.gov.cn/gkml/zhgl/jytabl/
tadf/201912/t20191206_345550.html.

70 "关于深化人才发展体制机制改革的意见," CPC Central Committee, March 21,
2016. www.gov.cn/xinwen/2016-03/21/content_5056113.htm.

71 "国家引进海外高层次人才参考目录." https://hr.pku.edu.cn/docs/201701061310
09584633.pdf.

72 Some municipal governments have issued their own talent catalogues to target
individuals that can fill technology gaps in specific sectors deemed a priority by those
locales. An example is the Suzhou City 2019 Catalogue of Demand for Professional
Talent Shortages in Key Industries (苏州市2019年重点产业紧缺专业人才需求目
录). www.jsszhrss.gov.cn/szwzweb/html/zxzx/gsgg/31552.shtml.

73 *Talent Catalogue*, Section 1, https://hr.pku.edu.cn/docs/20170106131009584633.pdf.

74 *Talent Catalogue*, Section 2, https://hr.pku.edu.cn/docs/20170106131009584633.pdf.

75 *Talent Catalogue*, Section 1, https://hr.pku.edu.cn/docs/20170106131009584633.pdf.

76 Ibid.

77 www.1000plan.org.cn/qrjh/section/4/list.

Bibliography

Committee of Concerned Scientists. "US Scientist Leaves US After Petty Felony Conviction," April 27, 2018. https://concernedscientists.org/2018/04/us-scientist-leaves-us-after-petty-felony-conviction/.

Committee of 100. "Committee of 100 Expresses Concern About Unfair Prosecution of Chunzai Wang," March 2, 2018. www.prnewswire.com/news-releases/committee-of-100-expresses-concern-about-unfair-prosecution-of-chunzai-wang-300607546.html.

Communist Party of China. 中国共产党章程 中国共产党第十七次全国代表大会部分修改, 2007 年 10 月 21 日通过 ("CPC Charter-Amendments to the 17th CPC National Congress, Passed on Oct. 21, 2007"), CPC, October 21, 2007.

Communist Party of China Central Committee. 关于深化人才发展体制机制改革的意见 ("Opinions on Deepening Reform of the Talent Development System"), CPC, March 21, 2016.

Department of Justice—US Attorney's Office of Southern District of Florida. "Former Research Oceanographer Sentenced for Accepting a Salary from the People's Republic of China," February 22, 2018. www.justice.gov/usao-sdfl/pr/former-research-oceanographer-sentenced-accepting-salary-people-s-republic-china.

Hvistendahl, Mara. "China's Programme for Recruiting Foreign Scientists Comes Under Scrutiny," *South China Morning Post*, November 3, 2014.

Jing, Shi. "Talent Pool the Cornerstone of Development," *China Daily*, December 28, 2018.

Office of the US Trade Representative. "Update Concerning China's Acts, Policies and Practices Related to Technology Transfer, Intellectual Property, and Innovation," November 2018.

PRC Ministry of Human Resources & Social Security. 留学人员回国工作"十一五"规划 ("11th Five-Year Plan on Working for the Return of Overseas Scholars"), MOHRSS, November 15, 2006.

PRC Ministry of Human Resources & Social Security. 关于加强留学人员回国服务体系建设的意见 ("Opinions on Strengthening Construction of the Overseas Scholar Returnee Service System"), MOHRSS (46), April 29, 2011.

PRC Ministry of Human Resources & Social Security. 人力资源社会保障部对政协十三届全国委员会第二次会议第 3819 号（社会管理类293号）提案的答复（人社提字〔2019〕30 号 ("Ministry of Human Resources & Social Security Reply to Proposal of Second Session of 13th National Committee of CPPCC"), MOHRSS (3819) (Social Management Category No. 293), August 6, 2019.

PRC State Council. 国家中长期人才发展规划纲要（2010–2020 年）("National Medium and Long-Term Talent Development Plan 2010–2020"), SC, June 6, 2010.

Puko, Timothy and Kate O'Keefe. "US Targets Efforts by China, Others to Recruit Government Scientists," *Wall Street Journal*, June 10, 2019.

Redden, Elizabeth. "Science vs. Security," April 16, 2019. www.insidehighered.com/news/2019/04/16/federal-granting-agencies-and-lawmakers-step-scrutiny-foreign-research.

Sharma, Yojana. "Panic over US Scrutiny of Science Talent Programme," *University World News*, October 18, 2018.

Strider Global Intelligence Team. "Quantum Dragon—How China Is Exploiting Western Government Funding and Research Institutes to Leapfrog in Dual-Use Quantum Technologies," *Strider Technologies*, November 2019.

Suzhou Municipal Department of Human Resources & Social Security. "苏州市 2019 年重点产业紧缺专业人才需求目录" ("Suzhou City 2019 Catalogue of Demand for Professional Talent Shortages in Key Industries"). Jiangsu Suzhou Department of Human Resources & Social Security, 2019.

United States Senate. "Threats to the US Research Enterprise: China's Talent Recruitment Plans," Staff Report Permanent Subcommittee on Investigations of the United States Senate Committee on Homeland Security and Governmental Affairs, November 2019.

Wang, Huiyao. "China's National Talent Plan: Key Measures and Objectives," Brookings, November 2010.

Wang, Jinhai (王金海) and Zhang Shi'an (张世安). "海外高层次人才创新创业基地发展论坛举行" ("Forum Held on Development of Overseas High-Level Experts Innovation and Entrepreneurship Bases"), *Renminwang*, June 30, 2010.

Yang, Fan. "Surveying China's Science and Technology Human Talents Programs," *SITC Research Briefs*, No. 3, 2015.

Zhao, Cheng (赵承), Chen Fang (陈芳), Yu Xiaojie (余晓洁). 海归梦, 中国梦, *Xinhua*, November 7, 2017.

Zhu, Xiaoshan (朱筱珊). "探究元禾控股:'千人计划'创业大赛项目已获得超过 8.5 亿元融资," *Securities Times*, April 30, 2016.

PART II

The system in operation

4

FOREIGN TECHNOLOGY TRANSFER THROUGH COMMERCE[1]

Karen M. Sutter

The government of the People's Republic of China (PRC) has a long-standing and well-developed set of policies and approaches to leverage trade and investment ties, in order to obtain foreign technology and capabilities that it identifies as critical to filling gaps and realizing national development goals. As China's market has developed, the government has recalibrated its trade, investment, and technology policies to target advanced and specialized foreign technology, significantly raising the costs and risks for foreign firms.

- Since joining the World Trade Organization in 2001, the PRC government has distorted the normal use of antidumping, antitrust, standards, and procurement tools to force technology transfer. The central role of the state in the business ecosystem and China's central position in global supply chains have allowed these approaches to root and gain traction.
- As Chinese firms have pushed offshore, the PRC government has leveraged state direction and funding to acquire foreign technology abroad, acquiring advanced capabilities in areas targeted in China's *Made in China 2025* plan—such as aerospace, advanced manufacturing, artificial intelligence (AI), biotechnology, data analytics, new materials, and semiconductors.

The imposition of tight market access controls has allowed China to play off global economic competitors by offering preferential market access terms in exchange for technology transfer. They have increased receptivity to China's acquisition bids as foreign firms assess that Chinese ownership is the only pathway to enter a restricted but undeniably important market.

This chapter highlights several aspects of China's commercial technology transfer policies that are sometimes misunderstood:

1   China's policies are organized and deliberate in requiring the transfer of targeted foreign intellectual capital to meet national development goals as a condition for market access.

2   The decision-making roots of China's current technology policies predate the rise of Communist Party of China (CPC) Chairman Xi Jinping in 2012. Indigenous innovation efforts have intensified under Xi, but the approach is more deeply rooted.

3   Many of China's commercial technology transfer policies are well documented and hiding in plain sight. The government's use of internal directives and informal authorities are well understood by market participants as "pay-to-play" requirements that the government imposes as a precondition for market access.

4   Technology decoupling goals and efforts originate in Beijing, not Washington. Chinese technology policies are clear in their intentions and instructions to take intellectual capital from foreign firms—through partnership, direct transfer, and acquisition—with the goal of displacing these firms over time as Chinese companies absorb and adapt this transferred knowhow to build independent or "indigenous" competencies.

5   The PRC state is directly immersed in commercial efforts to acquire foreign capabilities. State and non-state distinctions are blurred in the Chinese business ecosystem. The government is not an independent impartial regulator, often applying policies, regulations, and laws in ways that advance industrial policies, favor national champions, and influence corporate decision-making.

6   China's policies and approaches overlap and are mutually reinforcing. Legitimate commercial activity offers proximity that can be exploited to steal intellectual capital that foreign firms refuse to transfer.

7   China's technology transfer efforts have made important gains since 2006, as China has become more integrated into global research and production chains.

China's trade and investment regime: the plans

China's policy framework for commercial technology transfer took shape in the 1980s and 1990s. Even as the toolkit has evolved since 2001, key aspects of the approach—national plans, trade and investment policies, business structures, and special zones and projects—remain in place, offering a blueprint for government and commercial actions.

China's economic, industrial, and S&T plans are top-level policy documents that communicate the objectives, priorities, and targets for national development across the Chinese bureaucracy and business ecosystem. Ministries, commissions, and local government officials advance these objectives through relevant policies, rules and regulations. The plans signal to industry targets to incorporate in their commercial strategies.

China's Medium- and Long-Term Plan for S&T Development (MLP)—developed in 2003 under former Premier Wen Jiabao—established innovation as a national priority and set the strategic direction for the industrial policies China has enacted since 2006. The MLP reflected an assessment that China must own and control the IP and standards underlying global supply chains to gain a technology leadership position and leverage dual-use technologies independently for military modernization.

- The plan called for developing indigenous capabilities, decreasing dependency on foreign technology imports, and leapfrogging into emerging technologies.
- It featured long-standing priorities to acquire core knowhow in aerospace, advanced energy and manufacturing, biotech, lasers, microelectronics, semiconductors, computer software, quantum, and nanotechnology.
- It focused on the central role of the corporate sector in China's innovation, elevating the importance of commercial ties and technology transfer in implementing China's goals.
- It formally introduced a phased approach to innovation that involved the introduction, digestion, absorption and adaptation or "re-innovation" (再创新) of foreign IP and technology.[2]

In response to the MLP, China's 11th Five-Year Plan (FYP) of 2006–2010 adopted a more assertive approach to technology transfer. During this period, the Chinese government eliminated broad tax preferences for foreign investment—focusing preferences for companies transferring advanced technology—and tightened requirements for what qualified as "advanced technology." China revitalized plans to build a single-aisle aircraft, prompting new policies to increase foreign co-production and technology transfer. Following intense debate about would qualify as "indigenous," Chinese practice settled on a definition of technology transfer that is advanced, not otherwise available in China, and gives a Chinese entity access, ownership or control of the underlying knowhow.[3]

China's 12th FYP (2011–2015) sought to combine the role of markets with governmental guidance; increase international cooperation to attract technology and conduct re-innovation; and gather global innovation resources for core technology and relevant intellectual property (IP). China sought to compete in emerging technologies in which developed countries did not yet have an established presence, and the plan introduced incentives for foreign technology transfer and innovation partnerships in seven strategic industries: biotechnology, advanced materials, next-generation information technology (IT), advanced manufacturing equipment, renewable energy, energy conservation, and alternative fuel cars. In 2014 the government launched a National Semiconductor Plan.[4]

China's 13th FYP (2016–2020) continued to prioritize innovation and introduced new supporting plans, such as the *Internet Plus Action Plan*—that sought to integrate the Internet with industry in areas such as cloud computing, big data, and the Internet of Things[5]—and the *Made in China 2025* strategy[6] that set targets for ten strategic sectors (next-generation IT, high-grade computer numerical controls, machine tools and robotics, aerospace equipment, machine engineering equipment and high technology ships, advanced rail transportation equipment, energy efficient and new energy automobiles, electric power equipment, agricultural equipment, new materials, and biomedicine and high-performance medical equipment). That FYP launched the *S&T Innovation 2030* project to develop and commercialize technologies for jet engines, gas turbines, deep sea space station, quantum, AI brain science, biotech seed innovation, genomic sequencing, smart grid, robotics, new energy vehicles, smart manufacturing, space integrated networks, 5G, advanced sensors, wearable devices, and satellite remote sensing.[7] It introduced policies favoring domestic production using IP developed, owned, or registered first in China, unleashing procurement tools that required Chinese parties to control or own the IP in products and services sold in China.[8]

Funding

Priorities identified in plans receive preferential government approvals and funding as state banks and financial institutions are directed and incentivized to finance commercial activity in these sectors. In support of 11th FYP targets, the People's Bank of China (PBOC) issued a Guiding Opinion in December 2009 that encouraged financing of innovative technology-absorbing industries.[9] In response to the 12th FYP, the State Council announced in October 2011 that the government would fund up to $1.5 trillion over ten years to develop these industries.[10] Since 2014, the PRC government has increasingly used government guidance funds to develop or acquire specific foreign technology. To implement the National Semiconductor Plan, the government created the China Integrated Circuit Industry Investment Fund (CICIIF, 中国国家集成电路产业投资基金) with an estimated $150 billion under management—that funded domestic development, importation of semiconductor manufacturing equipment, and the acquisition of foreign companies.[11] In support of *Made in China 2025*, as of 2017, the Chinese government had established 800 state funds valued at an estimated $313 billion.[12]

Government funds facilitate commercial technology transfer by signaling economic rewards for those who obtain knowhow relevant to these priorities and by funding partnerships with foreign firms and the acquisition of capabilities abroad. Chinese investments in strategic sectors—such as aerospace, biotech, and semiconductors—typically have high levels of state financial support underpinning the transaction. Subsidies also set terms for domestic industry to seek foreign technology. For example, China's rail subsidies favor indigenously developed urban rail equipment projects that facilitate the digestion (消化) and absorption (吸收) of imported technology.[13] Subsidies fund imports of advanced manufacturing equipment, allowing China to leverage its role as a top customer to influence foreign firms with capabilities targeted in China's industrial plans. In 2015, San'an Optoelectronics—a CICIIF shareholder—canceled a large semiconductor equipment order from Aixtron, Inc., causing Aixtron's share price to tumble and pressuring Aixtron to accept a bid from a PRC firm tied to San'an and the CICIIF.[14]

China's foreign investment approvals

China's investment policies respond to the plans by promoting Chinese industry while seeking the transfer of specific foreign capabilities that China needs to meet its goals. The National Development and Reform Commission (NDRC) and Ministry of Commerce (MOFCOM) react to the plans by determining what areas of the economy will be open to trade and investment and on what terms to best advance China's development goals. Since 1995, *China's Catalogue for Guiding Foreign Investment* has established the sectors in which foreign investment will be encouraged, allowed, restricted or prohibited. Priority sectors, such as autos, aerospace, and biotech, often have restrictive foreign investment terms such as JV and technology transfer requirements. Even with the introduction of a negative list in 2018, China retained a catalogue to calibrate market access terms, including technology transfer, according to changing needs. China's overseas direct investment (ODI) catalogue facilitates technology transfer by encouraging investment in technology, advanced manufacturing, and R&D overseas.[15]

Chinese officials refine technology acquisition through sectoral and other laws, regulations, and requirements. For example, foreign seed companies must "transfer good quality seeds, advanced technologies and equipment from outside of China."[16] In the Neighorhood Electric Vehicle (NEV) sector, policies require Joint Ventures (JVs), cap foreign equity at 50 percent, and require the Chinese partner to control the IP in one of three key technologies: batteries, drive systems, and control systems. China requires manufacturers to demonstrate mastery of the development and manufacturing technology for a complete NEV and possess core R&D capabilities. These requirements force foreign companies to transfer core knowhow to their Chinese partners. China's requirements apply to whole vehicle control systems, interfaces and boundaries between NEV core components, engineer and power train control systems, and trial production, assembly and testing, which in essence prohibit using imports and require foreign companies to develop local suppliers' capabilities.[17] Tesla established a wholly foreign owned enterprise (WFOE) in Shanghai but is shifting to Contemporary Amperex Technology Co. Ltd. (CATL)—China's champion lithium-ion battery producer—and fully localizing production, likely transferring IP and expertise related to batteries, lightweight composites, electrical systems, and sensors.[18]

The Chinese government's approval process for business incorporation, expansion, and product certification allows it to formally or informally impose conditions. A foreign firm's contribution to its China operations often includes IP and proprietary manufacturing processes,[19] allowing PRC officials to review foreign technologies in detail and press for specific transfers.

Tax

The government calibrates tax policies to encourage technology transfer. In response to MLP goals to accelerate foreign technology transfer, China in 2007 introduced more selective tax criteria such that only foreign firms transferring advanced technology and R&D (or investments in the Northeast and Western China) would qualify for a preferential 15 percent corporate income tax rate.[20] NDRC tightened the definition of "advanced technology" and what investments would qualify for incentives, focusing on technology transfer in priority sectors.[21] China's R&D tax incentives support technology transfer through the full cycle of product research, development and commercialization with government cash grants at the initial research stage, a super tax deduction (150 to 175 percent) for eligible R&D expenses during the R&D stage, and preferential tax rates for particular IP for technology software, and integrated circuit firms.[22]

Corporate structures: JVs, investment zones, and special projects

The PRC government has long favored the JV corporate structure to require the transfer of foreign technology and expertise. In a wide range of industries— agriculture, aerospace, autos, energy, and IT—Chinese policies require foreign firms to partner, often with a state-owned competitor. China uses equity caps to ensure the Chinese side maintains control. China's rules and regulations require foreign firms to contribute advanced technology to a JV that is capable of (1) significantly improving the performance or quality of existing products; (2) significantly saving raw materials, fuel, or power; and (3) being applicable and advanced, such that the JV's products generate significant benefits in the domestic market or are competitive globally.[23] The Chinese partner handles the JV approval process, allowing the PRC government and partner to manage information to pressure the foreign company to transfer technology.[24] Technology regulations give the Chinese partner control over the foreign technology that is transferred, including adaptations that the JV or the Chinese partner independently makes.[25] JV regulations limit technology contracts to a defined period—generally ten years—and grant the Chinese partner the right to use the technology in perpetuity after the contract expires.

The Chinese partner exerts a strong influence over human resource and supplier decisions,[26] selecting employees, sometimes from competing businesses and interests, who have access to foreign knowhow within a JV. There have been numerous prominent examples of JV trade secret theft in which this type of proximity has opened up foreign firms to trade secret misappropriation.[27] For example, Chinese partners have exploited foreign company joint ventures and partnerships to misappropriate foreign technologies in mobile telecommunications, high speed rail, and nuclear power. These foreign capabilities were transferred, absorbed, adapted, and rebranded by the Chinese partner as Chinese indigenous technology supporting new Chinese standards and were used by Chinese firms to then compete against the corporate sources of this knowhow in China and third markets.[28] Influence over supplier decisions allows the Chinese partner to favor domestic suppliers who gain from foreign manufacturers sharing details about proprietary processes, standards, and requirements.[29]

Since the late 1990s, China has allowed wholly foreign-owned control to entice foreign companies to invest in advanced manufacturing,[30] making the WFOE the most popular foreign investment vehicle between 1997 and 2015.[31] Since the PRC government's antitrust action against Qualcomm in 2015, there has been a marked shift away from the WFOE structure in technology investments, toward JVs with the Chinese government and its research institutes. Under pressure to license its technology, Qualcomm in 2016 entered into a JV with the Guizhou government to design and develop server chips for the Southwest China Supercomputing Center, an entity tied to the China Academy of Engineering Physics (CAEP), China's nuclear weapons R&D facility. Qualcomm licensed its proprietary server chip technology and R&D processes[32] and gave the Guizhou government its server chip IP when it exited the JV in 2019.[33]

During this same period, IBM announced partnerships with Chinese state firms including Suzhou Powercore (tied to the Jiangsu Supercomputing Center), Inspur, and Teamsum.[34] Intel entered a partnership it eventually terminated in 2019 with Tsinghua Holdings—a state leader in CICIIF—to share 5G modem technology.[35] AMD entered into a JV with a Chinese government consortium that included CAS and Sugon, a state supercomputing firm, to share x86 chip knowhow.[36] After Softbank acquired ARM in 2017, the company licensed ARM's microprocessor architecture to the Chinese government through a JV with the Hopu Fund, a group that includes the China Investment Corporation (CIC), China Development Bank (CDB), State Administration of Foreign Exchange (SAFE), and the Shenzhen government.[37]

China incentivizes companies to transfer technology through special investment zones that offer preferential tax rates, fast-track approvals, and access to inputs and suppliers. Zones often specialize in particular industries and target specific technologies for acquisition and adaptation.

Many are tied to national S&T projects that foreign investments directly or indirectly support. For example, Wuxi has been a national center to develop semiconductor capabilities since the 1990s and hosts the Wuxi Integrated Circuit Design Center, a partnership with the PLA-tied electronics firm China Electronics

Technology Group Corporation (CETC). In 2012, the Wuxi government formed a JV with a US venture capital (VC) firm, Tallwood, to attract foreign investment and IP in semiconductors.[38] In July 2018, SK Hynix Inc., South Korea's second-largest memory chipmaker, announced a JV with the Wuxi government to build a foundry.[39] Beijing E-town, a government agent tasked to bring foreign technology to the Beijing Economic-Technological Development Area, is a shareholder in CICIIF and has been part of Chinese government consortiums that have bought US aviation and semiconductor firms.[40] AMD's x86 JV with CAS is located Chengdu's Science City, a national pilot for advanced technology integration and military–civil fusion in aerospace and microelectronics.[41]

China's effort to "indigenously" build a single-aisle aircraft—the C919—shows how China uses projects to facilitate technology transfer. The project is led by the Commercial Aircraft Corporation of China (COMAC), a state entity tied to China's national aviation champion AVIC that was created in response to the 11th FYP directive to build a single-aisle aircraft. Faced with significant capability gaps, China assessed it would need foreign contributions for most aspects of the project. Many areas in which China sought partnership—avionics, electronics, and flight control systems, composites, electronics, and engines—are controlled technologies and involve proprietary expertise that foreign firms are, generally, reluctant to share. China required JVs and technology sharing agreements that companies likely would not have considered in another market that increase technology spillover risks by locating production in China and using Chinese staff.[42]

Foreign technology is responsible for almost the entire plane: engine, engine thrust reverser, flight control system, weather radar, electricity system, cockpit, simulator system, wing de-icing, flight recorder, APU, fuel system, landing gear, gate signal, fire detection, and tires.[43] AVIC is providing the airframe, radar cover, wings, and tail assembly and these capabilities are not indigenous. AVIC has co-production agreements with Airbus and Boeing for wing and tail production as offsets for aircraft purchases.[44] China has played off global completion for additional concessions and targeted specialized areas where foreign firms refuse to share capabilities for illicit theft. In 2018, Boeing announced a $33 million aircraft completion plant with COMAC to install interiors before completing final delivery that potentially gives AVIC visibility and training on integrating interior systems, including power, electronics, and data.[45]

Corporate theft and espionage

By making IP and technology a national strategic imperative, Beijing has unleashed strong incentives for Chinese actors to acquire foreign companies' intellectual capital any way they can. According to a 2019 CNBC poll of CFOs of leading US companies, one in five companies had IP stolen from China in the past year.[46] The Commission on the Theft of American Intellectual Property estimates that total theft of US IP and trade secrets accounts for between $225 billion to $600 billion a year.[47] A review of publicly known Chinese IP thefts since 2000 shows how legitimate commercial partnerships in strategic areas can facilitate theft. A high volume of Chinese commercial espionage cases involve a corporate insider from a partnership in China. The specific knowhow that is stolen is targeted in China's plans, e.g., aerospace (including jet engines and satellites), automotive, chemicals, encryption, energy (oil and gas, solar), medical equipment, metals, microelectronics, new materials, nuclear, rail, robotics, semiconductors, software, and telecommunications.[48]

An IP theft case involving GE shows how Chinese efforts can coalesce. To operate and sell gas turbines in China, GE is partnered with state-owned Harbin Electric.[49] GE is also co-producing with Safran the Leap-1C jet engine for China's C919, one of the few C919 components that is not co-produced with a Chinese partner due to the sensitivity of the technology. In April 2019, the US Department of Justice charged a Chinese engineer working in GE's power business in New York and his counterpart in China with stealing GE gas turbine engine knowhow to benefit research institutes tied to AVIC and the government's jet engine program.[50]

Additionally, just after selecting foreign participants for the C919 program, Turbine Panda—a cyber threat actor that CrowdStrike ties to the Ministry of State Security (MSS) Jiangsu Bureau and the 2015 US Office of Personnel Management breach—targeted multiple foreign aerospace suppliers between 2010 through 2015.[51] In October 2018, the FBI charged a group of Chinese intelligence officers, hackers, and company insiders with breaking into the networks of 13 aerospace manufacturers, including GE Aviation, to steal proprietary foreign capabilities to advance China's jet engine program.[52] Concerns arose in December 2017 when AECC released its CJ-1000AX engine that shared design similarities—such as dimensions and turbofan blade sizes—with GE's Leap-1C jet engine.[53]

Procurement, standards, IP, and antitrust

China is using procurement rules tied to industry and product catalogues for computers, telecommunications, software, new energy equipment, lithium-ion batteries, medical equipment, NEVs, and other sectors to require technology transfer through inclusion and exclusion of targeted products and vendors. China can set qualification requirements such as levels of localization, disclosure, and transfer of knowhow. The PRC government adjusts its catalogues to reflect the extent to which domestic firms can meet demand and targets technology transfer to fill gaps. This approach tries to accelerate the transfer of foreign technology to Chinese industry from US technology leaders and eventually displace these firms with Chinese companies.[54]

Unlike other markets in which a qualification to be domestic depends on local production, the government requires the underlying knowhow be transferred to a Chinese entity to be included in catalogues and sell in China. China used procurement rules and catalogues to push the transfer of foreign lithium-ion knowhow to Chinese suppliers and, once domestic firms developed capabilities, to then favor these suppliers. In 2016 Chinese policies required foreign NEV manufacturers to source from an electric battery supplier list that excluded leading firms like Samsung SDI and LG Chem, undercutting these foreign battery companies' position in China.[55] In high-speed rail, China used design and manufacturing JVs with Bombardier, Kawasaki, Siemens, and Alstom to acquire, adapt, and rebrand foreign technology related to high-speed rail electric multiple units (EMUs).[56] European rail executives reported in 2016 that, under the February 2008 *Action Plan for the Independent Innovation of China's High Speed Trains*, the Chinese government imposed informal bidding requirements that required foreign rail firms to conduct R&D in China, place that R&D within a JV that can operate globally, and operate final products produced by JVs under the State-Owned Enterprise (SOE) brand.[57] When China merged its rail firms in 2015 under one state monopoly, CRRC, this consolidated earlier technology transfers and positioned CRRC to expand overseas with $30 billion in China ExIm Bank financing.[58]

Global standards leadership requires Chinese companies to hold relevant IP and technical competencies to shape national and global standards. China's focus on standards development has gone hand in hand with its push under the MLP to own the core IP underlying the technologies, industries, products, and services it seeks to adapt and re-innovate under its own brands. *Made in China 2025* includes a standards component led by the Chinese Academy of Engineering (CAE), *China Standards 2035*, that aims to develop Chinese standards to facilitate Chinese companies' expansion abroad. To reach these goals, China is using industry, technical, and security standards to establish requirements for the types and levels of technology required to be controlled by a Chinese entity to sell foreign products and services in China. Product verification and testing can require foreign firms to share sensitive IP and source code. In 2009 the government issued "secure and controllable" rules requiring a Chinese entity to control or own the underlying IP in a product sold in China, forcing firms who want to remain or expand in China to transfer their technology and intellectual capital.[59] In 2016, the China Banking Regulatory Commission (CBRC) established "secure and controllable" criteria for IT hardware and systems used by Chinese banks and required the disclosure of source code for software and firmware, the establishment of an R&D facility in China, government review and approval of foreign encryption, and regulator backdoors. CBRC set high domestic targets in technologies in which China had emerging capabilities (routers, wireless LAN equipment, and storage) and lower targets in software, likely because Chinese capabilities were insufficient.[60]

The PRC government uses IP regulations to push technology transfer and reduce China's reliance on foreign IP licensing. China's patent law requires foreign firms to file patents first in China and allows compulsory licensing—a requirement that a patent holder grant this right to the state. Beijing is pushing for greater disclosure of foreign patent information and more generous IP licensing terms. The government is trying to restrict foreign companies' use of exclusive IP rights and patent pools, making it difficult for foreign firms to refuse to license IP and allowing the government to set prices and terms for licensed IP. China's antimonopoly law states that IP should be shared when it promotes the public interest of creating common standards or meeting industrial goals.[61] Chinese firms are using design patents—that have a lower threshold of inventiveness and are easier to file and harder to invalidate—to sue and countersue foreign firms in Chinese courts to gain advantage in priority sectors like semiconductors.[62]

China's antimonopoly law allows the government to challenge foreign firms' market gains and innovation prowess under the guise of antitrust action. The law exempts domestic firms in many instances while subordinating foreign IP holders' interests to China's industrial development goals by focusing antitrust review on the effect a foreign companies' action has on Chinese firms' market access and technology progress.[63] China is using review of global M&A deals to impose terms that advance industrial policies.

MOFCOM's antitrust terms for Qualcomm in 2015 included a $975 million fine, pricing terms for licensing technology to Chinese users, and the establishment of two JVs for chip development with SMIC (R&D next-generation CMOS logic technology) and the Guizhou government (server chips).[64] China's 2015 review of NXP's acquisition of Freescale, prompted NXP to sell its RF power business to State Council-controlled Beijing Jianguang Asset Management Co., Ltd. (JAC Capital).[65] In 2017 Qualcomm, JAC Capital, and "state backbone telecom enterprise" Datang Telecom announced a JV to design, package, test, and sell smartphone chipsets in China, a venture that JAC Capital said would improve China's chip design capabilities, a key gap in China's semiconductor program.[66]

Trade barriers and market pressures

The Chinese government uses trade barriers to encourage technology transfer. In autos, China maintains a high import tariff on vehicles to encourage joint venture production.[67] China has used antidumping actions against key industrial inputs, like optical fiber and polysilicon, to pressure firms to bring specialized glass and solar production to China.[68]

The government uses export quotas and duties and vertical integration (mining, processing and production) under state firms like Minmetals to restrict exports of raw materials for which China dominates global processing—coking coal, fluorspar, and select rare earth elements (REEs)—and to pressure foreign firms reliant on these inputs to bring advanced production to China. Fluorspar is used in the chemical, specialty glass, ceramics and optical industries. Coking coal is a key ingredient in steel manufacturing. REEs are used in a range of technologies and defense production.[69]

Chinese subsidies have created overcapacity in industries including aluminum, steel, and solar. By driving margins lower, Chinese firms have undercut foreign industry and then acquired distressed assets in US bankruptcy proceedings. In 2017, Sun Edison sold 100 patents and 200 patent applications related to proprietary materials and processes for solar panels to GLC-Poly Energy Holdings, China's largest manufacturer of polysilicon and wafers.[70]

Overseas investment

Since 2004, China has looked to global markets to acquire foreign technology. AVIC has targeted gaps in aerospace design, R&D, avionics, engines, and maintenance, repair, and overhaul.[71] Chinese state consortiums have bought automotive knowhow in suspension and brakes, electronic steering, sensors, lithium-ion battery and other electric vehicle technologies. Semiconductor acquisitions have targeted the full value chain including materials, design, manufacturing and testing tools, memory and logic capabilities, storage, and sought niche capabilities in field programmable gate arrays (FPGAs), radio frequency (RF) power, and gallium nitride (GaN). China has sought emerging capabilities in biotech, health, data analytics, new materials, advanced manufacturing, AI, and robotics.

China's acquisitions in strategic sectors typically have government ties and funding. Sometimes that role is less visible. While Evergrande, as a large property developer, appears to be a passive investor in technology, in 2018 it signed a $16 billion agreement with CAS, to develop capabilities in aerospace, AI, biotech, integrated circuits, life science, quantum, new energy, and robotics.[72] Several investors in Evergrande are tied to new materials, rare earths, and semiconductors.[73] In emerging technologies, China has leveraged domestic barriers in gaming— platforms for data analytics—to incentivize acquisition. As strategic investors, venture capitalists tied to the PRC government gain insights from the large pool of deals they consider and the companies in which they invest, and are positioned to facilitate large technology transfer plays.[74] In 2015, Haiyin Capital—a Chinese VC firm operating with Chinese government funds—invested in Terrafugia—a US start-up conducting R&D on flying cars—and sponsored Terrafugia to meet with Geely in Hangzhou. Geely subsequently acquired Terrafugia in 2017.[75] In 2016, Haiyin invested in Neurala—a start-up that received US military funding to develop brain-based computational models—promising money and access to Haiyin's network in China. Neurala in 2018 provided its BrainBuilder platform to China's Software Developer Network to build capacity in a sector that China otherwise restricts.[76]

Overseas acquisitions have given China access to corporate technical teams with decades of experience in areas of strategic interest, and control over entire production systems and supply chains. Evergrande's purchase of Faraday Future in 2018 likely transferred full electrical vehicle capabilities including R&D, design, production, new materials, batteries, system on a chip, sensors, and autonomous systems.[77] In biotech—a sector China restricts—China now leads in agrochemicals, seed technology, and genomics with ChemChina's acquisition of Syngenta in 2016. Since BGI acquired Complete Genomics in 2013, China has emerged as a top global DNA sequencer. Acquisitions in aircraft assembly and semiconductor packaging that may seem low-end are not, in fact, because these final points of production occur when earlier, sophisticated functions are integrated on an airplane or a chip.

China is aggregating competencies through discrete transactions. In micro-electronics, CAS' acquisition of AMD's and IBM's x86 and server businesses, and ARM's JV with the Hopu Fund, and deepening collaboration with RISC-V offer China foundational intellectual capital for leading global computer architectures. Since buying Korvis (3D printing) in 2015, China Everbright, through the Burke Porter Group, has acquired automotive and aerospace capabilities in production assembly, automation systems, end of line testing, precision motion, and balancing systems.[78]

Conclusion

Chinese indigenous innovation policies downplay the importance of technology transfer to China's technological breakthroughs, understating China's dependence on the United States and overstating US dependencies on China. Chinese actors are using less visible and regulated paths for technology transfer such as private equity, VC, greenfield, R&D, open-source technology platforms, complex technology licensing, cross-border service, and JV arrangements. China is pursuing smaller transactions and discrete technologies to make key gains there and divert attention from its bigger activities. In China, the government is turning to internal guidance, verbal requests, and a corporate credit system that leverages a company's rating to influence corporate behavior on technology transfer. The tactics are shifting in response to increased scrutiny, but the Chinese drivers for technology transfer and the serious challenges they pose remain.

Notes

1 The views expressed in this chapter are those of its author and are not presented as those of the Congressional Research Service or the Library of Congress.
2 Cong Cao, Richard P. Suttmeier, and Denis Fred Simon, "China's 15-Year Science and Technology Plan," *Physics Today*, December 2006.
3 国民经济和社会发展第十一个五年规划纲要 ("Guidelines of the Eleventh Five-Year Plan for National Economic and Social Development").
4 国务院关于加快培育和发展战略性新兴产业的决定 ("State Council Decision on Accelerating the Process of Nurturing and Developing Strategic New Industries"), SC No. 32, October 2010.
5 国务院关于积极推进"互联网+"行动的指导意见 ("Guiding Opinions of the State Council on Promoting the Internet Plus"), SC No. 40, July 1, 2015.
6 中国制造 2025 ("Notice of the State Council on Issuing Made in China 2025"), SC No. 28, May 8, 2015.

7 Tang Shubiao, "China's New Vision for the Next Five Years," *China Today*, March 11, 2016; "13th Five-Year Plan on Science, Technology and Innovation," China Science and Technology Newsletter, No. 17, Ministry of Science and Technology (MOST), September 15, 2016; and "National Science and Technology Major Projects," MOST (www.nmp.gov.cn/).

8 国民经济和社会发展第十三个五年规划纲要（2016－2020 年）"The 13th Five-Year Plan for Economic and Social Development of the People's Republic of China (2016–2020)," March 16, 2016.

9 关于进一步做好金融服务支持重点产业调整振兴和抑制部分行业产能过剩的指导意见 ("Guiding Opinions on Further Supporting the Restructuring and Revitalization of Key Industries and Curbing Overcapacity in Some Industries through Financial Service"), PBOC, CBRC, CSRC and CIRC, No. 386, 2009.

10 国务院关于印发"十二五"国家战略性新兴产业发展规划的通知 ("Notice of the State Council on Printing and Issuing the 'Twelfth Five-Year' Development Plans for the National Strategic Emerging Industries"), SC No. 28, July 2012; Bruce Wilson and Taryn Koball Williams, "China announces $1.5 trillion development plan for seven strategic emerging industries," Trade and Manufacturing Alert, King & Spalding LLP.

11 US Chamber of Commerce, "Made in China 2025: Global Ambitions Build on Local Protections," Appendix 2, pages 63–64.

12 MERICS, pages 53–54.

13 关于城市轨道交通设备国产化的实施意见 ("Notice of General Office of the State Council on Forwarding the Opinions of National Planning Commission on Implementation of Localization of Urban Rail Traffic Equipment"), SC No. 20, 1999.

14 MERICS, pages 53–54.

15 "How to Use China's Negative Lists and Foreign Investment Encouraged Catalogue," China Briefing, Dezan Shira & Associates, December 10, 2019; and "Issuance of the Catalogue of Industries for Guiding Foreign Investment," NDRC and MOFCOM Order No. 27, June 30, 2019.

16 关于设立外商投资农作物种子企业审批和登记管理的规定 ("Examination, Approval and Registration of Foreign-invested Seeds Companies"), MOA, NDRC, et al., No. 9, 1997.

17 European Chamber of Commerce in China, "China Manufacturing 2025," 2017, pp. 47–49.

18 Trefor Moss, "The Key to Electric Cars is the Battery: One Chinese Firm Dominates the Industry," *Wall Street Journal*, November 3, 2019; Anjani Trivedi, "Heaven is a Made in China Tesla, But Only for Some," *Washington Post*, January 7, 2020; "Tesla is Said to Reach Preliminary Battery Supply Deal with CATL," *Bloomberg News*, November 5, 2019; and "Tesla Meets Output Goals for Its Model 3s in China," *Wall Street Journal*, December 30, 2019.

19 Tami Overby and Jeremie Waterman, "China's Approval Process for Inbound Foreign Direct Investment," US Chamber of Commerce, November 11, 2012.

20 Enterprise Income Tax Law of the People's Republic of China, March 16, 2007.

21 "Dissecting Foreign Investment," *Beijing Review*, No. 2, January 11, 2007.

22 www.pwccn.com/en/tax/china-rd-incentive-service/r-d-services-brochure.pdf.

23 USTR, pp. 48–51; and "Regulations for the Implementation of the Law of the People's Republic of China on Chinese-Foreign Equity Joint Ventures," State Council, Guofa [1983] No. 148, September 1983 (February 2014).

24 Overby and Waterman.

25 USTR, pp. 48–51; and "Regulations of the PRC on Administration of Import and Export Technologies," State Council Order, No. 331, amended in 2011.

26 Margaret L.H. Png, "Equity Joint Ventures in the People's Republic of China," *Case Western Reserve Journal of International Law*, Vol. 24, Issue 3, 1992.

27 USTR. Opcit.

28 Jeff Ferry, "Top Five Cases of Huawei IP Theft and Patent Infringement, "Coalition for a Prosperous America, December 13, 2018; "Did China Steal Japan's High Speed Train," Fortune, April 15, 2013; "Here's What Chinese Hackers Actually Stole From US Companies, Time, May 20, 2014; and Kenneth Rapoza, "Westinghouse Electric's Chinese 'Trojan Horse'," Forbes, May 17, 2016.

29 Stefan H. Kaiser, "Local Sourcing in China: The Case of Braun Electric (Shanghai) Co. Ltd." in Robert Strange, ed., Management in China: The Experience of Foreign Business, 1998, Frank Cass Publishers, Portland, Oregon.

30 Wilifried R. Vanhoneckar, "Entering China: An Unconventional Approach," Harvard Business Review, March–April 1997.

31 Kun Jiang, Wolfgang Keller, Larry Qiu, "International Joint Ventures and Internal vs. External Technology Transfer Evidence from China," Working Paper, NBER, May 2018; and Nicholas R. Lardy, "Does China Force Foreign Firms to Surrender Their Sensitive Technology," PIIE, December 10, 2018.

32 "Qualcomm and Guizhou Province Sign Strategic Cooperation Agreement and Form Joint Venture to Design and Sell World-Class Server Chipsets in China," Qualcomm, January 16, 2016.

33 Lucian Armasu, "Report: Qualcomm Ending Joint Server Chip Venture with China," Tom's Hardware, April 19, 2019.

34 Matthew Miller and Gary Shih, "IBM to Share Technology with China in Strategy Shift—CEO," Reuters, March 23, 2015; Paul Mozur, "IBM Venture with China Stirs Concerns," New York Times, April 19, 2015; Eva Dou, "IBM Allows Chinese Government to Review Source Code," Wall Street Journal, October 16, 2015; and "Inspur, IBM to Form Server Production and Sales JV," Marbridge Daily, September 11, 2017.

35 Don Clark and Eva Dou, "Intel Links Up With China in Serve Chip Venture," Wall Street Journal, January 21, 2016; Li Tao and Sarah Dai, "Intel Ends 5G Partnership with Chinese-Government-Linked Chip Maker Unisoc, Citing 'Business' Reasons," South China Morning Post, February 27, 2019.

36 Kate O'Keefe and Brian Spegele, "How a Big US Chip Maker Gave China the 'Keys to the Kingdom," Wall Street Journal, June 27, 2019.

37 Nina, Xiang, "CIC, Silk Road Fund Team up with ARM to Establish $800M Innovation Fund," China Money Network, January 27, 2017.

38 "Investment in New Model of Things Are Welcome Opportunity for the Semiconductor Industry," US R&K Holdings Group Co., Ltd.

39 "SK Hynix to Move Foundry to Wuxi, China in JV," Pulse, Maeil Business News Korea, July 11, 2018.

40 See www.crunchbase.com/organization/beiid#section-overview.

41 Hao Nan, "Civil Military Integration Boosts Science City's Growth," China Daily, May 23, 2017.

42 "New Investments are Flowing into the Aerospace Sector," Wharton Aerospace and Defense Report, Knowledge Wharton, August 2009; Mark Stokes," China's Commercial Aviation Sector Looks to the Future," Project 2049 Institute, February 2009.

43 Catalin Cimpanu, "Building China's Comac C919 Airplane Involved a lot of Hacking, Report says," Zero Day, October 14, 2019.

44 Dominic Gates, "Boeing Delivers First 737 Jet From Completion Center in China," Seattle Times, December 14, 2018.

45 Josh Horwitz, "Boeing Opens First 737 Plant in China Amid US Sino Trade War," Reuters, December 15, 2018.

46 Eric Rosenbaum, "1 in 5 Corporations Say China Stole Their IP Within the Last Year: CNBC CFO Survey," CNBC, March 1, 2019.

47 NBR, "The Theft of American Intellectual Property: Reassessments of the Challenge to the United States," 2017.

48 "Survey of Chinese-Linked Espionage in the United States Since 2000," CSIS, August 2019.

49 See http://en.harbin-electric.com/about_1.php.

50 These entities include Liaoning Tianyi Aviation Technology Co., Ltd., Nanjing Tianyi Avi Tech Co. Ltd., Shenyang Aerospace University, Shenyang Aeroengine Research Institute, and Huaihai Institute of Technology. "Former GE Engineer and Chinese Businessman Charged with Economic Espionage and Theft of GE's Trade Secrets," US Department of Justice (USDOJ), April 23, 2019.

51 Pierluigi Paganini, "China Linked Cyberspies Turbine PANDA Targeted Aerospace Firms for Years," SecurityAffairs.Co, October 18, 2019.

52 "Chinese Intelligence Officer Charged With Economic Espionage Involving Theft of Trade Secrets From Leading US Aviation Companies," USDOJ, October 10, 2018; Craig Cheatham, "I-Team: How the Cincinnati FBI Cracked the Chinese Spy Case at GE Aviation," *WCPO Cincinnati*, March 4, 2019.

53 Joel Hruska, "China's New COMAC C919 Jetliner is Built with Stolen Technology," Extreme Tech, October 16, 2019.

54 Li Xiaoxiao, "China Pulling the Plug on IBM, Oracle, Others," *MarketWatch*, June 26, 2014; and "Domestic Innovation and Procurement," *China Business Review*, March–April 2010.

55 "Notice on Adjusting the Financial Subsidy Policy for the Promotion and Application of New Energy Vehicles," Ministry of Finance, Cai Jian [2016] 958, January 11, 2017.

56 Zhenhua Chen and Kingsley Haynes, "A Short History of Technology Transfer and Capture: High Speed Rail in China," November 2016.

57 European Chamber of Commerce in China, pp. 44–45.

58 www.reuters.com/article/csr-corp-china-cnr-ma/chinas-trainmakers-complete-merger-adopt-crrc-as-new-name-idUSL5N0YN1WU20150601; www.railnews.in/china-exim-bank-sign-agreement-with-crrc-for-usd-30-billion-funding-to-shore-up-exports/.

59 *China Business Review*.

60 "China Introduces Comprehensive New Cyber Security Rules for Banking and Procurement," Freshfields, March 23, 2016.

61 Antimonopoly Law of the PRC, August 3, 2008. http://english.mofcom.gov.cn/article/policyrelease/Businessregulations/.

62 Mark Cohen, "On Avoiding 'Rounding Up the Usual Suspects in the Patent Law Amendments," *China IPR Blog*, January 23, 2013; and "Micron Provides Statement on Fujian Province Patent Litigation," Micron, July 5, 2018.

63 Antimonopoly Law of the PRC, August 3, 2008.

64 "Antitrust in China: 'NDRC v. Qualcomm—One All,'" Allen & Overy, March 18, 2015. Eva Dou, "Qualcomm Will Make China Customized Chips Through Chinese Venture," *Wall Street Journal*, May 27, 2016; and "SMIC, Huawei, IMEC, and Qualcomm in Joint Investment in SMIC's New Research and Development Company," SMIC, June 23, 2015.

65 MERICS, page 51; http://english.mofcom.gov.cn/article/policyrelease/announcement/201512/20151201203768.shtml.

66 "JAC Capital, Leadcore, Qualcomm, and Wise Road Capital Enter Agreement to Form Joint Venture to Design and Sell Smartphone Chipsets in China," Qualcomm, May 25, 2017.

67 "China: Automotive Industry," US Department of Commerce, Export.Gov, July 30, 2019.

68 Steven Mufson, "Chinese Tariffs May Hurt US Makers of Solar Cells' Raw Material, *Washington Post*, July 23, 2013; "China Accuses Corning of Dumping," *Wall Street Journal*, June 17, 2004.

69 Wang Zhuoqiong, "Government Approves Rare Earth Conglomerates," *China Daily*, August 6, 2014; "China Minmetals Heilongjiang Graphite Industry Project shareholders signing ceremony successfully held," SMM News, December 12, 2019; "WTO Case Challenge China's Export Restraints on Raw Materials Inputs, USTR, June 2009; Terence Stewart, "China's Export Restraints on Fluorspar," Presentation, October 22–24, 2012.

70 "What Patents Did Bankrupt SunEdison Sell to China's GCL-Poly Energy," Duane Morris Green IP, November 28, 2017.
71 Greg Levesque and Mark Stokes, "Blurred Lines: Military–Civil Fusion and the 'Going Out' of China's Defense Industry, Pointe Bello, December 2016.
72 恒大"牵手"中科院为高科技产业引最强"智库, ScienceNet.cn. http://news.sciencenet. cn/htmlnews/2018/4/408458.shtm.
73 Summer Zhen, "China Evergrande Raises a Further US$9 billion to Cut Debt Ahead of Shenzhen Listing," *South China Morning Post*, November 6, 2017.
74 Michael Brown and Pavneet Singh, "China's Technology Transfer Strategy," DIUx, January 2018.
75 Erin Rohr, "Report Shows Silicon Valley Beating Boston in Demand Startup Economy," Metis Communications, May 23, 2015; "Chinese Companies Line Up to Partner with Haiyin Tech Teams," Haiyin Capital, June 1, 2015; and "Zhejiang Geely Holding Group Completes Acquisition of Terrafugia," Terrafugia, November 13, 2017.
76 "Tim Draper and Haiyin Capital Lead $1.2 Million of New Investment in Neurala," Neurala, June 2, 2016; "Neurala Brings Brain Builder to AI Developers in Academia, Helping to Bridge AI Skills Gap," Neurala, November 8, 2018.
77 Sean O'Kane, "Faraday Future Reveals the Source of its $2 billion Investment as a Cofounder Steps Away," *The Verge*, June 26, 2018.
78 China bought Winterpark, Van Hoecke, CIMAT, and Titan. www.burkeportergroup. com/about/our-history/.

Bibliography

Brown, Michael and Pavneet Singh. "China's Technology Transfer Strategy: How Chinese Investments in Emerging Technology Enable a Strategic Competitor to Access the Crown Jewels of US Innovation," *Defense Innovation Unit Experimental DIUx*, January 2018.
Cao, Cong, Richard P. Suttmeier and Denis Fred Simon. "China's 15-Year Science and Technology Plan," *Physics Today*, December 2006.
European Chamber of Commerce in China. "China Manufacturing 2025," 2017.
Levesque, Greg and Mark Stokes. "Blurred Lines: Military–Civil Fusion and the 'Going Out' of China's Defense Industry," Pointe Bello, December 2016.
McGregor, James, "China's Drive for 'Indigenous Innovation': A Web of Industrial Policies," US Chamber of Commerce and APCO, 2010.
Mercator Institute for China Studies (MERICS). "Made in China 2025: The Making of a High-Tech Superpower and Consequences for Industrial Countries," December 2016.
NBR. "The Theft of American Intellectual Property: Reassessments of the Challenge to the United States," 2017.
Office of the US Trade Representative. "Findings of the Investigation Into China's Acts, Policies, and Practices Related to Technology Transfer, Intellectual Property, and Innovation under Section 301 of the Trade Act of 1974," March 22, 2018.
Overby, Tami and Jeremie Waterman. "China's Approval Process for Inbound Foreign Direct Investment," US Chamber of Commerce, November 11, 2012.
Stokes, Mark. "China's Commercial Aviation Sector Looks to the Future," Project 2049 Institute, February 2009.
Suttmeier, Richard P. and Yao Xiankui. "China's Post-WTO Technology Policy: Standards, Software, and the Changing Nature of Techno-Nationalism," NBR Special Report, No. 7, May 2004.
US Chamber of Commerce. "Made in China 2025: Global Ambitions Build on Local Protections," 2017.

5

THE MYTH OF THE STATELESS GLOBAL SOCIETY

Anna B. Puglisi

For many years, the US and Western nations' engagement with China has been predicated on certain core beliefs regarding globalization, market economics, transnational labor pools, Internet and scientific freedoms, and what it takes to be innovative.[1] As a result, discussions of China as a strategic competitor have often been shaped by an implicit bias for certain key assumptions underlying Western political theory: that you need democracy to be innovative and creative, that you need a market economy to be successful, and that we, especially the US, will always be able to out-innovate others.

In practice, these biases often take the form of the following memes:

- we are not a US business we are a global one;
- innovation comes from the private sector not government investments;
- everyone has the same driver—making money—and national, political, or ethnic ties are passé and no longer important.

The biggest assumption though was that China would change and acquiesce to the belief system of Western capitalism and globalization.[2,3] And had we taken the time, we might have discovered that China's views on these matters were quite divergent from our own.

In this chapter we examine some of the ways our failure to understand China's core beliefs has impacted our ability to respond to their actions. We will also explore what is at stake if China's view of zero-sum development becomes the global norm and the values of transparency, reciprocity, and open markets yield to an authoritarian system that uses commerce and science to exert national power and promote authoritarianism. Finally, we will look at the implications of the US losing "home field advantage" with US entities not viewing themselves as

American companies while China's businesses, universities and researchers do, and how this inhibits our ability to maintain our economic dynamism.

Technology as a national asset: the new geopolitical battlespace

We begin with the simple recognition that China has engaged with the global multilateral trading order not in order to transform itself into a liberal Western-style democracy, but rather to amass wealth and power for both the country and its citizens and to protect the core interests of the Communist Party of China (CPC). It is an error to conflate engagement with this order with acceptance.[4] As stated in a recent monograph on China's international objectives,

> [t]he Chinese leadership's critique of the existing international order reveals its unswerving objection to the values on which this order has been built. At stake is not only the predominant position of the US in the current system but more importantly the potential erosion of fundamental human rights, freedom of thought and expression, and self-government around the world.[5]

At the core of this challenge is that China views itself as engaged in a strategic rivalry with the US, centered on economic power, and, as documented in the preceding chapters, has adopted an all-of-society approach to target the foundation of that power—our technology, human capital, and open exchange of ideas.[6] China's management of its relationship with the US has been designed to mask key aspects of this rivalry—exploiting the West's core beliefs as a way to build its national innovation base.[7] Despite regularly violating the global norms of business and research, China has controlled the narrative with respect to how the world views its behavior through both carrots—the China market, and sticks—harshly striking back at its critics. As a result, much of the US does not perceive the growing challenge that this rivalry poses and often questions if there is actually a problem.[8] As a result, China through its policies and actions has succeeded in surreptitiously making industry and academia the new site of geopolitical rivalry, even a battlespace.[9]

The idea of this new battlespace is well documented. Both Beijing, and especially CPC general secretary Xi Jinping, view development as a zero-sum game with Chinese government support for key industries of the future—the emerging technologies and industries of the 4th Industrial Revolution[10] such as AI, next-generation communications, and biotechnology—giving it a distinct advantage over competing market economies.

This is clear from Xi's own words (our italics):

> In today's world, S&T innovation has become a critical support for increasing comprehensive national strength … *whoever holds the key*

to S&T innovation makes an offensive move in the chess game of S&T innovation and will be able to *take the lead and win the advantages.*

(*Xi Jinping, May 24, 2014*)[11]

In a May 30, 2016 speech at the National S&T Innovation Conference to the Chinese Academy of Sciences (CAS), Chinese Academy of Engineering (CAE), and China Association for Science and Technology (CAST), Xi Jinping stated that "*science and technology is a national weapon*" and that "if China wants to be strong … it must have powerful science and technology."[12]

"We should seize the *commanding heights* of technological competition and future development."

(*Xi Jinping, May 28, 2018*)[13]

Artificial Intelligence is a vital driving force for a new round of technological revolution and industrial transformation. China must control artificial intelligence and *ensure it is securely kept in our own hands.*

(*Xi Jinping, October 31, 2018*)[14]

The idea of this new battlespace is also embedded in key policy documents outlining China's industrial policy and international engagement objectives. The May 2016 *Outline of the National Innovation-Driven Development Strategy* (IDDS), a foundational yet often overlooked policy directive, renders this view in stark terms:

> Innovation drive is bound up with the fate of a country. The core support of national power is its scientific and technological innovation capabilities. If innovation is strong, the country will be prosperous. If it is weak, the country will fall into peril. [China's] backwardness and the beatings it suffered in modern times were because it lost contact with previous scientific and technological revolutions, which resulted in weak science and technology and weak national strength. To realize the Chinese dream of the great rejuvenation of the Chinese nation,[15] we must make good use of the revolutionary forces and powerful levers of science and technology.

The IDDS and other recent Chinese policy documents also focus on the historical opportunity now before China in a time of rapid technological change. According to the IDDS,

> As disruptive technologies continue to emerge, they are reshaping the world's competitive landscape, changing the comparison of national

power, and driving innovation as the core strategy of many countries seeking competitive advantage. China is facing both a rare historical opportunity to catch up and leapfrog [other nations], but there is also a serious challenge that the gap [between developed and developing countries] may widen.

According to the Outline of the National Informatization Development Strategy, released in July 2016,

> The global governance system has undergone profound changes with the development of global multipolarization, economic globalization, cultural diversification, and social informatization. Whoever occupies the commanding heights in informatization will be able to grasp opportunities, win advantages, win security, and win the future.[16]

Thus, it is no understatement that Beijing views technology—and the robust S&T infrastructure needed to develop it—as a crucial national asset to "catch up," and "leapfrog" the West and thereby "win the future." Many of the behaviors examined in this and other chapters can be ascribed to this goal.

Of course, it is every nation's sovereign right to target technological development as a means to increasing national wealth and power. And certainly, the leaders of the Communist Party of China (CPC) have made no effort to hide their views of the importance of technological and commercial dominance, and how they view a robust S&T infrastructure as key to building a modern advanced economy,[17] if not necessarily an open market economy. However, the way China has structured its system to reach this goal is inherently at odds with key assumptions of globalization including open markets, reciprocity, transparency, and findings being shared equally and unencumbered.

China's approach, which we have detailed in this and other chapters, stands in stark contrast to the United States' and European approach to S&T collaboration with China that assumed cooperation benefits both parties in the long term.[18] The US and the West, in formulating their S&T policies, do not describe S&T as a contest, something to grab for ones' self or where you have to preempt your rivals. For instance, recently the National Academy of Sciences reaffirmed six core values for research which are objectivity, honesty, openness, accountability, fairness and stewardship.[19] Xi's statements and Chinese policy illustrate a philosophical difference in which we enter into these agreements and in the purpose of these agreements.

The Medium- to Long-Term Plan for the Development of S&T (MLP), Made in China 2025, the IDDS, Strategic Emerging Industries. and the Five-Year Plans are all policies that support this worldview.[20] These are not isolated plans but a complementary web of development and industrial policies for emerging technologies to achieve technological leadership.[21] The policies focus not only on specific technology areas but seek to create the environment to foster innovation and development, and most importantly build a national innovation base that will be the foundation for future economic growth and military modernization.

We are not playing the same game: China's hybrid innovation system

Imagine for a moment you are playing a board game with established rules and you invite a new player to join. After explaining the rules, the new player, while enjoying and benefiting from the game, begins to ignore the rules. When you question them, they may say they are following the rules, claim that rule "x" means "y," or deny that they are cheating. Every three or four rounds they adhere to the rules or even the spirit of the game, but then when there is more at stake, they use the rules against you again and enlist others to say you are cheating, unfair, and most importantly, trying to make them lose. Finally, even in cases where they openly admit or acknowledge they are violating the rules, they outline a plan for change and then largely persist with the same behavior.

While perhaps a bit of an oversimplification, much of the CPC's behavior over the last two decades can be described in those terms.[22] To be sure, there is much to applaud in recent US engagement with China. After all, haven't US companies made a lot of money in China? And haven't there been some positive reforms and rising standards of living in China? While these are all true, they only tell one side of the story, and mask many of the underlying contradictions between how we view China and they view us.

Underneath the glossy veneer of modern China, the key assumptions made in most business and S&T agreements—rule of law, market driven competition, and accepted international scientific norms—as outlined in Chapter 4, are skirted, ignored, or outright challenged. The policies highlighted above and discussed throughout the book illustrate that despite the expectations of the last decades, China has its own view of the future, and it is one that does not appear to be leading to a more open society or an equal playing field for Western companies.[23] Indeed, there are significant signs that China's economic growth has empowered an increasingly authoritarian rule—one that sees "party leadership" (i.e., control) increasingly embedded across society including business, the mass incarceration of Chinese Muslims in Xinjiang province, and growing crackdowns on free-speech, including extra-territorial renditions of non-citizen booksellers for daring to publish and sell books critical of the Party. In the realm of economics, Chinese control of state-owned and state-invested companies in key sectors continues unabated, backed by a vast array of industrial subsidies that the US and other developed countries have had little success reducing.[24]

Naturally, this reality is inconvenient to those who desire to benefit in the short term.[25] The Communist Party of China is skilled at co-opting elite opinion, divide and conquer, controlling the narrative, and presenting engagements as "mutually beneficial" "win–win" which in reality means China wins twice—both by gaining technology and by not changing.

The US is in many ways losing the international debate with China by not talking about the structural differences in our systems and instead focusing on individual instances of bad behavior that can often seem anecdotal.[26] One area where this is most egregious is in our fundamental misunderstanding of the structure and recent reforms of the Chinese "socialist market economy."

For many in America, it seems that the view of China's economy is that of a former command economy that has seen the error of its ways and is slowly transitioning to a market economy that more resembles our own. To the extent that China may practice "state capitalism," this is seen as a withering legacy of its former system that will undoubtedly reduce in time if we can just convince the Chinese of the latent inefficiencies in their system. While a useful heuristic, this view of China's economy (so present during its World Trade Organization (WTO) accession) largely overlooks how China views its own economy—not as a command economy or as a market economy, but as a socialist market economy that is a historical synthesis of the two.

This widespread misunderstanding of the Chinese economic model prejudices our ability to understand and respond to shifts in Chinese economic policies. For instance, the CPC's 2015 call for "mixed ownership" as part of State-owned enterprise (SOE) reform has widely been viewed as a means to allow for partial privatization of state-owned enterprises.[27] And while this is true, many observers have failed to note that this "mixed ownership" flows both ways. On one hand, yes the mixed ownership reforms permit some partial private ownership of China's state-owned monoliths.[28] But on the other, it also permits Chinese SOEs to deploy their state-owned capital to invest in private companies, thereby increasing the role of the state in the domestic economy.[29] In the five years since this policy was announced, guess which direction has been more active?

The misunderstanding here calls to mind a classic story in US–China relations:

> When former US president George H.W. Bush met Chinese Premier Zhu Rongji in London during the Asia-Europe Meeting in 1998, his first questions to Zhu were "how are you proceeding with privatization in China? Is it going smoothly? Zhu, China's "economic czar," quite shocked by the question, managed to respond: "Mr. Bush, China does not go for privatization. Instead we promote the shareholding system (股份制), which is one of the various means to realize public ownership." Mr. Bush replied, "Well no matter how you describe it, we know what is going on."[30]

But we did not. In fact, Zhu's emphasis on public ownership remains a core attribute of the Chinese economy today. The CPC's landmark 2013 *Decision on Some Major Issues Concerning Comprehensively Deepening Reforms*, for example, was widely cited on its release for its statement that the market should "play a decisive role" in the economy. But read in full, the decision only spoke of letting the market play a "decisive role" for the "allocation of resources (资源配置)," while still stressing that China should "persist in the dominant position of public ownership (坚持公有制主体地位)," and "give full play to the leading role of the state-owned sector (发挥国有经济主导作用)."[31] In other words, the "decisive role" language only recognized that certain market-based components could be beneficial to China's existing socialist market economy; it did not represent further transition to a market economy as that term is generally understood in the West.[32]

Our inability to recognize these distinctive features of the Chinese economy, and our bias toward equating distinctive features of their system with more recognizable features of our own, has significantly hampered our ability to discuss and debate these issues globally and among our allies. The result has essentially been tactical and "whack a mole" instead of a strategic narrative that paints the full picture of how China flaunts the values of globalization and increasingly promotes an alternative, authoritarian system.

Inefficiency and its discontents[33]

How often do we hear economists argue that you can't pick winners and that China's economy is inefficient? By both word and action, it is clear that an efficient Western macroeconomy is not the CPC's end-goal. It is important to remember that China's policies—even if they do not produce national champions—can create long-lasting distortions in markets and supply chains. That is, China's economy can remain "inefficient" for many years, with the negative externalities effectively exported to US and other foreign companies, who are required to compete as market-based players against often heavily subsidized Chinese competitors. The resulting market dynamics can create "chokepoints" where China's mercantilist practices cause the hollowing out of US manufacturing of both key parts as well as basic things such as medicine—so not just the technological "cutting edge." When pushed, many economists admit that their definition of efficiency does not take into account US jobs lost or companies going out of business—this should be a concern.

One of many examples of how China's predatory policies impacted a US company is AMSC, an American energy technologies company. China's 11th Five-Year Plan (2006–2010) and related policies heavily emphasized the development of renewable energy, including wind. These measures incentivized domestic parties in China to invest in renewable energy, further abetted by a large domestic stimulus package passed by China in the wake of the Great Financial Crisis. According to one 2010 study, "[i]n 2007 an estimated 25 companies were producing wind turbines, with another 40 or 50 to add facilities, but by 2009 the number of producers had grown to be over 100."[34] Because of a recognized "technological and qualitative gap" between Chinese and foreign producers, the Chinese companies were focused on upgrading their technology through "absorbing and adapting foreign technology":[35]

> In 2005 AMSC entered into a partnership with the Chinese company Sinovel for wind turbine design and engineering services, including the software to regulate the flow of electricity between the turbines and the grid. By 2011 Sinovel was the largest wind Turbine manufacturer in China and the second largest in the world. In March of 2011, an employee was paid $15,000 to transfer the proprietary control software technology to Sinovel managers at which point Sinovel severed its business relationship with AMSC. AMSC went public with this information and its stock price dropped 40 percent in one day. Eventually 500 of AMSC's 700 employees lost their jobs in the two years afterwards.

AMSC illustrates how China's policies created a demand signal for action and how it played out in the real world. It is also a rare case of an American CEO willing to talk about China's actions.

As the old adage goes, "markets can remain irrational longer than you can remain solvent." Even if China's system is unsustainable and inefficient over the long run, it can still significantly damage US interests over the near term, if not irretrievably. The negative externalities likely to be felt by China's "inefficiencies" are even more concerning when you factor in the sheer size of the Chinese economy as well as their stated ambition to "leapfrog" their competitors and "win the future" in global technology.

While Americans pride themselves on their innovation abilities, there are places where China's "good enough" is, indeed, good enough and where writing a check can impact development or buy one's way to the front of a technology field. Perhaps the best explanation of how what China is doing not only works but also undermines the assumptions of the importance of efficiency, is put forth by Silicon Valley entrepreneur Kai-Fu Lee:[36]

> What these critics miss is that this process can be both highly inefficient and extraordinarily effective. When the long-term upside is so monumental, overpaying in the short term can be the right thing to do. The Chinese government wanted to engineer a fundamental shift in the Chinese economy, from manufacturing-led growth to innovation-led growth, and it wanted to do that in a hurry.... The process of pure force was often locally inefficient—incubators that went unoccupied and innovation avenues that never paid off—but on a national scale, the impact was tremendous.

What is at stake? The United States' S&T dominance since World War II has underpinned American strength and soft power. Losing our technological edge and the influence it entails will have implications beyond scientific disciplines. Increasingly this is not only about military technologies, but dual-use technologies and commercial applications. We have not lived in a world where the US has been number two in foundational technology and have trouble imagining its consequences. Yet in many ways we have forgotten our own history, whereas China has learned from it. The Manhattan project, space race, and the Internet were driven by government investment. The US economy still benefits from investments that happened decades ago.

Does innovation matter?

When China's S&T capabilities and its ability to challenge the US are discussed, the issue of innovation is always raised. The norms that underlie our Western beliefs of what it takes to be truly innovative are at times thrown around as fact rather than assumptions that we make about our own system. Ditto with efficiency, creativity, and the importance of democracy.

Discussing China's growth and development often devolves into a debate over who can do more of what. This capability-to-capability comparison should not be our focus. Instead, a true measure how well we are doing is the rate of change in these different areas. China is building its foundation—through investments and acquisitions—and we are letting ours decay by not making the investments that will enable future discovery.[37] As we reassess the current state of affairs, we would do well to remember the follow key points:

- Innovation comes from doing the research—if you are not doing it, and ceding whole disciplines to competitors, you will not be innovative or competitive.
- A society cannot be innovative if it is not training enough students.
- You cannot build an innovation base if you are not building big science facilities.[38,39]
- What we did 40 years ago is irrelevant to today's challenges. Indeed, the hubris of past success disadvantages the US.
- Technologies do not have to be cutting edge to matter.
- The funder of research, education, and the big science facility will not benefit if the transition points are not supported.
- A better design on paper counts for nothing on the battlefield or marketplace.

By only focusing on the commercially viable—or worse, the next quarter's profit—we hollow out our innovation base. Someone else will win by playing the long game, someone who doesn't see funding as a welfare program and has the will to see past "efficiency" for something bigger, namely, building a national innovation base. In this case all indicators point to China.

The question of innovation is more than a philosophical debate because whether a company, government, or individual thinks China is innovative or not impacts the risk calculation one makes in dealing with China. This has shaped early interactions and willingness to share technology and train students, researchers and technicians in China. If you believe you are 5–10 years ahead and that you inherently will "always out innovate them" you will make a different risk calculation than if you are dealing with a peer competitor.

As we point out in this book's introductory chapter, the ability to do radical innovation in the abstract—which has not been China's strong suit historically—has little or no impact in today's reality, because abstractions lack real world utility, because China is closing the theory "gap" in areas it sees as important and, as we are at pains to point out through this entire volume, because China has perfected techniques to access the "cutting-edge" breakthroughs done elsewhere. Our point is that clutching this myth of inherent technological superiority is nothing short of suicidal.

Losing home field advantage

Given the power of multinational corporations (MNC), the spectacle of US-based firms benefiting from our open society, its protections, and its taxed-funded infrastructure but not seeing themselves as American companies—even acting against US interests—cannot help but impact US competitiveness.[40] MNC's are described as having more power than some countries,[41] able to shape society not only through their business practices but through the persona and values they project. By failing to criticize or even publicly question China's actions in violating global norms of business, in its demands for technology and its violation of human rights, they support China's vision of the world, and its relative place in the world.

More incongruously, while refusing to work with the USG in matters of national defense,[42] they evince few qualms about supporting China's undemocratic polity. It has always been the case, and it is inherently assumed, that in times of conflict the United States can rely on its companies and institutions. What if this isn't true anymore? What if, for example, the same companies that led us to victory producing materiel 75 years ago decide next time to opt for China market share?

The risks of this disturbing trend to ignore the interests of the commonwealth while upholding those of a strategic competitor are an erosion of the innovation system that is the foundation of US national power, and a decline in global norms of transparency, reciprocity, and the principles of democracy themselves. The following are real-life examples of how we are losing our "home field advantage":

- refusal of a US company to work with the USG while working with China to build a search engine that would censor information at the behest of the Chinese government;
- discoveries funded by the USG (American taxpayer) at national labs commercialized by companies owned by China;

- US-based advocacy groups with ties to the Communist Party of China influencing with impunity local US governments and elected officials;
- "Sino-American" professional guilds requiring their members to exercise fealty and provide service to their alleged "ancestral" country;
- Chinese government use of US-based social media to push its propaganda in the US while many of these same social media companies are blocked in China;
- US universities canceling or censoring content on issues related to China due to the threat of losing China money.

In summer 2019, the Business Roundtable raised some of the issues at stake when they issued a statement that businesses should serve all their stakeholders, including workers and society.[43] They reaffirmed that "America's economic model, which is based on freedom, liberty and other enduring principles of our democracy, has raised living standards for generations, while promoting competition, consumer choice and innovation."

If that is indeed the case, there must be a re-envisioning of private-public partnerships to deal with the new reality of China.

Beijing has reasserted the CPC's role in decision-making as a way to ensure the best interests of the communist state, going as far as to establish party cells in Western companies. It is in the process of developing and implementing a Corporate Social System.[44] The system will apply to all foreign companies doing business in China and gauge their performance by considering a range of factors, including, for example, how many Communist Party members a company employs, its responses to politically sensitive issues, and willingness to hand over company data for scrutiny.[45] A company's score can lead to punishments and will impact its access to low cost loans, level of taxation and a host of other things. Like many rules and regulations in China, few details have been released.

China's legal system is also creating its own "home field advantage" and compelling support from its domestic companies and citizens.[46] Here are some examples:

1   National Security Law (2015).[47]
      - Article 77: Citizens and organizations shall perform the following obligations for safeguarding the national security: Provide national security authorities, public security authorities and military authorities with needed support and assistance.
2   Counterterrorism Law (2015)
      - Article 9: All work units and individuals are obligated to aid and assist the relevant departments in carrying out of counterterrorism work. If suspected terrorist activities or suspected terrorists are discovered they should be reported to relevant organs or relevant departments in a timely manner.

3   Cyber Security Law (2016).[48]
   - Article 28: Network operators shall provide technical support and assistance to public security organs and national security organs that are safeguarding national security and investigating criminal activities in accordance with the law.
4   National Intelligence Law (2017)
   - Article 7: All organizations and citizens shall support, assist, and cooperate with national intelligence efforts in accordance with the law, and shall protect national work secrets they are aware of.

One of the hardest concepts for citizens of open societies to accept—even those doing business in China on a regular basis—is that regardless of the personal view of the Chinese scientist, businessperson, or official interacting with you, they must respond to the government or security services if asked for information or data. In other words, the party and state potentially or immediately stand behind everyone. This is fundamentally difficult for people raised in democracies to comprehend. China intimidates and harshly silences its critics and those who do not comply, even more so in recent years, making it difficult for citizens to evade this responsibility, though some do try, at least some of the time.[49]

Conclusions

We are acutely aware of the win–win nature of international cooperation where assumptions, goals and talents are shared by all parties. But this system only works, when the goals are accepted and shared by all parties to the table. Today, the US and China exist in a state that can best be described by the Chinese idiom 同床异梦—same bed different dreams—a state of affairs first noted by sinologist David Lampton in 2002 and which remains true today.

Given what is at stake, a discussion among stakeholders is needed on how to mitigate the negative externalities of Chinese activity and protect US national interests. For this to happen, we will need to be open and honest about the nature of the threats we face while still recognizing the problems inherent in our own system. Thus, we should accept that it is not a "red scare" to call out China's bad behavior, and that when a largely homogenous country adopts policies to incentivize its citizens to purloin foreign technology for the "great rejuvenation" of the race, it is not "ethnic profiling" for the target heterogeneous country to defend against such actions.

These questions touch upon some of the most vexing and sensitive issues in today's America. But in discussing them, we should not forget the liberal Western values that permit a country as diverse as America to give voice to its polity and allow them to debate these issues on the national stage. These rights and the opportunities should be remembered when considering what the rise of an authoritarian China may bring to us in terms of our fundamental values. The inability to call out China's policies for what they are, see what is at stake and, most importantly, move beyond identity politics will give China the advantage and threaten our future.

Public perception will be a big part of addressing this challenge. In the preceding decades, China controlled the message. Silicon Valley has also dominated the conversation with the result that American society has learned to conflate private wealth generation with innovation. While apps are one form of innovation, they are not the foundational work that industries are supported by or capacity building for the future.[50] What should the US do about it?

One problem is that knowledge-based industries in their early stages provide a foundation for future trade, but do not always produce tradable goods, requiring remedies that support these technologies at earlier points in their development than do export controls or tariffs. These traditional remedies probably will be ineffective at correcting imbalances in high-tech industries that rely on knowhow and expertise and will have limited impact on major national initiatives, including Made in China 2025.

Addressing threats to our long-term technological leadership includes, crucially, increased investment in R&D and education, and more robust support for moving cutting-edge research out of the lab and into business. Public-private partnerships that protect intellectual property and provide incentives for moving technology from the lab to the market—to take a lesson from China's own "commercialization enclaves"—will also create the innovation environment to propel these industries.

As stated in this and previous chapters, the US, allies, and partners face unique challenges by competitors like China because of the scale and scope of its efforts, and the extent of government involvement, which challenge traditional policy remedies. Our open system of business, research and education is based on reciprocity, transparency, and meaningful exchange of ideas. We must ensure that our partners share these values—and hedge against the likelihood that they will not.

Notes

1 Alex Gray, "What is Globalization Anyway," World Economic Forum, January 10, 2017. www.weforum.org/agenda/2017/01/what-is-globalization-explainer.

2 James Mann, *The China Fantasy: How Our Leaders Explain Away Chinese Repressions*, New York: Viking, 2007.

3 Kenneth Roth, *China's Global Threat to Human Rights*. Global Report 2020, "China's Global Threat to Human Rights". John Pomfret, "What America Didn't Anticipate about China," *The Atlantic*, 16 October 2019. In recent years, some have attempted to downplay or reject the idea that America's support for China's WTO accession was based in part on a belief that economic engagement would eventually lead to political or social change. This argument finds little support in the record. See, e.g., https://1997-2001.state.gov/current/debate/chinsph.html.

4 See, e.g., Nadege Rolland, *China's Vision for a New World Order*, The National Bureau of Asian Research Special Report No. 83, January 27, 2020. ("In 2002, Jiang Zemin

already bemoaned the 'old international political and economic order, which is unfair and has to be changed fundamentally.' China's criticism of the US-led world order has only grown stronger and more pointed over the years. In 2016, for example, senior diplomat Fu Ying compared it to an old suit that no longer fits. The discontent with the current order, deemed 'unfair and unreasonable,' is unambiguous.").

5 Ibid.

6 China's technology acquisition policies and all-of-society approach are outlined in the preceding chapters.

7 We use the term "national innovation base" as opposed to "national security innovation base" because we believe that economic security is national security and narrowly defining what we should care about to military technologies will not address the problem the US is facing.

8 Numerous press statements by academic organizations, the Committee of 100, and others who question that these are more than isolated cases. For example: the website "supchina" has an entire section dedicated to "responses to rising sinophobia;" and despite concrete evidence of wrong doing, over a dozen university presidents have come out with statements that focus on alleged ethnic profiling instead of the violations of research integrity.

9 The Director of the US National Counterintelligence and Security Center called business and academia the new geopolitical battlespace in *Catalyst Magazine*, Fall 2019.

10 The fourth industrial revolution is described by Klaus Schwab as the era that will be characterized by the combining of the physical, digital and biological worlds. His book *The Fourth Industrial Revolution* has been the subject of discussion at DAVOS. Klaus Schwab, *The Fourth Industrial Revolution*, New York: Random House, 2017.

11 www.xinhuanet.com//politics/2014-05/24/c_1110843342_2.htm.

12 www.xinhuanet.com//politics/2016-06/06/c_129043555.htm.

13 www.xinhuanet.com/politics/leaders/2018-05/28/c_1122899973.htm.

14 www.xinhuanet.com/politics/leaders/2018-10/31/c_1123643321.htm.

15 Although officially translated as "Chinese nation," the word here is *zhonghua minzu* or "Chinese race."

16 国家信息化发展战略纲要 (*Outline of the National Informatization Development Strategy*), July 2016.

17 Cong Cao, Richard Suttmeier, and Denis Fred Simon. "China's 15-year Science and Technology Plan," *Physics Today*, December (2006), pp. 38–43.

18 It is important to make the distinction that we are talking about long-term benefits. While there are many examples of individual companies making money in the short-term what is at stake here are how these trade-offs now will impact the future sustainability of both industries and US competitiveness.

19 National Academies of Sciences, Engineering, and Medicine. 2017. *Fostering Integrity in Research*. Washington, DC: The National Academies Press. https://doi.org/10.17226/21896.

20 See 国家创新驱动发展战略纲要 (Outline of the National Innovation-Driven Development Strategy). CPC Central Committee & State Council, May 19, 2016; "十三五" 科技军民融合发展专项规划, MOST, CMC, 2017; 国务院关于印发"十三五"国家战略性新兴产业发展规划的通知, State Council, 2016; 国家科技创新基地优化整合案, MOST, MOF, National Development and Reform Commission, 2017.

21 Denis Simon and Cong Cao. *China's Emerging Technological Edge: Assessing the Role of High-End Talent*, Cambridge: Cambridge University Press, 2009.

22 See, e.g., Mark Wu, "The 'China, Inc.' Challenge to Global Trade Governance." *Harvard International Law Journal* 57, no. 2 (2016), pp. 261–224.

23 James Mann, Ibid.

24 See, e.g., David Lynch, "Initial US–China Trade Deal Has Major Hole: Beijing's Massive Business Subsidies," *Washington Post*, December 31, 2019.

25 What we mean here is there are many examples of CEOs making agreements that are not in the long-term interest of the company, industry, or US but instead makes their short-term stock prices look good. In academia this means taking research funds from an authoritarian government that does not allow true academic freedom.

26 William C. Hannas, James Mulvernon, and Anna B. Puglisi, *Chinese Industrial Espionage: Technology Acquisition and Military Modernization*, London and New York: Routledge, 2013.

27 See, e.g., Ann Listerud, "MOR Money MOR Problems: China's Mixed Ownership Reforms in Practice." CSIS, October 1, 2019.

28 See, e.g., David Stanway and Jing Wang, "China State Firms Complete 48 "Mixed Ownership", Reuters Business News, June 20, 2017. www.reuters.com/article/us-china-soe-idUSKBN19C09K. Reforms this Year, June 20, 2017 (But note the last paragraph "However, the head of the state-owned asset regulator said last week that SOEs should avoid 'erroneous' notions like 'privatization' and 'denationalization,' saying that the role of the Communist Party in state-run firms needed to be strengthened.").

29 See, e.g., Hao Peng, 加快实现从管企业向管资本转变形成以管资本为主的国有资产监管体. www.cnpc.com.cn/cnpc/gzdt/201911/e0f755afb8a043869f23ceeb0aa13787.shtml.

30 Jin Zeng, *State-led Privatization in China: The Politics of Economic Reform.* Oxford: Routledge, 2013.

31 www.china.org.cn/chinese/2014-01/17/content_31226494.htm.

32 In international fora, China now claims that "there are many forms of market economy" of which the socialist market economy is just one.

33 Mariana Mazzucato, "The Entrepreneurial State: Debunking Public vs. Private Sector Myths," *Public Affairs*, 2015.

34 Dewey & Lebouef LLP for the National Foreign Trade Council. "China's Promotion of the Renewable Electric Power Equipment Industry," March 2010.

35 Ibid. An overview of China's IDAR method (Introduce, Digest, Absorb, Re-innovate) for acquiring foreign technology is provided in the *Section 301 Report into China's Acts, Policies, and Practices Related to Technology Transfer, Intellectual Property, and Innovation.* Office of the U.S. Trade Representative. "Findings of the Investigation into China's Acts, Policies, and Practices Related to Technology Transfer, Intellectual Property, and Innovation Under Section 301 of the Trade Act of 1974," March 22, 2018.

36 Kai-Fu Lee. *AI Superpowers: China, Silicon Valley, and the New World Order*, Boston, MA: Houghton Mifflin Harcourt, 2018, p. 65.

37 This includes STEM education, funding for basic research and investments in big science facilities that enable discovery.

38 A history of China's investment programs and policies can be found in the following: Denis Simon and Cong Cao. *China's Emerging Technological Edge: Assessing the Role of High-End Talent*, Cambridge: Cambridge University Press, 2009; Applebaum et al., *Innovation in China*. Cambridge: Polity Press, 2018; and *Chinese Industrial Espionage: Technology Acquisition and Military Modernization*, London and New York: Routledge, 2013.

39 By "big science facilities" we mean light sources, HPC, colliders etc.

40 We lack attribution for the following quote: "Chinese companies work for China, US companies work for their shareholders, but who works for the US?"

41 Parag Khanna and David Francis, "The Rise of the Titans: These 25 Companies Are More Powerful Than Many Countries," *Foreign Policy*, March 15, 2016.

42 Project Maven, DUIX etc.

43 Press Release from Business Roundtable and WSJ editorial June 2019.

44 European Chamber of Commerce, "The 'Digital Hand' How China's Corporate Social Credit System Conditions Market Actors," 2019. www.europeanchamber.com.cn.

45 Klein, Jodi Xu, "Why US Business Should Be Worried about China's Corporate Social Credit System," *South China Morning Post*, October 14, 2019.
46 "Findings of the Investigations into China's Acts, Policies and Practices Related to Technology Transfer, Intellectual Property and Innovation under Section 301 of the Trade Act of 1974," March 22, 2018, USTR.
47 China's National Security Law (2015), Counterterrorism Law (2015), Cybersecurity Law (2016) and National Intelligence Law (2017).
48 Ibid.
49 Kenneth Roth, *China's Global Threat to Human Rights*. Global Report 2020.
50 Mariana Mazzucato, "The Entrepreneurial State: Debunking Public vs. Private Sector Myths," *Public Affairs*, 2015.

Bibliography

Alderman, Daniel. "An Introduction to China's Strategic Military–Civilian Fusion," in Joe McReynolds, ed., *China's Evolving Military Strategy*, Washington, DC: Brookings Institution Press, 2016.

Alderman, Daniel, Lisa Crawford, Brian Lafferty, and Aaron Straberg. "The Rise of Chinese Civil–Military Integration," in Tai Ming Cheung, ed., *Forging China's Military Might: A New Framework for Assessing Innovation*, Baltimore, MD: Johns Hopkins Press, 2014.

Applebaum, Richard P., Cong Cao, Xueying Han, Rachel Parker, and Denis Simon. *Innovation in China: Challenging the Global Science and Technology System*, Boston, MA: Polity Press, 2018.

Berger, Suzanne. "Why Manufacturing Matters," *MIT Technology Review*, July 1, 2011.

Cao, Cong, Richard Suttmeier and Denis Fred Simon. "China's 15-year Science and Technology Plan," *Physics Today*, December (2006), pp. 38–43.

Chamber of Commerce. *Made in China 2025: Global Ambitions Built on Local Protections*, 2017.

Cherif, Reda and Hasanov, Faud. "The Return of the Policy that Shall Not Be Named: Principles of Industrial Policy," IMF Working Paper, March 2019.

Cheung, Tai Ming. *Fortifying China: The Struggle to Build a Modern Defense Economy*, Ithaca, NY: Cornell University Press, 2009.

Cheung, Tai Ming. "The Chinese Defense Economy's Long March from Imitation to Innovation," *Journal of Strategic Studies* 34, no. 3, June 2011.

Cheung, Tai Ming. ed. *Forging China's Military Might: A New Framework for Assessing Innovation*, Baltimore, MD: Johns Hopkins Press, 2014.

Churchill, Owen. "Compel Chinese Companies Listed in US to Disclose Party Links, Congress Urged," *South China Morning Post*, November 15, 2019.

Department of Defense. "Annual Report to Congress: Military Power of the People's Republic of China," Washington, DC: GPO, 2009.

Department of Defense. *Annual Report to Congress: Military and Security Developments Involving the People's Republic of China 2019*, Washington, DC: GPO, 2019.

European Chamber of Commerce, "The Digital Hand: How China's Corporate Social Credit System Conditions Market Actors," 2019. www.europeanchamber.com.cn.

European Union Chamber of Commerce in China. *China Manufacturing 2025: Putting Industrial Policy Ahead of Market Forces*, 2017.

Feigenbaum, Evan. *China's Techno-Warriors: National Security and Strategic Competition from the Nuclear to the Information Age*, Stanford, CA: Stanford University Press, 2003.

Goldberg, Paul. "MD Anderson Researchers Ousted As NIH and FBI Target Diversion of Intellectual Property," *The Cancer Letter*, April 26, 2019.

Gorman, Lindsey. "5G is Where China and the West Finally Diverge," *The Atlantic*, January 5, 2020.

Hamilton, Clive. *"The Silent Invasion,"* Hardie Grant, March 20, 2018.

Hannas, William C., James Mulvenon, and Anna B. Publisi. *Chinese Industrial Espionage: Technology Acquisition and Military Modernization*, London and New York: Routledge, 2013.

Howell, Sabrina. "Financing Innovation: Evidence from R&D Grants," *American Economic Review*, 107, no. 4, 2017, pp. 1136–1164.

Hu, Jintao. "Hold High the Great Banner of Socialism with Chinese Characteristics and Strive for New Victories in Building a Moderately Prosperous Society in All Aspects," *Xinhua*, October 10, 2011.

Jencks, Harlan. "The General Armaments Department," in James C. Mulvenon and Andrew N.D. Yang, eds., *The People's Liberation Army as Organization*: Reference Volume v1.0, Santa Monica, CA: RAND, 2002.

Joske, Alex. "Picking Flowers, Making Honey—The Chinese Military's Collaboration with Foreign Universities," *Australian Strategic Policy Institute*, International Cyber Policy Centre, October 30, 2018.

Khanna, Parag and David Francis, "The Rise of the Titans: These 25 Companies Are More Powerful Than Many Countries," *Foreign Policy*, March 15, 2016.

Krugman, Paul. "Competitiveness: A Dangerous Obsession." *Foreign Affairs* 73, no. 2, 1994, pp. 28–44.

Krugman, Paul. "The Myth of Asia's Miracle," *Foreign Affairs* 73, no. 6, 1994, pp. 62–78.

Lee, Kai-Fu. *AI Superpowers: China, Silicon Valley and the New World Order*, Boston, MA: Houghton Mifflin Harcourt, 2018.

Mandiant. *APT1: Exposing One of China's Cyber Espionage Units*, February 18, 2013.

Mann, James. *The China Fantasy: How Our Leaders Explain Away Chinese Repressions*, New York: Viking, 2007.

Mazzucato, Mariana. "The Entrepreneutial State: Debunking Public vs. Private Sector Myths," *Public Affairs*, 2015.

OECD. "Science, Technology and Innovation in the New Economy," September 2000.

Office of the US Trade Representative. "Findings of the Investigation into China's Acts, Policies, and Practices Related to Technology Transfer, Intellectual Property, and Innovation under Section 301 of the Trade Act of 1974," March 22, 2018.

Plender, John. "Why Finance Has Resisted a Big Push towards Deglobalization," *Financial Times*, November 18, 2019.

PRC State Council. "国务院关于印发《中国制造2025》的通知 ("State Council Directive China Manufacturing 2025"), No. 28, 2015.

Romer, Paul. "Endogenous Technological Change," *Journal of Political Economy* 98, no. 5, 1990, pp. S71–102.

Roth, Kenneth. *China's Global Threat to Human Rights*, Global Report, 2020.

Rumbelow, Helen. "Don't Mess with Mariana Mazzucato, the World's Scariest Economist," *The Times*, November 17, 2017.

Simon, Denis and Cong Cao. *China's Emerging Technological Edge: Assessing the Role of High-End Talent*, Cambridge, Cambridge University Press, 2009.

Tait, Robert. "China Accused of Buying Influence after Czech Billionaire Funds PR Push," *Guardian*, January 5, 2020.

Truex, Rory. "Colleges Should All Stand up to China," *The Atlantic*, December 28, 2019.

Wang, Bijiun and Huiyao Wang. "Chinese Manufacturing Mirms' Overseas Direct Investment (ODI): Patterns, Motivations and Challenges," in Jane Golley and Ligang

Song, eds., *Rising China: Global Challenges and Opportunities*, Canberra, Australia: Australian National University, 2011.

Zwetsloot, Remco and Dahlia Peterson. "The US–China Tech Wars: China's Immigration Disadvantage: How the US Can Retain Technological Leadership Despite Its Demographic Deficit," *The Diplomat*, December 31, 2019.

6

TARGETING DEFENSE TECHNOLOGIES

James Mulvenon and Chenny Zhang

While economic development is the primary driver of China's non-traditional collection and espionage activity, improving the capabilities of its military is a close second. The combination of the shock of the first Gulf War in the early 1990s, the emergence of the ongoing cross-straits crisis with Taiwan, and the increasingly heavy demands created by the growth of China's strategic interests around the globe have driven Beijing to expand dramatically the resources devoted to military modernization and lay down aggressive benchmarks for success.

Yet from the 1990s forward, the People's Liberation Army (PLA) and the defense–industrial base faced significant structural impediments to modernization, especially access to advanced technologies. This chapter explores that struggle and the role of illicit technology transfer in overcoming the shortfalls, beginning with a critical examination of the existing literatures on Chinese defense innovation and strategic weapons development, followed by an analysis of the roles of defense technology planning and foreign sources of technology on the modernization process.

The China defense innovation literature: missing pieces

The field literature on Chinese defense innovation is robust, ranging from the early canon works of John Frankenstein and Bates Gill[1] to the strategic weapons canon (John Wilson Lewis, Xue Litai, Evan Feigenbaum[2]) to the "transition" literature about defense industries reform in the late 1990s[3] to the more recent publications from Tai Ming Cheung and his Minerva Initiative program ("The Evolving Relationship Between Technology and National Security in China") at the University of California, San Diego.[4]

The strategic weapons canon is notable for the lack of discussion of any illicit acquisition of technology as supporting China's historic defense technology successes (e.g., atomic and hydrogen bomb, satellite, intercontinental ballistic missile (ICBM), nuclear-powered ballistic missile submarine (SSBN)) in the Mao and early-Deng period, preferring to emphasize a COSTIND-friendly narrative highlighting remarkable individuals, innovative bureaucratic processes, and massive government resources.[5] While the works in the late-1990s and early-2000s can be excused for not mentioning illicit transfer or espionage, as they immediately predated the most intense period of illegal activity, the absence of mention in the more recent literature is striking. In the current gold standard work on Chinese defense innovation, Tai Ming Cheung's *Forging China's Military Might*, Eric Hagt's chapter discusses the development of the J-31 stealth fighter but fails to note the extensively documented link between the J-31 and the cyber breach against Lockheed-Martin's F-35 program.[6] In his conclusion, Cheung mentions the F-35 as a competing platform but also fails to mention Chinese cyber espionage.[7] Kevin Pollpeter's chapter on China's human spaceflight program omits any discussion of the remarkable similarities between the design of the *Shenzhou* flight capsule and the Russian *Soyuz*, and makes no mention of Dongfan "Greg" Chung's 30 years of espionage, which involved transferring over 300,000 Boeing documents to Beijing including information related to the Space Shuttle program and the Delta IV rocket.[8] The sole discussion of espionage occurs in the Richard Bitzinger et al., chapter, which acknowledges that the "final driver for China's indigenous naval S&T *could* be its defense technological espionage overseas," but then dilutes the point by asserting that espionage is "a strategy not unique to Beijing or even its Asian competitors."[9] Later in the chapter, Bitzinger only mentions cases of Chinese espionage against Japanese and Ukrainian targets but no US cases, despite their abundance.[10] Instead, Cheung and his co-authors conclude that "adaptation of foreign acquired technology" is a key element of Chinese "incremental innovation,"[11] without any clarification of where or how that technology was acquired. Given the massive scale of defense-related non-traditional collection and technology espionage documented in *Chinese Industrial Espionage* and the pages of this book, this is a significant and at times inexplicable oversight that needs to be corrected in order to present a truly comprehensive picture of Chinese defense innovation.

Role of defense technology planning in technology espionage

In responding to myriad perceived threats, both external and domestic, the default Chinese government reaction is long-term planning. The Chinese government's affinity for planning, befitting their centrally planned economic roots, remains remarkably robust, even in the market-oriented period of "socialism with Chinese characteristics." Indeed, many serious analysts have commented on the "retrogression" back to more central planning and a renewed focus on state-owned enterprises under the Xi Jinping regime, despite the gains from private enterprises that drove the early growth in the 1980s and 1990s. Within this larger state planning construct, defense and military planning have also been consistent features of the Chinese system. While detailed and long-term defense planning is a common feature of all professional military organizations, the Chinese system is particularly noteworthy for its explicit linkages of defense, economic, and science and technology planning. Kate Walsh correctly notes that Chinese defense planning seeks to "facilitate domestic and foreign technology transfers to, from, and across the defense sector."[12] Yet given the perceived external and internal threats detailed above, it is not surprising that demands on defense planning have become more serious and outcomes-focused in the last 20 years, resulting in a concomitant increase in defense-related non-traditional collection, cyber espionage, and technology espionage.

National S&T and industrial planning: MLP 2006–2020 and Made in China 2025

Supplementing the military and national defense planning programs are a series of national science and technology and industrial plans, which then further integrate into the military–civilian fusion programs outlined below. The two most prominent and important of these national plans are the Medium- and Long-Term Program (MLP) for Science and Technology Development (2006–2020)[13] and "Made in China 2025."[14] The MLP defines 16 "major special projects" for national defense research and innovation, including core electronic devices, high-end chips and software, large-scale integrated circuit manufacturing technology, next-generation mobile telecommunication, basic manufacturing technology, large passenger aircrafts, high-resolution satellites, and manned spaceflight, among others.[15] Chinese officials noted that foreign companies were more advanced in all of the listed "major special projects" technologies. Thus, the fastest means for China to leapfrog was to rely on tech transfer from foreign sources to accelerate China's technological development.

The PRC industrial plan "Made in China 2025" ("MIC2025") is "a high-level industrial policy aimed at transforming China into a global manufacturing leader."[16] Published by the State Council in 2015, MIC2025 lays out a multi-stage agenda for achieving this goal, beginning with policies to localize and indigenize supply chains, followed by rapid programs to substitute Chinese technologies for their foreign counterparts and then externalize the initiative by capturing global market share.[17] The planning documents identify ten priority sectors:

- next-generation information technology;
- high-end numerical control machinery and robotics;
- aerospace and aviation equipment;
- maritime engineering equipment and high-tech maritime vessel manufacturing;

- advanced rail equipment;
- energy-saving and new energy vehicles;
- electrical equipment;
- new materials;
- biomedicine and high-performance medical devices; and
- agricultural machinery and equipment.

While MLP or MIC2025 do not have a specific military or defense focus, many of these priority sectors have natural spin-offs for military research, development, and acquisition, particularly given the pervasiveness of "dual-use" technologies in twenty-first century warfare.

From civil–military integration to military–civil fusion

China's national industrial plans like MLP and MIC2025 directly benefit defense innovation through an evolving set of "bridge" policies, originally known as "civil–military integration" and more recently termed "military–civilian fusion." In 2001, China's 10th Five-Year Plan introduced guiding principles for its economic and military modernization: "军民结合、寓军于民、大力协同、自主创新" (civil–military integration, military adoption of civilian capabilities, vigorous collaboration, and indigenous innovation.)[18] The concept of civil–military integration (CMI; 军民结合) traces back to Mao Zedong and has since iterated over four generations of party leadership under Deng Xiaoping, Jiang Zemin, and Hu Jintao. Deng's policy is well summarized by Alderman et al:[19]

> Deng's CMI policy, encapsulated by the slogan 'combining the military and civilian sectors' [军民结合], emphasized encouraging China's defense industries to produce goods for the civilian market, as the government wanted to encourage the development of dual-use technologies and maintain defense industry capacities in an era of relative peace.

By contrast, Hu Jintao's policy of "civil–military integration" [军民融合] aimed to balance the equation back toward military technology development. In a prominent 2007 article, Hu argued:

> We will adjust and reform the national defense S&T industrial system and the weapons and equipment procurement system, and we will enhance the quality, efficiency, and indigenous innovation capability of our weapons and equipment development. We will establish and perfect a weapons and equipment research and manufacturing system that "combines the military and civilian sectors" and "locates military potential in civilian capabilities" … and we will take the development road of military and civilian integration with Chinese characteristics.[20]

According to Alderman et al., CMI therefore sought to break down barriers between the defense and civilian sectors, which were "preventing the defense industry from effectively tapping into the S&T boom that [was] rapidly emerging in the rest of the country."[21] The hope was that "increased collaboration between military and civilian actors [would] be a boon to development within both systems." (110) Specifically, this

> expanded conception of CMI … pursued 'overall coordination" by merging defense modernization planning with the country's broader economic planning. It [aimed] to join, integrate, and combine planning efforts in economic and military development in order to utilize capital, technology, human capital, facilities, and information most effectively at the national strategic level.
>
> *(111)*

Under Xi Jinping, military–civil fusion (MCF; 军民融合) is a variation on the same concept "寓军于民," (locate military potential in civilian capability), which leverages commercial innovation for its defense–industrial base. CMI and MCF, by design, are about creating an ecosystem for indigenous innovation that facilitates the transfer of commercial innovation to military capabilities. Under this system the PLA acts as a "funding source, a research partner, and an elite customer."[22]

Since taking power, Xi Jinping elevated MCF to a national strategy and expanded its scope beyond the defense industry.[23] Indeed, MCF reinforces the CPS's aim to build China into an economic, technological, and military superpower. This sharing of resources and collaboration in research and applications ensures the mutually beneficial coordination of economic and national defense development. Thus, China's economic growth is inextricably tied to the PLA's modernization and the Chinese defense–industrial base.

Foreign sources of defense technology: within China

China's military has relied on transferring technology from foreign sources as a means of achieving its modernization and development objectives. Tech transfer for defense happens in several ways—licitly and illicitly, within and outside of China.

Bureaucratic and regulatory pressure

In and of itself, tech transfer within the commercial sector may not be problematic. However, China's systemic nature of blending of civil and military affairs makes tech transfer concerning to foreign governments and multinational corporations. The Civil–Military Integration Department (军民结合推进司) within the

Ministry of Industry and Information Technology (MIIT) gives guidance on military–civilian dual-use technology transfer. The existence of this office, and its counterparts within other state ministries is an indicator of an explicit and encouraged relationship between commercial and defense sectors.[24] Indeed, this relationship enables the defense sector to leverage spin-on benefits from synergies with the commercial sector.

The regulatory and commercial environment in China is such that foreign companies must transfer technology to access the domestic market.[25] In fact, this has been the norm for so long that many foreign businesses simply accept tech transfer as the price of doing business with China, even though such practices would be considered predatory or unfair in their home countries.[26] For example, Chinese regulations often only allow foreign companies to operate in China through joint ventures or partnerships with their domestic counterparts. These partnerships include investments in R&D and labs, much like Huawei's technology cooperation agreements with Lucent, Motorola, Intel, IBM, AT&T, Texas Instruments, and Sun Microsystems.[27] Effectively, many foreign companies have to buy their way into the domestic market.

Coupled with an unfamiliarity with China's political economy, foreign companies unwittingly facilitate the development of Chinese national security capabilities by transferring technology, capital, or knowhow to domestic companies linked to the PLA or the state security apparatus. For example, multinational corporations have agreed to transfer core technologies in exchange for market access. Microsoft in 2015 initiated a partnership with the China Electronic Technology Group Corporation (CETC, 中国电子科技集团公司), which is China's defense electronics conglomerate. Ericsson agreed to release CDMA source code to its Chinese partner. In another instance, Network Solutions gave data of 300 computer viruses to the Ministry of Public Security in order to speed up the certification of its anti-virus products.[28] China also uses domestic mergers and acquisitions as a vehicle to transfer technology into its defense–industrial base. According to a 2019 report by C4ADS, state-owned defense contractors initiated almost 75 percent of domestic mergers over a sample ten-year period.[29]

Defense technology and China's talent programs

"Talent" programs are an essential supplement to legal technology transfer and technology espionage, since these individuals can provide key pieces of context that are essential for understanding the intangible aspects of the acquired technology. Examples of individuals from U.S defense technology organizations receiving compensation from Chinese talent programs abound. An analysis of Thousand Talents award recipients from 2009–2015 reveals that four individuals from the Department of Defense were recruited, with one concurrently employed by the Defense Threat Reduction Agency, and three others formerly employed by the Air Force Academy, the Air Force Research Laboratory, and the Naval

Research Laboratory, respectively. The same data show more than 230 recruited scientists were affiliated with Department of Energy-sponsored national labs, many of which work on sensitive and classified DoD projects. These datapoints confirm the suspicion that the Chinese talent programs are not simply focused on cutting-edge civilian R&D, but can contribute to defense R&D as well.

Outsourcing defense R&D

Besides bringing talent to the mainland, China also uses contracts with foreign firms to outsource its defense R&D, especially in the aviation, satellite, and shipbuilding sectors.[30] For example, Shanghai and Chengxi Shipyard Co. (SSCS, 上海船厂船舶有限公司) in 2009 had foreign contracts worth roughly RMB 22 billion compared to RMB 5.1 billion in domestic contracts.[31] MCF often muddies the nature of these contract activities, as many of these large shipyard corporations (e.g., Guangzhou Shipyard International) construct civilian vessels next to People's Liberation Army Navy (PLAN) vessels, often using the same common advanced infrastructure like chemical baths and migrating advanced construction techniques like modular hull assembly.

Likewise, access to foreign technology through development contracts combined with increased domestic competition aided the rapid expansion of China's missile industry in the 2000s. In the early-2000s, China pushed its domestic missile manufacturers to compete in the global commercial aerospace markets as a means to increase competition and thereby domestic innovation. In 2004, Alcatel signed a contract with the China Satellite Communication Corporation (ChinaSat) to design and produce a direct broadcasting satellite, the ChinaSat 9.[32] ChinaSat was a subsidiary of China Aerospace Science and Technology Corporation (CASC), which competed in the global commercial space launch vehicle (SLV) market. As a RAND report observes:

> Although Chinese missiles were not originally developed with the space launch market in mind, technological advances to improve the SLVs have likely been incorporated into ballistic-missile design and production as well. All China's SLVs are based on its ballistic-missile designs. The Long March (*Chang Zheng* 长征) 1 (LM-1) launch vehicle, for example, is based on the DF-4 missile, and the LM-2C, LM-2D, LM-2E, LM-3, and LM-4 are all based on the DF-5.[33]

The C4ADS report also analyzed postings on China's national and provincial-level defense procurement websites (similar model to FedBizOps in the United States). Example postings include calls for "ship targeting technology based on deep-learning."[34] Based on trade and investment data for a sample set of companies, the report found that 58 percent of 65,727 shipments to China from 2014–2019 were shipped from just five countries—the United States was the most frequent origin country and US allies accounted for eight of the top ten origin countries spots.[35] Moreover, based on HS (Harmonized Commodity Description and Coding System) codes, "potentially dual-use shipments account for approximately 60 percent of total exports from the United States, Japan, Germany, and South Korea."[36] Notably, Japan has sent multiple shipments of radio navigational aids (HS 852691) to Jiangnan Shipyard Group, which happens to be building China's third aircraft carrier and other warships.[37]

Foreign sources of defense technology: outside China

China employs illicit and licit means of tech transfer. Illicit methods often involve human insiders or cyber hacks that steal or monitor data. Notable examples include APT1, linked to the PLA's Unit 61398.[38] The US Department of Justice (DOJ), military law enforcement agencies, and large tech companies are largely aware of nefarious licit activities but are often less equipped to respond since these activities don't amount to criminal offenses. It should be noted that the scope of Chinese tech transfer activities goes beyond the United States, despite being the main target.[39] Chapters 7 and 8 examine the situation in Europe, a highly innovative science and technology region where awareness of the range of transfer behaviors is significantly lower than in the US.

Defense technical information collection[40]

The China Defense Science and Technology Information Center (CDSTIC, 中国国防科技信息中心), which operated from 1959 to 2017, was a defense research institution that collected, processed, stored, and managed domestic and foreign defense-related science and technology information.[41] For decades, CDSTIC served several information resource support functions, including management of military networks, drafting of technical standards on data storage and technical reports, and reporting and tracking of military S&T topics. CDSTIC served as a resource for military S&T information by hosting connections to numerous foreign and domestic databases. CDSTIC published several books on military topics such as weapons, defense science and technology management, and military procurement, in addition to publishing military-focused monthly magazines *Conmilit* and *Defense Point*. Even though it was reorganized into the Academy of Military Sciences (AMS) in 2017, the resulting organization, the Military Science Information Research Center (MSIRC, 军事科学信息研究中心), carries on CDSTIC's information collection, storage, and dissemination work. Additionally, MSIRC integrates data mining, web scraping, hacking,[42] information analysis and intelligence research,[43] provides consultation and support to the CMC,[44] and leads technical construction and service for defense S&T information work.[45] A closer look at MSIRC activities may indicate Chinese military directions for the large-scale collection and management of science and technology information.

Knowledge transfer through study abroad

One of Beijing's primary methods of knowledge transfer is by sponsoring its military and defense–industrial scientists to study abroad. While military personnel studying abroad as part of exchange programs are not inherently problematic, an ASPI report found that of the more than 2,500 Chinese military and defense–industrial scientists and engineers who have gone abroad since 2007, at least dozens used false credentials to work in sensitive defense-related technology areas.[46]

In response, some democratic countries have subjected Chinese visiting academics to greater scrutiny, particularly those from "defense–industrial universities" directly subordinate to Science, Technology and Industry for National Defense (SASTIND such as the "Seven Sons of National Defense" (国防七子): Beijing Institute of Technology, Beijing University of Astronautics and Aeronautics, Harbin Engineering University, Harbin Institute of Technology, Nanjing University of Astronautics and Aeronautics, Nanjing University of Science and Technology, Northwest Polytechnical University; and the "Seven Sons of the Armament Industry" (兵工七子): Beijing Institute of Technology, Changchun University of Science and Technology, Chongqing University of Technology, Nanjing University of Science and Technology, North University of China, Shenyang Ligong University, Xi'an Technological University; and more than 160 other defense-related research organizations such as national defense S&T key laboratories (国防科技重点实验室), national defense key discipline laboratories (国防重点学科实验室), and Ministry of Education national defense key laboratories (教育部国防重点实验室).[47]

Moreover, public websites like the Australian Strategic Policy Insitute's (ASPI) China Defense Universities Tracker seek to provide Western universities and governments with public, unclassified information about the military and defense–industrial affiliations of specific universities or institutes in China, permitting potential hosts to conduct their own detailed risk assessments.[48]

Defense-related investment and acquisition activities

In 2018, the Office of the US Trade Representative (USTR) released findings of its investigation into China's tech transfer related acts, policies, and practices. The USTR found these activities "unreasonable because they are directed and supported by the government, and unfairly target critical US technology with the goal of achieving dominance in strategic sectors," including directing Chinese outbound investment to acquire and transfer critical technologies. Moreover, much of Chinese outbound investment and acquisition decisions are not market driven, instead, serve the state's strategic objectives.[49] Often, Chinese firms making overseas acquisitions offset their lack of firm-specific ownership advantages (e.g., management skills or brand) with access to the Chinese market and substantial government financial or political backing.[50] In fact, Chinese overseas investment activity has been dominated by companies within the corporate networks of Chinese state-owned defense contractors.[51]

On one hand, it would be foolish for US companies to avoid international partnerships, given the globalized nature of today's markets. On the other hand, companies have an increased responsibility to assess the risk profile of each collaborative relationship, especially in a system where commercial and defense industries are intentionally blended. The US government alone is not resourced enough to effectively monitor and track all such activity, even with the introduction of the Foreign Investment Risk Review Modernization Act (FIRRMA). Nor are foreign companies resourced or staffed with the necessary language and regional expertise to navigate the MCF-enhanced Chinese market and its complex political economy. There is certainly a gap for federal agencies to support private companies in conducting enhanced due diligence.

Looking ahead

China's tech transfer system has successfully brought value to the country's overall economic growth in general and its military modernization effort in particular. Its new model of "cooperate, learn, master, and re-innovate" is far more self-sustaining and enabling for indigenous innovation than its traditional model of "steal, reverse engineer, and reproduce."[52] China may even find it impossible to reverse this behavior given the decades of MCF enculturation in its commercial and defense industries. Looking ahead, there are several trends worth considering. First, while China has invested substantially in its military modernization efforts, its capabilities are not driven by indigenous innovation.[53] As one China analyst puts it, Chinese shipbuilders are "technologically bound by the willingness of international firms to collaborate with China ... [and their capabilities] have always been a function of the international partnerships they maintained."[54] Second, commercial technology firms outside of traditional defense contractors will be increasingly pulled into national security policy. As defense systems increasingly rely on commercial off-the-shelf (COTS), (or as COTS become more dual-use) ties between commercial industry and government agencies will necessarily become tighter. Both of these factors will drive Chinese entities to continue to pursue both legal and illegal avenues to acquire foreign defense technology.

Notes

1 In the "oldies but goodies" bin, you will find: Joseph P. Gallagher, "China's Military Industrial Complex," *Asian Survey* XXVII, no. 9, September 1987; Barry Naughton, "The Third Front: Defense Industrialization in the Chinese Interior," *China Quarterly* no. 115, September 1988; Wendy Frieman, "China's Military R&D System: Reform and Reorientation," in Denis Fred Simon and Merle Goldman, eds., *Science and Technology in Post-Mao China*, Cambridge, MA: Harvard University Press, 1989; Benjam in A. Ostrov,

Conquering Resources:The Growth and Decline of the PLA's Science and Technology Commission for National Defense, Armonk, NY: M. E. Sharpe, 1991; John Frankenstein, "The People's Republic of China: Arms Production, Industrial Strategy and Problems of History," in Herbert Wulf, ed., *Arms Industry Limited,* New York: Oxford University Press for SIPRI, 1993; Wendy Frieman, "China's Defence Industries," *Pacific Review* 6, no. 1, 1993, p. 54; John Frankenstein and Bates Gill, "Current and Future Challenges Facing Chinese Defense Industries," *China Quarterly* June 1996, pp. 394–427; Bates Gill, "The Impact of Economic Reform on Chinese Defense Production," in C. Dennison Lane, ed., *Chinese Military Modernization,* London: Paul Kegan International, 1996, pp. 144–167; Arthur S. Ding, "Economic Reform and Defence Industries in China," in Gerald Segal and Richard S. Yang, eds., *Chinese Economic Reform,* New York: Routledge, 1996; Erik Baark, "Military Technology and Absorptive Capacity in China and India: Implications for Modernization," in Eric Arnett, ed., *Military Capacity and the Risk of War: China, India, Pakistan and Iran,* Oxford: Oxford University Press, 1997; Jorn Brömmelhörster and John Frankenstein, eds., *Mixed Motives, Uncertain Outcomes: Defense Conversion in China,* Boulder, CO: Lynne Rienner Publishers, 1997; Evan S. Medeiros, "Revisiting Chinese Defense Conversion: Some Evidence from China's Shipbuilding Industry," *Issues and Studies,* May 1998.

2 John Wilson Lewis and Xue Litai, *China Builds the Bomb,* Stanford, CA: Stanford University Press, 1988; John Wilson Lewis and Xue Litai, *China's Strategic Seapower:The Politics of Force Modernization in the NuclearAge,* Stanford, CA: Stanford University Press, 1995; John Wilson Lewis and Xue Litai, *Imagined Enemies: China Prepares for Uncertain War,* Stanford, CA: Stanford University Press, 2006; Evan Feigenbaum, *China's Techno-Warriors: National Security and Strategic Competition from the Nuclear to the Information Age,* Stanford, CA: Stanford University Press, 2003.

3 John Frankenstein, "China's Defense Industries:A New Course?" in James C. Mulvenon and Richard H. Yang, eds., *The People's Liberation Army in the Information Age,* Santa Monica, CA: RAND, CF-145-CAPP/AF, 1999; David Shambaugh, "Defense Industries and Procurement," in David Shambaugh, *Modernizing China's Military: Progress, Problems, and Prospects,* Berkeley, CA: University of California Press, 2003; Bates Gill, "Chinese Military–Technical Development:The Record for Western Assessments, 1979–1999," in James C. Mulvenon and Andrew N. D. Yang, eds., *Seeking Truth from Facts:A Retrospective on Chinese Military Studies in the Post-Mao Era,* Santa Monica, CA: RAND, CF-160-CAPP, 2001; Roger Cliff, *The Military Potential of China's Commercial Technology,* Santa Monica, CA: RAND, 2001; Harlan Jencks, "The General Armaments Department," in James C. Mulvenon and Andrew N.D. Yang, eds., *The People's Liberation Army as Organization: Reference Volume v1.0,* Santa Monica, CA: RAND, 2002; Evan Medeiros, Roger Cliff, Keith Crane, and James Mulvenon, *A New Direction for China's Defense Industry,* Santa Monica, CA: RAND, 2005.

4 Tai Ming Cheung, *Fortifying China: The Struggle to Build a Modern Defense* Economy, Ithaca, NY: Cornell University Press, 2009; Tai Ming Cheung, "The Chinese Defense Economy's Long March from Imitation to Innovation," *Journal of Strategic Studies* 34, no. 3, June 2011, pp. 325–354; Tai Ming Cheung, ed., *Forging China's Military Might:A New Framework for Assessing Innovation,* Baltimore, MD: Johns Hopkins Press, 2014.

5 COSTIND refers to the former Commission on Science, Technology, and Industry for National Defense, which Feigenbaum describes as "single, unified military industry headquarters for both defense R&D and industry." Feigenbaum, p. 108. The Lewis, Xue, and Feigenbaum works do emphasize the critical role of foreign technology and technical information in the development of China's strategic weapons systems, but only provide the most general data about how the technology and information was acquired. It is highly unlikely that the official COSTIND materials used as the primary sources for the books would mention classified topics like technology espionage.

6 Eric Hagt, "The General Armament Department's Science and Technology Committee: PLA-Industry Relations and Implications for Defense Innovation," in Cheung, *Forging China's Military Might*, p. 75.

7 Tai Ming Cheung, "Conclusion," in Cheung, *Forging China's Military Might*, p. 278.

8 Kevin Pollpeter, "Organization as Innovation: Instilling a Quality Management System in China's Human Spaceflight Program," in Tai Ming Cheung, ed., *Forging China's Military Might: A New Framework for Assessing Innovation*, Baltimore, MD: Johns Hopkins Press, 2014, pp. 213–240.

9 Richard Bitzinger, Michael Raska, Collin Koh Swee Lean, and K. Weng, "Locating China's Place in the Global Defense Economy," in Tai Ming Cheung, ed., *Forging China's Military Might: A New Framework for Assessing Innovation*, Baltimore, MD: Johns Hopkins Press, 2014, p. 182.

10 Ibid, pp. 182–183.

11 Tai Ming Cheung, ed., *Forging China's Military Might: A New Framework for Assessing Innovation*, Baltimore, MD: Johns Hopkins Press, 2014, p. 33.

12 Katherine Walsh, "China's Emerging Defense Innovation System: Making the Wheels Turn," in Cheung, ed., *Forging China's Military Might*, pp. 136–168. There were at least two major breaches involving the F-35. For information about the 2009 breach of Lockheed-Martin's network, see: www.reuters.com/article/2013/06/19/usa-fighter-hacking-idUSL2N0EV0T320130619. Information about the 2016 hack of F-35 information in Australia in November 2016 can be found here: https://arstechnica.com/information-technology/2017/10/australian-defense-firm-was-hacked-and-f-35-data-stolen-dod-confirms/. For speculation about the design origins of the J-31, see www.defenseone.com/threats/2015/09/more-questions-f-35-after-new-specs-chinas-copycat/121859/.

13 国家中长期科学和技术发展规划纲要 (2006–2020). For a translation of the MLP text, see www.itu.int/en/ITU-D/Cybersecurity/Documents/National_Strategies_Repository/China_2006.pdf.

14 State Council, 国务院关于印发《中国制造2025》的通知 (State Council Directive "China Manufacturing 2025"), No. 28, 2015.

15 Department of Defense, *Annual Report to Congress: Military Power of the People's Republic of China*, 2009, 39; Department of Defense, *Annual Report to Congress: Military and Security Developments Involving the People's Republic of China*, 2019.

16 US Chamber of Commerce, *Made in China 2025: Global Ambitions Built on Local Protections*, 2017. For additional analyses of MIC2025 and its implications, see European Union Chamber of Commerce in China, *China Manufacturing 2025: Putting Industrial Policy Ahead of Market Forces*, 2017; and Jost Wübbeke, Mirjam Meissner, Max J. Zenglein Jaqueline Ives, and Björn Conrad, *Made in China 2025: The Making of a High-Tech Superpower and Consequences for Industrial Countries*, MERICS: Mercator Institute for China Studies, December 2016.

17 National Advisory Committee on Building a Manufacturing Power Strategy, "Made in China 2025 Major Technical Roadmap," October 2015. www.cae.cn/cae/html/files/2015-10/29/20151029105822561730637.pdf.

18 National People's Congress, 国民经济和社会发展第十个五年计划纲要 (China's 10th Five-Year Plan), March 15, 2001.

19 Daniel Alderman, Lisa Crawford, Brian Lafferty, and Aaron Shraberg, "The Rise of Chinese Civil–Military Integration," in Tai Ming Cheung, ed., *Forging China's Military Might: A New Framework for Assessing Innovation*, Baltimore, MD: Johns Hopkins Press, 2014, pp. 109–135.

20 Hu Jintao, "Hold High the Great Banner of Socialism with Chinese Characteristics and Strive for New Victories in Building a Moderately Prosperous Society in All Aspects." www.zzzxy.gov.cn/ar/2345.htm.

21 Daniel Alderman, Lisa Crawford, Brian Lafferty, and Aaron Shraberg, "The Rise of Chinese Civil–Military Integration," in Tai Ming Cheung, ed., *Forging China's Military*

Might: A New Framework for Assessing Innovation, Baltimore, MD: Johns Hopkins Press, 2014, p. 109.

22 James Mulvenon and Rebecca Samm Tyroler-Cooper, "China's Defense Industry on the Path of Reform," *Center for Intelligence Research and Analysis*, October 1, 2009, p. 39.

23 Daniel Alderman, "An Introduction to China's Strategic Military–Civilian Fusion," in *China's Evolving Military Strategy*, ed. Joe McReynolds, Washington, DC: Brookings Institution Press, 2016, 334–348; Yu Chuanxin, ed., *Military–Civilian Fusion in Actual Combat* (实战化的军民融合), PLA Press, 2015, 1–3.

24 The MIIT (known at the time as the Commission for Science, Technology and Industry for National Defense) gave guidance on a stipulation in the 2007 Science and Industry Law (科工法), stressing the importance of commercial participation in China's defense sector. Guidance included "encourage and guide private companies and capital to participate in competition and in cooperative projects involving military production and R&D." (www.most.gov.cn/ztzl/gjzctx/ptzctcxt/200802/t20080222_59248.htm).

25 Office of the US Trade Representative, "Findings of the Investigation into China's Acts, Policies, and Practices Related to Technology Transfer, Intellectual Property, and Innovation under Section 301 of the Trade Act of 1974," March 22, 2018, 147–148.

26 Ibid.

27 Evan Medeiros, Roger Cliff, Keith Crane, and James Mulvenon. *A New Direction for China's Defense Industry*, Santa Monica, CA: RAND, 2005, 241–242.

28 Ibid.

29 Marcel Angliviel de la Beaumelle, Benjamin Spevack, and Devin Thorne, "Open Arms: Evaluating the Global Exposure to China's Defense Industrial Base," *C4ADS*, 2019, 42.

30 For more examples in the aviation and satellite sectors see Mulvenon and Tyroler-Cooper, "China's Defense Industry," *Center for Intelligence Research and Analysis*, 43–45.

31 Mulvenon and Tyroler-Cooper, "China's Defense Industry," *Center for Intelligence Research and Analysis*, 46.

32 "Alcatel Reinforces Cooperation with China by Providing the ChinaSat 9 Satellite," *Alcatel Space*, June 11, 2004.

33 Medeiros et al., *A New Direction*, RAND Corporation, p. 71. For more cases of foreign commercial contracts that have aided Chinese defense industries in space (e.g., China Aerospace Science and Technology Corporation), nuclear (e.g., China National Nuclear Corporation), and telecommunications (e.g., Huawei, ZTE, Datang) sectors, see the 2019 US–China Economic and Security Review Commission report.

34 Beaumelle, et al., "Open Arms," *C4ADS*, p. 38.

35 Ibid., p. 41.

36 Ibid., pp. 38–42.

37 Ibid., p. 41; 新浪军事 (Sina Military News), "江南造船厂产能有多强: 10多艘神盾舰与航母同时开工 (How Strong is Jiangnan Shipyard's Production Capacity: More than 10 Aegis Ships and Aircraft Carriers Start Construction at the Same Time)," 新浪军事 (Sina Military News), March 14, 2019.

38 Mandiant, *APT1: Exposing One of China's Cyber Espionage Units*, Mandiant, February 18, 2013.

39 Elsa Kania, "Written Testimony for the US–China Economic and Security Review Commission Hearing on Technology, Trade, and Military–Civil Fusion," June 7, 2019.

40 This section on DTIC is taken with permission from the excellent work of Katherine Atha, Johanna Cox, Debra Geary, and Brian Lafferty.

41 Information accessed at http://web.archive.org/web/20160401023129/www.cdstic.cn/cdstic-zyjsfw.html on December 18, 2019.

42 Information accessed at www.cnki.com.cn/Article/CJFDTOTAL-QBLL201002029.htm accessed on December 7, 2019.

43 Information accessed at http://211.103.242.144:1010/zxdt/tzgg/index_138.html on November 21, 2019.

44 Information accessed at http://he.huatu.com/2019/1112/896478.html on November 18, 2019.
45 Information accessed at http://webcache.googleusercontent.com/search?q=cache: xu5JVr5OQfwJ:www.sxgkw.net/2019/1112/38834.html on December 18, 2019.
46 Alex Joske, *Picking Flowers, Making Honey*, Australian Strategic Policy Institute, October 30, 2018; Kania, "Written Testimony for the US–China Economic and Security Review Commission Hearing on Technology, Trade, and Military–Civil Fusion."
47 www.aspi.org.au/report/china-defence-universities-tracker.
48 Ibid.
49 Office of the US Trade Representative, "Findings of the Investigation into China's Acts, Policies, and Practices Related to Technology Transfer, Intellectual Property, and Innovation under Section 301 of the Trade Act of 1974," March 22, 2018, 147–148.
50 Bijiun Wang and Huiyao Wang, "Chinese Manufacturing Firms' Overseas Direct Investment (ODI): Patterns, Motivations and Challenges," in *Rising China: Global Challenges and Opportunities*, ed. Jane Golley and Ligang Song, Australian National University, 2011, pp. 105, 107; Jan Bogaert, "China Newsletter: Challenges to Chinese Outbound M&A in the Year of the Rooster," *Lexology*, 2017; David Rothnie, "China Re-Defines the M&A Landscape," *International Financing Review*, 2016; Fang Xue, Yuefan Wang, and Qi Yue, "Recent Trends and Issues in Outbound Acquisitions by Chinese Companies," *The M&A Lawyer* 10, no. 10, 2016.
51 Beaumelle et al., "Open Arms," *C4ADS*, 42.
52 Medeiros et al., "A New Direction," *RAND Corporation*, 245; A combination of concepts in Medeiros, et al., "A New Direction," *RAND Corporation*, 245 and C4ADS's IDAR concept.
53 David M. Finkelstein, "Breaking the Paradigm: Drivers Behind the PLA's Current Period of Reform," in Saunders et al., *Xi Remakes the PLA*, Washington, DC: National Defense University Press, 2019, pp. 56–58.
54 Alex Osborn, "Shipbuilding Part 2: Can Tech Transfer Get China to the Cutting Edge?" ChinaEconTalk, December 19, 2019. https://chinaecontalk.substack.com/p/shipbuilding-part-2-can-tech-transfer?

Bibliography

Daniel Alderman, Lisa Crawford, Brian Lafferty, and Aaron Shraberg. "An Introduction to China's Strategic Military–Civilian Fusion," in Joe McReynolds, ed., *China's Evolving Military Strategy*, Washington, DC: Brookings Institution Press, 2016.

Alderman, Daniel, et al. "The Rise of Chinese Civil–Military Integration," in Tai Ming Cheung, ed., *Forging China's Military Might: A New Framework for Assessing Innovation*, Baltimore, MD: Johns Hopkins Press, 2014.

Angliviel de la Beaumelle, Marcel, Benjamin Spevack, and Devin Thorne. "Open Arms: Evaluating the Global Exposure to China's Defense Industrial Base," *C4ADS*, 2019.

Baark, Erik. "Military Technology and Absorptive Capacity in China and India: Implications for Modernization," in Eric Arnett, ed., *Military Capacity and the Risk of War: China, India, Pakistan and Iran*, Oxford: Oxford University Press, 1997.

Bitzinger, Richard, et al. "Locating China's Place in the Global Defense Economy," in Tai Ming Cheung, ed., *Forging China's Military Might: A New Framework for Assessing Innovation*, Batimore, MD: Johns Hopkins Press, 2014.

Brömmelhörster, Jorn and John Frankenstein, eds., *Mixed Motives, Uncertain Outcomes: Defense Conversion in China*, Boulder, CO: Lynne Rienner Publishers, 1997.

Cheung, Tai Ming. *Fortifying China: The Struggle to Build a Modern Defense Economy*, Ithaca, NY: Cornell University Press, 2009.

Cheung, Tai Ming. "The Chinese Defense Economy's Long March from Imitation to Innovation," *Journal of Strategic Studies* 34, no. 3, June 2011.

Cheung, Tai Ming. ed., *Forging China's Military Might: A New Framework for Assessing Innovation*, Baltimore, MD: Johns Hopkins Press, 2014.

China's State Council Information Office. *China's National Defense in the New Era*, July 2019.

Cliff, Roger. *The Military Potential of China's Commercial Technology*, Santa Monica, CA: RAND, 2001.

Department of Defense, *Annual Report to Congress: Military and Security Developments Involving the People's Republic of China 2019*, Washington, DC: GPO, 2019.

Department of Defense. *Annual Report to Congress: Military Power of the People's Republic of China*, 2009.

Department of Defense Inspector General. "Audit of the DoD's Management of the Cybersecurity Risks for Government Purchase Card Purchases of Commercial Off-the-Shelf Items," July 26, 2019. www.oversight.gov/sites/default/files/oig-reports/DODIG-2019-106.pdf.

Department of Justice. "Former U.S. Navy Contractor and its President Sentenced for Scheme Related to Transfer of U.S. Navy Submarine Rescue Technology," December 4, 2019. www.justice.gov/usao-dc/pr/former-us-navy-contractor-and-its-president-sentenced-scheme-related-transfer-us-navy.

Ding, Arthur S. "Economic Reform and Defence Industries in China," in Gerald Segal and Richard S. Yang, eds., *Chinese Economic Reform*, New York: Routledge, 1996.

Erickson, Andrew S. and Ian Burns McCaslin. "The Impact of Xi-Era Reforms on the Chinese Navy," in Phillip C. Saunders, Arthur S. Ding, Andrew Scobell, Andrew N.D. Yang, and Joel Wuthnow, eds., *Xi Remakes the PLA*, Washington, DC: National Defense University Press, 2019.

European Union Chamber of Commerce in China. *China Manufacturing 2025: Putting Industrial Policy Ahead of Market Forces*, 2017.

Fang, Xue, Yuefan Wang, and Qi Yue, "Recent Trends and Issues in Outbound Acquisitions by Chinese Companies," *The M&A Lawyer* 10, no. 10, 2016.

Feigenbaum, Evan. *China's Techno-Warriors: National Security and Strategic Competition from the Nuclear to the Information Age*, Stanford, CA: Stanford University Press, 2003.

Finkelstein, David M. "Breaking the Paradigm: Drivers Behind the PLA's Current Period of Reform," in Saunders, et al., eds., *Xi Remakes the PLA*, Washington, DC: National Defense University Press, 2019.

Frankenstein, John. "The People's Republic of China: Arms Production, Industrial Strategy and Problems of History," in Herbert Wulf, ed., *Arms Industry Limited*, New York: Oxford University Press for SIPRI, 1993.

Frankenstein, John. "China's Defense Industries: A New Course?" in James C. Mulvenon and Richard H. Yang, eds., *The People's Liberation Army in the Information Age*, Santa Monica, CA: RAND, CF-145-CAPP/AF, 1999.

Frankenstein, John and Bates Gill. "Current and Future Challenges Facing Chinese Defense Industries," *China Quarterly*, 146, June 1996.

Frieman, Wendy. "China's Military R&D System: Reform and Reorientation," in Denis Fred Simon and Merle Goldman, eds., *Science and Technology in Post-Mao China*, Cambridge, MA: Harvard University Press, 1989.

Frieman, Wendy. "China's Defence Industries," *Pacific Review* 6, no. 1, 1993.

Gallagher, Joseph P. "China's Military Industrial Complex," *Asian Survey*, XXVII, no. 9, September 1987.

Gallagher, Sean. "Australian Defense Firm Was Hacked and F-35 Data Stolen, DOD Confirms," *Ars Technica*, October 13, 2017.

Gill, Bates. "The Impact of Economic Reform on Chinese Defense Production," in C. Dennison Lane, ed., *Chinese Military Modernization*, London: Paul Kegan International, 1996.

Gill, Bates. "Chinese Military–Technical Development: The Record for Western Assessments, 1979–1999," in James C. Mulvenon and Andrew N. D. Yang, eds., *Seeking Truth from Facts: A Retrospective on Chinese Military Studies in the Post-Mao Era*, Santa Monica, CA: RAND, CF-160-CAPP, 2001.

Hagt, Eric. "The General Armament Department's Science and Technology Committee: PLA-Industry Relations and Implications for Defense Innovation," in Tai Ming Cheung ed., *Forging China's Military Might*, Baltimore, MD: Johns Hopkins Press, 2014.

Hebei Public Institution. "2019中国人民解放军军事科学院军事科学信息研究中心招聘6人公告" ("2019 People's Liberation Army Academy of Military Sciences Military Science Information Research Center Recruitment Posting for 6 Positions"), November 12, 2019. http://he.huatu.com/2019/1112/896478.html.

Highlander (海兰信). "海兰信与上海船舶研究设计院签署战略合作协议" ("Highlander and Shanghai Merchant Ship Design and Research Institute Sign Strategic Cooperation Agreement"), Highlander.com, January 21, 2019. www.highlander.com.cn/newsmes. html?id=1472.

Hu, Jintao. "Hold High the Great Banner of Socialism with Chinese Characteristics and Strive for New Victories in Building a Moderately Prosperous Society in All Aspects," *Xinhua*, October 10, 2011.

Jencks, Harlan. "The General Armaments Department," in James C. Mulvenon and Andrew N. D. Yang, eds., *The People's Liberation Army as Organization*: Reference Volume v1.0, Santa Monica, CA: RAND, 2002.

Joske, Alex. *Picking Flowers, Making Honey*, Australian Strategic Policy Institute, October 30, 2018.

Kania, Elsa. "Written Testimony for the U.S.–China Economic and Security Review Commission Hearing on Technology, Trade, and Military–Civil Fusion," June 7, 2019.

Lewis, John Wilson and Xue Litai, *China Builds the Bomb*, Stanford, CA: Stanford University Press, 1988.

Lewis, John Wilson and Xue Litai. *China's Strategic Seapower: The Politics of Force Modernization in the Nuclear Age*, Stanford, CA: Stanford University Press, 1995.

Lewis, John Wilson and Xue Litai. *Imagined Enemies: China Prepares for Uncertain War*, Stanford, CA: Stanford University Press, 2006.

Li, Qingshan. 新军事革命与高技术战争 *(The New Military Revolution and High Tech Warfare)*, Beijing, China: 军事科学出版社 (Military Science Press), 1995.

Mandiant. "APT1: Exposing One of China's Cyber Espionage Units," February 18, 2013.

Medeiros, Evan S. "Revisiting Chinese Defense Conversion: Some Evidence from China's Shipbuilding Industry," *Issues and Studies*, May 1998.

Medeiros, Evan, Roger Cliff, Keith Crane, and James Mulvenon. *A New Direction for China's Defense Industry*, Santa Monica, CA: RAND, 2005.

Mulvenon, James and Rebecca Samm Tyroler-Cooper, "China's Defense Industry on the Path of Reform," Center for Intelligence Research and Analysis, October 1, 2009.

National Advisory Committee on Building a Manufacturing Power Strategy. "Made in China 2025 Major Technical Roadmap," October 2015. www.cae.cn/cae/html/files/2015-10/29/20151029105822561730637.pdf.

National People's Congress. "China's 10th Five-Year Plan," March 15, 2001. www.people. com.cn/GB/shizheng/16/20010318/419582.html.

Naughton, Barry. "The Third Front: Defense Industrialization in the Chinese Interior," *China Quarterly*, No. 115, September 1988.

Office of the US Trade Representative. "Findings of the Investigation into China's Acts, Policies, and Practices Related to Technology Transfer, Intellectual Property, and Innovation under Section 301 of the Trade Act of 1974," March 22, 2018.

Ostrov, Benjamin A. *Conquering Resources: The Growth and Decline of the PLA's Science and Technology Commission for National Defense*, Armonk, NY: M. E. Sharpe, 1991.

Pollpeter, Kevin. "Organization as Innovation: Instilling a Quality Management System in China's Human Spaceflight Program," in Tai Ming Cheung, ed., *Forging China's Military Might: A New Framework for Assessing Innovation*, Baltimore, MD: Johns Hopkins Press, 2014.

PRC Ministry of Industry and Information Technology. "关于非公有制经济参与国防科技工业建设的指导意见." https://baike.baidu.com/item/关于非公有制经济参与国防科技工业建设的指导意见/2387392?fr=aladdin.

Shaanxi Civil Servants Examination Website. "2020 中国人民解放军军事科学院军事科学信息研究中心招聘工程师公告(6名)" ("2020 Announcement of Recruiting Engineers for the Military Science Information Research Center of the PLA Academy of Military Sciences (6 positions"), Shaanxi Civil Servants Examination Website, November 12, 2019.

Shambaugh, David. "Defense Industries and Procurement," in David Shambaugh, ed., *Modernizing China's Military: Progress, Problems, and Prospects*, Berkeley, CA: University of California Press, 2003.

Shou, Xiaosong. *The Science of Military Strategy* (战略学), Military Science Press, 2013.

"江南造船厂产能有多强: 10多艘神盾舰与航母同时开工" ("How Strong is Jiangnan Shipyard's Production Capacity: More than 10 Aegis Ships and Aircraft Carriers Start Construction at the Same Time"), 新浪军事 *(Sina Military News)*, March 14, 2019.

State Council. "The National Medium- and Long-Term Program for Science and Technology Development (2006–2020)," PRC State Council, 2006.

State Council. "国务院关于印发《中国制造2025》的通知" ("State Council Directive China Manufacturing 2025"), No. 28, 2015.

US Chamber of Commerce. *Made in China 2025: Global Ambitions Built on Local Protections*, 2017.

Walsh, Katherine. "China's Emerging Defense Innovation System: Making the Wheels Turn," in Tai Ming Cheung, ed., *Forging China's Military Might*, Johns Hopkins Press, 2014.

Wang, Bijiun and Huiyao Wang. "Chinese Manufacturing Firms' Overseas Direct Investment (ODI): Patterns, Motivations and Challenges," in Jane Golley and Ligang Song, eds., *Rising China: Global Challenges and Opportunities*, Canberra, Australia: Australian National University, 2011.

White House. "President Donald J. Trump is Signing a Landmark Phase One Trade Agreement with China," The White House, January 15, 2020.

Wübbeke, Jost, Mirjam Meissner, Max J. Zenglein Jaqueline Ives, and Björn Conrad. *Made in China 2025: The Making of a High-Tech Superpower and Consequences for Industrial Countries*, MERICS: Mercator Institute for China Studies, December 2016.

Yu, Chuanxin. *Military–Civilian Fusion in Actual Combat* (实战化的军民融合), Beijing: PLA Press, 2015.

Zhao, Ruitao, Sun Yujun, and Zhao Boqiao. "构建新时期科技情报工作的科学技术体系" ("Constructing an S&T System for Technological Intelligence Work in the New Era"), China National Defense Science and Technology Information Center, February, 2010.

Zhongguancun Yunti Technology Innovation Alliance (中关村京企云梯科技创新联盟). "北京海兰信数据科技股份有限公司" ("Beijing Highlander Technology Stock Corporation Co., Ltd." Zhongguancun Yunti Technology Innovation Alliance. https://perma.cc/2P3U-MGF7.

PART III

China's worldwide transfer networks

7

EUROPE

A technology transfer mosaic

*Didi Kirsten Tatlow, Hinnerk Feldwisch-Drentrup
and Ryan Fedasiuk*

Technology transfer from Europe to China is an understudied field, as are the intricate CPC structures and wide political influencing that enable it.[1] Chinese diplomats in Europe, and officials in China including those belonging to the United Front and "friendship associations,"[2] actively guide networks of overseas Chinese students, researchers, and professionals, and connect to European institutions and officials from Ireland to Czech Republic, Norway to Greece. The aim: remind overseas Chinese to "repay the motherland" (回报祖国 or 报效祖国)[3] by sending back technology, human talent, and skills, and shape the broader socio-political environment in Europe to make that possible. This raises important questions of political values and strategic intent for European governments, challenging simple notions of "win–win" techno-globalism.

The European Union is one of the most innovative regions of the world, with about two million R&D researchers (one-third more than a decade ago), and 750,000 science and technology Ph.D. students.[4] Some major technologies have been vigorously copied in China in a process of "introduction, digestion, absorption, re-invention" (引进消化吸收再创新).[5] This has enabled the Chinese government and state-owned companies to build about two-thirds of the world's high-speed railway network and sell "intelligent" security systems which have national security implications, globally.[6]

Historically, interest in European science was sparked in part by sophisticated and gorgeously embellished mechanical clocks brought by Jesuit missionaries to the Qing court; fascination fought with rejection until the Communist revolution of 1949 when contacts largely broke off.[7] Yet Eastern European countries continued to send technicians and engineers to China for over a decade after 1949, building electrical engineering factories and power plants until the Sino-Soviet split of 1960 forced them too to withdraw.[8] Diplomatic relations between the European Union and China were established in 1975, broadly re-starting the flow of ideas and technology.

There is scant awareness in European governments and society of these transfer and political processes. Economic and industrial espionage from China (the "sharp" end of the phenomenon) is rarely prosecuted.[9] One study estimated economic losses of 60 billion euros and hundreds of thousands of jobs in the European Union (EU) in 2018 due to cybertheft by various actors, noting, "the time lag between intrusion and detection in Europe is three times longer than in the rest of the world: 469 days against an average of 146."[10] As the United States grows wary of collaboration with China, one study shows more Chinese researchers are coming to Europe.[11]

A talent pipeline

Europe-wide networks of Chinese Student and Scholar Associations (CSSAs, 中国学生学者联合会 or 中国学生学者联谊会) gather up students starting at the undergraduate level. There are between 80 and 88 in Germany,[12] 96 in the United Kingdom,[13] about 50 in France[14] and 38 in Italy,[15] according to reports by the groups, Chinese embassies, and consulates. For some members, CSSAs are mostly about making friends and practical advice, and not all students join. Yet their function in the eyes of the CPC is clear: diplomats offer students a low-key yet assiduous mix of pastoral and political attention, including but not limited to staffing suggestions, "guidance" on study and travel, organizing social events such as picnics to welcome visiting Chinese leaders, modest financial support for parties. At annual Chinese New Year galas or end-of-year meetings at Chinese missions, diplomats exhort students to "repay the motherland."[16] Students are required to register with local embassies in Europe on arrival and deregister on departure, to receive a certificate proving the authenticity of their degree for future employers, and other benefits.[17] In practice, not all do.[18]

Professional associations

Many students return to China, but for those who stay in Europe, a network of at least 95 Chinese professional associations, or guilds, gathers up scientists with family roots in China.[19] United Front, science and education, and local government officials connect broadly to these structures and attend events. At least 47 guilds state on their websites they are involved in transferring technology.[20] The authors estimate at least 25,500 people are involved.[21] Like the CSSAs, the guilds offer practical and community support, as well as opportunities to share research and skills with Chinese institutions.

We examined three key networks: the Federation of Chinese Professional Associations in Europe (FCPAE, 全欧华人专业协会联合会),[22] the Overseas Chinese Science and Technology Organization Federation (OCSTOF, 海外华人科技组织联合会),[23] and China's "Haizhi Plan," (海智计划), which aims "to mobilize the participation of national societies and local science and technology associations to build a platform for overseas talents."[24] Some identifying language, with numbers:

- Thirty-eight associations representing approximately 20,050 experts facilitate "technology transfer" (技术转让), "technology exchange" (技术交流), "knowledge transfer" (知识传输), or other kinds of industrial "exchange and cooperation" (交流与合作) with China.
- Twenty-six associations representing approximately 17,000 experts "return" (返回中国) foreign-born, ethnically Chinese "Overseas Chinese" (华侨) people, to found businesses or work at Chinese research universities.
- Eleven associations representing approximately 3,370 experts contribute to Chinese state-run talent spotting plans, such as the "Hundred Talents Plan" (百人计划) or "Chunhui Cup" (春晖杯).[25]

Three examples of individual associations, drawn from scores, include: The China–Sweden Life Science Association (中瑞生命科学协会), 200 members. They partner with the Chinese firm BGI Genomics and have been contacted under China's Haizhi Plan.[26] Set up in 2010 with the support of the Chinese Embassy in Sweden: "Our members have also shown great interest in returning to China for cooperation and development opportunities. Some members have returned to China to start their own businesses or take the lead in national scientific research."[27]

The French–Chinese Association of Science and Technology (全法中国科技工作者协会). With more than 300 members it claims to have "returned" foreign-born Chinese scientists to the Western provinces of China, and sent delegations to participate in the Chunhui Cup, a major talent-spotting competition discussed below.[28]

The China–Switzerland International Technology Transfer Center (CSITTC, 中瑞技术转移中心).[29] CSITTC's website outlines a 14-step process for transferring a technology project including intellectual property certification and technology market prospects.[30] It aims "to promote the docking of high-tech companies in science and technology parks between China and Switzerland, promote technology transfer and innovation cooperation between the two countries, and explore new models of China–Switzerland technology cooperation." It focuses on acquiring technologies related to precision manufacturing, clocks, food, printing and dyeing, and biotechnology.

Seven chapters of the Western Returned Scholars Association (WRSA, 欧美同学会), part of the CPC's United Front and focusing on knowledge and technology transfer, also operate in 21 European countries (for more on the WRSA see Chapter 15).

Talent plans

A chief purpose of the CSSAs and the professional guilds (above) is to connect members to China's many "talent plans" by urging them to register for talent-spotting competitions. According to a 2020 US district court indictment, these are "various diverse plans designed by the Chinese government to attract, recruit, and cultivate high-level scientific talent in furtherance of China's scientific development, economic prosperity, and national security."[31]

Some of the largest include:

The "Haizhi Plan."[32] Instituted in China in 2004 by the China Association for Science and Technology, CAST (中国科学技术协会) and 35 overseas science and technology groups,[33] "the Haizhi Plan revolves around the party and state's human talent work," its website says. The plan aims "to build a platform to serve the country and bring back overseas Chinese to work." In 2017, it said it had organized a total of 8,651 trips by scientists back to China from overseas (including Europe), yielding 1,267 projects and 2,880 persons engaged on the ground, 145 of them top scientists belonging to the Thousand Talents Plan.[34]

The Chunhui Cup (春晖杯).[35] Now in its 14th round, Chunhui is one of China's most prestigious entrepreneurship and innovation competitions. In 2018, 287 people were selected as finalists, with people from European countries accounting for one-third of all award winners.[36] It appears very significant to Communist Party of China leadership: at its tenth anniversary, in 2015, Liu Yandong (刘延东), a deputy premier of the State Council, former head of the United Front and a Politburo member, flew to the United States to participate in the award ceremony in person.[37]

The Hangzhou International Talents Exchange and Project Cooperation Conference (杭州国际人才交流与项目合作会议),[38] sometimes referred to as "Maker World." This aims to attract foreign students with innovative technology products and patents to found businesses in China. In 2019, the head of the province-level branch of the important CPC Organization Department presided over its meeting.[39] Annually about 300 applicants compete for 200,000 to five million RMB in venture capital funding from Chinese investors.[40] The authors procured a list of 100 competition finalists in 2017 and descriptions of their projects: 41 were from European countries. Finalists' projects included a "mass drone operation management platform system" (大规模无人机运营管理平台系统), a "molecular diagnostics and eugenics health care system" (分子诊断和优生保健系统), and a "fintech data mining and prediction system" (金融科技数据挖掘和预测系统). Most finalists hold patents registered in their home country and/or duplicate patents in China.

The FCPAE: umbrella organization

The Federation of Chinese Professional Associations in Europe (FCPAE) is a key vector in this activity, gathering more than 60 guilds under its roof.[41] The FCPAE aims "to build an interdisciplinary, multi-science, Chinese knowledge group to contribute to China's reform and construction" and, somewhat jarringly, describes its members in physical, even racialized, terms: "a group of yellow-skinned, black-haired people among whom are some of the best students and scholars in the world."[42]

Registered in a residential home in a suburb of Frankfurt-am-Main, Germany,[43] the federation organizes an annual "Europe Forum" attended by hundreds of overseas Chinese scientists and officials, as well as officials and business people from the host country.[44] Its 11th forum, in October 2019 in Dublin, Ireland, focused on "AI, 5G, life sciences, and how Brexit will affect China–Europe relations."[45] The next is in Manchester, Britain, at the end of 2020. In Dublin, the FCPAE awarded ten prizes to leading Europe-based Chinese scientists, "in hopes of encouraging more outstanding talents to bring forth mutually beneficial innovation and entrepreneurship for a win–win science and technology future." While talent is the number one reason for winning an award, organizational ability counts too, or being "the chairman or general convener of a major, specialist international conference."[46]

Li Zhuobin (李卓彬), a deputy chairman of the United Front's All-China Federation of Returned Overseas Chinese in Beijing (中华全国归国华侨联合会), which plays a key role in connecting and organizing ethnic Chinese communities overseas, gave a keynote address in Dublin,[47] exhorting attendees to innovate for China. Yet he also struck a decidedly non-scientific note: "Actively introduce China's development model and concept to overseas friends," Li said.[48] "Rely on the intelligence, financing and technology of overseas Chinese to create resource advantages … pay closer attention to Chinese strategic development and opportunities, use all ways and forms (以各种途径和形式) to be part of China's economic reform … seek the correct integration point between yourself and China's economic development and social progress."[49]

The FCPAE coordinates talent recruitment drives and advertises competitions on its website. It co-runs four "Double Innovation Bases" (创新创业基地), two in China (Jinan and Xuzhou, established 2004 and 2008), and two in Europe.[50] The European bases are more recent. One set up in 2016 in Louvain-la-Neuve, Belgium, the "CAST–FCPAE European (Belgium) Base for Entrepreneurship and Innovation" (中国科协-FCPAE 欧洲 (比利时) 海智创新创业基地), "symbolizes how Chinese companies can directly make use of Europe's technological resources and its strong research," according to an article on the website of the Association of Chinese-European Innovation and Entrepreneurship.[51] Services: project docking, technology transfer, education collaboration, and acquisition. A fourth base, set up in 2018 in Switzerland, is the "CAST–FCPAE European (Switzerland) Life Sciences Haizhi Double Innovation Base" (中国科协-FCPAE 欧洲生命科学 (瑞士) 海智创新创业基地). Both European bases were earmarked as Haizhi Plan projects in 2019.[52]

An overseas proxy: the Zhigong Party[53]

The Zhigong Party (致公党) is one of the eight non-Communist political parties in China that are part of the United Front (UF).[54] In addition to gathering non-party voices to support the party (the traditional function of the UF), the Zhigong Party gathers up science and technology, and investment, as well as focusing on education and the Chinese diaspora more broadly. Two deputy chairpersons of the Zhigong Party, Yan Xiaopei (闫晓培) and Li Zhuobin (mentioned above) officiated at the Dublin meeting of the FCPAE in 2019. Yan also briefed the Chinese ambassador to Ireland on "the Zhigong Party's work connecting to experts in the overseas Chinese world."[55]

A new, "Nordic Zhigong Association" (北欧致公协会) was founded in Stockholm in 2017. "Northern Europe is an important innovation base for Europe," according to the association website,[56] which says its "stable development" is "inextricably linked to the care and leadership of Zhigong Party central" in China. The Nordic Zhigong Association meets with Zhigong Party delegations to Europe. A four-person delegation from the Chongqing party branch traveled to Helsinki in 2018 where it also attended the annual FCPAE meeting in the Finnish capital.[57] Nordic Zhigong Association members met with another four-person delegation, from the Guizhou branch, in Helsinki at the same time,[58] telling them that in the short time since its founding the association had set up "strategic partnerships with major companies and social groups" in China, "extending top level science and technology talents and the most sophisticated projects from Northern Europe into China via the Zhigong Party."[59] The association "supported" the FCPAE's Helsinki meeting in 2018.

With the establishment of the Nordic Zhigong Association, it seems reasonable to ask if the Zhigong Party's role is growing overseas. Overall, this scenario is a continuation, or reanimation, of history: the Zhigong Party was originally founded in San Francisco in 1925, with its roots thus predating the founding of the CPC, reaching back to 1876 in North America and the founding there of a "Hongmen Zhigong Hall" (洪门致公堂).[60] The Hongmen (洪门) were early, patriotic secret societies that are still active today. The word "hall" (堂), also means "clan," suggesting, perhaps, connections to the activities of the early, patriotic movements aimed at rejuvenating China, as the Qing dynasty ossified, then fell in 1911, to be replaced by the Republic of China. "Zhigong Halls were also called Righteous Rise companies or Hongmen," according to the Nordic Zhigong Association website ("致公堂又称义兴公司、洪门"). Today, Zhigong Halls (致公堂) remain part of overseas Chinese networks.[61] Fully co-opted by the CPC after the revolution, the chairman of the Zhigong Party in China is Wan Gang (万钢), a former Minister of Science and Technology and engineer who studied and worked in Germany for about 17 years. Wan presided over at the Nordic Zhigong Association's anniversary meeting in Stockholm in September 2019.

The European Union: Horizon 2020 and beyond

EU–China science and technology cooperation includes joint nuclear, aviation, agriculture, energy, and environmental research, all taking place under an agreement signed in 1998 and renewed several times since.[62] Two specialist Chinese technology transfer organizations were involved in EU–China talks that led to the latest renewal of the 1998 cooperation agreement, in 2018/2019: the "China Science and Technology Exchange Centre" (中国科学技术交流中心), which runs the international talent plan "Talented Young Scientist Program," and the "China International Talents Exchange Centre" (中国国际人才交流中心).[63]

In 2013, the year after Xi Jinping became general-secretary of the CPC, the EU and China upgraded overall relations to a "Comprehensive Strategic Partnership" to raise the level and intensity of research and innovation exchange.[64] MOST is the main partner, in a range of research areas; the Ministry of Information Industry and Technology (MIIT) in aviation; and the Natural Science Foundation of China (NSFC) in basic research including biotechnology.[65]

It is outside the scope of this chapter to look at all of the cooperation between European and Chinese scientists since 1998. Overall, Chinese entities have been involved at least 464 times in projects within Horizon 2020 (H2020), the EU's global research and innovation program from 2014–2020. This was a 26 percent increase over Chinese participations in the EU's previous funding program, the 7th Framework Program (2007–2013), though China is now paying significantly more for this cooperation.[66] By now, apart from nearly four million euros in direct EU funding, China mostly funds its own researchers for joint projects, EU officials say. Broadly, since 2016, the EU and China have committed about 400 million euros in joint research, with the EU paying some two-thirds and China one third. In this way, however, the EU may not always know exactly who the Chinese partner is. "Chinese participants can enter for example into a project as partner not signing the grant, and therefore we cannot easily track them."[67] European scientists can apply for Chinese state funding to research in China but should adhere to national strategic industrial policy goals if they want to succeed. Being "truly and fully committed to the Chinese innovation ecosystem" is a prerequisite to secure funding; failure to do so may have consequences for the person or institution's social credit rating system.

Joint "flagship initiatives" agreed by the EU and China in 2017 focus on food, agriculture and biotechnologies. Concerned about China's increasingly technologized and digitalized security state, the EU says it does not want to fund "technical" AI research with China but only "ethical" aspects.[68] Yet there is a somewhat different flavor to MOST's priorities in 2019, which also included, "New generation information network; intelligent and green manufacturing; safe, clean and efficient energy; advanced, effective, safe and convenient health technologies; marine equipment; space; new materials; large scientific research infrastructures; public security."[69] The latter areas appeared to be earmarked to receive a lion's share of China funding for joint projects in 2019.[70]

China is also a principal nuclear research interlocutor for the European Atomic Energy Community (Euratom). It is a full member of ITER, the France-based magnetic fusion energy project, and plans to build its own fusion device, the

"Chinese Fusion Engineering Testing Reactor (CFETR)."[71] Some smaller-scale projects stand out for their potential for specific technology transfer such as "Exciting," an "EU–China study on IoT and 5G" with about one million euros in European financing.[72] "Exciting will study the research and innovation ecosystem for IoT and 5G in China and compare it with the European model," focusing on "standardization and interoperability."[73] The project had eight partners in Europe and six in China. China-based partners included the telecommunications company Huawei and two universities, the Huazhong University of Science and Technology (HUST, 华中科技大学) and the Beijing University of Posts and Telecommunications (BUPT, 北京邮电大学). Both are identified by one database as "very high" risk for collaboration.[74] Other, current, S&T research cooperation between China and three European nations stands out: with Norway (energy innovation including intelligent operation control technologies, and "digital area"), Austria (quantum information science and ICT) and Sweden (life sciences and ICT).[75]

China's policy of "military–civilian fusion development" (军民融合发展) has profound implications for cooperative research.[76] Horizon 2020 outlawed the joint development of technologies with military applications,[77] yet it is unclear if it is possible to truly differentiate between civilian and military technology under "fusion" conditions, and EU officials appear to have no good solution to this problem. Research on defense-related topics with Chinese partners can still qualify for funding: "Research on defense related subjects may still qualify for funding, as long as its aims are exclusively focused on civil applications," according to the Commission.[78] "All relevant projects are being closely monitored by the Commission services," it added.

The EU appears to be increasingly—belatedly—aware it does not sufficiently understand China's system or goals. A "reflexion [sic] is needed in the area of Research & Innovation," according to a Commission document circulating internally before a workshop in Brussels in December 2019. "Europe–China cooperation in research and innovation increasingly raises a number of issues such as … the need for better knowledge on China and its academic system, or the understanding of the relationship and collaboration goals of the Chinese partners."[79]

Member states: some examples

The cooperation picture on the ground in EU member states is intricate, reflecting the mosaic of realities that is Europe. In some countries, such as *Austria*, cooperation appears virtually unchecked. Austrian physicists have worked with the China Academy of Sciences to develop "unhackable" quantum communication systems, an area where it is hard to overlook military or national security interests. The technology also has uses in quantum cryptography.[80] The project, QUESS, a collaboration between CAS, the Austrian Academy of Sciences (OeAW) and the University of Vienna, sent a satellite into space from China's Jiuquan launch facility in Inner Mongolia in 2016 using a "backbone" of ground stations in China, achieving "the world's first inter-continental quantum call," according to a report on the website of the Austrian academy.

In *France*, a spokesperson for the Centre national de la recherche scientifique (CNRS), the country's largest research organization, says researchers "maintain close and fruitful relationships" with Chinese colleagues.[81] China is CNRS's second-largest partner in terms of the number of joint publications outside of Europe, after the United States; each year CNRS conducts about 1,500 research visits to China, of a total of 60,000 international visits (mostly within Europe).[82] "At the institutional level, the CNRS is trying to structure scientific partnerships of excellence with Chinese research institutions, and above all the Chinese Academy of Sciences (中国科学院), in all research fields," the spokesperson said.[83] However, its president, Antoine Petit, said officials at CNRS institutes carry out security checks on incoming Chinese scientists, and after deliberation with government ministries may refuse cooperation. CNRS declined to say how often cooperation is refused, or to give details on cases of espionage or intellectual property theft.

In *Greece*, a member of the "17 + 1" EU–China bloc, the "ASEM Cooperation Centre for Science, Technology and Innovation" (ASEM–CCSTI)[84] opened in 2016, two years after Premier Li Keqiang called for an innovation and transfer mechanism between Asia and Europe within the "Asia–Europe Meeting" (ASEM).[85] (Founded in 1996, ASEM is a dialogue and cooperation platform between Asia and Europe.)

ASEM–CCSTI is located in Athens, the capital of one of China's closest partners in Europe. However, the ASEM–CCSTI headquarters are in Beijing at the municipal Science and Technology Commission. The ASEM–CCSTI website advertises "cross-state transferring of technology achievements."[86] Multiple technologies are advertised there though it's not clear who is offering or asking. One example is a lightweight, cryogenic transmitter for UAVs, useful for "radio astronomy Defense Communications science" (sic).[87] Its purpose:

> Excavate the needs for technique cooperation of the enterprises, universities and the research institutes in their own country; organize the relevant activities for skill match-making; provide the relevant follow-up services … [and] Establish coordination mechanism with secretariat of ASEM-CCSTI and keep sustainable communication in science and technology cooperation (*sic*).[88]

The first of several planned "national points of contact" in Europe, ASEM–CCSTI advertises other transfer events and co-hosted the FCPAE forum in Helsinki in 2018,[89] holding a special, side event for Southern European countries including Greece, Italy and Portugal.[90] Curiously, the Helsinki meeting was not listed on the ASEM Infoboard, meaning it was not formally an ASEM event. EU officials in Brussels said they were unaware of the group.[91]

Focusing on *Italy*, the "China–Italy Technology Transfer Center" (CITTC, 中意技术转移中心) is also headquartered in Beijing, at the municipal Science and Technology Commission.[92] In November 2019 CITTC co-organized a four-day, dual location (Beijing and Jinan), "China–Italy Science, Technology and Innovation Week."[93] Scores of projects were reportedly discussed, including intelligent manufacturing, life sciences, energy conservation, aviation, and "semiconductor illumination." Over the last decade nearly 1,000 agreements have been reached, according to STDaily.com, (中国科技网), a web portal affiliated with *Science and Technology Daily* (科技日报), China's science and technology newspaper.[94]

Overall, the flow of European talent to China is increasing. In 2019, for the first time, an Austrian and a Norwegian received China's "International Science and Technology Cooperation Award," called "the nation's highest honor for foreign scientists" in China.[95] Five recipients were from Europe (also scientists from the United Kingdom, Finland, and Italy). Seven Europeans were among 20 new additions to the ranks of foreign CAS academicians, bringing the total of all foreign academicians to 108.[96] CAS has ministry rank in China; Chinese academicians "have the duty" to serve as consultants on government policies, its website notes. CAS's motto, in part: "Facing the frontiers of global science and technology, facing the major demands of the country, facing the main battlefield of the national economy."[97]

The impact

Transferred technologies have enriched China greatly and today are a springboard for further innovation at home.[98] This process is highly significant; technologies originally from Europe are now returning, reshaped, to the world, impacting the global market and sometimes carrying with them a strong national security element mostly invisible to citizens of the new host country.[99]

A specific question that should be asked here is, how successful is the activity of recruiting talent via "talent plans"? Worldwide, the best known is the "Thousand Talents Plan" (千人计划). This has attracted more attention in the United States but is widespread in Europe, too (recently, at least partially, rebranded as the "High-end Foreign Experts Recruitment Plan" (高端外国专家引进计划). The EU has supported cooperation with these plans: an 18-month "China Innovation Project," operated in Beijing, aimed to help explain the Chinese research funding landscape to European scientists seeking to work in China and included talent plan information, was funded by the EU.[100]

Talent plans offer real money. By awarding 500,000 to one million RMB as a "subsidy," plus one to five million RMB in research funding (depending on experience) for researchers to work full-time in China,[101] the Thousand Talents

Plan has successfully recruited an estimated 7,000 scholars worldwide over a nine-year period.[102] Other talent plans, cups, and competitions, like the national Chunhui Cup and regional Hangzhou Maker-World competitions examined above, have recruited fewer people, but still approximately 1,000 foreign scientists each over the past ten years.[103]

Do they truly matter for China's technological development? And do top talents from abroad (most of whom are considered "Overseas Chinese") selected under national talent plans and competitions tend to be more prolific or effective at their jobs than average Chinese academics? The evidence is mixed. In one example, the authors were able to procure the master list of scholars recruited to work at Ningbo University from 2001 to 2018. Of the 708 scholars recruited, 81 (11 percent) were trained at foreign universities.[104] Compared to researchers at China's state key labs, recruits under the Youth Thousand Talents Program tend to produce more highly cited research papers at a faster pace.[105] On the other hand, foreign-trained recruits who return to China may not be as prolific as their Chinese counterparts who remain abroad working, for example, in Europe or in the United States.[106] The quality of their papers may suffer.[107]

Although top European talents represent a fraction of China's academic workforce, they have the potential to make significant contributions to the Chinese economy, possibly at the expense of the countries where they have studied, or their home countries. Efforts to transfer this talent outflow are systematic and large, and virtually unchecked. They are organized by the CPC, often via its United Front, and associated groups. The EU is in a state of "systemic rivalry" with China's party-state, suggesting that Europeans must get better at asking, and figuring out the important question: What is the PRC's strategic intent? It is especially important to be clear as scrutiny of the practice grows, and recruitment is aimed increasingly at non-Chinese overseas persons in Europe, as well as the United States.

Notes

1 Didi Kirsten Tatlow, "The Chinese Influence Effort Hiding in Plain Sight," *The Atlantic*, July 12, 2019. www.theatlantic.com/international/archive/2019/07/chinas-influence-efforts-germany-students/593689/ By the same author, "Mapping China in Germany," October 2, 2019, https://sinopsis.cz/en/mapping-china-in-Democracy: the European Parliament China Friendship Cluster. November 26, 2019, https://sinopsis.cz/en/ep/.
2 Jichang Lulu, "Repurposing Democracy: the European Parliament China Friendship Cluster. November 26, 2019, https://sinopsis.cz/en/ep/ Tatlow, "Mapping China in Germany," October 2, 2019, https://sinopsis.cz/en/mapping-china-in-germany/.
3 For a discussion of "repay the motherland" that shows enthusiasm for the cause among Chinese citizens, see Zhihu.com, www.zhihu.com/question/20331694.
4 Includes Britain, which left the EU in 2020. https://ec.europa.eu/eurostat/statistics-explained/index.php/R_%26D_personnel#Science_and_technology_graduates.
5 Ministry of Railways media event, April 29. 2007, www.gov.cn/wszb/zhibo59/content_601548.htm.
6 See also Chapter 12, NucTech.

7 Catherine Pagani, *Eastern Magnificence and European Ingenuity, Clocks of Late Imperial China*, Ann Arbor, MI: Michigan University Press, 2001; Tang Kaijian, *Setting Off from Macau: Essays in Jesuit History during the Ming and Qing Dynasties*, Koninklijke Brill NV: Leiden, 2016; and Joseph Needham, *Heavenly Clockwork: The Great Astronomical Clocks of Mediaeval China*, Cambridge: Cambridge University Press, 1960.

8 Joachim Krüger (ed.), "Beiträge zur Geschichte der Beziehungen der DDR—VR China—Erinnerungen und Untersuchungen," *Berliner China Studien* Nr. 41, 2002 (www.geschkult.fu-berlin.de/e/oas/sinologie/publikationen/bchst/bchst41/index. html). See also a brief *People's Daily* account of the Beijing North China Wireless Joint Equipment Factory built by East German technicians (in German): http://german. people.com.cn/209048/8594661.html For Czechoslovakia and Eastern Europe more generally, see: www.wilsoncenter.org/publication/central-europeans-and-the-sino-soviet-split-the-great-friendship-international-history.

9 "The Scale and Impact of Industrial Espionage and Theft of Trade Secrets through Cyber," March 2019, European Commission/PwC (www.pwc.com/it/it/publications/docs/ study-on-the-scale-and-Impact.pdf) The full study, sadly redacted: https://op.europa. eu/en/publication-detail/-/publication/4eae21b2-4547-11e9-a8ed-01aa75ed71a1/ language-en. See also, Susanne Knickmeier, "Spies without borders? The Phenomenon of Economic and Industrial Espionage and the Deterrence Strategies of Germany and other Selected European Countries," *Security Journal*, 33, no. 1 (2020): 6–26. And Chapter 8, the Lanxess case.

10 Ibid, EC/PwC study.

11 Cong Cao et al., "Returning Scientists and the Emergence of China's Science System," in *Science and Public Policy*, 47, no. 2 (202): 172–183.

12 Didi Tatlow, "The Chinese Influence Effort Hiding in Plain Sight," *The Atlantic*, July 12, 2019.

13 Website of the Chinese Student and Scholars Association UK, March 2, 2020: http:// cssauk.org.uk/.

14 第八届在法中国留学人员团体联席会成功举 (The 8th Joint Meeting of the Chinese Study in France Overseas Groups Successfully Held), French Overseas Student Service portal, December 4, 2019. http://france.lxgz.org.cn/publish/ portal116/tab5722/info141588.htm.

15 意大利中国学生学者联谊会 (CSUUI Chinese Students and Scholars Union in Italy), accessed March 2, 2020, www.cssui.org/.

16 "The motherland" could be translated as "the fatherland," due to patriarchal tradition. A literal translation: 祖国 is "ancestral country." We leave it up to readers to decide.

17 "Austria Overseas Students Service Network," Education Section, Chinese embassy in Vienna: http://austria.lxgz.org.cn/publish/portal29/tab5245/info94284.htm. Also, CSSA handbooks and author interviews with Chinese students in Germany. The authors believe that the same rules apply, at least in theory, wherever there are Chinese students abroad.

18 Author interviews.

19 Figure based on authors' own calculations, by compiling a unique list of Chinese professional associations in Europe who are members of the FCPAE (全欧华人专业 协会联合会), OCSTOF (海外华人科技组织联合会), or connected to the Haizhi Plan (海智计划). Information from each association's public-facing website, including the Chinese-language "About Us" pages.

20 To determine which associations are involved in technology transfer, the authors conducted systematized keyword searches in Mandarin for phrases including "technology transfer," "technology exchange," "return to China," and the names of specific state-run talent programs. This turned up a number of 47.

21 Of the 47 associations in our dataset that engage in technology transfer, 19 list the number of dues-paying members in their organizations, while 28 do not. The median

number of members in a Chinese professional association was 350, and the average was 823, with high variance in our sample despite a narrow IQR. We could confirm that at least 15,639 people are members of technology transfer associations. For the remaining 28 groups, we used the median (350 people) to estimate that an additional 9,800 people may be members of the associations with unknown membership counts. For more detail contact the authors.

22 www.fcpae.com/.
23 "About" page of OCSTOF. www.co-st.org/index.php?s=/home/about/partner. html.
24 Haizhi Plan: in Chinese-language texts the English name is also given as "HOME Program—Help Our Motherland through Elite Intellectual Resources from Overseas, 简称:海智计划."
25 For more on "talent" plans, and the Chunhui Cup, see the section "Spotting, and reeling in, the talent."
26 BGI Genomics is headquartered in Shenzhen, China and has three regional HQs, including in Copenhagen, Denmark. www.bgi.com/global/company/about-bgi/.
27 www.cbas.se/helix3/index.php/component/spsimpleportfolio/item/7-about-us.
28 The "Association des Scientifiques et des Ingénieurs Chinois en France" (ASICEF) was set up in 1992, according to its homepage: https://asicef.fr/.
29 http://csittc.com/en/index.php.
30 Homepage: http://csittc.com/en/index.php For specific services, http://csittc.com/service.php.
31 United States of America vs. Feng "Franklin" Tao: www.justice.gov/opa/press-release/file/1197256/download.
32 http://hzb.cast.org.cn/. Also known as "HOME Program." See also Chapter 1.
33 Homepage: www.cast.org.cn/ A core part of the party-state S&T system, CAST "serves as a bridge that links the Communist Party of China and the Chinese government to the country's science and technology community." Through 210 national member societies and local branches all over the country, CAST maintains close ties with millions of Chinese scientists, engineers and other professionals working in the fields of science and technology. See: http://english.cast.org.cn/col/col471/index.html.
34 http://before.cast.org.cn/n200685/c57776903/content.html and www.sohu.com/a/210350400_749128.
35 http://cyds.cscse.edu.cn/.
36 www.czzht.com/index.php?c=content&a=show&id=34089.
37 www.chinadaily.com.cn/world/7thcused/2015-06/22/content_21072747.htm.
38 Website of the Hangzhou city government: www.hangzhou.gov.cn/art/2019/11/10/art_812255_39996465.html.
39 Ibid, "Opening Ceremony of the 2019 Hangzhou International Talent Exchange Program Cooperation Meeting," November 10, 2019.
40 www.cutic.org/en/enroll/id-1.html.
41 FCPAE homepage: www.fcpae.com/.
42 Ibid.
43 Author trip to Bad Vilbel, outside Frankfurt, April 2019. According to a neighbor, the inhabitants of the house, who include the federation founder, are rarely seen. After gaining a Ph.D. in computer science and working in Germany for some years, Zhou Shengzong (周盛宗) appears to have at least partially returned to China some years ago, working at a branch of the Chinese Academy of Sciences in Fujian. See: www.cas.cn/rc/gzdt/201309/t20130929_3942570.shtml.
44 www.fcpae.com/?p=2261.
45 www.fcpae.com/?p=2227.
46 FCPAE website, report on the award ceremony in Dublin, October 2019. www.fcpae.com/?p=2261.

47 中华全国归国华侨联合会 (All-China Federation of Returned Overseas Chinese), long tasked with keeping overseas Chinese loyal. Set up under the State Council, in 2018 it became part of the United Front Work Department. www.chinaql.org/.
48 www.chinaql.org/n1/2019/1026/c419643-31421945.html.
49 "以各种途径和形式," similar, more detailed, than "以多种方式."
50 "Double innovation" (双创). Shorthand for a national slogan dating from 2014, "Mass Entrepreneurship, Mass Innovation" (大众创业, 万众创新).
51 The "Association of Chinese-European Innovation and Entrepreneurship "may be interchangeable with, or otherwise part of, the "CAST–FCPAE European (Belgium) Base for Entrepreneurship and Innovation" (中国科协-FCPAE 欧洲 (比利时) 海智创新创业基地,) since its website mirrors the "base." The website is sparse and not always accessible): www.aceie.eu/2018/05/12/post-3/.
52 http://news.sciencenet.cn/htmlnews/2019/9/430892.shtm. See also Chapter 1 for the Haizhi Plan (HOME).
53 Zhigong Party website: www.zg.org.cn/. Can also be written "Zhi Gong Party."
54 Gerry Groot, 1997, *Managing Transitions: The Chinese Communist Party's United Front Work, Minor Parties and Groups, Hegemony and Corporatism*, New York and London: Routledge, 2004. See also Bibliography for more.
55 Accessed on the Ministry of Foreign Affairs website, October 17, 2019. Source: PRC embassy in Ireland. www.fmprc.gov.cn/web/zwbd_673032/nbhd_673044/t1708760.shtml.
56 北欧致公协会 (Nordic Zhigong Association), www.nordiczg.org.
57 致公党重庆市委员会 (China Committee of Chongqing Zhigong Party), www.cqzgd.gov.cn/article/14-644.html.
58 北欧致公协会与致公党贵州省委会在芬兰进行会晤 (The Nordic Zhigong Association and the Guizhou Province Zhigong Party committee hold a meeting in Finland), October 2, 2018, https://wemp.app/posts/6cf719cd-78c5-4ca9-b0f4-fdac6253406b.
59 Ibid.
60 致公堂历史简介 (A brief explanation of Zhigong Halls). This describes connections between the Hongmen and the Zhigong Party. www.nordiczg.org/?p=87.
61 This is not the place for a detailed discussion of this fascinating topic, but for more see Groot, (above), or Emmanuel Jourda (in French), "Le Parti Communiste Chinois, le Front Uni et les Triades: Patriotisme, Business et Crime Organisé," *Sociétés politiques comparées*, January/April, 2019.
62 European Union, "Agreement for Scientific and Technological Cooperation between the European Community and the Government of the People's Republic of China," December 22, 1998. https://ec.europa.eu/research/iscp/pdf/policy/china-agreement.pdf#view=fit&pagemode=none.
63 中国科学技术交流中心 (China Science and Technology Exchange Centre): www.cistc.gov.cn/Scientist/ and www.cistc.gov.cn/Scientist/details.asp?column=917&id=98085 For the "China International Talents Exchange Centre" (中国国际人才交流中心) see: www.most.gov.cn/kjbgz/201904/t20190424_146218.htm.
64 "Roadmap for EU–China S&T Cooperation," European Commission, p. 2. https://ec.europa.eu/research/iscp/pdf/policy/cn_roadmap_2018.pdf#view=fit&pagemode=none.
65 EU S&T officials, via email and telephone interviews, January 2020.
66 Horizon 2020 Dashboard: https://webgate.ec.europa.eu/dashboard/sense/app/a976d168-2023-41d8-acec-e77640154726/sheet/d23bba31-e385-4cc0-975e-a67059972142/state/0.
67 EU S&T officials, via email and telephone interviews, January 2020.
68 Ibid.
69 国家重点研发计划政府间国际科技创新合作/港澳台科技创新合作重点专项2019年度第一批项目申报指南 ("Notice of the Ministry of Science and

Technology on Application Guidelines for the 1st Batch of Projects for year 2019 under the 'Key Project on Intergovernmental International Science, Technology and Innovation (STI) Cooperation/STI Cooperation with Hong Kong, Macao and Taiwan' of the National Key R&D Programme").

70 Ibid.

71 ITER = Latin, "the way." An energy project, ITER is a France-based, 35-nation collaboration building a magnetic fusion device. See: www.iter.org/ and www.iter. org/proj/inafewlines.

72 European Union, Cordis (Community Research and Development Information Service), https://cordis.europa.eu/project/id/723227 Cordis tracks projects funded by the EU's framework programs for research and innovation (FP1 to Horizon 2020).

73 Ibid.

74 "The database is designed to capture the risk that relationships with these entities could be leveraged for military or security purposes, including in ways that contribute to human rights abuses ..." Defence Universities Tracker of the Australian Security Policy Institute, https://unitracker.aspi.org.au/.

75 Ibid.

76 "习近平主持召开中央军民融合发展委员会第一次全体会议," ("Chairman Xi Jinping convenes the first full meeting of the Central Military–Civilian Fusion Development Committee"), June 20, 2017. www.gov.cn/xinwen/2017-06/20/content_5204059.htm.

77 Regulation (EU) No 1291/2013 of the European Parliament and of the Council of December 11, 2013 Establishing Horizon 2020—the Framework Programme for Research and Innovation (2014–2020). https://eur-lex.europa.eu/legal-content/ EN/TXT/?uri=CELEX%3A32013R1291.

78 Spokesperson for Directorate-General, Research & Innovation, via email, January 6, 2020.

79 "Workshop with Member States and EU R&I Institutions on R&I cooperation with China—Wednesday December 18, 2019," European Union Commission, Directorate-General for Research and Innovation.

80 www.oeaw.ac.at/en/detail/news/erstes-abhoersicheres-quanten-videotelefonat-zwischen-wien-und-peking-geglueckt-1/ In 2019, China passed a Cryptography Law. The law classifies cryptography into core, common and commercial. Core and common cryptography are used to protect the country's confidential information, and are state secrets, according to *Xinhua*. www.xinhuanet.com/english/2019-10/26/c_ 138505655.htm.

81 Email communication with CNRS spokeswoman, January 15, 2020.

82 Ibid.

83 Author interview with CNRS president Antoine Petit, April 4, 2019.

84 See "About Us," ASEM–CCSTI website, accessed February 23, 2020. http://en.asem innovation.org.cn/sites/english/about.html?part=about4.

85 European External Action Service (EEAS), Asia–Europe Meeting (ASEM). https:// eeas.europa.eu/diplomatic-network/asia-europe-meeting-asem/2051/asia-europe-meeting-asem_en.

86 ASEM–CCSTI website, "European office of ASEM innovation cooperation center inaugurated in Athens," November 15, 2015. http://en.aseminnovation.org.cn/web/ detail/1660.html.

87 Posted 18 May 2017, accessed 23 February 23, 2020. http://en.aseminnovation.org. cn/sites/english/projectContent.html?id=8a8a9f045c140f68015c1a982bb40025.

88 "About Us," ASEM–CCSTI website. http://en.aseminnovation.org.cn/sites/english/ about.html?part=about4.

89 www.asem-ccsti.gr/index.php/2nd-asem-seminar/objectives/. See also: www.asem-ccsti.gr/wp-content/uploads/2018/06/EN-1.pdf.

90 Author interview in April 2019 with Finnish organizers working for the Helsinki city government. The FCPAE meeting took place in Helsinki Town Hall.
91 EU spokesperson on background, emails and telephone interviews, April and May 2019.
92 There are more. For example, the "International Technology Transfer Network" (国际技术转移协作网络), which is global in scope, was set up in 2010 by the Beijing city government's Science and Technology Commission.
93 CITTC website: www.cittc.org.cn/sites/2019/index.html#.
94 Authorized by State Council Information Office (国务院新闻办公室) 2010, STDaily. com is managed by MOST together with *Science and Technology Daily*. STDaily.com describes itself as "a 'national team' that undertakes the science and technology news propaganda task of the party and state," ("承担党和国家科技新闻宣传任务的国家队"). www.stdaily.com/index/yqlj2/2016-09/02/content_143065.shtml For the China–Italy event, www.stdaily.com/qykj/qianyan/2019-11/28/content_831871.shtml.
95 *China Daily*, "China's Top Scientific Award for Foreign Scientists Given to 10," January 10, 2020.
96 "CAS Adds More Diverse Group of New Academicians," CAS website, November 26, 2019. http://english.cas.ac.cn/newsroom/cas_media/201911/t20191126_226250.shtml.
97 Chinese Academy of Sciences (中国科学院), www.cas.cn/.
98 See NucTech (同方威视), Chapter 12.
99 For examples of the interplay of technology and national security in China, and its growing impact on the outside world, see Samantha Hoffman, "Engineering Global Consent: The Chinese Communist Party's Data-driven Power Expansion," ASPI, October 14, 2019.
100 Ibid.
101 www.rvo.nl/sites/default/files/2017/01/1000-Talents-Policy-Article.pdf.
102 US Senate Permanent Subcommittee on Investigations, "Threats to the US Research Enterprise: China's Talent Recruitment Plans," p. 2. David Bekkers, "China's Pursuit of Overseas Brains: The 1,000 Talents Policy," Government of The Netherlands, January 31, 2017, www.rvo.nl/sites/default/files/2017/01/1000-Talents-Policy-Article.pdf Includes case studies of European participants.
103 Based on authors' own estimations, extrapolating data from the 2018 and 2019 Chunhui Cups, and the 2009 and 2017 Hangzhou Maker World competition finalists.
104 Data generated from Ningbo University Talent Service Declaration System, accessed December 12, 2019. https://hrs.nbrc.com.cn/download/35rc.xls.
105 Bekkers, above.
106 Lili Yang and Giulio Marini, "Research Productivity of Chinese Young Thousand Talents," *International Higher Education: China Focus* 97, pp. 17–18.
107 Cong Cao, "China's Approaches to Attract and Nurture Young Biomedical Researchers," 6 (2018). See See: https://www.hsgac.senate.gov/imo/media/doc/2019-11-18%20PSI%20Staff%20Report%20-%20China%27s%20Talent%20Recruitment%20Plans.pdf.

Bibliography

Cheng, Ganyuan (程干远). 中共统战部揭秘–统战干部回忆录, (*Secrets of the CCP's United Front Work Department*), Washington, DC: Citizen Press 公民社, 2019.

European Union. "Agreement for Scientific and Technological Cooperation between the European Community and the Government of the People's Republic of China," December 22, 1998. https://ec.europa.eu/research/iscp/pdf/policy/china-agreement.pdf#view=fit&pagemode=none.

European Union. *Cordis*, Community Research and Development Information Service. https://cordis.europa.eu/project/id/723227.

European Union. "Establishing Horizon 2020—the Framework Programme for Research and Innovation 2014–2020," December 11, 2013.

European Union/PwC. "The Scale and Impact of Industrial Espionage and Theft of Trade Secrets through Cyber," Publications Office of the European Union, March 11, 2019.

Groot, Gerry. *Managing Transitions—The Chinese Communist Party, United Front Work, Corporatism, and Hegemony*, New York and London: Routledge, 2004.

Groot, Gerry and Ray Wang. "Who Represents? Xi Jinping's Grand United Front Work, Legitimation, Participation and Consultative Democracy," *Journal of Contemporary China*, 2018.

Hannas, William C., James Mulvenon, and Anna B. Puglisi, Anna B. et al. *Chinese Industrial Espionage: Technology Acquisition and Military Modernization*, London, New York: Routledge, 2013.

Hoffman, Samantha. "Programming China: The Communist Party's Autonomic Approach to Managing State Security," *MERICS*, December 12, 2017.

Joske, Alex. "The China Defence Universities Tracker: Exploring the Military and Security Links of China's Universities," Australian Strategic Policy Institute, November 25, 2019.

Jourda, Emmanuel. "Le Parti Communiste Chinois, le Front Uni et les Triades: Patriotisme, Business et Crime Organisé," *Sociétés Politiques Comparées*, January/April 2019.

Jüris, Frank. "Handing over Infrastructure for China's Strategic Objectives: 'Arctic Connect' and the Digital Silk Road in the Arctic," March 7, 2020; Sinopsis conference "Beyond Huawei: Europe's Adoption of PRC Technology and its Implications," Prague, 2019.

Knickmeier, Susanne. "Spies without Borders? The Phenomena of Economic and Industrial Espionage and the Deterrence Strategies of Germany and Other Selected European Countries," *Security Journal*, 33, no, 1 (2020): 6–26.

Krüger, Joachim (ed.). "Beiträge zur Geschichte der Beziehungen der DDR-VR China—Erinnerungen und Untersuchunge," *Berliner China Studien* Nr. 41. 2002.

PRC Central Committee of the CPC and State Council. 中共中央、国务院关于进一步加强人才工作的决定 ("Decision on Further Enhancing the Development of Human Resources"), December 26, 2003.

Sarek, Łukasz. "5G and the Internet of Things: Chinese Companies' Inroads into 'Digital Poland'," January 3, 2020; Sinopsis conference "Beyond Huawei: Europe's Adoption of PRC Technology and its Implications," Prague, 2019.

Sinopsis. Conference Papers, conference "Beyond Huawei: Europe's Adoption of PRC Technology and Its Implications," December 4, 2019.

Tatlow, Didi Kirsten. "Manufacturing Creativity and Maintaining Control: China's Schools Struggle to Balance Innovation and Safeguard Conformity," *MERICS*, February 14, 2019.

US Senate Permanent Subcommittee on Investigations. "Threats to the US Research Enterprise: China's Talent Recruitment Plans," 2019.

8

TECHNOLOGY TRANSFER FROM GERMANY

Didi Kirsten Tatlow, Hinnerk Feldwisch-Drentrup and Ryan Fedasiuk

This chapter maps technology transfer from Germany, Europe's most populous country and biggest economy with 83 million people, and a strong scientific and industrial tradition. It deepens the exploration begun in Chapter 7, similarly including many primary sources and original research. This is an understudied field.

Germany's history of ties with the PRC is not uniform, as we touched on (see Chapter 7): East Germany (the German Democratic Republic, GDR) and the PRC established diplomatic relations soon after the founding of the two Communist states, days apart, in October 1949—the PRC on October 1, the GDR on October 7. For about 20 years, East Germany was the only official representative of Germany in Beijing.[1] It sent scores of engineers, architects, and other specialists to aid the CPC's early industrialization and state-building. A well-known example is the North China Wireless Joint Equipment Factory in Beijing built by East Germans, today the 798 Arts District.[2]

West Germany (the Bundesrepublik Deutschland) re-established diplomatic relations with China in 1972. Eighteen months later, in April 1974, Reimar Lüst, the president of a storied research institute, the Max-Planck-Gesellschaft, traveled to China with an eight-person delegation, beginning a new phase of cooperation.[3] Around one-third of senior and directorial positions in the Chinese Academy of Sciences (CAS, 中国科学院) have been filled with scientists trained in Germany.[4]

An intergovernmental agreement on scientific and technological cooperation, signed in 1978, laid the foundations for today's wide-ranging cooperation.[5] By March 2020 there were more than 1,400 ventures between German universities and Chinese counterparts (not including research institutes and businesses) including in life sciences, environment, and vocational training.[6] Cooperation has taken place in ultra-sensitive technologies, such as lasers and the realm of nuclear engineering physics.[7]

A transfer pipeline

The technology transfer system between Germany and China operates on multiple levels and in multiple areas, simultaneously. These include "licit" or "gray zone" activities such as student, scholar, and professional associations, both traditional (from the 1980s) and new style (AI-oriented starting in the mid-2010s); individual activities; government-organized outfits such as the China International Talent Exchange Association (CAIEP [sic], 中国国际人才交流协会); and a busy illicit extraction scene, examined at the end of this chapter.

Students and scholars

As noted in Chapter 7 there are between 80 and 88 Chinese Student and Scholar Associations in Germany (CSSA), according to the Federation of Chinese Student and Scholar Societies in Germany (CASD, 中国留德学者学生团体联合会) and other sources;[8] 71 in German university towns, 7 "specialized scholarly associations," and 6 alumni associations of Chinese universities, according to the CASD website. Officials at German universities and research centers seem largely unaware of these groups in their midst. A spokesperson for the RWTH Aachen University, a leading S&T institution, said it had no accredited CSSA; it "is not possible, if a student group is supported substantially by a political party," the spokesperson said.[9] However, the university hosts a website belonging to the Federation of Chinese Students and Scholars in Aachen" (Verein der Chinesischen Wissenschaftler und Studenten in Aachen, 亚琛学生学者联合会) which says it was set up in the 1980s and is "recognized and supported by the Chinese embassy and by the university's foreign students office."[10] RWTH Aachen has about 15 cooperation programs with mainland China. In the winter semester of 2019–2020 they comprised 1,753 Chinese students.[11]

Sometimes the role played by Chinese diplomats in the CSSAs concretizes. In September 2019, the CSSA at the Forschungszentrum Jülich (FZJ, Jülich research center, a leading S&T institute),[12] thanked Chinese diplomats for their "support" for a "study abroad information sharing exchange" event marking the Mid-Autumn, or Moon, Festival at a research center within the institute.[13] Its chairman, Zhou Xiaoran (周潇然), addressed the gathered Chinese students on "overseas student security, ability forging and patriotism" (留学安全，锻炼能力和爱国). Zhou introduced attendees to the FZJ's CSSA (CSSAFZJ), "its structural composition and all kinds of rich and varied activities." The report ended: "Thanks to the Düsseldorf general consulate for its support and help for this activity which was organized by the students themselves, for giving us a feeling of home in a foreign place, for such a substantial and happy Mid-Autumn

Festival."[14] FZJ has about 500 Chinese visiting scientists and Ph.D. students. Here too, officials were vague. Whether organizations at the center welcomed diplomatic visitors was not on record, a spokesperson said. "Representatives of the Chinese consulate or the embassy have not been at the research center during the last three years in order to hold talks with its board," she said, and, "We are not aware of any organizational structures within the research center," referring to queries about the CSSA.[15] Curiously, the report about the Moon Festival party was deleted from the CSSAFZJ WeChat account after the authors of this chapter contacted the FZJ for comment.[16]

Professional associations

In Chapter 7 we estimated at least 47 professional guilds of overseas Chinese throughout Europe were involved in transferring technology to China. Of these, 17 are in Germany, with approximately 5,500 Germany-based experts.[17] The following examples show the language and provide figures:

- Fifteen associations representing approximately 5,100 German experts mention they facilitate "technology transfer" (技术转让), "technology exchange" (技术交流), "knowledge transfer" (知识传输), or other kinds of industrial "exchange and cooperation" (交流与合作) with China.
- Six associations representing approximately 2,300 German experts state their intent to "return" (返回中国) foreign-born, ethnically Chinese overseas Chinese people to China, to found businesses or work at Chinese research universities.
- Seven associations representing approximately 2,000 German experts highlight their contributions to specific Chinese state-run talent spotting plans, such as the "Hundred Talents Plan" (百人计划) or "Chunhui Cup" (春晖杯).

In Germany as in Europe more broadly, the Frankfurt-based Federation of Chinese Professional Associations in Europe (全欧华人专业协会联合会) is a key umbrella group.[18] Set up in late 2001, in June 2002 it took part in an "Overseas Chinese specialists persons return (come) to China entrepreneur network symposium," a transcontinental event in Beijing, Washington, Tokyo and Frankfurt, organized by the Overseas Chinese Affairs Office (then part of the State Council and today part of the United Front Work Department under the Central Committee of the CPC. The OCAO is a key United Front organization).[19] The FCPAE bylaws state it is politically neutral ("联合会独立于任何党派，在政治和宗教方面保持中立"); this is hardly likely, given its close ties to the CPC.[20] The FCPAE has 60+ guilds; a quarter are located in Germany. They include:

- The Association of Chinese Chemists and Chemical Engineers in Germany (GCCCD, 中国旅德学者化学化工学会). This 400-person guild founded in 1988 has an address in Limburgerhof, a small town near Ludwigshafen, the headquarters of BASF, the world's largest chemical company.[21] It organizes "excellent experts and scholars" into a "Chunhui Plan delegation" that travels to China each year "to cultivate high-level talent services."[22] A five-person delegation in 2019 included scientists from the Max Planck, the German Aerospace Center (DLR, Deutsches Zentrum für Luft- und Raumfahrt), and the Swiss chemical company Clariant AG.[23] The trip was "supported" by the Ministry of Education in China and the Chinese embassy in Germany; members held meetings at half a dozen Chinese universities including several classified medium or high risk in a study by ASPI.[24] The focus: "new materials, new energies, analog computing, toxicology and chemical product safety." "Though the members of the Chunhui Plan delegation have lived and worked in Germany for many years, they have always wanted to repay their country, and hope with practical actions to promote cooperation and exchanges between China and Germany in chemistry and chemical engineering," the GCCCD website says.

- The "Society of Chinese Physicists in Germany" (Gesellschaft Chinesischer Physiker in Deutschland, 留德中国物理学者学会), has 130 members who work or study in German universities, research institutes, or companies.[25] "Many have already begun to employ different ways to serve the country," according to its website.[26] Its website says: "On May 11, 1990 the founding ceremony & the first annual meeting of GCPD took place in the Education Section of Chinese Embassy in Bonn in a simple decorated room but in a solemn atmosphere."[27] It exists "to contact Chinese physics (and similar, interdisciplinary) scholars in Germany, to promote Sino-German academic exchanges and the modernization of the motherland."

Within the FCPAE, the "Society of Chinese Computer Scientists in Germany" (Gesellschaft Chinesischer Informatiker in Deutschland, GCI, 中国留德学者计算机学会), is of special interest. Founded in 1986 and headquartered in Karlsruhe in the Southwestern state of Baden-Württemberg, 12 years after Reimar Lüst's historic trip to China, the GCI essentially set up the FCPAE, "in order to unite more overseas Chinese students in Europe."[28] A key figure in both associations is Zhou Shengzong (周盛宗),[29] a computer expert who completed a Ph.D. and worked for decades in Germany. Zhou is the former chairman (today deputy chairman) of the GCI and the longtime, founding chairman of the FCPAE. Its 500 members include many who obtained their Ph.D. in Germany, "large numbers of talents [sic] proficient in data storage, big data, digital commerce, office automatization, advanced intelligent manufacturing and robotics," according to its website.

The GCI stands out for its longevity, scale, and coordinating role. "Under the care and guidance of the education section of the Chinese embassy in Germany, the GCI has always strongly developed and promoted the scholarly exchange of overseas students and overseas Chinese in Germany."[30] It is a "work station"

(工作站) for overseas Chinese talent in Germany serving Chinese provinces and cities, with the aim of "introducing" (引进) overseas Chinese science professionals to China, and links to about 11 "stations" in Germany and China.[31] The GCI co-organized a foundational trip to China for the FCPAE 2002, establishing two "Europe Innovation Parks" (欧洲华人创业园), in Tianjin and Shanghai, and a cooperation agreement in Zhejiang province.

In a letter from December 2017 prominently displayed on the GCI website, Xi Jinping urges Chinese students overseas to repay the "ancestral country" (祖国) by bringing home knowledge. Ostensibly a Lunar New Year greeting prompted by a letter from Chinese students to the chairman, Xi repeats Mao Zedong's saying that overseas students are "the morning sun of eight or nine o'clock" (八九点钟的太阳) full of talent and promise.[32] Such correspondence between young students and leaders is part of a time-honored ritual aimed at reminding overseas students of their duty to the "motherland."[33] An accompanying text interprets the letter:

> Firstly, Chairman Xi's attention to overseas students has risen to a new level. Secondly, Chairman Xi put a focus, and specific, operational requirements, on the role of overseas students, which is to mature early in order to endure the great responsibility of becoming exceptional talents, consecrateing their skills to the motherland and the people.

The GCI's 2019 annual meeting in Hamburg was "strongly supported" by the education section of the Chinese embassy in Germany, as well as by "Morningsun Technology" (the name echoes Mao's saying), a natural language processing (NLP) and AI company that does business intelligence, sentiment analysis and text mining.[34] Morningsun's projects have included: "Building the complete simplified Chinese syntax & sentiment analysis … which connects to Facebook/Tweets and provides the real-time service. Providing deep complex analysis for social media data, big enterprises and governments."[35] Its address is the same as the GCI: a photo shows a white, brown-roofed house, on a leafy road in Karlsruhe.[36]

A traditional talent exchange organization

The China International Talent Exchange Association (known in Chinese by an older acronym, CAIEP), has a branch in Germany. Nominally an NGO, the CAIEP is a front organization for the State Administration of Foreign Experts Affairs (SAFEA, 国家外国专家局), in Beijing (see Chapter 11).

Its representative, Yuan Xudong (袁旭东), described his work in a 2018 article on the website of International Talent online media[37] as procuring "foreign talent" for China and organizing the records and contacts of "Thousand Talents" plan scientists in Germany and Chinese "friendship prizes" recipients, among other things. CAIEP maintains a close relationship to ALBA Recycling Gmbh, a waste management business in Berlin, according to the report, which marked the 30th anniversary of the association's Germany office. Alba sponsors the capital's beloved basketball team, which bears its name.

The city of Cologne appears also to play a significant role in the CAIEP's work: Yuan has organized "city management" and "foreigner management" personnel exchanges between Cologne and Beijing, Tianjin and Hangzhou for China's "Chengguan" city management force (城管) and Germany's "Ordnungsamt."[38] At a 2012 event in Cologne to mark the 25th anniversary of the founding of the CAIEP in Germany, Li Bing (李兵), the deputy head of SAFEA, noted that since 1987 the organization had helped bring 5,000 of "all kinds of German retired experts" to China to work, and China had sent tens of thousands of "trainees" to Germany."[39] Li did not specify in what areas.

A new style technology exchange association

Reflecting changes in a global technology and business landscape increasingly driven by AI, in 2018, a new association began work: the Berlin-based, "German–Chinese Association of Artificial Intelligence," (GCAAI, 德中人工智能协会, also addressed in Chapter 11).[40] Its slogan: "We boost the exchange of education, research and public resources between Germany and China in the field of Artificial Intelligence."[41] GCAAI says it has more than 400 members, "academic researchers, industry entrepreneurs, tech leaders, who live or work in Germany or China." Berlin has a flourishing start-up scene.

Its deputy chairman, Wu Hao (吴昊), is a "National Youth Thousand Talents" member and the former head of a research group at the Zuse Institute Berlin (ZIB).[42] Wu obtained a Ph.D. from the Free University of Berlin. The chairman of the GCAAI, Xiao Han (肖涵), works at Tencent's AI laboratory in China,[43] after obtaining his Ph.D. at the Technical University Munich before working for the Berlin-based fashion and digital company Zalando.[44] In 2018, the association organized a trip for Germany-based start-ups in Shenzhen and Beijing. In a telephone interview, a German participant on the trip said the key interest among Chinese counterparts the Germans met was in domain expertise, and the application of technologies.[45]

Austria: a politics and technology transfer organizational cluster

In Austria, "PASCO," the "Promotion Association for Scientific and Technological Cooperation between Austria and China" (奥中科技交流协会), set up in 2011, provides "strategic consulting and collaboration services for both governments and enterprises."[46] Its more than 100 members are:

> variously active in Austrian universities, research institutes, industrial companies and government agencies as full professors, associate professors,

internationally-known company executives, high-level engineers at multinational companies, as well as department heads and technical officials in government agencies, and high-level technical officials in United Nations agencies.[47]

In addition to working in classic S&T areas such as IT and energy, members work in architecture, geography, economics and translation, illustrating the CPC's "whole of society" approach.[48]

PASCO held its 2019 annual gathering at the Chinese Culture Center in Vienna (维也纳中国文化中心) belonging to the European Times Group (欧洲时报集团),[49] a Paris-based overseas Chinese, pan-European media in frequent contact and cooperation with the China News Service (中中国通信社) which is part of the United Front. According to a first-hand account, *European Times* was founded at the suggestion of diplomats at the cultural section of the Chinese embassy in Paris.[50] Diplomats from the science and technology section of the Chinese embassy in Vienna participated in the 2019 PASCO event, attended by around 100 overseas Chinese professionals in Austria.[51]

Another organizational cluster is the Austria–China International Economic and Trade Promotion Association (OECGIW, 奥中国际经济贸易促进会). Founded in 2002 it is located in Bad Schallerbach in Upper Austria; its 150 members are expected "to introduce foreign advanced technology and various forms of foreign economic and technological cooperation, and promote Austria's cooperation with China and other countries."[52] This is also UF territory: the OECGIW appears to have several overlapping identities, being connected also to the "Chinese Association for Cross Strait Relations in Austria" (奥地利华人海峡两岸关系促进会)—the organizations share a logo and acronym—with the OECGIW reportedly the first overseas organization founded by, or "upon the basis of," the United Front's core "China Council for the Promotion of Peaceful National Reunification (中国和平统一促进会), in Beijing.[53] This clutch of Austria-based, overseas S&T and UF, organizations shows clearly how technology and political influence are intimately tied for the CPC— the goal is state building. These CPC-linked structures exist in all European countries.

Professors

A "Society for German Professors of Chinese Origin" (GDPCH, 德国华人教授学会), founded in 2006, aims "to act in an interdisciplinary way at the nexus of science, economy, politics and society," according to its website.[54] It "especially supports the scientific and academic exchange between Germany and China."[55] Today its members, full professors at German universities, number about 50.[56] A founding deputy chairperson studied and taught for ten years as a cartographer at the Institute of Surveying and Mapping of the People's Liberation Army.[57] GDPCH events have been supported by the German government and major academic organizations and foundations, including the Alexander von Humboldt-Stiftung and the DAAD.[58] According to a 2019 report in *European Times* (欧洲时报), it aims to be more than a mutual support group: "We hope to turn the forum into a think tank for scholarly, educational, science and technology exchanges, and furnish recommendations to both the governments and all levels of society."[59] Its annual meeting at the University of Göttingen that year was also attended by representatives of universities in China, a diplomat from the Chinese embassy in Berlin and a handful of German academics, and supported by the Confucius Institute Göttingen.[60] From the society's website it appears these fora are held in alternate years in Germany and China; host universities in China have been identified as "medium" to "very high" security risk.[61]

At the Göttingen meeting, Hou Zhengmeng (侯正猛), an professor of engineering at the Clausthal University of Technology (TUC), introduced cooperation between TUC and Sichuan University.[62] Hou is reportedly a recipient of both the Thousand Talents Plan and Chunhui Plan, according to a Chinese media report,[63] and helped set up a joint campus between Sichuan University and the TUC, the TUC/SCU Sino-German International College.[64] In 2018, Hou traveled to Sichuan University's College of Electronics and Information Engineering to discuss "lasers and matter" (激光与物质) with scientists at its photoelectronic technology laboratory.[65] Sichuan University has been assessed as "very high" risk in terms of collaboration.[66] Hou is also the head of an institute for environment, energy and technology at the Sichuan University College of Architecture and Environment, according to the international office of the university.[67]

Technology transfer at German research institutes

Germany has a large network of research institutes outside of universities.[68] Some major ones:

Forschungszentrum Jülich (FZJ), mentioned above, is one of the largest publicly funded ones.[69] In 2017, Wang Shunbing (王顺兵), who works at a science management center belonging to the Ministry of Science and Technology (MOST),[70] studied Germany's science research management system (德国的科研管理体制) at FZJ. Addressing its CSSA he compared the German and Chinese research systems; China should learn from Germany's focus on talent resource creation and support for small-and-medium enterprises, the CSSAFZJ WeChat account said. Wang gave a not-so-subtle hint to students to take their technology and knowledge home: "Use your own science and technology hard power" (用自己的硬实力) "and the state's great support for science and technology to push forward the remarkable undertaking of China's science research development."[71]

After its early start in China in 1974, the *Max-Planck-Gesellschaft* has sought to train Chinese researchers and, effectively, transfer skills, providing them "with an attractive opportunity to return to their home country."[72] "In order to intensify cooperation and bring about enduring changes to the Chinese research system," it set up "partner groups" with CAS in areas including cosmology, material and plant research, chemistry and mathematics. It co-founded a Partner Institute for Computational Biology (PICB) with CAS in Shanghai in 2005. The institute focuses on "the interface between biology, theory and modelling."[73]

In September 2019, the German National Academy of Sciences Leopoldina signed a "Beijing Declaration" vowing to pursue basic science with CAS. The declaration describes plans for apparently untrammeled cooperation.[74] Significantly, the document includes a key Chinese political phrase in its foundational goals, which demonstrates how the CPC's political language and concepts are being mainstreamed in Europe along with practical cooperation: "With the clear vision of a common future for all of humankind" (人类命运共同体) "we have to break down barriers, support research cooperation across disciplines, institutions and national boundaries, allow the free and independent interaction of scientific schools and cultures and foster long-term, stable, reliable and trustful collaboration."[75] The Beijing Declaration is prefaced with a pithy, eight-character, traditional-style Chinese couplet: "面向未来, 探索未知" (Face the future, Explore the unknown).[76] A spokeswoman for Leopoldina said that the institute had made sure to anchor concepts in the declaration "which have not been put into practice in China," such as academic freedom.[77]

The state-funded *Helmholtz-Gemeinschaft*,[78] with about 18 centers in Germany, opened an office in Beijing in 2004.[79] "China is a miracle," said its Beijing representative.[80] "We should always bear in mind that one fifth of the world population lives here and that the country has an unbelievably dynamic economy and tremendous research potential. From either perspective, our scientists and researchers should not hesitate to go to China, to establish contacts and to start-up win–win projects," he said.[81]

Yet German universities and research institutes often lack expertise and caution in selecting Chinese partners. In 2016, the *Helmholtz–Zentrum Dresden–Rossendorf*[82] (HZDR) signed a memorandum of understanding[83] with the Chinese Academy of Engineering Physics (CAEP, 中国工程物理研究院),[84] in the Chinese consulate in Hamburg.[85] The CAEP develops China's nuclear weapons and high-energy lasers[86] and is on the US Department of Commerce's Entity List.[87]

The Helmholtz International Beamline for Extreme Fields (HIBEF) laboratory, where the cooperation was to take place, said it was pleased about the "substantial international interest."[88] On the German side, the project also involved DESY *(Deutsches Elektronen-Synchrotron)*, an advanced physics institute (and also part of the Helmholtz-Gemeinschaft).[89] DESY, in turn, is part of the world's largest X-ray laser project, the European XFEL. This aims to produce the world's fastest, brightest X-ray flashes, to study processes occurring deep inside planets, see the atomic structure of viruses,[90] and investigate matter under extreme conditions including high pressure, temperatures, or electromagnetic fields.[91]

"We very much welcome the renewed interest from China as our CAEP colleagues have knowhow in high-intensity lasers and high energy density physics that will help make HIBEF possible," Roland Sauerbrey of the HZDR scientific management board.[92] The European XFEL scientific director Thomas Tschentscher said, "We are happy to see the planned cooperation between CAEP, and Helmholtz–Zentrum Dresden–Rossendorf as the lead organization of HIBEF, complementing planned and existing cooperation and collaboration with European XFEL," adding, "We would welcome if these were the first steps to make China a partner in European XFEL." A student exchange was also planned. Yet the cooperation ended in 2019 after discussions with the Federal Ministry of Education and Research (BMBF), "due to security concerns" and "to exclude all eventualities," a HZDR spokesperson said.[93]

European XFEL itself has other links to the CAEP that began in 2015, when its director, Liu Cangli (刘仓理)[94]—Liu has deputy minister status—and European XFEL signed a collaboration agreement on "future exchange of staff and students" and the "development of instrumentation for European XFEL" by the CAEP. The academy aimed to "spearhead" research into X-ray lasers of this type across China.[95] "We are very happy about the involvement of the CAEP, and we greatly appreciate their interest in the European XFEL. Their expertise across many areas of physics and engineering will be of considerable value to the research at this facility," European XFEL managing director Massimo Altarelli said in 2015.[96] DESY also has contacts with CAEP through individual researchers.[97] The status of some of the above ties is currently unclear.

There is also collaboration between European XFEL and scientists from the Chinese Academy of Sciences (CAS). In 2018, German and Chinese scientists agreed to set up a "CAS Helmholtz International Laboratory for FEL [free-electron laser] research," CHILFEL. The partners are DESY, European XFEL, the Shanghai Institute for Applied Physics (SINAP, part of CAS),[98] and ShanghaiTech University; in all 25 scientists from China and Hamburg, where XFEL and DESY are located, are to be involved.[99] DESY has cooperated with CAS since 1977, according to the website of the Chinese consulate in Hamburg.[100] "All our Chinese partners emphasize the civilian use of their work," a DESY spokesperson said.[101] CAS and Sichuan University (see above) are among CAEP's many collaboration partner in China.[102]

Other German researchers have cooperated with CAEP. In 2017, for more than a year, a visiting researcher from CAEP worked at the Max-Born-Institut (MBI) in Berlin, which conducts basic research on the interaction of light and matter. The researcher was funded by a stipend from the Chinese government, according to MBI director Stefan Eisebitt.[103] Eisebitt said there was no indication the Chinese researcher was involved in military research.[104] Researchers from Chinese military universities have in the past worked at German universities while concealing their military affiliations.[105] One is professor Hu Changhua (胡昌华), who in scientific publications—like a book he co-authored for SpringerNature[106]—said he worked for a "High-Tech Research Institute" in Xi'an (西安高技术研究所).[107] This apparently is a cover name of the PLA Rocket Force Engineering University

(RFEU, 火箭军工程大学), where Hu was a professor; he is reported to be a Major General of the People's Liberation Army and head of the Military Key Lab on Missile Testing and Control Technology.[108] Hu spent about 3 months in 2008 at the University of Duisburg-Essen, according to his CV. The university was not aware of Hu's background, a spokesperson said in 2019.[109] There were no special background checks. Hu stayed at the university's guest house, paying his own expenses.[110]

Espionage: the sharp end

Relatively little attention is paid at Germany's research institutes or universities (and elsewhere in Europe) to possible espionage by visiting researchers, according to a study by legal scholars at the Max-Planck-Gesellschaft.[111] Researchers are urged by institutions to cooperate, despite espionage concerns, in order to receive grant money: "The German state in this way finances spying on research results in their own country," one said.

Researchers quoted in the study said they did question incoming applications critically. A particular problem is transfer of knowhow by employees after leaving an organization. Yet if legends were created, with fake certificates, there was "no chance of finding out" about deception, an interviewee said.[112] An Austrian interviewee said that negligent handling of data by research partners was also sometimes a problem, leading to a loss of trust in the collaborator. The "worst-case scenario" was the outright loss of confidential data, in this case belonging to industry partners, the person said. One interviewee said that their organization had observed Chinese scientists sometimes brought with them other "forces that guide the researchers," with elaborating. Others spoke about illegal photographing on campus or theft of laptops containing research data, prototypes, or drafts of devices. Theft has also been uncovered by detecting the outflow of a large amount of data, a missing laptop, violations of regulations on the use of equipment, or by finding research results at a competing research organization.

"With a few exceptions," awareness was lacking "at all levels of the hierarchy, including at institutes belonging to the large German research associations," the report noted.[113] German research institutions see their mission as to educate and consider themselves more or less "open houses." In Germany and in Denmark, some organizations said they did not file legal complaints, since they assumed that police would not help anyway.

Its 2018 annual report, the domestic counterintelligence agency, the Federal Office for the Protection of the Constitution (Bundesamt für Verfassungsschutz, BfV), warned that China's secret services "intensively elicit the work areas and knowledge potential of Chinese scientists who work in Germany. Through friendly relationships and informal contacts, they try to win selected persons from these circles to work with them ('non-professionals')."[114]

A case study: Lanxess

Few cases of economic or industrial espionage come to public attention, making a recent case at Lanxess, a chemical company in Cologne that was part of Bayer until 2004, unusual.

According to court documents obtained by the authors, a Chinese employee who had been in charge of a Lanxess production site in Shanghai between 2004 and 2008 moved to Germany in 2010 to work as a senior technical employee at headquarters. He stole trade secrets that helped accomplices back in China build a parallel production site.[115] The intellectual property (IP) in question is marketed by Lanxess under the name Velcorin; the chemical substance, dimethyl dicarbonate, can be used as a beverage preservative or sterilant.

Between 2011 and 2013 the employee copied about 1,000 documents to a hard disk and sent emails with scientific information to a former colleague in Shanghai, including a customer list for the product.[116] In 2016, the accomplices approached Lanxess customers at a congress of the International Society of Beverage Technologists in the United States, offering the dimethyl dicarbonate produced in China. In 2018, the Düsseldorf Labor Court convicted the man on "unfair competition" laws, ordering him to pay more than 166,000 euros in compensation.[117] According to court documents, Lanxess succeeded in enforcing an order for preservation of evidence at a court in China, however, any outcome is so far unknown.[118] Lanxess also filed a criminal complaint in the state of North Rhine-Westphalia, where Cologne is located, that led to raids and an arraignment at a district court in Cologne in 2018.[119] As of March 2020, that case was still ongoing.[120]

Overall, according to one report, "Ascertaining the scope of industrial and economic espionage is challenging in Europe, as researchers are faced with a lack of statistical data."[121] Prosecution rates are low. One sample of 713 cases of industrial espionage from all sources found just 7.2 percent resulted in prosecution.[122] In "economic espionage," where state actors are involved, as opposed to "industrial espionage" (commercial espionage), the difficulties are even more extreme.

Weak law enforcement

Economic and scientific espionage involving foreign state agents can be prosecuted either as espionage or treason in Germany. In addition, the forbidden transfer of trade secrets (industrial espionage) as well as espionage of data and violation of private or official secrets, can be persecuted as a criminal offense.[123] However, there are gaps in criminal liability, according to academics researching the field.[124]

"Due to the close intertwining of the state and the economy in China, it's hardly possible in individual cases to differentiate between state-driven, economic espionage, and spying by competing firms," the BfV has said.[125] The Lanxess case demonstrated this perfectly: In its 2018 report, the BfV noted that "despite diverse indicators of involvement of Chinese state bodies," charges could, initially, only be brought under competition laws. As China strives to realize its ambitious program to dominate key high-tech industries by 2025 ("Made in China 2025"), Germany's security interests may be impaired, the BfV warns. China's "secret services occupy a special position" in achieving the goal of technological leadership. These are supported by both state-owned and private companies at home, and their methods are diversifying.[126] "While in the past, people with Chinese roots have been recruited as agents, the services now increasingly try to recruit persons from Western countries."

Like the United States, Germany is federally structured country, meaning that action at the states level is important. According to the Baden-Württemberg State Office for the Protection of the Constitution (Landesamt für Verfassungsschutz, LfV), "there is a high risk" that people with specific, sought-after expertise will be deceived into sharing information, forced to release it, or recruited for espionage.[127] Its counterpart in North Rhine-Westphalia warns against giving confidential information to a "friend" who has in reality merely been cultivating political and economic contacts for the PRC. "In addition, China uses Chinese permanently living here, guest scientists, students or interns temporarily in Germany for illegal transfer of knowledge."[128]

A key reason for difficulty bringing charges in all these situations is a veritable jungle of responsibilities, with victims sometimes unsure who to turn to. In brief, the choice is whether to appeal to the state (Länder) or federal (Bund) authorities, with police, prosecutors and intelligence agencies at all these levels. The agencies all gather statistics and may record events according to different parameters. The issues reflect something profound about Germany; its highly federal structure, established after 1945 to distribute power across the country and avoid dictatorship ever growing again. Amid rising power competition and tensions in the transatlantic relationship that has long underpinned Germany's security, this arrangement raises questions about national security and S&T management.

Notes

1 Joachim Krüger (ed.), "Beiträge zur Geschichte der Beziehungen der DDR—VR China—Erinnerungen und Untersuchungen," *Berliner China Studien* Nr. 41, 2002. www.geschkult.fu-berlin.de/e/oas/sinologie/publikationen/bchst/bchst41/index.html.
2 *People's Daily*, http://german.people.com.cn/209048/8594661.html.
3 "40 Years of Cooperation between the Max Planck Society and the Chinese Academy of Sciences," Max-Planck-Gesellschaft. www.mpg.de/8198951/40-years-cas-mpg. The society says Europe is losing ground to China: "Europe is facing fierce global competition and losing ground to the USA and China in scientific and technological terms," www.mpg.de/13558942/horizon-Europe. However, concern centers on whether the European Union's "Horizon Europe" funding program, to begin in 2021, will commit enough funds, rather than loss of research through technology transfer. Anecdotal reports told to the authors suggest the leaders of some institutes

and universities are aware of large-scale, deliberate technology extraction by "teams of Chinese scientists," but decline to go public.

4 Ibid.

5 Federal Ministry of Education and Research, BMBF. www.bmbf.de/en/china-cooperating-closely-to-meet-global-challenges-2211.html.

6 BMBF, "The China Strategy 2015–2020," www.bmbf.de/en/the-china-strategy-2015-2020-2345.html. For updated figures, see www.internationale-hochschulkooperationen.de/statistik/act/stat.html?tx_szcooperationsearch_pi2%5Bcontroller%5D=CooperationResults.

7 For German cooperation in fusion (军民融合) or military-use areas, see the section "Technology Transfer at German Research Institutes." Partners have included the Chinese Academy of Engineering Physics (CAEP 中国工程物理研究院). www.caep.ac.cn/.

8 https://liudediy.com/Organization/xuelian_detail/id/b295djJrMHhMNkFtSg%253D%253D.html. See also, Didi Kirsten Tatlow, "The Chinese Influence Effort Hiding in Plain Sight," *The Atlantic*, July 12, 2019.

9 Communication with the authors, December 9, 2019.

10 www.vcwsa.rwth-aachen.de/.

11 Ibid.

12 Portal of the Forschungszentrum Jülich, www.fz-juelich.de/portal/EN/Home/home_node.html;jsessionid=308AFC0A502B660DEF8130D0AD4A9CF2.

13 Accessed January 2020, CSSAFZJ, https://mp.weixin.qq.com/s/XnwULpwbupWDsWTbpTVdhw by March 2020 this WeChat post had been deleted. Archived here: https://archive.is/rTJGG.

14 Ibid.

15 Communications with the authors, December 3 and 6, 2019.

16 Ibid, CSSAFZJ, above.

17 Of the 17 associations in Germany that engage in technology transfer, eight list the number of dues-paying members in their organizations, nine do not. The median number of members in a Chinese professional association was 334, and the average was 317. We could confirm that at least 2,538 people are members of technology transfer associations in Germany. For the remaining nine groups, we used the median (334 people) to estimate that an additional 3,000 people may be members of the associations with unknown membership counts. For more detail contact the authors.

18 www.fcpae.com.

19 全欧华人专业协会联合会大事记, "Major event record of the FCPAE," www.fcpae.com/?page_id=666.

20 全欧华人专业协会联合会章程, FCPAE bylaws, www.fcpae.com/?page_id=660.

21 In German: Gesellschaft Chinesischer Chemiker und Chemieingenieure in der Bundes republik Deutschland. www.gcccd.de/cn/.

22 中国旅德学者化学化工学会2019年"春晖计划"代表团短期回国访问, www.gcccd.de/cn/newsgcccd/276-2019chunhui.html.

23 Deutsches Zentrum für Luft- und Raumfahrt (DLR): www.dlr.de/DE/Home/home_node.html.

24 https://unitracker.aspi.org.au/ and www.aspi.org.au/report/china-defence-universities-tracker.

25 GCPD website accessed 4 March, 2020, www.gcpd.de/about/.

26 Ibid.

27 www.gcpd.de/about/founding.htm.

28 www.gci-online.de/index.php?option=com_content&view=article&id=124:2016-01-09-15-25-35.

29 周盛宗 (Zhou Shengzong), 闽侨网 (Minqiao wang), http://minqw.fjsen.com/2014-11/07/content_15178889.htm.

30 关怀指导下, "Under the care and guidance."
31 For a list of the "overseas talent work stations" (海外人才工作站). www.gci-online. de/index.php?option=com_content&view=article&id=124&Itemid=410. Described variously as 工作站, 联络处, 联络站, 联络点 or 合作中心.
32 世界是属于你们的 (The world belongs to you), Mao Zedong, Moscow, Nov. 17, 1957, www.people.com.cn/GB/shizheng/252/7955/7958/20020422/714354.html.
33 Didi Kirsten Tatlow, "From Chinese Students in Germany, a Technology Promise to the Motherland," Sinosphere, *New York Times*, January 20, 2014.
34 www.morningsun-technology.com/.
35 http://morningsun-technology.com/projects.html.
36 Addresses can be compared here: http://morningsun-technology.com/contact.html and www.gci-online.de/index.php?option=com_contact&view=contact&id=1&Ite mid=349.
37 www.caiep.net/.
38 https://wenku.baidu.com/view/838ffab0814d2b160b4e767f5acfa1c7ab0082c6.html.
39 http://frankfurt.china-consulate.org/chn/sbwl/t941863.htm.
40 Deutsch-Chinesische Verein zur künstlichen Intelligenz, www.gcaai.org/ LinkedIn, www.linkedin.com/company/gcaai.
41 Ibid.
42 The Zuse Institute Berlin (ZIB). Specializes in mathematics, data, and computing: www. zib.de/.
43 GCAAI board: www.gcaai.org/#board.
44 Zalando, founded in Berlin in 2008: "We want to become the operating system for fashion." https://corporate.zalando.com/en/company/who-we-are.
45 Interview with the author, on background, 2019.
46 For "PASCO," see logo on homepage, www.pasconet.at/ Austrian-Chinese Association of Exchange Promotion of Science and Technology (ACST, 奥中科技交流促进协会), www.chinaqw.com/hqhr/2014/04-23/1580.shtml. Also on a United Front website for overseas Chinese, www.chinaqw.com/kong/2014/06-10/6015.shtml.
47 www.pasconet.at/2017/03/27/new-blog-post2/.
48 Ibid.
49 欧洲时报维也纳中国文化中心 (European Times Vienna China Culture Center). www.oushinet.com/static/activitySpace/Vienna.html.
50 Interview with the author, on background. "'Tell the Chinese Story Well': China's Great External Propaganda in Europe," Henry Jackson Society, December 2019. https://henryjacksonsociety.org/wp-content/uploads/2019/12/HJS-Sharp-Power-Report-FINAL.pdf.
51 www.pasconet.at.
52 www.oecgiw.com/indexmain0.html.
53 OECGIW and China Council for the Promotion of Peaceful National Reunification (中国和平统一促进会), www.oecgiw.com/news/20091106/20091106rmw.htm. Wu Ken (吴恳), appointed ambassador to Germany in 2019, attended the founding ceremony in 2009 as ambassador to Austria.
54 德国华人教授学会, Gesellschaft für Deutsche Professoren Chinesischer Herkunft. (GDPCH), http://gdpch.de/en/verschiedenes/Gu-Rede-Festakt.pdf.
55 http://gdpch.de/en/index.htm.
56 http://gdpch.de/en/mitglieder/mitglieder.htm.
57 The first chairman, Gu Xuewu (辜学武) is head of the Center for Global Studies at the University of Bonn. www.politik-soziologie.uni-bonn.de/de/personal/prof.-dr.-xuewu-gu Gu is also listed as an "expert" on the website of the Center for China & Globalization (全球化智库) in Beijing, a United Front organization. www.ccg.org. cn/Expert/Eview.aspx?Id=607). The founding deputy chairperson, Meng Liqiu (孟立秋) has been a professor of cartography at the Technical University of Munich for over two decades. www.professoren.tum.de/en/meng-liqiu/.

58 DAAD, the German Academic Exchange Service, www.daad.de/en/.

59 欧洲时报 (European Times) www.oushinet.com/qj/qjnews/20190517/321506.html.

60 The Georg-August-Universität Göttingen, www.uni-goettingen.de/en/80169. html?id=5430.

61 https://unitracker.aspi.org.au/.

62 Hou Zhengmeng (侯正猛) is Professor and Head of Rock Mechanics, Energy Research Center of Lower Saxony & Institute of Petroleum Engineering, http://gdpch.de/en/mitglieder/ZhengmengHou.htm.

63 For an account of Hou's status as a recipient of the Thousand Talents Plan and Chunhui Plan: https://nanchong.scol.com.cn/sdxw/201909/57061220.html. According to the report, Hou received funding from the Chunhui Plan in 2003 bringing him back to China, and has been professionally engaged there since.

64 A report by the International Office of Sichuan University, http://global.scu.edu. cn/?channel/63/115/_/2161.

65 College of Electronics and Information Engineering, Sichuan University, in English, www.scu.edu.cn/eneieen/. In Chinese, http://eie.scu.edu.cn/index. jsp?urltype=tree.TreeTempUrl&wbtreeid=1001 Hou's 2018 visit, http://eie.scu.edu. cn/info/1038/5477.htm.

66 https://unitracker.aspi.org.au/.

67 College of Architecture and Environment, Sichuan University, http://acem.scu.edu. cn/ International Office: http://global.scu.edu.cn/?news/1673.

68 "Research in Germany, Land of Ideas," Federal Ministry of Education and Research, www.research-in-germany.org/en/research-landscape/research-organisations. html.

69 www.fz-juelich.de/portal/EN/Home/home_node.html.

70 Wang Shunbing (王顺兵), 德国科技管理特点及启示 (Characteristics and Lessons of German Science and Technology Management), in 全球科技经济瞭望 (*Global Science, Technology and Economy Outlook)*, April 2017.

71 WeChat account of CSSAFZJ, 22 May, 217, https://mp.weixin.qq.com/s/_Xusu6ncs1 yg8VsXdJ0f7w.

72 Max-Planck-Gesellschaft, www.mpg.de/china.

73 Ibid.

74 The 2019 Beijing Declaration, Chinese: www.leopoldina.org/uploads/tx_leopubli-cation/2019_Beijing_declaration_chin_signed_web_01.pdf English: www.leopoldina. org/en/publications/detailview/publication/beijing-declaration-on-basic-science-2019-1/.

75 Xinhua, "A community of shared future for all humankind," www.xinhuanet.com/ english/2017-03/20/c_136142216.htm For critical analysis, www.hongkongfp. com/2017/10/14/china-pushes-human-rights-chinese-characteristics-un/.

76 For a discussion of the socio-political significance of this kind of language: Perry Link, "An Anatomy of Chinese, Rhythm, Metaphor, Politics," 2013.

77 Email communication with Leopoldina spokeswoman, January 8, 2020.

78 Homepage: www.helmholtz.de/en/.

79 www.helmholtz.de/ueber_uns/die_gemeinschaft/internationale_bueros/buero_ peking/.

80 "Helmholtz and China, Strategic Alliances for a Better Future," Helmholtz Association of National Research Centers, www.helmholtz.de/fileadmin/user_upload/publikationen/ pdf/Helmholtz_and_China.pdf.

81 Ibid.

82 Helmholtz-Zentrum Dresden-Rossendorf, www.hzdr.de/db/Cms?pNid=0.

83 www.hzdr.de/db/Cms?pNid=139&pLang=de Agreement to be part of European XFEL, a project to create the world's fastest X-ray laser. www.xfel.eu/facility/ overview/index_eng.html.

84 中国工程物理研究院 (China Academy of Engineering Physics), www.caep.ac.cn/ According to the Entity List of the US Department of Commerce, CAEP has 17 aliases, www.ecfr.gov/cgi-bin/retrieveECFR?gp=1&SID=9ae4a21068f2bd41d4a5ae e843b63ef1&ty=HTML&h=L&n=15y2.1.3.4.28&r=PART.

85 Photo of signing ceremony, www.hzdr.de/db/Cms?pOid=46412&pNid=99&p Lang=de.

86 "CAEP's four main tasks are to develop nuclear weapons, research microwaves and lasers for nuclear fusion ignition and directed-energy weapons, study technologies related to conventional weapons, and deepen military–civil fusion." https://web. archive.org/web/20190926042240/http:/www.job.sdu.edu.cn/info/1016/1239. htm Via Joske, www.aspi.org.au/report/china-defence-universities-tracker.

87 The Entity List "identifies foreign parties that ... present a greater risk of diversion to weapons of mass destruction (WMD) programs, terrorism, or other activities contrary to US national security and/or foreign policy interests." www.bis.doc.gov/index. php/policy-guidance/lists-of-parties-of-concern/entity-list.

88 www.hzdr.de/db/Cms?pOid=46412&pNid=99&pLang=de For a list of those present: www.hzdr.de/db/Cms?pNid=no&pOid=46413.

89 DESY: www.desy.de/about_desy/desy/index_eng.html.

90 www.xfel.eu/facility/overview/index_eng.html.

91 www.xfel.eu/news_and_events/news/index_eng.html?openDirectAnchor=1294& two_columns=0.

92 Ibid.

93 Hinnerk Feldwisch-Drentrup, "Wenn der Gastprofessor Generalmajor der Volksbefreiungsarmee ist," *Die Welt*, December 27, 2019.

94 刘仓理院长 (Director Liu Cangli), See Liu's appointment by the State Council in 2015. www.gov.cn/xinwen/2015-09/15/content_2931983.htm?agt=2/.

95 www.xfel.eu/news_and_events/news/index_eng.html?openDirectAnchor=1208& two_columns=0.

96 Ibid.

97 Hinnerk Feldwisch-Drentrup. "Soft Power aus dem Reich der Mitte," *Frankfurter Allgemeine Zeitung*. February 15, 2020.

98 Shanghai Institute for Applied Physics. http://english.sinap.cas.cn/.

99 www.xfel.eu/news_and_events/news/index_eng.html?openDirectAnchor=1633.

100 科技合作需要开放 ("Science and Technology Cooperation Must Be Open"), May 22, 2019. http://hamburg.china-consulate.org/chn/zlgxx/t1665662.htm.

101 Ibid.

102 ASPI, https://unitracker.aspi.org.au/universities/chinese-academy-of-engineering-physics/.

103 Author communication, July 29, 2019.

104 Ibid.

105 Alex Joske, "Picking Flowers, Making Honey, Australian Strategic Policy Institute, October 30, 2018.

106 Kong Xiangyu, Hu Changhua, and Duan Zhansheng, *Principal Component Analysis Networks and Algorithms*, Berlin, Germany: Springer, 2017. www.springer.com/de/ book/9789811029134.

107 *International Journal of Systems Science*, Taylor & Francis Online. www.tandfonline. com/doi/abs/10.1080/00207721.2012.749547.

108 Alex Joske, citing CCTV, www.aspi.org.au/report/picking-flowers-making-honey.

109 Hinnerk Feldwisch-Drentrup, "Wenn der Gastprofessor Generalmajor der Volksbefreiungsarmee ist," *Die Welt*, December 27, 2019.

110 Hinnerk Feldwisch-Drentrup. "Soft Power aus dem Reich der Mitte," *Frankfurter Allgemeine Zeitung*, February 15, 2020.

111 https://wiskos.de/en/publications_presentations/publications.html.

112 Ibid.
113 Ibid.
114 Bundesministerium des Inneren, für Bau und Heimat, Verfassungsschutzbericht 2018. www.verfassungsschutz.de/embed/vsbericht-2018.pdf.
115 Landesarbeitsgericht Düsseldorf (State Labor Court Düsseldorf), June 28, 2019, https://openjur.de/u/2179569.html.
116 Ibid.
117 https://openjur.de/u/2179569.html.
118 Ibid.
119 https://de.reuters.com/article/deutschland-lanxess-spionage-idDEKCN1PT0MR.
120 Communication by the author with the court.
121 Susanne Knickmeier, "Spies without Borders? The Phenomena of Economic and Industrial Espionage and the Deterrence Strategies of Germany and Other Selected European Countries," *Security Journal*, 33, no. 1 (2020): 6–26.
122 Ibid, Table 6.
123 Sabine Carl, "Wissenschaftsspionage—Risiken für den deutschen Forschungsstandort?" www.mpg.de/12584445/Handlungsleitfaden_Wissenschaftsorganisationen_final.pdf.
124 Ibid.
125 BfV, www.verfassungsschutz.de/embed/vsbericht-2018.pdf.
126 Ibid.
127 Baden-Württemberg LfV, www.baden-wuerttemberg.de/fileadmin/redaktion/m-im/intern/dateien/pdf/20190606_Verfassungsschutzbericht_2018.pdf.
128 North Rhine-Westphalia LfV, www.im.nrw/system/files/media/document/file/VS_Bericht_2018.pdf.

Bibliography

Baden-Württemberg Ministerium für Inneres, Digitalisieren und Migration. *Verfassungs-schutzbericht 2018*, published 2019.

Bundesministerium des Inneren, für Bau und Heimat. *Verfassungsschutzbericht 2018*, published 2019.

European Union. "Agreement for Scientific and Technological Cooperation between the European Community and the Government of the People's Republic of China," December 22, 1998. https://ec.europa.eu/research/iscp/pdf/policy/china-agreement.pdf#view=fit&pagemode=none.

European Union/PwC. *The Scale and Impact of Industrial Espionage and Theft of Trade Secrets through Cyber*, Publications Office of the European Union, March 11, 2019.

Joske, Alex. "Picking Flowers, Making Honey," Australian Strategic Policy Institute, October 23, 2018.

Knickmeier, Susanne. "Spies without Borders? The Phenomena of Economic and Industrial Espionage and the Deterrence Strategies of Germany and other Selected European Countries," *Security Journal*, 33, no. 1 (2020): 6–26.

Krüger, Joachim (ed.). "Beiträge zur Geschichte der Beziehungen der DDR-VR China—Erinnerungen und Untersuchunge," *Berliner China Studien* Nr. 41. 2002.

Landesarbeitsgericht Düsseldorf. *openJur* 2019, 30835, June 28, 2018–8 Sa 379/17. https://openjur.de/u/2179569.html.

Meissner, Werner and Anje Feege. *Die DDR und China, 1949 bis 1989: Politik-Wirtschaft-Kultur*, Berlin: Akademie Verlag, 1995.

Nordrhein-Westfalen Innen Ministerium. *Verfassungsschutzbericht des Landes Nordrhein-Westfalen über das Jahr 2018*.

PRC Central Committee of the CPC and State Council. 中共中央、国务院关于进一步加强人才工作的决定 ("Decision on Further Enhancing the Development of Human Resources"), December 26, 2003.

Sinopsis, and Oriental Institute of the Czech Academy of Sciences. Conference papers, "Mapping China's Footprint in the World II," Prague, 2019.

US Senate Permanent Subcommittee on Investigations. *Threats to the U.S. Research Enterprise: China's Talent Recruitment Plans*, 2019.

Wallwaey, Elisa, Esther Bollhöfer, and Susanne Knickmeier (eds). *Wirtschaftsspionage und Konkurrenzausspähung. Phänomenologie, Strafverfolgung und Prävention in ausgewählten europäischen Ländern*, Max Planck Institute for the Study of Crime, Security and Law, Vol. K 187, Berlin: Duncker & Humblot, 2020.

9

JAPAN AND SOUTH KOREA

William C. Hannas and Huey-Meei Chang

China's technology transfer activities in Northeast Asia mimic its behavior elsewhere in the world, as chronicled in this book's preceding chapters. The same pattern of state initiatives and diaspora support used in its dealings with the United States and Europe are evidenced in its approach to Japan and South Korea.

Ironically, many transfer techniques fielded by China were pioneered by Japan in the post-war era, and later by South Korea, during their own rise to prominence, albeit with differences in scale. And just as the United States until recently abetted China's technological development, or turned a blind eye to the matter, so too did Japan and Korea at first welcome the "cooperation" that both countries are now beginning to regret.

This chapter describes a litany of measures used by China against its near neighbors to expedite its technological rise. The subtext here, beyond demonstrating that Chinese technology transfer is a general phenomenon, is that China has alternatives to the US and Europe for S&T support—a fact to take into account when contemplating mitigation. We also hope that by airing these two nations' concerns, we can drive a stake into the claim that the US harbors bias or racial animus against China.

Japan: official support and collaboration

Japan was a favorite destination for Chinese students at the turn of the 19th century, due to its proximity to China and, by comparison with the West, its many elements of shared culture.[1] The number of Chinese studying there grew rapidly, reaching some 100,000 by the end of Japan's Taishō (1912–1926) era.[2] This promising beginning in Sino-Japanese educational and technical exchanges was interrupted by the Pacific war and post-war turmoil, resuming only in October

1978, when Chinese Vice Premier Deng Xiaoping signed the China–Japan Treaty of Peace and Cooperation, ushering in another era of "learning from Japan" (向日本请教).[3]

Technical ministries of both countries were quick to act. In 1979, the Japanese International Cooperation Agency (JICA), which gives technical aid to developing countries, began supporting China as part of Japan's Official Development Assistance (ODA). China responded the same year by standing up a China–Japan Technology Cooperation Affairs Center (中日技术合作事务中心), authorized by the State Council to manage the relationship. In June 2003, it became a part of the Ministry of Science and Technology's (MOST) "China Science and Technology Exchange Center" (中国科学技术交流中心), where it continues to function as a "Japan Office" (日本处), albeit without the Japanese ODA assistance.[4] The office has a broad mandate:

- manage China–Japanese intergovernmental cooperation projects;
- organize China–Japanese intergovernmental S&T exchange activities;
- receive Japanese S&T delegations to China;
- manage the introduction of Huajia (花甲) Experts (see below) and dispatch of trainees;
- manage the organization and implementation of "JICA channel" projects;
- manage the everyday work of the China–Japan Technology Cooperation Affairs Center;
- participate in non-governmental research on current status, trends, and major issues of Japanese science and technology cooperation, and propose related policies.[5]

From the Japanese side, interaction between JICA and China's science ministry is coordinated through JICA's "China Office" (日本国際協力機構, 中華人民共和国事務所) in Beijing.[6] The arrangement has lent significant support to China's S&T development through "cooperation in projects, development surveys, personnel exchanges, and by training and receiving experts."[7]

One aspect of this cooperation is a "formal alliance" between the China Science and Technology Exchange Center and an association of retired ("*huajia*," i.e., 60 or over) Japanese experts, set up in October 1983 for technology support by sending S&T personnel to China directly. By the end of 2017, the program had dispatched more than 4,700 experts, laying down "glorious achievements" in all areas of technology.[8]

Although billed as "cooperation," the benefits of these programs appear to be mostly one-sided, as the following suggests:

> Through the cooperation of the JICA channel, many advanced practical technologies and industrial methods from Japan have been introduced, a number of practical projects have been implemented in China, and a

number of high-level practical technologies have been established and expanded using Japanese technology and funds.[9]

The Japan Science and Technology Agency (JST) supports China's S&T development through its Beijing Representative Office, which publishes a list of "Strategic International Cooperation Research Programs," and a year-by-year catalog of relevant China–Japan S&T events.[10] It also sponsors a "Sakura Science Plan" (櫻花科技计划, or "Cherry Blossom Plan"), an annual program that brings to Japan "students, researchers and others engaged in science and technology" who are 40 years of age or younger from primarily Asian countries. From its inception in 2014 to 2019, some 30,000 persons worldwide were involved, of whom about 10,000 were Chinese.[11]

Meanwhile, at the invitation of China's MOST, in 2016 Japan began a reciprocal initiative to send young scientists and engineers to "visit" China. The first year saw 78 delegations make the pilgrimage, climbing to 150 by 2018.[12] According to Chinese ambassador to Japan Cheng Yonghua (程永华), these delegations—part of a "Sino-Japanese Young Scientist Exchange Plan" (中日青年科技人员交流计划)—are for "short period exchanges" (短期交流) aimed at "innovative cooperation," code for providing targeted Japanese solutions to practical Chinese problems.[13]

BOX 9.1 KAZUKI OKIMURA (沖村憲樹)

Former director of the JST and staunch advocate of China–Japan S&T cooperation. Okimura has been involved personally in many such projects. They include establishing the:

- JST representative office in Beijing;
- China Research and Sakura Science Center (中国研究与樱花科技中心, www.keguanjp.com/crc/);
- China–Japan University Exhibition and Forum (中日大学展暨中日大学论坛, www.keguanjp.com/jcff/cn/);
- China–Japan Large-scale Flagship Projects Joint Research Plan (中日大型旗舰项目的联合研究计划);
- Sakura Science Plan.

He is also credited with a "new model of cooperative projects" between China and Japan called "joint solicitation, joint review, and joint funding" (联合征集、联合评审、共同资助).

(www.most.gov.cn/ztzl/gjkxjsjldh/jldh2015/jldh15jlgg/201601/t20160106_123352.htm)

Japan is also a willing host for other formal Chinese transfer initiatives. In September 2019, the China Association for Science and Technology (CAST), a nominal non-governmental organization (NGO) that advertises its links to China's Communist Party and government, announced a plan to establish a Japan Haizhi Innovation and Entrepreneur Base (日本海智创新创业基地建设) in Tokyo. "Haizhi" is an abbreviation of a CAST plan, supported by China's central and local governments, to "Help Our Motherland through Elite Intellectual Resources from Overseas" (see Chapters 1 and 2).

CAST's program for transfer bases in Japan is not unique. In 2001, a Zhongguancun (ZGC) Liaison Office was established in Tokyo (北京中关村科技园区驻东京联络处) to "build a bridge" for bilateral cooperation, draw ethnic Chinese in Japan to China to found companies, and motivate ZGC-based Chinese entrepreneurs to conduct exchanges with Japanese industry.[14] The office remains active after two decades, engaging Japan's ethnic Chinese community (2013),[15] hosting exchange forums (2014),[16] and brokering formation of a "ZGC International Innovation Fund" with Japan's financial sector (2019).[17]

Another example is the Japan–China Science, Technology, and Culture Center (日中科学技术文化中心) founded in 1978. The Center specializes in bringing to Japan "Chinese technical interns" to train in Japanese companies. The center acknowledges on its website its transfer mission and status as an appendage of the Chinese state:

> The center was one of the first Japanese organizations to join China's SAFEA network. To actively meet China's domestic needs for overseas experts, in 1999 the center became a designated overseas training venue of China's State Administration of Foreign Experts Affairs (venue number: 998106), and in 2001 it became a venue for introducing [foreign] talent (certificate number: SAFEA 034).[18]

Japan: the "academic" dimension

China's links—access points—to Japanese technology extend well beyond these government-sponsored initiatives into the academic and commercial sectors. We cite two examples, from China's North and South, to illustrate: Beijing's Tsinghua University (清华大学) and Shenzhen's Southern University of Science and Technology (南方科技大学).

After years of collaboration, Tsinghua University via its TusStar (启迪之星) and Tokyo University IPC (Innovation Platform Company) agreed on November 30, 2018 to move cooperation to the "next level" and build a joint innovation center. On the same day, Tsinghua signed a second agreement with Japanese SoftBank Group's subsidiary Deepcore, a machine learning incubator company, to back AI companies moving into China and Japan.[19] The deals signaled Tsinghua's intent to become a top supporter of high-tech start-up companies in Japan, with plans to invest four billion RMB ($584 million) in Japanese AI and robotics.[20]

It is unclear what Japan hopes to gain from Chinese investment in its fabled robotics industry. Nonetheless, some five months later, in a move to support China's burgeoning but technology-starved automobile industry, Toyota Motors signed an agreement with Tsinghua for a Tsinghua University–Toyota Joint Research Institute.[21] This was followed by a meeting of Tsinghua's chancellor Qiu Yong (邱勇) and Toyota president Akio Toyoda (豊田章男) in August 2019, in which Qiu proposed more "talent" training and deepened cooperation in AI, new energy cars, and autonomous vehicles. In meetings with other Japanese business leaders, Qiu, who in 2006 was a Chiangjiang Fellowship Program selectee, went on to express a wish for "multi-faceted in-depth exchanges and cooperation with Japan's business community, to explore the new win-win situation afforded by the internationalization of innovation."[22]

Then in November 2019, Chen Shiyi (陈十一), president of the Southern University of Science and Technology, led a delegation of Chinese officials and scholars on a visit to Tokyo, Nagoya, and Tohoku Universities, where multiple agreements were signed for training and R&D.[23]

Linkups between Chinese educational institutions and Japanese industry aim at tapping the latter's technological expertise. That, however, is hardly the whole of it. As we noted at this chapter's beginning, Chinese students have a long history of study in Japan and the debt owed to Japanese educators for China's S&T advancement, while impossible to calculate, is enormous. Here are ten contemporary examples of Japan-educated returnees—dozens more could be cited.

BOX 9.2 CHEN SHIYI (陈十一)

SUSTech President Chen has an interesting and storied background. He is a CAS academician, a fellow at the American Physical Society and England's Institute of Physics, and was among the first selectees of the Thousand Talents Program.

After earning a Ph.D. from Beijing University, Chen worked at the US government's Los Alamos National Laboratory in 1987, where he was an Oppenheimer Fellow and recipient of an Outstanding Research Reward.

Chen was tenured at Johns Hopkins (1999–2005) while concurrently serving as chair of Beijing University's Center for Computational Science and Engineering until 2011, when he assumed a series of administrative posts before becoming president of SUST.

(baike.baidu.com/item/陈十一)

- Professor Gao Wen (高文), director of Information and Engineering Sciences at Beijing University, CAE academician, and formerly vice-director of China's National Natural Science Foundation (NNSF), was awarded a Ph.D. from Tokyo University in 1991. (eecs.pku.edu.cn/info/1419/6282.htm)
- Hu Zhenjiang (胡振江), Changjiang fellow and chair of computer science at Beijing University, spent most of his career at Japanese academic institutions, including Tokyo University and the National Institute of Informatics. (sei.pku.edu.cn/~hu/)
- Gong Yihong (龚怡宏), dean of Xi'an Jiaotong University's School Software Engineering, a Thousand Talents selectee and Chief Scientist of the 973 Program, studied at Tokyo University from 1983 to 1992. (gr.xjtu.edu.cn/web/ygong)
- Xue Qikun (薛其坤), Tsinghua University VP for research, CAS member, and director of the State Key Lab of Quantum Physics, worked at Japan's Tohoku University from 1992 to 1999, and served in Japan's MOE. (www.stmbe.tsinghua.edu.cn/members/qi-kunxue)
- Wan Lijun (万立骏), CAS academician, former president of the University of Science and Technology of China, and chair of All-China Federation of Returned Overseas Chinese (侨联) is also a Tohoku University alumnus. (spm.iccas.ac.cn/wanlijun/People/wljys/)
- Wei Yuezhou (韦悦周), Shanghai Jiaotong University professor of nuclear chemistry and engineering, and Thousand Talents selectee, is another Tohoku University graduate who spent most of his earlier career in Japan. (baike.baidu.com/item/韦悦周)
- Zha Hongbin (查红彬), Changjiang fellow and professor in Beijing University's School of Electronics Engineering and Computer Science. Zha received a Ph.D. from Kyushu University in 1990, where he continued to teach. (eecs.pku.edu.cn/info/1342/6104.htm)

Three more notables were educated by Akira Fujishima (藤嶋昭), president of Tokyo University of Science: Yao Jiannian (姚建年), CAS academician and VP of China's NNSF; Jiang Lei (江雷), CAS academician and dean of Beihang University's School of Chemistry; and Liu Zhongfan (刘忠范), another CAS academician, former Changjiang fellow, and director of a series of technical departments at Beijing University.

What of Japanese-educated Chinese who do not go back? Are there venues to support the ancestral country? Here we enter, once again, the world of the ethnic support guilds, the generic Sino-Japanese professional associations, whose declared fealty is not to their host country. A description of five such groups follows.

Union of Chinese residing in Japan (全日本华侨华人联合会)[24]

This is a Tokyo-based umbrella organization for 62 groups that has existed for 16 years (as of 2019). Its extended leadership cadre of 60 persons, with two exceptions, is made up of people with ethnic Chinese names. Its original name Japanese New Overseas Chinese Association (日本新华侨华人会) was changed in 2013. The federation's purpose as stated in its Union charter is to support friendship and exchange among ethnic Chinese in Japan, protect their legal interests, and "promote Sino-Japanese development in economy, culture, S&T, and other fields." Affiliated groups—mostly technical PhDs., professorial, student, and professional organizations—are listed on the site's "member-list" page.[25]

Association of Chinese scientists and engineers in Japan (在日中国科学技术者联盟)[26]

ACSEJ was established in 1993 and is also Tokyo-based. There are chapters for machine technology, bioscience, electronics and computer applications, materials, and others. The group has "repeatedly assisted the Chinese government," helped China–Japan non-governmental friendship groups return to China to create enterprises, go back "for short periods to work and do joint research" (短期工作和开展共同研究), and perform "exchanges in the service of China" (为国服务的交流)—standard phrases for technology transfer understood by all. It has been recognized by China's MOST, National Natural Science Foundation, and CAS for its notable contributions, and is affiliated like many of these groups with CAST's Haizhi Plan (above).[27]

All-Japan federation of overseas Chinese professionals (中国留日同学总会)[28]

This organization dates back to 1915. It was resurrected after World War II in May 1946 and claims continuous close contact with the Chinese government "under the direction of the China Central Committee's United Front, the Western Returned Scholars Association, and other units." The group, which helped sponsor some 27 "scientific research bases" (科研基地) and another five returnee parks in China,[29] sees itself as "a broad platform for serving China" (为国服务的广阔平台). Its goals are "to organize and promote overseas scholars to return to China to render services or serve in other ways (以各种方式为国服务), and actively participate in the construction of the ancestral country."

Ph.D. and experts group in Japan (留日博士专家团)[30]

Made up of specialists in Japan with advanced degrees engaged "in transfer activities to China and committed to serving the further development of China's economy." The group acts as a "bridge for technology flows," "digging out" (挖掘) talent in Japan where China's skills are in short supply. Its leader Zhao Xinwei (赵新為), a professor at Tokyo University of Science, reflected on their 16 years of service at a reception at the Chinese embassy in February 2018, promising that "All those who study abroad will do their utmost to make great strides in the new era of their homeland" (海外で学ぶ者はみな祖国の新時代の大発展に微力ながら力を尽くすだろう).[31] Zhao was back at the embassy a few months later for a "Chunhui Plan (春晖计划) work exchange seminar" to claim credit on behalf of the group's 300 members for supporting 1,215 exchange projects. Platitudes about "patriotic feelings" (爱国之情) were shared.[32]

Japan–China Innovation Centre (日中イノベーションセンター)[33]

Established in 2016 and subtitled "Startup School Tokyo," the organization's stated goal is to move beyond the traditional formula of "high technology Japan and China as a market" to a new paradigm of "contributing to the two countries through an innovation network" (イノベーションネットワークを通じた日中両社会への貢献). This will be achieved by fostering an "alliance between China's and Japan's governments and industry." Services include consulting, talent spotting, and management support to Chinese getting started in Japan.

Other notable transfer-oriented groups are: the Japan Chinese Society of Automotive Engineers (在日华人汽车工程师协会),[34] CAST Japan (全日本华人科学技术促进会),[35] China–Japan Association for Artificial Intelligence (中日人工智能协会),[36] China–Japan Organization for High-Tech Promotion (日中ハイテク促進機構),[37] All-Japan Chinese Doctors [Ph.D.s] Association (全日本中国人博士协会),[38] All-Japan Federation of Overseas Chinese Professionals (留日同学总会),[39] and Chinese Students' Association in Japan (日本新华侨华人会).[40]

Space will not permit a full account of the venues China uses to facilitate transfer of Japanese technology.[41] Suffice it to note that the full spectrum of techniques directed at the rest of the industrialized world are used against Japan to good effect. Here we give examples of the latest such venue—start-up competitions—sponsored by the aforementioned diaspora organizations.

- The Japan–China Innovation Centre announced the 3rd "Red Boat Cup (红船杯) Global Innovation and Entrepreneurship Competition" in Jiaxing, Zhejiang Province scheduled to run May through September 2019. Goals are to attract domestic and overseas talent.[42]
- The All-Japan Federation of Overseas Chinese Professionals registered support for a "Yellow Crane Cup (黄鹤杯) International Entrepreneurship Competition held in Tokyo in November 2019. The event was sponsored by the Wuhan city government and has attracted "more than 5,000 innovative projects" worldwide since 2015.[43]
- The same Japanese organization backed a "China Guilin Innovation and Entrepreneurship Competition," sponsored by Guilin's city government in November 2019. The event is one of six subsidiary competitions to be held in Japan, South Korea, Shenzhen, Wuhan, Changchun, and Guilin itself in

early November 2019. These six subsidiary competitions all fed into the final competition in Guilin in late November 2019.[44]

- The Japan Overseas Chinese Service Network on May 6, 2019 announced the 14th Chunhui Cup (春晖杯) "Chinese Overseas Scholar Innovation and Entrepreneurship Competition" run by the PRC embassy in Japan for the benefit of OCS in Japan.[45]
- An early example of diaspora group sponsorship is Chinese Entrepreneurs in Japan's (全日本中国留学人员创新创业协会)[46] support for the "Premier China Shenzhen Overseas Innovation Talent Competition—Japan Branch" held at Waseda University in January 2016.[47] The event reportedly elicited a "positive response" from Chinese residents.[48]
- Harbin's city government held an "Overseas Talent Innovation and Entrepreneurship Competition" in Japan and South Korea in early 2019. The Japan event was organized by the Japan–China Science, Technology, and Culture Center in Tokyo with participation from 16 Sino-Japanese cooperation groups.[49]

China–South Korea technology transfer

China's technology transfer posture vis-à-vis the Republic of Korea (hereafter "ROK," "South Korea," or "Korea") parallels in most respects that toward Japan. This may be deliberate, or because there are only so many ways to skin a cat. We look at state venues first.

In November 1991, while negotiating the establishment of diplomatic relations between the two countries, South Korean President Roh Tae-woo (노태우) presented a symbolic golden key to China Foreign Minister Qian Qichen (钱其琛) in Seoul.[50] This figurative exchange also opened the door to technological "cooperation" that has continued to this day. A description of what followed appears on the Chinese Embassy in Korea website:

> On September 30, 1992, a month after the two countries had established diplomatic relations, their respective science ministers signed an "Agreement on Science and Technology Cooperation between the Governments of the People's Republic of China and the Republic of Korea" (中华人民共和国政府和大韩民国政府科学技术合作协定). Cooperation grew rapidly to encompass today basic research, applied technologies, and new-high technology, realized through "joint research, joint research centers, mutual visits by delegations, exchange of skilled experts, training, and seminars." Avenues of exchange extend to the government and private sectors, including universities, research institutes, and industry.[51]

The agreement called for convening every two years a state-level "Joint S&T Committee Meeting" (科技合作联委会) to determine areas of cooperation. True to plan, in October 2012 the two countries' science ministries hosted a "4th S&T Innovation Forum" (제4차 한중 과학기술 혁신 포럼) in Pusan to celebrate 20 years of China–Korea S&T cooperation that began in 1992, during which the Joint S&T Committee met 11 times.[52] This continues to be the main formal venue through which the two countries interact on matters of technology exchange.[53]

Other arrangements exist. In January 2018, China's science ministry issued a "Notification on the 'China–Korea Young Scientist Exchange Program' Solicitation Guidelines in 2018 for Young Chinese Scientists to Visit Korea and Carry Out Academic Exchange Work"[54] aimed at enabling "young" scientists to elevate their research abilities and "raise the S&T level in their respective countries."[55] The program was supported by the science ministries of both countries and the call was repeated in March 2019.[56] The 2018 notice defines "young" as under 40. In 2019 it was raised to under 45. Requirements are having a Ph.D. and current work experience.

"Exchange" activities similar to what China does with Japan (and everyone else) occur today in Korea without respite—a reflection of the "internationalization of S&T" or, as we see it, China's unwillingness or inability to abandon its traditional paradigm. In April 2019, the PRC ambassador officiated a forum in Seoul titled "'One belt, one road' and Korea—Outlook and Prospects for Cooperation." Speakers included faculty from Beijing University's Institute of International and Strategic Studies (国际战略研究院) to discuss "opportunities for international cooperation and the future direction of China–Korean cooperation within the framework."[57]

That same month, the People's Daily online site "people.cn" described a "1st KIC China–Korea S&T Innovative Industrialists Forum" (第一届KIC中韩科技创新企业家论坛大会) held in Seoul, attended by representatives from "93 Chinese entrepreneurial and 20 Korean innovative technology organizations."[58] KIC is the Korea Innovation Center in China (在华韩国创新中心), established in Beijing under the ROK's science ministry in 2016 as a joint venture designed to create a "global startup ecosystem" and support host country market access.[59] At the forum, a member of China's General Chamber of Commerce—in a statement meant to acquaint Korean companies with China's trade-for-technology rule—reminded attendees:

> Chinese companies themselves are constantly filling market gaps, so if you want to enter the Chinese market, you should look for industrial gaps to make your move (进行布局).

In other words, look for areas where the Chinese technology lags and be ready to part with your technology at some point. Driving it home, a Zhongguancun S&T service representative added:

> The best way to speed up your China localization operation is to work with Chinese companies and entrepreneurial industries to learn how to commercialize and market your technology.[60]

A chronology of the S&T relationship from Korea's perspective is available on a Korea–China Science & Technology Cooperation Center (한중과학기술협력센터) portal, managed by Korea's Ministry of Science and ICT, on aspects of past and current China S&T cooperation.[61] On the China side, the country's Ministry of Commerce hosts a website on Sino-Korean industrial parks, with information on joint facilities in China's Yancheng (Jiangsu), Yantai (Shandong), Huizhou (Guangdong), and Korea's Saemangeum, meant to serve as platforms for high-tech industrial cooperation and as a key element (again) of China's "Belt and Road Initiative" (一带一路).[62]

These parks have their statutory basis in a Korea-specific China State Council directive issued in 2017,[63] a recent example being an agreement between the Suzhou Industrial Park Administrative Committee (苏州工业园区管委会) and the Korea Advanced Institute of Science and Technology (한국과학기술원, KAIST) in August 2019 to establish a "China–Korea Industrial Technology Innovation Research Institute" as a "new platform for industrial cooperation and talent exchange." The Suzhou park itself houses over 400 Korean companies with a total investment $6.6 billion.[64]

As noted above, pay-to-play is de rigueur for Korean companies accessing China's market, as it is for other nations operating there. In 2018 a "China–Korea Artificial Intelligence Exchange Center" (中韩人工智能交流中心) was established in Chengdu to bring Korean start-up companies into China for "incubation" and to promote cooperation "in the areas of technology R&D and market expansion," a reference to trade-for-technology.[65] Samsung Electronics also is "paying more attention to R&D of key technologies" at its 800-person Beijing facility instead of "just" doing product commercialization.[66]

Then there is SK Hynix (SK 海力士), the world's third-largest semiconductor company with subsidiaries in San Jose, Shanghai, and Wuxi. On May 16, 2019 the firm signed an agreement with Jiangsu Province's Industry Information Office to create a "Jiangsu Semiconductor Talent Development Platform" to alleviate the province's acute shortage of skilled personnel. The goal is to train 100 Chinese engineers and another 250 "elite" technicians.[67]

Interestingly, one area where Korea appears to differ markedly from Japan is in the number and composition of Chinese support guilds. There is the "Chinese Students and Scholars Association in Korea" (전한중국학생학자연합회) founded in 1993—an obligatory feature of the landscape; a China–Republic of Korea Friendship Association (中国韩国友好协会)—ditto; and the expected Korea Branch (朝韩分会) of the Western Returned Scholars Association (欧美同学会). But we find no pattern comparable to the ethnic technological support groups detailed above for Japan, probably because China and South Korea did not establish relations until 1992. Prior to that the ROK government was not disposed to countenance diaspora support to communist nations.

Threat awareness

There are signs Japanese and South Koreans are becoming sensitized to the threat Chinese technology transfer poses to their economic and national security. The release of translations of our 2013 book *Chinese Industrial Espionage* (中国の産業スパイ網, 2015; 중국 산업스파이, 2019) is perhaps one indication of an awakening. High-profile spy cases in Japan involving fruit seeds,[68] Kobe beef DNA,[69] and machine technology[70] also draw attention to the overall problem of technology loss. Examples of concern are easy to find:

An August 2018 expose on NHK's News Web titled "'S&T Powers' China's Leap Ahead and Japan's Harsh Reality" ('科学技術強国'中国の躍進と日本の厳しい現実) describes for Japanese readers China's Thousand Talents Plan, through which overseas scientists are given "exceptional" (破格の) treatment including resettlement compensation, high salaries, and the option to maintain "a dual appointment with their existing research facility." (それまでの研究機関との兼任). The plan originally targeted ethnic Chinese, but reporter Hiroshi Yokogawa (横川浩士) warns it now seeks "foreign persons" (non-Chinese) with the requisite skills. The article depicted a Japanese professor co-opted by Thousand Talents to work at Fudan University, with a research budget of more than 100 million yen over five years, and compensation, work conditions, and lab facilities superior to Japan's. As a consequence, Japan is seeing an "overseas exodus of young researchers who hold the future of Japan."[71]

Another article in Tōyō Keizai on June 6, 2019 reported how Hisao Ishibuchi (石渕久生), a top Japanese AI expert whose papers have been cited over 25,000 times, was poached by the Southern University of Science and Technology (Dr. Chen Shiyi's outfit; see Box 9.2), with the promise of a research budget "ten times" higher than what he received at Osaka University.[72]

Other examples are publicized in the Chinese media itself. A sina.com clip on October 23, 2018 cites a Japan specialist claiming at the 15th China Manufacturing Industry International Forum that Huawei's success in mobile phones can be credited to hiring Japanese researchers and their use of Japanese technology. As the news source put it, Huawei founder and CEO:

> Ren Zhengfei is very clever. Instead of buying people's production lines, he buys people's minds.

Sina.com went on to note that Huawei currently operates a research facility in Yokohama, Japan employing 400 Japanese cellphone engineers working on intelligent phones.[73] Ren himself reportedly stated that Huawei's success depends on foreign technology and advice:

> Every year we spend many hundreds of millions of US dollars on consulting fees.[74]

The same complaints about China wooing away talent with high salaries and benefit packages are surfacing in the South Korea media as well. The December 4, 2019 Hankyoreh Sinmun cites a Korea International Trade Association report stating that since launching its "Made in China 2025" program in 2015, China has stepped up its poaching of technical experts worldwide. For Korea this has been especially true of battery, semiconductor, and aviation technologies, where experts going to China can expect three or four times their Korean salary.[75] China's BOE Technology Group (京东方), an electronic parts manufacturer, reportedly hired away more than 100 South Korean technical personnel—half from Samsung Electronics and the other half from LG and SK Hynix—at salaries multiples higher than the comparable rate in Korea.[76]

The impact of these losses was underscored in a Hyundai Research Institute report, which noted that the gap between China and Korea on 120 strategically important technologies (국가전략기술) shrank from 1.4 years in 2014 to 1.0 year in 2016.[77] A report by Korea's National Intelligence Service in 2018, which looked at 152 core technologies leaving the country, noted that some 60 percent of them went to China.[78]

Sympathy for the Devil[79]

In response to vocal concerns within Japan of technology loss to China, Chinese media allege that Japan itself set a precedent for technology predation when the country was recovering from its war losses. The message is: can China be blamed for taking its cues from Japan?

For example, a June 16, 2013, *People's Daily* online article "Japan's Economic Spies May Be Hiding Next to You" (日本经济间谍或许就藏在你身边) cited a series of Western authorities, including an unnamed "former CIA official," to the effect that "Japan became one of the top economic powers through the collection and use of advanced foreign technology by industrial espionage." The article cited cases that mostly petered out in the late 1980s.[80]

A (China) Nikkei article dated June 30, 2016 reported similarly that China is countering Japanese claims of industrial theft by asking "Didn't Japan do the same thing?" The article gave examples of Japanese misappropriation of trade secrets in the 1950s by Toyota and Sony, but went on to point out that Japan later progressed to develop its own technologies.[81]

We will go a step further and play devil's advocate by citing research done by one of the present authors two decades ago, based on older sources, that supports these historical accusations—and then some:

> We can gauge the magnitude of Japan's reliance on foreign sources of technology by examining the mechanisms used to effect these transfers. Some twenty such venues or techniques have been identified, including access to foreign labs, benchmarking, company buyouts,

corporate intelligence networks, database exploitation, direct licensing, foreign-based research institutes, government collection support, imitation, industrial espionage, investment in high-tech foreign firms, involvement in international scientific projects, leveraging institutional inequities, liaisons with foreign universities, membership in professional societies, partnerships and coproduction agreements, patents research, rejection of foreign patent applications (while gleaning their ideas and finding workarounds), reverse engineering, sending researchers abroad, technology offsets, and trading technology for market access. This formidable list could be expanded by refining individual categories....[82]

If these techniques were pioneered by the current victims of foreign transfer operations, what is the basis of their complaint? The logic of this argument—morally bankrupt in any case—falls apart, however, on several levels:

- The US turned a blind eye to Japan's early predations to shore up a Cold War ally and advance the global innovation system. No such rationale exists with China today.
- The distortions to global incentives for R&D caused by Japan's post-war behavior cannot compare to the damage done by China's undermining of the global innovation ecosystem.
- As the chronologies suggest, Japan stopped poaching from the world when its economy and R&D base achieved global prominence. The country is a contributor.
- Japan never rose to significance in the US government's National Counterintelligence Executive[83] reports. China has always held the lead—by enormous margins.
- Japan's diaspora population in the US is 30 percent that of China's,[84] well assimilated, and not subject to the same state-sponsored pressure to contribute to the "ancestral country."

Let's look now at how South Korea stacks up in the guilt competition.

For a period of five years (1993–1998), when the Republic of Korea (ROK) was transitioning from a low- to high-tech economy, one of this chapter's authors was one of only two people in the US federal government following South Korean technology transfer. The other person was at the US Department of Commerce. Despite this lack of resources—a reflection of a lack of concern—we identified and tracked through press reports and other unclassified venues the country's transfer operations in great detail.

We eventually were able to forecast transfer events before they happened and, in some cases, participate in them as registered observers. When the ROK government was considering a new measure, we would follow the matter in the open press, had the legislative document in hand soon after it was released, tracked how media analysts (whose habits were known to us) reported the event, and observed the measure as it was being implemented.

Corporate initiatives were also tracked, thanks to the Korean media's assiduous reporting and, in some cases, our contact with the principals themselves, who were aware of the colleague's role at Commerce and would vie to get their views in front of her. Other machinations are best left unsaid. Our whole point is that with just two people working this "account," we had a better grip on what was happening than any ten persons in the ROK. Our understanding was so granular that we had to caveat a chapter on Korea in a 2003 book by stating that our chief concern was "to avoid giving the impression Korea is any more active in this respect" than other countries.[85]

By contrast, a decade later with a staff much larger, a research budget, and the benefit of experience working the transfer issue from multiple perspectives, we and our colleagues never once felt we had more than a bare fraction of the *openly available* and readily accessible data on China's technology transfer apparatus, let alone the actual operations. Frankly, we were happy just to catalog the venues and access points by type. Even in the new age of computers and data algorithms, we knew just enough to guess how much we were missing. No one left the office satisfied. More telling was the spontaneous head shaking that happened on a regular basis on hearing yet another China tech transfer horror story, just when we thought we had heard it all.

None of these comments pertains to China's human and technically enabled espionage acts, knowledge of which we eschewed by design so as not to compromise the objectivity of our own methodology and ability to disseminate what little we did learn. Our argument here is that the China data are so voluminous, reflecting operations that are so widespread and comprehensive in scope, that even groups of trained staff across multiple agencies were overwhelmed by it (not to mention 17 people trying to capture its outlines in a book). While we concede that the disparity between China's transfer operations and that of other countries is partly a function of China's greater size, from a threat perspective how does that matter?

"Apples-to-oranges" is an inadequate metaphor to compare Japan's and Korea's prior, and diminishingly small present, foreign technology transfer posture to that of China. Grapes to a watermelon is closer. We hope these comments will help lay to rest an argument we hear from time to time—most recently from the commandant of a military training academy[86]—that China is no different than other countries in its appetite for "stealing" foreign technology. Whatever advantages Japan and South Korea took of the developed world decades ago they are repaying now to China with interest.

Notes

1 Paradoxically, China's defeat by Japan in the "First Sino-Japanese War" (1894–1895) led to an exodus of Chinese students to Japan, encouraged in part by Zhang Zhidong,

proponent of China's "ti-yong" movement to learn from the West (see chapter 1). Japan by then had been "Westernized" by comparison.

2 https://en.wikipedia.org/wiki/Chinese_people_in_Japan, citing Marius B. Jansen, *The Japanese and Sun Yat-sen*. Stanford, 1970.

3 Quote attributed to Deng. http://world.people.com.cn/GB/14549/8422429.html.

4 Data from Japan's Ministry of Foreign Affairs reveals that between 1979 and 2018, when the program ended, Japan provided China ODA assistance of 3.65 trillion yen in "yen loans, grant aid, and technical cooperation." www.nippon.com/en/features/h00321/after-40-years-japan-stops-aid-to-china.html.

5 www.cstec.org.cn/infoDetail.html?id=1387&column=1036.

6 www.jica.go.jp/china/index.html.

7 https://baike.baidu.com/item/中日技术合作事务中心. See also "Overview of Sino-Japanese Intergovernmental JICA Channel Technical Cooperation" (中日政府间 JICA 渠道技术合作概述), a 178-page document published by the JICA China Office (introduction by China's Technology Cooperation Affairs Center) in 2013 covering the previous decade of joint projects. www.jica.go.jp/china/chinese/office/others/pr/c8h0v m0000al4mq9-att/report_01.pdf.

8 http://sino-jp.com/news-14-352.html.

9 https://baike.baidu.com/item/中日技术合作事务中心.

10 www.jst.go.jp/inter/beijing/activity.html.

11 http://world.people.com.cn/n1/2019/1112/c1002-31451419.html.

12 www.xinhuanet.com/world/2018-10/26/c_1123619166.htm.

13 www.china-embassy.or.jp/chn/jykj/t1596231.htm.

14 www.xinhuanet.com/world/2018-10/26/c_1123619166.htm.

15 www.jnocnews.jp/news/show.aspx?id=70118.

16 http://niigata.china-consulate.org/chn/jjjsfw/t1176794.htm.

17 www.xinhuanet.com/local/2019-06/10/c_1124603354.htm.

18 State Administration of Foreign Expert Affairs (see Appendix 1). www.jcst.or.jp/cn/page.php?id=1.

19 www.tusholdings.com/h/qdnews/show-60-1107-1.html.

20 https://tech.huanqiu.com/article/9CaKrnKfC9N.

21 http://news.tsinghua.edu.cn/publish/thunews/11494/2019/20190422090406917215 461/20190422090406917215461_.html.

22 http://news.tsinghua.edu.cn/publish/thunews/11494/2018/2018081814390787875168 268/20180818143907875168268_.html.

23 www.sohu.com/a/355965943_100226214.

24 www.ucrj.jp.

25 www.ucrj.jp/members/member-list.

26 www.npo-ohp.com/acsej/cn/.

27 See: 海智计划联系的海外科技团体名单 (http://hzb.cast.org.cn/art/2019/1/7/art_265_9870.html).

28 www.obcs.jp/about-us/introduction/.

29 http://ww2.obcs.jp/关于我们-2/工作内容/.

30 https://spc.jst.go.jp/cdb/group/detail/241. The English name is a translation; the group does not have its own website.

31 www.china-embassy.or.jp/jpn/tpxw/t1536664.htm.

32 www.chisa.edu.cn/rmtnews1/haiwai/201905/t20190527_236930.html.

33 www.ceinjp.com.

34 www.jcsae.org/.

35 www.castjp.org/ Established in July 2015 by Tokyo University Chinese faculty and students. The group was involved in promoting Huawei's Japan-based research institute (www.ut.castjp.org/).

36 http://cjaai.com/.

37 www.npo-ohp.com/.

38 www.casej.jp/jp/.

39 www.obcs.jp/.

40 www.acajapan.org/.

41 A sense of the options available to Chinese in Japan to support their homeland can be glimpsed on the Japan Overseas Chinese Service Network's (日本留学服务网) portal, especially the "return home to render services" (回国服务) page, which besides specific employment opportunities also lists talent programs and instructions on how to apply for "short-term visits back to China." http://japan.lxgz.org.cn/.

42 www.ceinjp.com/zh-hans/info/redboat/.

43 www.obcs.jp/20191117wuhan/.

44 www.obcs.jp/20191103guilin.

45 http://japan.lxgz.org.cn/publish/portal112/tab5732/info140712.htm.

46 Established in 2014 "under the MOE's Chinese Service Center for Scholarly Exchange and the Education Section of the Chinese Embassy's guidance." www.weibo.com/ttarticle/p/show?id=2309404005832307154468.

47 www.chinaqw.com/hqhr/2016/01-28/78412.shtml.

48 www.jnocnews.jp/news/show.aspx?id=84393.

49 www.jcst.or.jp/cn/article.php?id=33.

50 http://ckxx.net/pinglun/p/137892.html.

51 "Outline of China–Korea S&T Cooperation." http://kr.china-embassy.org/chn/kjjl/kjhz/t815244.htm.

52 The event was attended by some 40 Chinese scientists who used the occasion to visit Korean S&T facilities and discuss in detail areas for future cooperation. https://baike.baidu.com/item/韩中科学技术合作周.

53 On December 27, 2019 the "14th China–Korea Joint S&T Committee Meeting" (中韩科技合作联委会第14次会议) took place in Seoul, aimed as usual at "deepening scientific and technological innovation and talent exchange and cooperation between the two countries." www.gov.cn/xinwen/2019-12/27/content_5464572.htm.

54 "'中韩青年科学家交流计划' 2018 年中国青年科学家赴韩进行学术交流工作征集指南的通知."

55 www.most.gov.cn/tztg/201801/t20180112_137658.htm.

56 www.most.gov.cn/tztg/201903/t20190311_145567.htm.

57 www.xinhuanet.com/2019-04/18/c_1124386188.htm.

58 http://world.people.com.cn/n1/2019/0423/c1002-31045952.html.

59 www.kicchina.org/.

60 http://world.people.com.cn/n1/2019/0423/c1002-31045952.html.

61 http://kostec.re.kr/.

62 http://yzs.mofcom.gov.cn/article/zt_zhcyy/.

63 国务院关于同意设立中韩产业园的批复 (State Council Approval to Establish China–Korea Industrial Parks), SC (142) December 11, 2017.

64 http://std.jiangsu.gov.cn/art/2019/8/8/art_12282_8662127.html.

65 https://cbgc.scol.com.cn/news/96130.

66 www.shixiseng.com/com/com_eve87rkzmkan.

67 www.dramx.com/News/IC/20190516-16548.html.

68 https://matome.naver.jp/odai/2157352701226735701.

69 www3.nhk.or.jp/news/html/20190311/k10011844031000.html.

70 http://cn.nikkei.com/politicsaeconomy/politicsasociety/34505-2019-02-28-01-00-50.html.

71 www3.nhk.or.jp/news/special/nobelprize2018/tokushu/tokushu_01.html.

72 https://premium.toyokeizai.net/articles/-/20827.

73 http://news.sina.com.cn/c/zj/2018-10-29/doc-ifxeuwws9346047.shtml.

74 "我们每年花好多亿美元的顾问费." www.guancha.cn/zhaohongwei/2016_06_04_362839.shtml.

75 http://hani.co.kr/arti/english_edition/e_international/919603.html.

76 https://epochtimes.com/gb/18/6/28/n10520084.html.

77 https://biz.chosun.com/site/data/html_dir/2018/11/07/2018110700398.html.

78 Cited in http://mil.news.sina.com.cn/china/2018-12-04/doc-ihmutuec5969622.shtml.

79 Opening track on the Rolling Stones 1968 album *Beggars Banquet*.

80 http://finance.people.com.cn/n/2013/0616/c1004-21852698.html.

81 http://cn.nikkei.com/columnviewpoint/column/20286-2016-06-30-04-51-30.html.

82 William C. Hannas, *The Writing on the Wall*, Philadelphia: University of Pennsylvania Press, 2003, p. 16.

83 NCIX, predecessor to the present DNI's National Counterintelligence and Security Center.

84 Figures for the United States are 1,469,637 Japanese (https://en.wikipedia.org/wiki/Japanese_diaspora) to 5,025,817 Chinese. https://en.wikipedia.org/wiki/Overseas_Chinese.

85 Hannas, op. cit., 2003, p. 62.

86 Hannas and Puglisi, Q&A session following a counterintelligence lecture at a US Navy advanced officer training facility a few years ago.

Bibliography

Hannas, William C. *The Writing on the Wall*, Philadelphia: University of Pennsylvania Press, 2003.

Jensen, Marius. *The Japanese and Sun Yat-sen*, Palo Alto: Stanford University Press, 1970.

JICA China Office. "中日政府间 JICA 渠道技术合作概述" ("Overview of Sino-Japanese Intergovernmental JICA Channel Technical Cooperation"), 2013.

PRC State Council. 国务院关于同意设立中韩产业园的批复 ("State Council Approval to Establish China–Korea Industrial Parks"), SC (142) December 11, 2017.

PART IV

Case studies

10

SINO-FOREIGN RESEARCH COLLABORATION

Jeffrey Stoff

This chapter surveys problem areas in Sino-foreign science and engineering research collaboration, especially with regard to the United States. The open and collaborative nature of international scientific research has afforded China opportunities to engage with foreign academics in ways that present challenges and risks to the foreign partner. These challenges and risks include unequal starting points characteristic of a "developing" country in basic science, where China lags, different attitudes toward ownership of scientific discoveries, and unreported or concealed ties to the PRC military. For overseas collaborators eager to advance science, these problems are difficult to reconcile with scientists that are under pressure to protect national equities, particularly in defense research, or in cases where the foreign component is funded by state grants not judged to be in the public interest.

In this chapter, we present examples of US–China scientific collaboration, identified through co-authorship of published research, that represent potential threats to US national security yet reside in a gray zone currently unaddressed by existing regulations or practices. These examples reveal collaboration between US institutions with defense-affiliated entities in the PRC, and uncover research pathways through which the latter can tap US research at its source and potentially divert it to PRC defense programs and surveillance technologies. Such diversions could erode US military superiority with lethal consequences and can be used to further ongoing human rights abuses carried out in Xinjiang and other provinces. Often the technology gained by these collaborations is commercialized, posing potential deleterious economic effects as well.

The cases discussed are a sampling, selected to highlight problematic collaborations. A more rigorous study across the entire literature, conducted in both English and Chinese, is needed to fully assess the scope of the problem.

Understanding the challenges

American universities are among the best in the world and their research programs attract a highly talented, global pool of applicants. The openness of the US system has undoubtedly contributed to the country's economic, technological, and military superiority. Recognizing the benefits it derives from foreign scholarship, the USG facilitates and encourages collaboration with PRC-based researchers and institutions as matters of policy and soft power diplomacy.[1]

That said, China has been exploiting the open nature of international scientific collaboration in ways that erode the collaborative relationship. For example, in 2018, the director of the US National Institutes of Health (NIH) in a letter addressed to thousands of research institutions noted that some recipients of NIH funding had diverted intellectual property (IP) to other countries, shared confidential application information with foreign entities, tried to influence funding decisions, and failed to disclose resources from foreign governments, thereby distorting decisions on the use of NIH funds.[2] These concerns were behind a growing number of cases receiving public attention, including the termination of three scientists at the MD Anderson Cancer Center,[3] two Emory University professors,[4] and the resignations of the Moffitt Cancer Center president and director.[5] In addition, the NIH and US Senate Homeland Security Committee's findings on China's talent programs indicate that some collaboration and concurrent China-based employment of US researchers is not being reported to US institutions.[6]

The NIH problems highlight a key challenge for US institutions generally, namely, that basic research is unregulated and unprotected per a 1985 policy that remains in effect today. National Security Decision Directive 189 (NSDD-189) states that fundamental research should be shared (published) globally as a matter of policy, unless the research in question has national security implications, in which case the material should be classified.[7]

Another problem is that formal assessments, when done at all, hinge on the *legality* of an activity, not on its inherent risk. If no US law is violated, the hazards are assumed to be negligible or manageable. This crude binary test is an inadequate measure of risk.

Scholarship on the problem is sparse. A study by the Australian Strategic Policy Institute (ASPI) estimates that the PLA has sent over 2,500 scientists and engineers overseas to collaborate with researchers and institutes worldwide, and the US is their top destination.[8] Another ASPI study identified 115 PRC research institutions that pose "high" or "very high" risk to potential Western partners,[9] due to their links with the PLA, defense conglomerates, and China's intelligence and security apparatus.

Surveying problematic US–China research collaboration

China's unfettered access to foreign research risks spillage into defense programs and weapons development. China also steers collaboration to applications that can violate democratic norms or values, such as those that enable or enhance domestic surveillance and rights abuse (Chapter 14). Much of this goes unnoticed, however, if the collaboration involves fundamental research. Accordingly, methodologies are needed to evaluate the risk involved in academic collaboration generally, if not as a prophylactic device, then at least as a baseline to inform policymaking.

One way to survey US–PRC scientific collaboration is through co-author affiliations in published scientific and engineering literature. Our aim here is to provide a few such case studies to demonstrate the methodology. We shall focus on US collaboration with seven PRC institutions that support China's defense R&D and public security apparatus:

1   Harbin Institute of Technology (哈尔滨工业大学)
2   Northwest Polytechnical University (西北工业大学)
3   Beijing Institute of Technology (北京理工大学)
4   Nanjing University of Aeronautics & Astronautics (南京航空航天大学)
5   Xidian University (西安电子科技大学 or Xi'an University of Electronic Science & Technology)
6   Engineering University of the People's Armed Police (武警工程大学)
7   Academy of the People's Armed Police (武装警察部队学院)

The first four universities were founded either as the People's Liberation Army (PLA) institutes or from mergers of military engineering academies.[10] They later became civilian universities, typically in the late 1970s or 1980s. All four state their core mission as supporting the PRC's defense research and industrial base and promoting or executing civil–military fusion policies, which channel civilian research into military applications. From the early 1980s until 2008, the four universities were managed by the Commission for Science, Technology and Industry for National Defense (COSTIND, 国防科学技术工业委员会)—a State Council organ responsible for formulating policies and regulations for defense industries; drafting annual plans for R&D, production, investment, and "foreign fund utilization" of defense industries; coordinating military procurement; formulating polices and plans for nuclear, aerospace, aviation, shipbuilding, ordnance, and military electronics industries; and organizing "international exchange and cooperation concerning defense industries."[11]

In 2008, COSTIND was absorbed by the new Ministry of Industry and Information Technology (MIIT, 工业和信息化部), which administers seven schools supporting defense R&D,[12] referred to as the "seven Sons of National Defense" (国防七子)[13] or "Seven Schools of National Defense" (国防七校).[14]

We chose Xidian University as our fifth example because of its key role in defense electronics and information systems. The university is now administered by several government organs including the State Administration of Science & Technology Industry for National Defense (SASTIND, 国家国防科技工业局—the successor to COSTIND) and the state-owned defense conglomerate

China Electronics Technology Group Corporation (CETC, 中国电子科技集团公司).[15]

Supporting China's defense–industrial base and advancing civil–military fusion are core missions of the first six universities listed here. As such, "civilian" research will, as a matter of policy, be examined for military applications. Hence as a matter of simple logic, any joint research, student exchanges, or any other form of facility or resource sharing between these universities and US institutions should be viewed as a risk.

Schools affiliated with the People's Armed Police (PAP), our sixth and seventh examples, were selected owing to the PAP's function as a paramilitary force that performs domestic security and surveillance, and the probability it is also involved in the human rights abuses in Xinjiang.

Summary of methodology, findings

Bibliographic data[16] was extracted from English and Chinese-language science and engineering journal articles made available by two digital aggregators: Elsevier's ScienceDirect and the China National Knowledge Infrastructure (CNKI).[17] Searches were run in these repositories for any articles that name a co-author affiliated with (at least) one of the aforementioned PRC universities, plus a US institution. Supplemental research was conducted primarily through Chinese-language sources, focusing on the PRC-based co-authors in the data and their institutional affiliations.

Our survey was limited to peer-reviewed scientific journal articles and theses/dissertations. Conference proceedings and patents were not included. We also excluded third nation co-authored articles. Given our small (trial) sample, we cannot state with certainty these cases are not outliers, although we consider it unlikely. Any future surveys of this subject would ideally include professional content evaluations to assess the degree of risk—that would require more institutional support, including funding, for this important work.

That aside, we believe the cases present compelling evidence of the need for scrutiny even in so-called "basic" areas of collaborative scientific research.

Key findings are:

- Evidence of co-authorship with employees at sensitive USG research facilities, and citations crediting USG funding support for the research.
- Co-authorship with PRC scientists involved in missile design and other PLA programs, some of which appear to be classified.
- Collaboration with Chinese laboratories that obfuscate actual names and associations with PRC defense programs in the articles' English versions but generally claim these affiliations in the Chinese versions.
- Employees of private U.S companies publishing research with the PAP and Xidian University, i.e., known suspect actors.

Example 1: US collaboration with Harbin Institute of Technology

The Harbin Institute of Technology (HIT) was founded in 1920 and came under Communist Party of China (CPC) administration in 1950. Although also engaged now in arts and sciences,[18] HIT at its core "primarily serves national defense construction and civil–military integration" to "strengthen the needs of national defense modernization."[19] In 2008, the university began a partnership with the state-owned defense conglomerate China Aerospace Science and Technology Corp. (CASC, 中国航天科技集团公司) and founded the Joint Technology Innovation Center.[20]

The first sample article, on conductive thin films, names authors affiliated with HIT and the US Department of Energy (DoE) Lawrence Berkeley National Laboratory's (LBNL) Plasma Applications Group and Molecular Foundry.[21] While the research may be benign, examination of the HIT-affiliated authors reveals direct ties to PRC defense programs.[22]

No further information was found on one of the authors who claims dual LBNL and HIT affiliations. It is possible this author was a visiting Ph.D. student at LBNL while studying at HIT since the article credits the "Ph.D. Programs Foundation" of China's MOE for funding support, and other co-authors of the article appear to hold faculty positions.

A second co-author's situation is more problematic. According to his curriculum vitae (CV), the co-author is a professor at HIT's School of Astronautics, where he studies photonics and thin-film materials, and has worked with the former PLA General Armament Department (GAD, 总装备部) on multiple projects.[23] The CV lists "major positions" and projects that presumptively disqualify him from participation in USG-funded research, including:

- served as a PLA GAD Stealth Technology Experts Group member;
- served as a PLA GAD military use electronic components technology expert evaluator;
- oversaw five PLA GAD Preliminary Research Fund projects (总装预研基金5项) and two SASTIND projects.[24]

The second sample article entitled, "Weakly Supervised Codebook Learning by Iterative Label Propagation with Graph Quantization," was published in the English-language journal *Signal Processing*. The article's authors are affiliated with HIT, Harbin Engineering University (another "Seven Sons of National Defense" school), Columbia University, and the University of Texas at San Antonio.[25] The author associated with Harbin Engineering University was completing a Ph.D. degree at the time of publication and subsequently became a professor and researcher focused on spatial data science, remote sensing image interpretation, cloud data management, and multimedia content retrieval.[26]

The other PRC-based co-authors have direct ties to Chinese defense programs. One of them claimed both Columbia University and HIT affiliations for this article. He received a Ph.D. in 2011 from HIT, where he worked with his advisor (another co-author of this article). From late 2010 through 2013, he held a post-doctoral researcher position at Columbia University.[27] Now employed at Xiamen University's School of Information Science and Technology as a 2017 "youth" selectee of the PRC state-run Ten Thousand Talents Plan (万人计划),[28] he has worked on several defense projects, including:

- a "Central Military Commission S&T Committee Strategic High Technology Special Project" (中央军委科技委战略高技术专项);
- research under the 13th Five-Year Plan for PLA General Staff Headquarters;
- research under the 12th Five-Year Plan for the PLA's GAD.

Another PRC-based co-author is a professor at HIT's School of Computer Sciences Center for Intelligent and Human Machine Interface. The professor's CV lists work on multiple defense projects. Some of these projects listed below use "X" in their project names or funding codes, indicating that program is sensitive and probably classified.

- PLA General Armament Department "panoramic view XXXXXX system" preliminary research project (March 2011–December 2015);[29]
- PLA Unit 65927 "Border Crossing Automated Warning System" project (January 2007–December 2009);
- MIIT "242 Project" (no title given) with funding code "XXXXX (2005C41)."[30]

Given that both HIT-affiliated co-authors are actively involved in defense programs, it would be prudent to assume the research published in collaboration with US universities may flow to the PRC military. Information on these co-authors was derived exclusively from Chinese-language sources; it is not known if the US universities were aware of their associations with the PLA, which is not expressed in the English-language articles themselves. Assuming the collaboration complied with US export controls, this case nevertheless demonstrates the inadequacy of that standard as a test for assessing risk.

Example 2: US collaboration with Northwest Polytechnical University

Northwest Polytechnical University (NWPU), a merger of schools that date from 1938, has research programs in aeronautics, astronautics, and marine technology engineering.[31] The PLA's Air Force Engineering Department, part of the former Harbin Military Engineering Institute, became part of NWPU in 1970 and is now in NWPU's School of Aeronautics.[32] Two associated articles are described below, one appearing in Chinese only that shows collaboration with PRC weapons research, and the other an English-language article involving US Navy support.

The Chinese-language article was published in the PRC *Journal of Projectiles, Rockets, Missiles and Guidance*—a cause for concern in of itself. The article names co-authors affiliated with the NWPU National Defense Science & Technology Key Laboratory of Airfoil and Cascade Aerodynamics (西北工业大学,翼型/叶栅空气动力学,国防科技重点实验室), the Beijing Institute of Nearspace Vehicles System Engineering, and the University of California, Irvine.[33]

Several co-authors and the two PRC institutions named in this article warrant scrutiny. NWPU's National Defense Science & Technology Key Laboratory of Airfoil and Cascade Aerodynamics was established in 1992 by COSTIND and NWPU.[34] This laboratory is part of NWPU's School of Aeronautics and has two name variants. Some sources (on NWPU websites and scientific publications) substitute "national" or "state" (国家) for the "national defense" (国防) term appearing in the name "National Defense Science & Technology Key Laboratory."[35] In English, this full name is translated as "state key laboratory" instead. This mistranslation suggests a deliberate effort to obfuscate the laboratory's ties to defense programs. The article in question used the "national defense" designation *only in the Chinese-language version*.[36]

One co-author of the article is a professor at NWPU's School of Aeronautics and deputy director of the Academic Committee of the Key Laboratory of Airfoil and Cascade Aerodynamics. The professor specializes in aerodynamics and fluid mechanics research and has worked extensively on defense projects, including what appears to be classified weapons programs.[37] The NWPU faculty webpage highlights some of the defense projects he has worked on, including:

- national defense major fundamental research (国防重大基础研究);
- PLA GAD Key Fund (总装重点基金) projects;
- five "major projects" with "XXX" designators (likely classified programs) involving computational software systems integration, high-speed wind tunnels, fluid dynamics, and aerodynamics;
- a high-speed airfoil and wind tunnel project ("XXX连续式高速翼型风洞, 2014 国防科学技术奖二等奖, 排名第一") for which he won a 2014 National Defense S&T award.[38]

Another PRC-based collaborator is affiliated with the Beijing Research Institute of Near Space Aircraft Systems Engineering (北京临近空间飞行器系统工程研究所). This institute falls under the China Academy of Launch Vehicle Technology (CALT) (中国运载火箭技术研究院) (schematic on CALT website).[39]

CALT is a missile design and production academy under the state-owned China Aerospace Science and Technology Corporation.[40] According to the Nuclear Threat Initiative, a US-based weapons of mass destruction (WMD) threat advisory group, CALT is the PRC's "largest, most important organization for the research, development and production of space launch vehicles (SLVs), liquid-fueled surface-to-surface missiles, and solid-fueled surface-to-surface and submarine-launched ballistic missiles." CALT produces short-and medium-range ballistic missiles along with ICBMs.[41]

The participation of researchers from a NWPU defense laboratory and a component of China's missile design academy raises questions about the potential weaponization of this research, and concerns about the nature of the collaboration between these researchers and their co-authors at the University of California, Irvine.

The second identified article, published in English in 2019, names co-authors belonging to the US Naval Research Laboratory's Chemistry Division, NWPU, and Université de Lyon in France.[42] The NWPU co-authors are affiliated with departments that conduct defense research projects, which raises a fundamental question: should the US Navy collaborate on research of any kind with scholars from an institution on the Department of Commerce's Entity List, more specifically, from units known to participate in the defense programs of a strategic competitor?

Example 3: US collaboration with Beijing Institute of Technology

The Beijing Institute of Technology's (BIT) official Chinese-language website claims it is the first PRC institute of higher education to specialize in national defense industries. BIT has developed high-altitude solid rockets, low-altitude radars, the first light tank, advanced military use information systems and other national defense technologies. BIT also claims to have filed more national defense-related patents than any other PRC university. BIT is also involved in "military–civilian fusion and innovation development" (军民融合与创新发展), which are efforts key to the PRC's military modernization.[43] In short, BIT has a stated mission to transfer civilian research to defense applications. The example below is a master's thesis that raises questions about the role of US federally funded research in training graduate students from BIT.

The identified master's thesis was published in Chinese[44] by a BIT student in December 2016. The thesis credits support from the US National Science Foundation (NSF), National Natural Science Foundation of China, and the PLA GAD Preliminary Research Fund (总装预研基金).[45] Its author subsequently earned a Ph.D. in electronics engineering at BIT's School of Information and Electronics. He was a visiting researcher at Temple University in 2015–2016 funded by the PRC state-run China Scholarship Council.[46] His work on NSF-funded research may date to this time. He also spent a year at the University of Edinburgh (UK), from 2017 to 2018.

The author of the thesis is now an associate professor at the PRC's Southeast University and does research in artificial intelligence, radar signal processing, and image reconstruction.[47] We cite this as an example of a graduate student, whose education was funded by the PRC state—*including the PLA*—while also benefiting from USG-funded training and/or research. It is not clear what the National Science Foundation (NSF) or United States gains from supporting this student, given his prompt return to China to complete his studies and work on AI research with defense applications.

Example 4: US collaboration with Nanjing University of Aeronautics and Astronautics

The Nanjing University of Aeronautics and Astronautics (NUAA), founded in 1952, has focused on aerospace engineering throughout its history. In 2004, COSTIND claimed oversight of the school. Its English webpage notes the school "will deeply implement the military–civilian integration development strategy … in aeronautics, astronautics and aviation."[48] The Chinese version describes its National Defense S&T Industry Technology Research Applications Center (国防科技工业技术研究应用中心) and its ten "national defense special disciplines." Among the university's achievements are China's first large unmanned target drone, first unmanned nuclear materials testing drone, first unmanned helicopter, first unmanned microaircraft, and launch of an independently developed microsatellite.[49] We selected one article for this case study showing its co–authors' involvement in PRC defense R&D programs including hypersonic vehicles.

The identified Chinese-language article, published in 2018, is titled, "Research Progress of Adaptive Control for Hypersonic Vehicle in Near Space." The subject's sensitivity requires no explanation. The article named three authors affiliated with NUAA and one author affiliated with the University of Virginia.[50] Supplemental information confirms their extensive work on PRC defense projects and weapons systems.

Two of the article's co-authors are professors doing "weapon systems and applications engineering" in NUAA's College of Automation Engineering.[51] The first researches carrier-based aircraft, large passenger aircraft, hypersonic flight vehicles, drones/unmanned aerial vehicles (UAVs), and aircraft guidance and control. This researcher has directed projects for the PLA Air Force's Equipment Development Department.[52]

The second co-author studies carrier-based aircraft and UAV take-off (from ships) guidance and control, drone swarm coordination, control and strategic decision-making, hypersonic flight vehicles, fighter aircraft, large passenger aircraft, guided missiles, and related advanced flight controls. From February 2015 to February 2016, he was visiting scholar at the University of Virginia where the third co-author had an affiliation. His CV notes co-authorship of numerous Chinese and English-language publications, many of which relate to UAVs and aircraft carrier-related technologies.[53] Additionally, this co-author claims to have won four "National Defense Science and Technology Progress Awards" in 2010,

2011, 2012, and 2017 relating to aircraft guidance and control techniques, load simulators, aircraft carrier technologies, and ship-based drone technologies.[54]

The article lists the "First Academy Higher Education Joint Innovation Fund (CALT201603)" as its funding source.[55] "CALT" refers to the China Academy of Launch Vehicle Technology described above, also known as the "CASC First Academy" (中国航天科技集团有限公司第一研究院 or "航天一院").[56] The extensive defense research undertaken by both NUAA co-authors, coupled with their apparent partnership with CALT, suggests that the research in the identified article is intended for military-use hypersonic vehicles.

Example 5: US collaboration with Xidian University

Xidian University's current civilian form (originally a Radio School for the PLA) was jointly established by MOE, SASTIND, the Xi'an municipal and Shaanxi provincial governments, and state-owned defense conglomerate China Electronics Technology Group Corporation (CETC). Xidian conducts R&D on network and information security, wireless communications, cognitive radar, microwave antennas, electronic countermeasures, and other defense disciplines,[57] and claims to have "made important contributions to China's military modernization" (国防现代化做出了重要的贡献).[58] Two articles, one in Chinese and the other in English were selected[59] both for their research on radar development and their obfuscation of defense affiliations.

The articles name co-authors from Xidian University's "National Laboratory of Radar Signal Processing" (雷达信号处理国家重点实验室); the Chinese-language article also names a co-author with dual affiliation at the University of Delaware and the Xidian University laboratory.[60] That article posts brief biographies of the co-authors, all of whom focus on radar research, such as adaptive signal processing, automatic target identification and recognition radars, MIMO, and other radar imaging systems. The English-language article also involved MIMO radar research with co-authors from the same National Laboratory of Radar Signal Processing, the University of Science and Technology of China, and the University of Florida.[61] Both articles neglected to use the official name of the laboratory, in English or Chinese, which can be translated as the National Defense Science and Technology Key Laboratory of Radar Signal Processing (雷达信号处理国防科技重点实验室).[62]

Example 6: US collaboration with People's Armed Police schools

Foreign collaboration with research institutions subordinate to the People's Armed Police (PAP) raises national security and ethical concerns, as the PAP is a paramilitary police force that performs domestic security, monitors civil order, and carries out surveillance functions for the CPC and the domestic security apparatus. We examine two articles involving PAP collaboration with US partners.

The first article was published in Chinese in 2013, and names researchers from NWPU, Xi'an Engineering College of the People's Armed Police (武警工程大学), Tianjin University, and the University of California Merced.[63] No biographical information was found on the co-author affiliated with the PAP school. According to the school's website, in 2017 (after the identified article was published), the university was reorganized and merged with the former People's Armed Police Ürümqi Command College (武警乌鲁木齐指挥学院).[64]

The implications of this collaboration between UC Merced, NWPU, and a PAP institution are serious. The PAP school merged with an Ürümqi-based PAP training unit, which is located in the capital of the Xinjiang region. The PAP in Xinjiang is deeply involved in what many in the international community consider to be the most oppressive surveillance regime in the world, including widespread extrajudicial detentions and forced mass internments of millions of ethnic Uyghurs in reeducation camps.[65] This publication appeared in a domestic Chinese source in Mandarin and no information was found on the PAP-affiliated co-author; this raises questions about the degree of due diligence UC Merced might have been able to perform on this collaboration, if any.

Another article, published in English in 2018, named co-authors from Xidian University, Xi'an Jiaotong University, the Engineering University of People's Armed Police, Peking University, and the US NIH-funded Ultrasonic Transducer Resource Center at the University of Southern California.[66] Only one of the 14 co-authors is affiliated with the PAP school; however, eight co-authors claim a Xidian University affiliation, one of whom has a dual affiliation with the NIH center. This suggests both the PAP and Xidian University may be benefiting from NIH-funded programs, a potentially alarming ethical issue.

Example 7: US private sector collaboration with PRC schools

We have focused on collaboration between US and PRC academic institutions. There are also Sino-foreign R&D partnerships in the private sector reflected in the scientific literature. Surveys of those arrangements are beyond the scope of this chapter, though it needs urgently to be done. However the information gathered to date is enough to say that a subset of the partnerships include research between foreign companies and Chinese universities, and includes co-authors from the same schools profiled in this chapter.

Xidian University claims to host 74 joint laboratories with multinational corporations, including Infineon, Intel, IBM, and HP.[67] Searches in CNKI's portal identified articles with co-authors at the US firm National Instruments Co. and Xidian's Network and Information Security Virtual Simulation Center and School of Telecommunications Engineering.[68] The US firm FM Global has employees publishing research with the PAP Academy's[69] Department of Fire Protection Engineering.[70] It is unknown if this collaboration was sanctioned by the US firms. Regardless, it raises the same ethical and security concerns.

Conclusion

Regardless of whether US-based scientists or their employers intend such an outcome, S&T collaboration with the institutions profiled in this chapter jeopardizes the integrity of their research and the federal funding that supports it. A more extensive study will no doubt expand this list well beyond the few examples and institutions presented here.

A common argument for collaboration in basic science is that the results are published for all to use.[71] This overlooks the important issue of who or what is using the research and for what specific purpose, and bypasses the fact that the hands-on, unpublished input, knowledge, and experience that goes into conducting research in collaborative environments is not easily replicable through passive reviews of published literature. In other words, raw data and knowhow exist and may be transferred, in ways that lie outside of the published result. Additionally, China may be better resourced to convert technology into viable applications than collaborating countries, whose researchers are likely to view cooperation with government, on defense especially, as beneath the dignity of their posts.

The examples given here demonstrate, at a minimum, a need for more rigorous risk assessment of research collaboration with China, including a defined process that looks beyond a technical interpretation of legality to ethical and national security implications.

Notes

1 For an overview of the history of scientific collaboration with China and US policies that promoted this collaboration, see Richard Suttmeier, "Trends in US-China Science & Technology Cooperation: Collaborative Knowledge Production for the Twenty-First Century?" a report prepared for the US–China Economic and Security Review Commission, September 2014.

2 HHS memo, letter from Director of NIH Francis Collins on research integrity, August 20, 2018. www.nih.gov/about-nih/who-we-are/nih-director/statements/statement-protecting-integrity-us-biomedical-research.

3 www.houstonchronicle.com/news/houston-texas/houston/article/MD-Anderson-fires-3-scientists-over-concerns-13780570.php.

4 www.ajc.com/news/state-regional-govt-politics/new-findings-emory-researchers-didn-disclose-chinese-funding-ties/QQ58XiznSllTLYv5rARfjL/.

5 "Moffitt Cancer Center CEO, Center Director Resign after Compliance Review," December 18, 2019. https://moffitt.org/newsroom/press-release-archive/2019/moffitt-cancer-center-ceo-center-director-resign-after-compliance-review/.

6 Not all collaboration between US and PRC research institutions needs to be disclosed, as US employers or federal funding agencies' reporting requirements vary.

7 https://fas.org/irp/offdocs/nsdd/nsdd-189.htm.

8 Alex Joske, "Picking Flowers, Making Honey; The Chinese Military's Collaboration with Foreign Universities," Report No. 10, 2018, Australian Strategic Policy Institute.

9 www.aspi.org.au/report/china-defence-universities-tracker.

10 The exception is Harbin Institute of Technology, which was founded in 1920 (seven years before the PLA) but has focused on supporting defense research for most of its history.

11 http://english1.english.gov.cn/2005-10/01/content_212487.htm.

12 Space limits the present survey to four of the "seven sons." All seven, including Beihang University, Harbin Engineering University, and Nanjing University of Science & Technology are covered in a study by Jeffery Stoff and Glenn Tiffert, "Re-Assessing Risks to US-China Research Collaboration: A Look at the PRC's 'Seven Sons of National Defense' Universities and US Institution Partnerships," Hoover Institution, (forthcoming).

13 A MIIT web page (now unavailable) used the term "国防七子" along with the names of the seven schools. http://jmjh.miit.gov.cn/web/newsInfoWebMessage.action?newsId=493942&moduleId=1062. Other mentions are here: www.sdxgktb.com/index.php?id=2310 and here: www.jdxzz.com/gkzx/2019/1216/10038.html.

14 https://baike.baidu.com/item/国防七校.

15 "School Introduction." www.xidian.edu.cn/xxgk/xxjj.htm.

16 Bibliographic data used here includes article title, authors, affiliated institutions, publication source, date, and funding details (if provided).

17 Other aggregator holdings such as Wanfangdata (万方数据), CQVIP (维普资讯), and Web of Science were not consulted in this preliminary survey.

18 www.hit.edu.cn/236/list.htm.

19 "由于加强国防现代化建设的需要, 哈工大及时进行了专业调整, 由多学科性的工业大学转变为主要为国防建设服务, 军民结合." www.hit.edu.cn/240/list.htm.

20 http://en.hit.edu.cn/pdf/2017HIT%20Brief%20Introduction.pdf.

21 Yuankun Zhu, Rueben J. Mendelsberg, Jiaqi Zhu, Jiecai Han, and André Anders, "Transparent and Conductive Indium Doped Cadmium Oxide Thin Films Prepared by Pulsed Filtered Cathodic Arc Deposition," *Applied Surface Science* 265, 2013.

22 Bibliographic information also at: www.sciencedirect.com/science/article/abs/pii/S0169433212020545.

23 PLA's General Armament Department is now the Equipment Development Department of the Central Military Commission.

24 http://school.freekaoyan.com/heilongjiang/hit/daoshi/2016/04-01/1459455102545914.shtml.

25 Bibliographic information at: www.sciencedirect.com/science/article/pii/S0165168412001454 This article was also published in 2013.

26 https://information.xmu.edu.cn/info/1019/3182.htm.

27 http://mac.xmu.edu.cn/rrji-cn.html.

28 Ibid. The Ten Thousand Talents Plan (万人计划) is another nationally run recruitment program that although focused on domestic-based talents, appears to support the careers of individuals employed or educated overseas who have recently returned to China.

29 "全景 XXXXXX 系统 (ZLY2011324)" 总装预研. The X's presumably are redacted characters.

30 http://homepage.hit.edu.cn/yaohongxun.

31 Note that NWPU is on the US Department of Commerce Entity List with a presumption of denial for export control purposes.

32 http://hangkong.nwpu.edu.cn/home/overview/view.htm.

33 Wang Zhongyi (王中一), Zheng Borui (郑博睿), Gao Chao (高超), Fang Hong (方洪), Xiong Juntao (熊俊涛), Liu Feng (刘锋), and Luo Shijun (罗时钧), "圆锥前体大攻角绕流的数值计算与分析" ("Numerical Computation and Analysis of Flow over

A Conical Forebody at High Angle-of-attack"), *Journal of Projectiles, Rockets, Missiles and Guidance* (弹箭与制导学报) 33, no. 3, 2013.

34 http://hangkong.nwpu.edu.cn/info/1368/8220.htm.

35 For example, this NWPU page removes "national defense." http://hangkong.nwpu.edu.cn/info/1053/1309.htm.

36 US government analysts refer to the practice of mistranslating (or not translating) sensitive text as "hiding behind the soft encryption of the Chinese language." Examples could fill the rest of this book. Studying China through English sources provides you everything China wants you to know.

37 https://teacher.nwpu.edu.cn/gaochao.html.

38 Ibid.

39 www.calt.com/n481/n490/index.html.

40 Ibid.

41 www.nti.org/learn/facilities/59/.

42 J.C. Qiao, Y.H. Chen, R. Casalini, J.M. Pelletier, and Y.Yao, "Main α relaxation and slow β relaxation processes in a La30 Ce30 Al15 Co25 metallic glass," *Journal of Materials Science & Technology* 35, no. 1, 2019.

43 www.bit.edu.cn/gbxxgk/gbxqzl/xxjj/index.htm.

44 Full text of the thesis can be found at: www.doc88.com/p-8901799755474.html.

45 Liu Shengheng, "稀疏分数傅里叶变换理论及其在探测中的应用" ("Sparse Fractional Fourier Transformation and Its Applications in Exploration"), BIT Master's Thesis, December 2016.

46 https://sites.google.com/site/shenghengliu/.

47 Ibid.

48 http://iao.nuaa.edu.cn/nuaas-history/.

49 www.nuaa.edu.cn/479/list.htm.

50 Zhen Ziyang, Zhu Ping, Jiang Ju, and Tao Gang, "基于自适应控制的近空间高超声速飞行器研究进展" ("Research Progress of Adaptive Control for Hypersonic Vehicle in Near Space"), *Journal of Astronautics* (宇航学报) 39, no. 4, 2018.

51 http://caegl.nuaa.edu.cn/list/471.

52 http://caegl.nuaa.edu.cn/showSz/471-1073.

53 An illustrative example is "Self-Organization Method for Multiple Reconnaissance—Attack UAVs under Adversarial Environment," *Aerospace Science and Technology*, 2016.

54 http://caegl.nuaa.edu.cn/showSz/471-1060.

55 Funding information was listed in Chinese as "一院高校联合创新基金 (CALT201603)."

56 www.calt.com/n481/n489/index.html.

57 None of these facts are mentioned on the "about us" page on Xidian University's English-language website.

58 www.xidian.edu.cn/xxgk/xxjj.htm.

59 Example 7 that follows includes private sector research collaboration with Xidian University.

60 Liu Yuan (刘源), Jiu Bo (纠博), Liu Hongwei (刘宏伟), and Xia Xianggen (夏香根), "基于杂波的收发分置 MIMO 雷达阵列位置误差联合校正方法" ("Joint Transmit and Receive Array Position Error Calibration for Bistatic MIMO Radar Based on Clutter"), *Journal of Electronics & Information Technology* (电子与信息学报) 37, no. 12, December 2015. Full text here: http://jeit.ie.ac.cn/fileDZYXXXB/journal/article/dzyxxxb/2015/12/PDF/150347.pdf.

61 Jun Liu, Jinwang Han, Zijing Zhang and Jian Li, "Target Detection Exploiting Covariance Matrix Structures in MIMO Radar," *Signal Processing* 154, January 2019. www.sciencedirect.com/science/article/pii/S0165168418302457.

62 A news item on Xidian University's website described this lab's history and uses the official name that adds the "national defense S&T" designation. https://news.xidian.edu.cn/info/1013/3150.htm.

63 Xu Wei (徐伟), Sun Chunyan (孙春艳), Sun Jianqiao (孙建桥), and He Qun (贺群), "胞映射方法的研究和进展" ("Development and Study on Cell Mapping Methods"), *Advances in Mechanics* (力学进展) 43, no. 1, 2013.

64 www.wjgcdx.com/zhongxuejianjie/daxuejianjie/2018-06-07/47.html.

65 Human Rights Watch, "'Eradicating Ideological Viruses': China's Campaign of Repression Against Xinjiang's Muslims," 2018. www.hrw.org/report/2018/09/09/eradicating-ideological-viruses/chinas-campaign-repression-against-xinjiangs.

66 Chunlong Fei, Tianlong Zhao, Junshan Zhang, Yi Quan, Danfeng Wang, Xinyu Yang, Qiang Chen, Pengfei Lin, Di Li, Yintang Yang, Shuxiang Dong, Wei Ren, K. Kirk Shung, and Qifa Zhou, "0.36BiScO3-0.64PbTiO3 Piezoelectric Ceramics for High Temperature Ultrasonic Transducer Applications," *Journal of Alloys and Compounds* 743, April 2018. www.sciencedirect.com/science/article/abs/pii/S0925838818304122.

67 www.xidian.edu.cn/xxgk/xxjj.htm.

68 For example, see: Li Xiaohui (李晓辉), Li Yi (李毅), Liu Nai'an (刘乃安), and Liu Jindong (刘晋东), "无线局域网虚拟仿真实验平台设计与实现" ("Design and Realization of Virtual Simulation Experiment Platform for WLAN"), *Experimental Technology and Management* (实验技术与管理) 36, June 2019; and Meng Meimei (孟梅梅), Li Xiaohui (李晓辉), Liu Nai'an (刘乃安), and Xu Zheng (徐征), "NI USRP Based Experiment Platform of Multi-mode Adaptive Wireless Communication" (基于NI USRP的多模式自适应无线通信实验平台), *Modern Electronics Technology* (现代电子技术) 39, no. 1, January 2016.

69 "武装警察部队学院" is the official name of the PAP Academy.

70 Liang Zhou, Dong Zeng, Dongyang Li, and Marcos Chaos, "Total Radiative Heat Loss and Radiation Distribution of Liquid Pool Fire Flames," *Fire Safety Journal* 89, April 2017. www.sciencedirect.com/science/article/abs/pii/S0379711217301169.

71 Editor's note: the same claim is made by co-optees of China's talent programs, who argue that the research they do in China is published, hence accessible worldwide. The argument is absurd—if publication were all that mattered, China would save billions by monitoring the published scientific literature (which it does in any case; see *CIE*, chapter 2) of the experts its talent programs target, instead of going to the bother and expense of having them work in (or for) China.

Bibliography

Ackerman, Todd. "MD Anderson Ousts 3 Scientists Over Concerns About Chinese Conflicts of Interest," *Houston Chronicle*, April 19, 2019.

Cao, Liujuan, Ji Rongrong, Liu Wei, Yao Hongxun, and Tian Qi. "Weakly Supervised Codebook Learning by Iterative Label Propagation with Graph Quantization," *Signal Processing* 93, no. 8, August 2013.

Fei, Chunlong, Zhao Tianlong, Zhang Junshan, Quan Yi, Wang Danfeng, Yang Xinyu, Chen Qiang, Lin Pengfei, Li Di, Yang Yintang, Dong Shuxiang, Ren Wei, Shung K. Kirk, and Zhou Qifa. "0.36BiScO$_3$-0.64PbTiO$_3$ Piezoelectric Ceramics for High Temperature Ultrasonic Transducer Applications," *Journal of Alloys and Compounds* 743, April 2018.

Hart, Ariel. "New Findings: 2 Emory Researchers Didn't Disclose Chinese Funding, Ties," *Atlanta Journal-Constitution*, May 23, 2019.

Human Rights Watch. "'Eradicating Ideological Viruses': China's Campaign of Repression Against Xinjiang's Muslims," September 9, 2018. www.hrw.org/report/2018/09/09/eradicating-ideological-viruses/chinas-campaign-repression-against-xinjiangs.

Joske, Alex. "Picking Flowers, Making Honey; The Chinese Military's Collaboration with Foreign Universities," Australian Strategic Policy Institute, October 30, 2018.

Levesque, Greg and Mark Stokes. "Blurred Lines: Military–Civil Fusion and the 'Going Out' of China's Defense Industry," Pointe Bello, December 2016.

Li, Xiaohui (李晓辉), Li Yi (李毅), Liu Nai'an (刘乃安), and Liu Jindong (刘晋东). "无线局域网虚拟仿真实验平台设计与实现" ("Design and Realization of Virtual Simulation Experiment Platform for WLAN"), *Experimental Technology and Management* (实验技术与管理) 36, June 2019.

Liu, Jun, Han Jinwang, Zhang Zijing, and Li Jian. "Target Detection Exploiting Covariance Matrix Structures in MIMO Radar," *Signal Processing* 154, January 2019.

Liu, Shengheng. "稀疏分数傅里叶变换理论及其在探测中的应用" ("Sparse Fractional Fourier Transformation and Its Applications in Exploration"), Beijing Institute of Technology Master's Thesis, December 2016. www.doc88.com/p-8901799755474.html.

Liu, Yuan (刘源), Jiu Bo (纠博), Liu Hongwei (刘宏伟), and Xia Xianggen (夏香根). "基于杂波的收发阵列分置 MIMO 雷达阵列位置误差联合校正方法" ("Joint Transmit and Receive Array Position Error Calibration for Bistatic MIMO Radar Based on Clutter"), *Journal of Electronics & Information Technology* (电子与信息学报) 37, no. 12, December 2015.

Meng, Meimei (孟梅梅), Li Xiaohui (李晓辉), Liu Nai'an (刘乃安), and Xu Zheng (徐征). "基于 NI USRP 的多模式自适应无线通信实验平台" ("NI USRP Based Experiment Platform of Multi-mode Adaptive Wireless Communication"), *Modern Electronics Technology* (现代电子技术) 39, no. 1, January 2016.

National Security Decision Directive 189. *National Policy on the Transfer of Scientific, Technical, and Engineering Information*, September 21, 1985.

Office of the United States Trade Representative. *Section 301 Report into China's Acts, Policies, and Practices Related to Technology Transfer, Intellectual Property, and Innovation*, March 27, 2018.

Qiao, J.C., Y.H. Chen, R. Casalini, J.M. Pelletier, and Y. Yao. "Main α Relaxation and Slow β Relaxation Processes in a $La_{30} Ce_{30} Al_{15} Co_{25}$ Metallic Glass," *Journal of Materials Science & Technology* 35, no. 6, June 2019.

Stoff, Jeffrey and Glenn Tiffert. "Re-Assessing Risks to US-China Research Collaboration: A Look at the PRC's 'Seven Sons of National Defense' Universities and US Institution Partnerships," Hoover Institution, 2020 (forthcoming).

Suttmeier, Richard. "Trends in US-China Science & Technology Cooperation: Collaborative Knowledge Production for the Twenty-First Century?" Report to US-China Economic and Security Review Commission, September 2019.

United States Senate Judiciary Committee Hearing. "China's Non-Traditional Espionage Against the United States: The Threat and Potential Policy Responses," December 12, 2018.

Wang, Zhongyi (王中一), Zheng Borui (郑博睿), Gao Chao (高超), Fang Hong (方洪), Xiong Juntao (熊俊涛), Liu Feng (刘锋), and Luo Shijun (罗时钧). "圆锥前体大攻角绕流的数值计算与分析" ("Numerical Computation and Analysis of Flow over A Conical Forebody at High Angle-of-attack"), *Journal of Projectiles, Rockets, Missiles and Guidance* (弹箭与制导学报) 33, no. 3, June 2013.

Xu, Wei (徐伟), Sun Chunyan (孙春艳), Sun Jianqiao (孙建桥), and He Qun (贺群). "胞映射方法的研究和进展" ("Development and Study on Cell Mapping Methods"), *Advances in Mechanics* (力学进展) 43, no. 1, March 2013.

Zhen, Ziyang, Zhu Ping, Jiang Ju, and Tao Gang. "基于自适应控制的近空间高超声速飞行器研究进展" ("Research Progress of Adaptive Control for Hypersonic Vehicle in Near Space"), *Journal of Astronautics* (宇航学报) 39, no. 4, April 2018.

Zhou, Liang, Zeng Dong, Li Dongyang, and Marcos Chaos. "Total Radiative Heat Loss and Radiation Distribution of Liquid Pool Fire Flames," *Fire Safety Journal*, Vol. 89, April 2017.

Zhu, Yuankun, Rueben J. Mendelsberg, Zhu Jiaqi, Han Jiecai, and André Anders. "Transparent and Conductive Indium Doped Cadmium Oxide Thin Films Prepared by Pulsed Filtered Cathodic Arc Deposition," *Applied Surface Science* 265, January 2013.

11

CHINA'S 'ARTIFICAL' INTELLIGENCE

William C. Hannas and Huey-Meei Chang

The preceding chapters describe Chinese foreign technology acquisition in structural terms. Examples are given to demonstrate how transfer venues and techniques further China's strategic capabilities and commercial competitiveness.

The present chapter views the matter differently, from the perspective of a single (suite of) technologies, namely, artificial intelligence (AI). We chose AI because it illustrates perfectly how China, having identified an emergent technology of global and national importance, is able quickly to marshal its transfer apparatus to ensure state and commercial ventures are privy to foreign developments and to the international "talent" driving the field.

As will be shown, AI-related transfer initiatives have occurred across each of the legal and extralegal access points described in this volume.[1] Practices developed over decades, along with new techniques aimed at today's talent and capital markets, are leveraged by China to achieve parity or leadership in this latest arena of competition.

The chapter begins by examining state policy support for foreign AI transfers, the mobilization of transfer offices and state key labs, and the triangular relationship between "talent" programs, overseas technical support guilds, and China's technology commercialization enclaves. We then consider Chinese corporate initiatives, "angel" investments, start-up competitions, and the role of multinationals in China's AI development. A final section examines Chinese scholars' views on the country's ability to do high-tech innovation.

Chinese government statutory support for foreign AI access

Artificial intelligence (AI), with its focus on machine learning (ML), burst into prominence in recent years after a long gestation thanks to demonstrable progress in the field that promises to transform human society and the nature of humanity itself.[2] It is impossible today to research any technical discipline, or browse a technology forum, without encountering references to AI. This is as true of Chinese-language sources as it is of material in English.

Beyond the technical literature, popular media is also rife with commentary about the opportunities and dangers AI poses.[3] The discourse on AI inevitably includes comparisons of the relative strengths and advantages of different countries—the major players being the United States and China—leading to concern that competition between the two may create the civilian equivalent of an "AI war." While these matters warrant discussion, our concern here is more limited, namely, to explore the degree to which China's AI development, in basic research especially, is informed by access to foreign AI resources.

Our inquiry begins with a review of statutory enactments. The earliest appearance of "artificial intelligence" (人工智能) in a ministry-level notification is the July 1, 2015 "State Council Guiding Opinions on Positively Promoting 'Internet +' Activity" (No. 40),[4] wherein "AI and other technologies" are promoted as components of, or catalysts for, commercial products. The following year a supplement to the notice was issued by a consortium of ministries titled "Three-Year Action Implementation Plan for 'Internet +' Artificial Intelligence,"[5] elaborating on the role AI would play in nine areas of application. Again, the focus was on AI as an enabler, not as a standalone discipline, although the document already referenced the need to "go global" (走出去), "integrate domestic and foreign innovative resources," and build a "service platform" (服务平台) to spot opportunities for international cooperation.

Similarly, on July 28, 2016, two months later, a "State Council Notification on National Science and Technology Innovation Programs for the 13th Five-Year Plan," (No. 43) was issued.[6] The document is relevant in this context mostly for what it does <u>not</u> emphasize: although AI is mentioned, it is not included among the six major S&T or nine major engineering projects (项目). What appears instead is "brain science and brain-inspired research," listed in the fourth position of importance, defined in the document as "brain-inspired computing" (类脑计算) and "brain-computer intelligence" (脑机智能), which are AI-dependent. In other words, China, remarkably, had identified the nexus between "wet" and machine intelligence as a topic for concentrated research *before* designating AI itself as a priority research area.[7] Meanwhile, we note the usual calls for "a strategy to internationalize S&T innovation," strengthening China's overseas S&T institutions, giving Chinese organizations more play in "international innovation cooperation," and facilitating the introduction of more Chinese scientists in international S&T organizations.[8]

By the end of the year, it was clear the Chinese government was moving toward acceptance of AI as a discipline in its own right. On November 29, 2016, the State Council released another notification related to the 13th five-year plan, this time for "National Strategic Emerging Industry Development Projects"

(No. 67).[9] Among 21 projects listed, the fifth called specifically for "innovative engineering in artificial intelligence," in particular:

> Promote basic theoretical research and core technology development, realize the commercialization of neuromorphic computing chips, intelligent robots and intelligent application systems, embed new artificial intelligence technologies in various fields.[10]

"International cooperation" was listed 13 times in the document. Section 9— the penultimate part of the document typically reserved for priority elements in Chinese state discourse—laid out the framework for "expanding new cooperation paths." Its four paragraphs call for "actively introducing global resources," "creating new platforms for international cooperation," "building a global innovation and development network," and "deep integration into the global industry chain." The nation was encouraged to:

- introduce, digest, absorb and re-innovate[11] foreign technology;
- promote R&D centers in China by multi-national corporations (MNCs) and foreign research institutions;
- step up the introduction of high-end overseas "talent";
- induce leading Chinese companies to build overseas cooperation parks;
- beef up mechanisms to transfer and incubate "international" S&T achievements;
- build various international technology exchange and cooperation platforms;
- build international cooperation and innovation centers;
- develop high-level international intermediary service agencies;[12]
- establish overseas R&D centers (the reciprocal of the second bullet point);
- build a global R&D system;

and "create new means of cooperation" in case these and two dozen other recommendations prove inadequate. A final recommendation puts the transfer enterprise into perspective:

> Help aligned industries "go global" and feed back to China high-quality assets, technology, and management experience gained thereby, to create a comprehensive competitive advantage.

By 2017, AI had come into its own in China, as attested by a sharp jump in the number of AI colleges and academic research institutes,[13] and by the appearance of new state enactments that focused on AI specifically, such as a February 2017 amendment to the "National Science and Technology Innovation Programs" (above, State Council No. 43) adding "artificial intelligence 2.0" to the disciplines targeted for world status by 2030.[14]

The defining document for China's AI program was issued by the State Council on July 8, 2017, titled "The New Generation AI Development Plan" (No. 35).[15] It describes a three-step project to: "synchronize" (同步) AI technology and applications with the world's advanced levels by 2020; make breakthroughs in basic AI theory with some technology and applications reaching world-leading levels by 2025; and lead the world in AI theory, technology, and applications by 2030, a decade from now.

As expected, under "Key Tasks" in Section 4, the plan called for "speeding up the introduction of top AI talent and younger AI talent worldwide" to form China's "high ground" (高地) of AI experts. This goal will be achieved through:

- cooperation and interaction with major AI institutes worldwide;
- use of "special channels and policies" to recruit top AI persons;
- "flexible introduction" (柔性引进) of AI talent via projects and consultation;
- coordination with China's foreign talent programs ("Thousand Talents Plan").

Under "Resource allocation" (Section 3, "Coordinate international and domestic innovation resources"), the plan reads in part:

> Support cooperation between domestic AI enterprises and international AI leading universities, research institutes and teams. Encourage China's AI companies to go global. Facilitate overseas mergers and acquisitions, equity investments, venture capital investments, and the establishment of overseas R&D centers. Encourage foreign AI companies and scientific research institutes to set up R&D centers in China.

This State Council plan was followed on December 14 of that year by a Ministry of Industry and Information Technology (MIIT) action plan[16] for "full use of bilateral and multilateral international cooperation mechanisms" and "attracting high level AI talent and innovative entrepreneurial talent by various means." The plan recommended using the "Thousand Talents" and "Ten Thousand Talents" plans to support its staffing goals.

Another example of state support for access to foreign AI resources is the Education Ministry's "AI Innovation Action Plan for Institutes of Higher Education" issued on April 2, 2018 (No. 3).[17] Its "Key Tasks" are largely foreign-oriented. They include:

> Increase international academic exchanges and cooperation. Support the establishment of 111 Project 'foreign intellect bases' (引智基地, see Chapter 2)[18] and joint laboratories for international cooperation in the field of AI; cultivate international science programs and major scientific projects; accelerate the introduction of internationally renowned scholars to join in establishing scientific disciplines and scientific research;

organize high-level international academic AI conferences; promote Chinese scholars to important posts in relevant international academic organizations, etc.

One more document completes our chronology of AI statutory "notifications." On October 12, 2018 the Ministry of Science and Technology issued "Project Application Guidelines for S&T Innovation 2030—'New Generation Artificial Intelligence' 2018 Major Projects" (No. 208),[19] as a follow up to the July 2017 "New Generation AI Development Plan." The document is interesting for two reasons: among the three categories funded, the first is "fundamental theory of new generation AI" (新一代人工智能的基础理论), which notwithstanding China's primary interest in applications should dispel the idea that, in this case at least, China cares about applications *only*. Both this and the next category "key generic technologies serving major needs"—the expected "practical" research— list an equal number of projects.

A second key feature is that while applicants are restricted to "China mainland-registered R&D institutes, universities, and enterprises," project leaders can be foreign scientists (外籍科学家) employed by a Chinese entity or concurrently "by both a foreign and Chinese employer."[20] This caveat is reiterated in an English posting, where the entire passage is underlined presumably for emphasis,[21] and helps explain what talent award recipients and "two bases" (两个基地) co-optees end up doing.[22] It also clarifies the paradox of how a country, long poor at abstract science (see Chapter 1), can keep abreast of—and potentially lead—theory-driven international science.

As in Chapter 1, we have devoted considerable space to document the statutory record of support for China's foreign technology transfers here, since the issue of state sponsorship is sometimes called into question, yet is very important to liberal governments that need to justify mitigation.

Other state-sponsored AI technology transfers

State Council pronouncements affecting China's S&T development are followed by notifications from cognizant ministries "implementing" (落实) their expressed and implied aspects. Each of the three examples (immediately above) of MIIT (14 December 2017), Ministry of Education (MOE) (2 April 2018), and Ministry of Science and Technology (MOST) (12 October 2018) directives puts into effect elements of the general plan—here, the State Council's "New Generation AI Development Plan"—that impact their ministerial domains.[23]

These ministry documents are cited at provincial and municipal levels, often with a link to the original State Council directive, and are propagated downward in "talent" program calls, conference announcements, on the websites of China's overseas consulates, and in the communications of Sino-foreign professional associations abroad to rally support for PRC state-backed programs. Given the ubiquity of this pattern and its transparency, it is hard to understand the reluctance of some people outside China, even policymakers, to identify these projects and the transfer recommendations embodied in them with deliberate state sponsorship. Let's examine these connections further.

Each of China's technical ministries, and others focused on general aspects of governance, have offices charged with supporting China's foreign technology transfer program.[24] In MOST's case, there are seven: the Department of International Cooperation (国际合作司), Department of Overseas Intellectual Resources Cooperation (引进国外智力管理司),[25] Department of Foreign Expert Services (外国专家服务司), a Foreign Talent Research Center (国外人才研究中心), China Science and Technology Exchange Center (中国科学技术交流中心), a Service Center for S&T Personnel Exchange and Development (科技人才交流开发服务中心), and an affiliated China International Talent Exchange Foundation (中国国际人才交流基金会).[26] A survey by the present authors of online postings show most of these units involved in facilitating access to foreign AI technology.[27] This finding is consistent with (former) science minister Wan Gang's (万钢) call at an AI kick-off meeting (启动会) in 2017 to "deepen international AI cooperation."[28]

MOST's commitment to support AI development crystallized in an August 2019 notification establishing 20 "New Generation AI Innovation Development Experimental Zones"[29] nationwide to serve as "repeatable models" for adapting AI technology to local circumstances. The zones will offer opportunities for "international cooperation," "converting S&T achievements," and "bringing in talent." The program mirrors a MOST project started in 1988 to create "innovation service centers for new and high technology" (高新技术创业服务中心), which began as models or "demonstrators" (示范) and numbered in the hundreds by the turn of the century. The centers invariably became co-located with "pioneering parks for overseas Chinese scholars" (海外留学人员创业园), i.e., technology commercialization enclaves, and eventually merged with them.[30]

Similarly, the State Administration of Foreign Experts Affairs (国家外国专家局, SAFEA), China's premier foreign technology transfer authority, sponsors forums with foreign groups on AI-related topics[31] beyond its role as an AI talent spotter and recruiter. A Google search on the organization's (Chinese) name and 人工智能 (AI) yielded 90,300 hits in December 2019. The China International Talent Exchange Association (中国国际人才交流协会),[32] a SAFEA front with chapters in 45 China locations and ten offices abroad, gives examples of commercialized foreign AI technologies among 6,570 cases listed on its website.[33] Formally a non-governmental organization (NGO), the association provides co-optees with plausible deniability, although there is no question that it is an appendage of the Chinese state.[34]

The Chinese Academy of Sciences (中国科学院), an umbrella group for several hundred research institutes and other S&T enterprises, engages in foreign transfers through its "Hundred Talents Plan" (百人计划), dedicated transfer offices such as its International Cooperation Bureau (国际合作局), and sponsorship of scholarships that are tantamount to talent recruiting.[35] In 2019, it hosted international symposia on a range of AI disciplines, including high-performance computing, topological quantum computing, non-human primate brain science, connectomics (brain mapping), intelligent robotics, pattern recognition, computational neural modeling, advanced mathematics, brain-inspired AI, and computational intelligence.[36] CAS's Institute of Automation (CASIA) actively promotes collaboration across a range of AI-related disciplines. It operates joint laboratories with Australian, French, Swiss, Hong Kong, and Singaporean universities on connectomics, intelligent recognition, and data-intensive neuroscience in addition.[37]

Here is an excerpt from the Institute's "Introduction to International Cooperation" page:

> More than 320 of CASIA's R/D staff are annually sent abroad on *short-terms for scientific and technological exchanges*. CASIA annually hosts more than 700 overseas guests for scientific visits, and chairs more than ten international conferences each year. Meanwhile, CASIA has actively worked in partnership with a number of internationally well-known research organizations and worldwide companies.[38]
>
> *(our emphasis)*

While the institute engages in academic collaboration, there can be no question that it and its parent function as an appendage of the PRC government.[39] What is true of CAS is true of China's "state key labs" (重点实验室) as well, which numbered 253 in 2016.[40] Several focus on AI directly or related disciplines[41] while conducting worldwide collaboration. Xidian University's MOE Key Laboratory of Intelligent Perception and Image Understanding (智能感知与图像理解教育部重点实验室) is typical. The lab is part of SAFEA and MOE's "Program to Introduce Foreign Intellect for Disciplinary Innovation in Colleges and Universities" (the "111 Project"), is staffed by Changjiang Scholar recipients, and visited by foreign scientists.[42]

The examples can be multiplied. Given these clear links between Chinese research programs and state-directed activity—not to mention its transfer apparatus—the default presumption of foreign governments evaluating cooperative programs should be that a state connection exists.

AI-focused "talent" programs, support guilds, and returnee enclaves

The direct hand of the Chinese state in foreign technology transfers is evident not only in its statutory pronouncements and the declarations of ministries; state sponsorship also extends through to the grassroots and working level. This pattern plays out in AI as in other disciplines.

The operational venues can be analyzed in various ways. Here we introduce one such—a triangular construct involving China's state-run "talent" programs, Sino-foreign overseas support associations, and China's own commercialization or "innovation" centers—2,000 or more interlocking enclaves that dot China's landscape.[43] These venues are described earlier in this volume; here we offer a brief recap to situate them in the context of AI.

China's "talent" recruitment programs, stripped of the jargon, are distinguished from corporate hiring by their programmatic execution and administration by PRC party and state actors. Sponsorship is at the national, provincial, and municipal levels. Persons residing outside China,[44] regardless of citizenship and ethnicity, who have the technical knowledge or managerial skills—or simply access to the needed knowhow—are induced with financial and emotional propositions to go to China and share their expertise for periods of weeks or a year or more. Estimates puts the number of such active, individual programs at well over 500.[45]

Best known is the "Thousand Talents Plan" (千人计划), short for the "Recruitment Program of Global Experts" (海外高层次人才引进计划), founded in 2008 as an arm of the Central Talent Work Coordination Group (中央人才工作协调小组), itself governed by a consortium of 20 ministry-level organizations. Other top-line plans, or programs, are MOE's Chunhui Plan (春晖计划), the Changjiang Scholars Award Program (长江学者奖励计划), and the progenitor of the series: the CAS's "Hundred Talents Plan" (百人计划) founded in 1994 with over 2,200 participants.[46]

Many of these plans and programs post annual lists of co-opted participants along with details of their employment, i.e., their regular overseas jobs, besides the PRC-funded sinecures. The present authors have seen a compilation of extracts from one that included the names of more than 100 sitting US government employees, some of whom were holding sensitive posts in facilities that typically require security clearance. Unsurprisingly, the lists are disappearing as China confronts pushback from aggrieved foreign parties.

As a workaround to the blackout, the authors ran an online search on "thousand talents" in Chinese and English and on specific AI disciplines. The names of multiple persons appeared, which we capped at 100. Within this sample, program selectees were largely from the United States and Europe, typically university professors with specialties in deep learning, intelligent robotics, blockchain, or applied aspects of AI. Some already had dual appointments at Chinese facilities. Others had resumes with a history of support from both the US and Chinese governments, including the US Department of Defense. Searches run on Changjiang Scholars and the Chunhui Plan elicited similar results.

These talent calls appear on ministry-run "exchange" websites, foreign consulate pages, and in the "announcements" or "employment opportunities" sections of Sino-foreign professional groups worldwide. Counts of these latter organizations vary depending on criteria; a recent survey lists over 200 (see Chapter 1). Composed of diaspora Chinese, these associations (协会) of technical experts are viewed by Beijing as important conduits for technology transfer and are feted accordingly. The groups themselves, with few exceptions, align with China's interests as stated in their charters ("serve the ancestral country") and demonstrated in their actual behavior.

As with talent program participants, the members of these overseas technical support guilds include a spectrum of corporate figures, university researchers, entrepreneurs, and government employees. Participants number from a few hundred to many thousands. Some associations have PRC officials on their advisory boards. Others act as advisors to the Chinese government.[47] Entry thresholds are high—generally Ph.D. in hand or in progress—coinciding with China's talent program requirements, making the organizations and their members prime targets for co-option, although the motivation to collaborate owes as much to local initiatives organized by officers and staff of the associations themselves.[48]

The growth in AI's importance to China parallels an increase in the attention given it by these associations. The North American Chinese Scholars International Exchange Center (北美洲中国学人国际交流中心), headquartered in McLean VA, funneled to China only two AI projects in 2010.[49] In 2019, the number was eight.[50] In 2017, the Federation of Associations of Chinese Professionals in Southern USA (美南中国专家协会联合会), an Atlanta-based group, pitched ten AI projects in China's Jiangsu Province.[51] Houston's Chinese Association of Professionals in Science and Technology (中国旅美专家协会) in 2018 demonstrated AI and ML products at a forum attended by persons from Anhui, with which the group collaborates.[52]

The Association of Chinese–American Scientists and Engineers (旅美中国科学家工程师专业人士协会), a Midwest group with 12 chapters, featured AI at its meeting on October 13, 2018—one day after MOST formally released its application guidelines for "New Generation AI Projects." Two weeks later, it stood up a dedicated AI branch to "promote exchange of cutting-edge S&T and strengthen strategic cooperation."[53] A month earlier, the Chinese Association for Science and Technology USA (中国留美科技协会), an affiliate of its China-based namesake,[54] convened a forum on AI's future,[55] while its engineering counterpart, the Chinese Institute of Engineers USA (美洲中国工程师学会), met to discuss AI applications.[56]

The initiatives were not limited to US-based associations. In 2017–2018, when Beijing was publicizing its "New Generation AI Development Plan" and related implementation protocols, some 400 Chinese students and experts in Japan created the China–Japan Association for Artificial Intelligence (中日人工智能协会) to facilitate "exchanges, cooperation and globalization" of AI projects.[57] A China–Britain AI Association (中英人工智能协会) was founded by Chinese nationals in London "interested in the development of artificial intelligence by utilizing the resources and innovations being made in both countries."[58] The German–Chinese Association of Artificial Intelligence (德中人工智能协会) was also set up for "cooperation and exchange" (see Chapter 8 for more).[59]

Both talent selectees and guild collaborators are assigned to Chinese academic posts, vacancies in key labs, or positions in China's commercialization facilities, known variously as "national technology transfer centers" (国家技术转移中心), "innovation service centers" (创业服务中心), "innovation service centers for new and high technology" (高新技术创业服务中心), and "pioneering parks for overseas Chinese scholars" (海外留学人员创业园). The different genres, a function of era and sponsorship, share a common mission of transforming technology and ideas—domestic or foreign—into marketable products. Here, in these subsidized enclaves, is where China's gift for practical creativity comes into play.[60]

As expected, the uptick observed in 2017–2018 among overseas ethnic associations' AI support work and associated talent program calls is seen in the activities of these "innovation" enclaves. In July 2017, Jiangsu's Center of International Technology Transfer (江苏省跨国技术转移中心) held a forum attended by experts from Carnegie Mellon and UCLA on transfer opportunities in robotics and AI.[61] In 2018, MOST hosted a conference at Beijing's China International Technology Transfer Center (中国国际技术转移中心) to "establish communication channels and mechanisms for international technology transfer, and promote transformation of international innovation cooperation results." AI was featured."[62]

Looking at the returnee parks, an online search conducted by the authors in 2019 returned data on AI, machine learning, and intelligent manufacturing start-ups in facilities located in Beijing, Changchun, Changsha, Chengdu, Dalian, Fujian, Hangzhou, Hefei, Hohhot, Jiangyin, Jieyang, Kunshan, Nanjing, Ningbo, Shanghai, Shenzhen, Tangshan, Tianjin, Wuhan, Xiamen, Yantai and Zhuhai. Each of these cases involves IPR created abroad or as a result of having done research abroad.

Although causation is hard to establish, there is no denying that these three key elements of China's technology transfer apparatus—talent co-option programs, foreign support guilds, and commercialization enclaves—function in lockstep to promote Beijing's AI agenda.

Foreign AI "talent flows"

China's AI companies and the Chinese state itself are aware of opportunities for technology transfer by recruiting from, and investing in, foreign high-tech sectors, and spare no effort to exploit this venue. While the techniques used—direct hires, overseas "workstations," joint ventures, start-up competitions, corporate, state-backed, and angel fund investments—are legal, their scope and success in redirecting AI foreign talent to China are alarming. Although our focus here is the US, the phenomenon is worldwide. Let's look first at company staffing.

China's top AI companies—the so-called "BATH" group—consisting of Baidu (百度), Alibaba (阿里巴巴), Tencent (腾讯), and Huawei (华为), often compared to Google, Amazon, Facebook, and Apple, and others such as JD Research (京东AI研究院) and iFlytek (科大讯飞) all have AI staffs comprised heavily of foreign-resident or foreign-educated persons. Baidu's AI umbrella group (AIG) has labs in Silicon Valley and is advised by a board of American scientists.[63] Most of Alibaba's Damo Academy and Tencent's AI Lab have US pedigrees and both run outreach programs to co-opt global research.[64,65] JD AI Research recruits from its offices in the US and Europe.[66] A China Nikkei article notes that these top companies occupied half the recruiting stalls at the American Association for Artificial Intelligence's 2018 meeting, adding that:

> China's students train in AI in the United States, the world's leading country in AI research, then return to China to further improve their technical strengths.[67]

Less euphemistically, their training benefits Chinese—not US—companies. Beyond direct hires, China's AI companies also maintain overseas labs to gauge markets and access foreign talent. Baidu has an Institute for Deep Learning and a Silicon Valley Artificial Intelligence Lab in Sunnyvale, Alibaba has outposts in Seattle and Sunnyvale, and Tencent runs an AI Lab in Seattle. Sensetime (商汤科技), a computer vision and deep learning company, has an AI lab in New Jersey and synchronizes development (同步开拓) between its China and Silicon Valley locations.[68] Smaller China-invested AI companies in the US number in the hundreds.[69]

The influx is not limited to China's private sector firms—the Chinese state is also directly involved on the ground. An example is the ZGC Innovation Center @ Silicon Valley (中关村硅谷创新中心),[70] a 7,000 square meter facility set up in 2015 in Santa Clara.[71] The center has hosted 55 start-ups and invested in another 40.[72] According to its director Luo Wei (罗炜), at this and other "overseas workstations" (海外工作站) "not only can scientists with exemplary achievements contribute to China's scientific research while in America, they can at the same time continue to train talent, and link up the steady stream of overseas talent with Chinese innovation, entrepreneurship, and capital." The official summarized his joyful points with an aphorism:

> In bringing "talented people" (人才) overseas back to China, the key is to bring back the 'talent' (才). The "people" (人) don't need to go back (引进海外人才回国，关键是引才，人不一定要回去).[73]

This maxim, captured in the motto 引才留人 ("bring back the skills, leave the people there"), restates China's "two bases" (两个基地) or "work in place" model enacted in the early 1990s.[74] The strategy makes a mockery of US government countermeasures that see "retention" of foreign talent as the cornerstone to technological security (see also Chapter 2).

Angel funds

These government and company facilities—sometimes called accelerators—are complemented by "angel fund" consortia supporting Chinese–American AI start-ups, which in balance are at least as effective. Prominent among them are Beijing's ZhenFund (真格基金);[75] TechCode (太库科技) with offices in Beijing, Boston, and Silicon Valley;[76] and Sinovation Ventures (创新工场) with locations in Beijing, Shanghai, Shenzhen, Palo Alto and Seattle. By 2017, these China-oriented investors had made 641 AI tech investments in the US totaling $19 billion.[77]

Start-up competitions

Meanwhile, the confluence of two Chinese memes, namely, "innovation and entrepreneurship" (创新创业) among small-and-medium enterprises (SME), and "maker China" (创客中国), which depicts a garage shop spirit of collaborative discovery, helped foster another form of technology transfer that has found a niche in tech culture—the start-up competition.

In May 2018, MIIT launched a "'Maker China' International Innovation and Entrepreneurship Competition" under the theme "Make your story happen in China" (创新机遇在中国) to meet the "knowledge and technology needs" of China's international cooperation zones (中外合作区) and SME Advanced Manufacturing International Cooperation Zones (中小企业先进制造业中外合作区). The

---

BOX 11.1 THE "INNOVATION" IMPERATIVE

The Chinese phrase "innovation and entrepreneurship," abbreviated "*shuangchuang*" ("double create" from "create novelty, create enterprises"), is enshrined as one of "ten major popular sayings" (十大流行语) governing economic activity. The concept won statutory support from the State Council in 2016 (No. 43) and 2018 (No. 32).

The term "maker China" (*chuangke zhongguo*)'s first word (创客) is "a comprehensive interpretation of the English words 'maker' and 'hacker'," i.e., people "happy to share technology and exchange ideas." (zh.wikipedia.org/wiki/创客)

These terms highlight the importance—near fanaticism—China attaches to the need to innovate, a proposition taken for granted elsewhere. We believe it is meant to counter a cultural bias *against* innovation that China addresses by accessing foreign models, as the context suggests.

announcement was posted to the Xi'an Hi-Tech Industries Development Zone (西安高新技术产业开发区) website and reported the selection of 26 projects for a nationwide "road show" (巡回路演), i.e., the competition's final stage. Half were AI or IT related.[78]

The following year, a "2019 Anhui Innovation and Entrepreneurship Competition" took off at the behest of Hefei's municipal government, one of several China start-up competitions held in California's Silicon Valley and elsewhere by China state entities. The runoffs proceeded as follows: (June 1–September 1) registration; (September 1–September 14) evaluation by expert panel and investors; (September 14–September 28) road shows by the participants.[79]

"AI and Big Data" was one of three categories. Of 350 initial participants, 45 made it to the second round, and nine (three teams for each category) joined the final competition in Hefei.[80]

Hefei's events are managed by the Button Group, a "cross-border investment and consulting company" with offices in Mountain View, CA and on Hefei's University of Science and Technology of China (USTC) campus. Here is their description of accomplishments:

> Through the 2017 "Creating China" Anhui Innovation and Entrepreneurship Competition we brought back 30 overseas projects; 16 landed in the Hefei Hi-tech Zone, and 9 settled in other provinces. The 2018 event brought back 40 overseas projects. Button helped 16 overseas companies land in China.[81]

We surmise from the forgoing that China perceives benefit from its ability to access foreign AI talent—the skills (才) with or without the persons (人). What of the foreign AI presence in China? Most major US companies doing AI research have an R&D facility there, which they use to adapt products to local conditions and to expand their innovation base. IBM, Google, Amazon, Intel, and Apple are all represented.[82] Among these companies, Microsoft stands out for its:

- Microsoft Research Asia (MSRA, 微软亚洲学院) facility, established in Beijing in 1998, long before AI became a household word, with more than 200 scientists and some 300 visiting scholars and students;[83]
- National Engineering Laboratory for Brain-inspired Intelligence Technology and Application (类脑智能技术及应用国家工程实验室, NEL-BITA) co-founded with China's CAS, Fudan University, Baidu, and iFlytek at Hefei's USTC campus in 2017;[84]
- Next Generation AI Open Research and Education Platform (新一代人工智能开放科研与教育平台) founded with Beijing University, USTC, Xi'an Jiaotong University, and Zhejiang University under MOE auspices in 2018;[85] and
- Microsoft–INESA AI Innovation Center, co-located with MSRA's Shanghai branch, established in 2018 with INESA, "a large-scale state-owned

enterprise group affiliated with the Shanghai State-owned Assets Supervision and Administration Commission."[86]

Cui bono?

It's fair to ask who gains most from the relationship. Matt Sheehan poses this question, in a highly interesting article that traces the impact of an MSRA paper, and the subsequent careers of the paper's authors. His response is a lack of "granular data" precludes a definitive answer.[87]

We would argue, however, that even with better data, Sheehan may be comparing apples and oranges, since it doesn't follow that what benefits Microsoft—a multinational company with a multinational perspective—helps the US, whereas it is clear that China the nation benefits strategically from the training, creative atmosphere, accumulated knowhow, and international contacts available to those doing a stint at the Microsoft China facilities.

So how does Microsoft see its role? The following is from its Chinese news site: "Microsoft endeavors to be a reliable partner to the Chinese government, using its technical prowess to help solve the major problems in the country's development."[88] The company's intent was also captured in a 2002 memorandum of cooperation signed with MOE—the "Great Wall Plan" (长城计划)—focused on "talent training, scientific research cooperation, curriculum building, and academic exchanges, with MSRA serving as the precursor platform."[89]

Now let's look at China's side of the balance sheet. According to Hsiao-Wuen Hon (洪小文), present director of MSRA, Microsoft Research's role in China compares to that of the Whampoa Military Academy (黄埔军校) in the early Republican era, where China's future military leaders first trained.[90] Statistics from the MSRA website bear this out:

> In the past 20 years, of the 7,000-plus persons [at MSRA], more than 55 have been honored as IEEE fellows, ACM fellows, and Thousand Talents [selectees]; 115 became entrepreneurs; 18 served as CEOs and CTOs of China's top-ranking Internet companies; five were founders of "unicorn" companies;[91] and 200 taught at top universities.[92]

Let that sink in. It's hard to fathom any company—or for that matter, any constellation of state policies and incentives—playing a greater role in a nation's high-tech development. It raises the question of what contribution the company's new China-based AI, and especially brain-inspired AI, facilities will make toward US security and prosperity.

Chinese scholars on the matter of Chinese innovation

Space precludes discussing every venue and technique used by China to access foreign AI technology, for example, international conferences, transfer forums, AI think tanks with foreign ties, co-authorship, academic exchanges[93] and, obviously, espionage. Instead, we conclude this survey by presenting what Chinese scholars see as the main dynamic missing in China's AI program, which may shed light on the direction in which transfer initiatives are headed.

In a nutshell, the consensus is that China still lacks the motivation and talent to innovate in the theory and mathematics that support AI.

According to Xu Kuangdi (徐匡迪), former head of the Chinese Academy of Engineering (CAE), "The cornerstone of artificial intelligence is mathematics, and the key element is algorithms. But China's investment in this field is far behind the United States."[94]

Zheng Nanning (郑南宁), AI and robotics professor at Xi'an Jiaotong University and another CAE academician, believes it will take China another five to ten years to reach "Anglo-American" levels in basic theoretical and algorithmic research. Hardware design is also an issue.[95]

Sun Maosong (孙茂松), professor at Tsinghua University's Department of Computer Science and Technology, argues that China lacks leaders in world-class scientific research and falls way behind in training "top talent in the basic sciences."[96]

Yau Shing-Tung (丘成桐), Harvard professor and Fields Medal winner, after acknowledging China's achievements in applied AI technologies, concludes that China "is still some distance from the United States and Britain in terms of basic theory and algorithm innovation."[97]

These claims accord with Sinovation founder and AI author Kai-Fu Lee's argument that China's forte—and decisive advantage—lies in its ability to churn out practical implementations, not in AI theory.[98] We predict China will address this deficit as it always has: by seeking the "talent" it needs from abroad.

Notes

1 This chapter is a follow-up to William Hannas and Huey-Meei Chang, "China's Access to Foreign AI Technology." Georgetown University, Center for Strategic and Emerging Technology. September 2019.

2 AI as an academic discipline dates from the mid-1950s. The field passed through several boom and bust cycles as hype and speculation led to disappointments and loss of funding.

3 The present authors were first inspired by Oxford philosopher Nick Bostrom's 2014 book *Superintelligence: Paths, Dangers, Strategies* and more recently by Kai-Fu Lee's 2018 volume *AI Superpowers: China, Silicon Valley, and the New World Order*, albeit for different reasons.

4 国务院关于积极推进"互联网+"行动的指导意见. State Council (40), July 1, 2015.

5 四部门关于印发《"互联网+"人工智能三年行动实施方案》的通知. National Development and Reform Commission, Ministry of Science and Technology, Ministry of Industry and Information Technology (MIIT), and the Cyberspace Administration of China, May 23, 2016. (Authors' note: AI as it relates to China's "Internet +" program, not "Internet plus AI.").

6 国务院关于印发"十三五"国家科技创新规划的通知. State Council (43), July 28, 2016.

7 For a full-length treatment of Chinese research in BI-AI, connectomics, and BCI, see William Hannas and Huey-Meei, "China AI-Brain Research." Georgetown University, Center for Strategic and Emerging Technology. (July) forthcoming.

8 国务院关于印发"十三五"国家科技创新规划的通知. State Council (43), July 28, 2016.

9 国务院关于印发"十三五"国家战略性新兴产业发展规划的通知. State Council (67).

10 Ibid.

11 "再创新," i.e., innovative use of someone else's innovation.

12 i.e., technology spotters and transfer brokers.

13 The number of new AI colleges grew at one per year in 2015 and 2016, rose to eight in 2017, and reached 28 new colleges or research institutes in 2018, according to the MOE's China Education and Research Network (www.edu.cn/rd/gao_xiao_cheng_guo/gao_xiao_zi_xun/201904/t20190429_1656772.shtml). In 2019, the Ministry of Education approved an additional 180 "new AI-related majors" to undergraduate curricula. www.moe.gov.cn/srcsite/A08/s7056/202003/t20200303_426853.html.

14 www.most.gov.cn/ztzl/lhzt/lhzt2017/hkjlhzt2017/hkj_fbh02/201702/t20170228_131502.htm.

15 国务院关于印发新一代人工智能发展规划的通知. State Council (35).

16 促进新一代人工智能产业发展三年行动计划 (Three-Year Action Plan to Promote the Development of New-Generation AI Industry), MIIT, December 14, 2017. Section 4, "Accelerate the cultivation of talent." (No. 315).

17 高等学校人工智能创新行动计划. MOE, (No. 3), April 2, 2018.

18 The "111 Project" or "Overseas Expertise Introduction Project for Discipline Innovation" (see chapter 1) was started in 2006 by the MOE and MOST's State Administration of Foreign Experts Affairs to recruit some 1,000 top international scientists to serve at 100 centers, with the goal of "introducing foreign intellect" (引进国外智力) at Chinese universities.

19 科技部关于发布科技创新2030—"新一代人工智能"重大项目2018年度项目申报指南的通知, MOST (No. 208), October 12, 2018.

20 www.most.gov.cn/mostinfo/xinxifenlei/fgzc/gfxwj/gfxwj2018/201810/t20181012_142131.htm.

21 http://chinainnovationfunding.eu/project/2030-megaproject-new-generation-artificial-intelligence.

22 Accepting concurrent employment and undertaking research projects entrusted by PRC institutions while working overseas is incentivized activity discussed in Chapter 2 under the "Serve the Homeland Action Plan."

23 The directives share a common format. After naming its targeted audience, the documents read: "So as to implement (为落实) such-and-such a higher level notification," followed by a short list of objectified goals, and an itemized presentation of the content. Their stereotyped nature is a gift to analysts, as these documents are easily traced and compared, and can generally be taken at their face value.

24 See *CIE*, Chapter 3 "PRC-based Technology Transfer Organizations."

25 Literally the "Department for Managing the Introduction of Foreign Intellect."

26 SAFEA, a quasi-independent organization, was placed under MOST in 2018.

27 Hannas and Chang, "China's Access to Foreign AI Technology—an Assessment," op. cit.

28 www.most.gov.cn/kjbgz/201711/t20171120_136303.htm.

29 科技部关于印发《国家新一代人工智能创新发展试验区建设工作指引》的通知, MOST (298), August 29, 2019.

30 *CIE*, p. 176.

31 www.safea.gov.cn/content.shtml?id=12750366.

32 Formerly the "China Association for the International Exchange of Personnel" (CAIEP). The Chinese name itself remained unchanged.

33 www.caiep.net/achieve/index.

34 *CIE*, pp. 95–96.
35 *CIE*, pp. 87–88.
36 www.bic.cas.cn/gjhy/jqgjhylb/201907/P020190725742660780529.pdf.
37 http://english.ia.cas.cn/ic/introduction/.
38 Ibid. Passage edited for English grammar.
39 The controversy over CAS's status was laid to rest on October 22, 2019, when *Nature* published a rebuttal penned by CAS's Zhang Qingquan to the journal's assertion that CAS was independent. In Zhang's words: "CAS is not run independently of government, as you imply. The establishment and development of CAS have been entirely based on the wisdom and support of the central government.... CAS has never sought or achieved financial autonomy. Over the past 40 years, half of its income has come directly from central government investment; the rest has been from competitive funding or technology transfer." www.nature.com/articles/d41586-019-03205-z.
40 2016 国家重点实验室年度报告, MOST, December 2017.
41 E.g., the State Key Laboratory of Cognitive Intelligence (认知智能国家重点实验室) set up by MOST in 2017 under Iflytek's management.
42 http://see.xidian.edu.cn/iiip.
43 See Chapter 1 of the present volume.
44 Inward-facing calls for "talented persons" (人才) needed by this or that employing "unit" (单位) are everyday fare. We focus here on dedicated programs aimed at people living outside mainland China, including Taiwan, Hong Kong, and Macao.
45 Testimony from FBI Director Christopher Wray, cited in "The Chinese Threat to US Research Institutions Is Real," *Washington Post*, December 19, 2019. Author's unclassified discussions with currently serving analysts.
46 Data as of 2014. www.gov.cn/xinwen/2014-06/08/content_2696361.htm.
47 *CIE*, p. 125.
48 Decades of employment within the USG have given the authors a close-up view of the relationship between data collection requirements and the behavior of downstream collectors. As often as not, the requirements are written on the basis of what the collectors say is available. We would expect that principle to apply here and indeed have seen evidence of local associations pitching technologies to China in advance of specific calls.
49 http://tsrcw.com/zgjrc/Detial.aspx?id=4211.
50 http://fn.tsrcw.com/html/detail_12197.html.
51 www.wxhsdj.gov.cn/detail.php?id=3205.
52 www.xinhuanet.com/overseas/2018-05/02/c_129862909.htm.
53 www.acse.org/index.php?sub=bulletin&type=news#Oct%2013,%202018.
54 China Association for Science and Technology (中国科学技术协会).
55 www.yuanshihui.cn/detail/84b68b883d9f8ecb1efe7e1f.
56 https://chineseradioseattle.com/2018/09/10/cie_sea_2018-2/.
57 "日本と中国の間の交流「連携及びグローバル化" http://cjaai.com協会について.
58 www.cbaia.org.uk/en/cbaia.
59 www.gcaai.org/zh/index.html#about.
60 See www.tt91.com for a fuller description.
61 http://std.jiangsu.gov.cn/art/2017/7/13/art_7528_3661085.html.
62 www.cittc.net/news/detail/2467.
63 http://research.baidu.com/Blog/index-view?id=108.
64 https://damo.alibaba.com/labs.
65 https://ai.tencent.com/ailab/en/about.
66 http://air.jd.com/#index.
67 http://cn.nikkei.com/china/company/29181-2018-02-11-05-00-50.html.
68 www.sensetime.com.
69 Hannas and Chang, "China's Access to Foreign AI Technology—an Assessment," p. 20.

70 Zhongguancun (中关村), a major high-tech development zone in Beijing, is operated jointly by the municipal government and private sector.
71 www.chinadaily.com.cn/micro-reading/interface_yidian/2016-01-04/14454124.html.
72 https://de.reuters.com/article/us-usa-trade-china-startups/in-silicon-valley-chinese-accelerators-aim-to-bring-startups-home-idUSKCN1II0UG.
73 http://world.people.com.cn/n1/2017/0307/c1002-29129869.html.
74 *CIE*, pp. 171–174.
75 www.zhenfund.com.
76 www.techcode.com.
77 "From China with Love: AI, Robotics, AR/VR Are Hot Areas for Chinese Investment In US," CB Insights, August 1, 2017. www.cbinsights.com/research/chinese-investment-us-tech-expert-research/.
78 www.xdz.gov.cn/info/20498/195744.htm.
79 www.cxzghw.com/en/index.html.
80 www.xinhuanet.com/tech/2019-09/29/c_1125057757.htm.
81 www.cxzghw.com/en/about-button.html (English edited for grammar and style.).
82 Hannas and Chang., "China's Access to Foreign AI Technology—an Assessment," p. 15.
83 www.microsoft.com/en-us/research/lab/microsoft-research-asia.
84 http://leinao.ustc.edu.cn.
85 www.msra.cn/zh-cn/connections/academic-programs/ai-research-and-education-platform.
86 https://news.microsoft.com/apac/2018/09/17/microsoft-establishes-microsoft-research-asia-shanghai-and-a-new-ai-innovation-center/.
87 Matt Sheehan, "Who Benefits from American AI Research in China?" *Macro Polo*, October 21, 2019.
88 https://news.microsoft.com/zh-ch/微软中国介绍/.
89 www.msra.cn/zh-cn/news/executivebylines/msra-20th-anniversary.
90 Ibid.
91 Privately held start-up companies valued at over $1 billion. (en.wikipedia.org).
92 www.msra.cn/zh-cn/about/alumni/headlines/刚20岁的她，为何在计算机研究领域如此杰出？
93 See Hannas and Chang, "China's Access to Foreign AI Technology—an Assessment" for a comprehensive listing.
94 www.caeshc.com.cn/news_view.php?id=7997.
95 www.nature.com/articles/d41586-019-02360-7.
96 https://mp.weixin.qq.com/s/YtXW8HlWlRGGxQn5aOeabA.
97 http://news.stcn.com/2019/1017/15436849.shtml.
98 www.voachinese.com/a/kai-fu-lee-on-ai-development-2018116/4662278.html.

Bibliography

Bostrom, Nick. *Superintelligence: Paths, Dangers, Strategies*, Oxford: Oxford University Press, 2014.
Hannas, William C. and Huey-Meei Chang. "China's Access to Foreign AI Technology," Georgetown University, Center for Strategic and Emerging Technology, September 2019.
Hannas, William C. and Huey-Meei Chang. "China AI-Brain Research" Georgetown University, Center for Strategic and Emerging Technology, (forthcoming 2020).
Lee, Kai-Fu. *AI Superpowers: China, Silicon Valley, and the New World Order*, Boston, CO: Houghton Mifflin Harcourt, 2018.
PRC Ministry of Education. 高等学校人工智能创新行动计划 ("AI Innovation Action Plan for Institutes of Higher Education"), MOE (3), April 2, 2018.

PRC Ministry of Industry and Information Technology. 促进新一代人工智能产业发展三年行动计划 ("Three-Year Action Plan to Promote the Development of New-Generation AI Industry"), MIIT (315), December 14, 2017.

PRC Ministry of Science and Technology. 2016 国家重点实验室年度报告, ("2016 State Key Laboratories Annual Report"), MOST, December 2017.

PRC Ministry of Science and Technology. 科技部关于发布科技创新2030—"新一代人工智能"重大项目2018年度项目申报指南的通知 ("Project Application Guidelines for S&T Innovation 2030—'New Generation Artificial Intelligence' 2018 Major Projects"), MOST (208), October 12, 2018.

PRC Ministry of Science and Technology. 科技部关于印发《国家新一代人工智能创新发展试验区建设工作指引》的通知, ("New Generation AI Innovation Development Experimental Zones"), MOST (298), August 29, 2019.

PRC National Development and Reform Commission, et al. 四部门关于印发《"互联网+"人工智能三年行动实施方案》, ("Three-Year Action Implementation Plan for 'Internet +' Artificial Intelligence"), May 23, 2016.

PRC State Council. 国务院关于积极推进"互联网+"行动的指导意见 ("State Council Guiding Opinions on Positively Promoting 'Internet +' Activity"), SC (40), July 1, 2015.

PRC State Council. 国务院关于印发"十三五"国家科技创新规划的通知 ("State Council Notification on National Science and Technology Innovation Programs for the 13th Five-Year Plan"), SC (43), July 28, 2016.

PRC State Council. 国务院关于印发"十三五"国家战略性新兴产业发展规划的通知 ("Notification on National Strategic Emerging Industry Development Projects for the 13th Five-Year Plan"), SC (67), November 29, 2016.

PRC State Council. 国务院关于印发新一代人工智能发展规划的通知("The New Generation AI Development Plan") SC (35), July 8, 2017.

Sheehan, Matt. "Who Benefits from American AI Research in China?" *Macro Polo*. October 21, 2019.

12

THE IMPACT OF CHINA'S POLICIES

*Didi Kirsten Tatlow, Greg Walton and
Anna B. Puglisi*

In previous chapters we cataloged ways in which the Chinese government uses state policies and programs to extract foreign technology and knowhow, and how this behavior challenges global norms of commerce and research. Here we present two case studies and two vignettes involving emerging technologies that show how these practices are not "rogue acts" but derive from a comprehensive technology acquisition strategy designed and carried out by the Chinese state to expand its domestic economy and strengthen the influence of the CPC at home and abroad.

The examples illustrate the magnitude of the challenge. Yet nations targeted by this behavior are ill equipped to counter it. Mitigation tools available to government agencies, law enforcement, and research institutes are typically geared toward individual transgressions of law, policy, or ethics, and have not been designed to address, or even grasp, coordinated state-driven acts of this size. While individual cases may not appear problematic, taken together—viewed through a strategic lens—they expose common threads that reflect China's developmental priorities:

Set strategic priorities

All of the cases involve technology and industries the Chinese government identified as a strategic priority in policies, often over decades. While some fall into broad categories, China also seeks out less cutting-edge or niche technologies that can fill in gaps or provide scalable opportunities. Decision are not made based on economic viability alone; the Party will accept inefficiency if it results in the acquisition of identified technology. China's willingness to overbid or overinvest in targeted technology allows it and its proxies to undercut global prices (or overpay for global assets). As a result, other private enterprises are unable to compete without sustained funding or other state support.

Use a diverse set of actors

All of these cases involve multiple actors working in unison to meet a common goal. This is not to imply that there is a "puppet-master" in Beijing, but rather that China's efforts include a wide range of participants from academia, state-owned or supported enterprises, and small businesses overseas. While understanding that not every overseas PRC citizen or organization is acting on behalf of the party-state at all times, we must also acknowledge that such parties have been and will continue to be used to serve the broader goals of the CPC. By better understanding strategic policy and tactics we hope Western policymakers and law enforcement authorities will design more efficient and fair mitigation strategies to combat these new forms of espionage.

Promise the China market

The lure of the China market looms large in many cases. Because we treat China as a neutral actor and assume it will acquiesce to global norms, foreign companies or researchers willing to engage with China believe—or want to believe—that they enter transactions and collaboration with shared goals and play by the same rules, when in fact they are up against a nation-state that exploits these arrangements.

Operate within plausible deniability

While some cases show clear violations of laws or policies, many questionable transfers take place in gray areas that offer the Chinese state, its actors on the ground, and co-opted foreigners plausible deniability, thanks to an opaque web of political or institutional affiliations, and the obfuscation of financial ties. Add to this computer network exploitation ("cybertheft"), the use of front organizations to obscure state identities, and influence campaigns that push false narratives, and attribution is often hard to establish.

Build capacity for the future

China's overall acquisition strategy may not be readily apparent through initial individual transactions. In some cases, it may unfold over time, acquiring related technologies and putting in place the building blocks of a specific industry. While individual foreign companies can benefit, China's S&T infrastructure is the overall winner, as Chinese entities capitalize on the new information, technology and skills sets.

These principles are manifested in the case studies that follow.

The Nortel case: technology appropriation and company collapse

For more than 110 years, Nortel Networks Corporation, a multinational telecommunications and networking equipment manufacturer founded in Canada, was inextricably linked to Canada's economic development.[1] In 2009 it collapsed.[2] Most business school case studies or media reporting blamed mismanagement, failure to keep pace with changing times, loss of consumer confidence, a failed restructuring, and auditing scandals.[3]

We focus on another factor—a steady loss of technology and IP to the PRC, as a result of a coordinated and clandestine state campaign by China. We highlight how "extralegal" and "informal" technology transfer practices—neither "normal" joint venture company-style transfer nor clandestine operations—worked *in parallel* with one of the earliest and longest running, "Advanced Persistent Threat" (APT) cyberespionage campaigns. Nortel was the target of a decade-long corporate cyberespionage operation that began at least in 2000, possibly in the late 1990s, and continued until at least 2009.[4]

Founded 1895 as the "Northern Electric and Manufacturing Company Limited," a manufacturer of telephones and telephone equipment for its parent company, Bell Telephone, (founded in turn by Alexander Graham Bell, the inventor of the telephone), Nortel invented Canada's first vacuum tube. This was a foundational technology essential to early computing, and for the repeaters in long-distance telephone networks needed to connect the far-flung country's telegeography.

In the 1970s, Nortel was the first company to produce early digital telecommunications products, pivoting in the 1990s into fiber optic solutions for multiprotocol global networking equipment. These included the first fully digital telephone systems, Internet protocol routers, and telecommunications management software. In parallel with the epoch-defining rise of telecommunications in the twentieth century, Nortel went from being a small telephone equipment manufacturer to being a leading architect of global digital networks. At its height in 2000, it was the ninth most valuable corporation in the world and the world's largest telecommunication company, with sales of more than $30 billion. By 2002, its stock price, overvalued during the dot-com bubble despite the company's failure to show a profit, had collapsed from CAD$124 to CAD$0.47 per share. Two-third of its workforce was laid off. In January 2009, Nortel filed for bankruptcy protection in Canada, the US, and the UK. Today, Nortel networks exist in corporate form only, most of its assets long parceled out to competing enterprises.

Nortel's decline coincided with Huawei's meteoric rise, from a US$100 million reseller in 2000 to the largest telecommunications manufacturer in the world today. Coincidence? No, or, at least, not entirely. Underlying the other, undeniable, factors contributing to Nortel's collapse was an APT attributed to actors in China that exploited vulnerabilities in the company's network to systematically infiltrate and steal intellectual property and other sensitive information. (Huawei's rise was accompanied by other scandal: in 2004 it settled out of court a patent infringement suit brought by Cisco Systems alleging Huawei stole Cisco technology to develop its own suite of routers and switches).[5]

Technology loss through an Advanced Persistent Threat (APT)

Before describing the APT against Nortel, we briefly review the history of China's APT campaigns. APTs are unique in that, unlike other cyberattacks, they may remain dormant for months or years in targeted computers in order to gain access to as much sensitive data as possible without attracting suspicion or triggering alerts. Traditionally, they were targeted to address domestic security concerns and aimed at groups of people seen as threatening CPC control, such as the Falun Gong, or Tibetan or Uyghur exiles. The objective of these programs was to separate overseas civil society networks from like-minded people in China thereby weakening them.

Mulvenon and Chase provided an early account of malware and distributed denial of service (DDOS) attacks on overseas Falun Gong computers in the summer of 1999, noting that Falun Gong organizations received information that the Public Security Bureau "had paid two network security companies to hack the group's sites abroad."[6] A leading cyber threat intelligence vendor, FireEye, says, "China's cyber espionage apparatus most likely came initially out of the ruling party's own internal security needs."[7] China's state-sponsored hackers tested new tools and tactics on these groups before deploying them, likely in the early 2000s, for industrial espionage against Western corporations and governments, it says.[8] Official intelligence on Chinese industrial espionage-linked APT appears later in the timeline, with the first advisory in 2005 in the UK.[9]

Yet evidence suggests that the APT hacks on Nortel began prior to the reported attacks on exile communities. Thus, the timing of the initial breaches appears to challenge the timeline of the evolution of China's cyber espionage capability, suggesting that strategic technology transfer through APT commenced earlier than is generally known—at least by the public.[10] Chinese state actors, or their proxies, accessed Nortel's systems remotely, eventually installing rootkits (spyware designed to make processes running on a device invisible to basic inspection) on employees' computers, to enable ongoing surveillance of infected computers via remote encrypted connections to systems in China. The malign actors accessed internal research and development (R&D) reports, business plans, emails, and technical data from computers throughout the company, including the CEOs. The infiltration was not said to have impacted Nortel's day-to-day operations or compromise manufacturing processes or supply chains. However, the stolen data passed to its competitors would have significantly undermined its competitive advantage after 2000—and would be the key factor that led to its collapse, undermining its core business strength—its IP portfolio—which might otherwise have survived even the corporate shenanigans that took place.

Nortel was an excellent target due to its lax cybersecurity. In September 1991, its Australian network was allegedly compromised by a small group of Australian hackers led by WikiLeaks founder Julian Assange, in an attempt to gain access to information that would allow them to manipulate telephone exchanges and install backdoors in software to control Nortel telephone switches worldwide. Once inside the system, Assange found the company's internal security to be relaxed.[11] He was able to access Nortel's systems worldwide, including those at company headquarters in Brampton, Ontario. The three hackers who participated in this operation were eventually caught and convicted but not before they had installed password-cracking software on computers in Canada, thereby obtaining 5,000 passwords to Nortel computers worldwide.

Nortel management repeatedly dismissed the risk of espionage. A former official of the Canadian Security Intelligence Service (CSIS) said that as early as the mid-1990s the agency reported its concerns but these were dismissed by executives more interested in doing business with China: "at that time, we noticed there was quite a lot of activity around Nortel, and we tried to approach Nortel, but we were brushed off," Michel Juneau-Katsuya, ex Asia-Pacific bureau chief at CSIS, said.[12] Yet Brian Shields, the former head of cyber security at Nortel, tells a different story: after cyberbreaches were discovered, in 2004, "We went to the RCMP and turned everything over.... There was no help. CSIS came to us in 2009, finally, five years later, to offer to help just before the bankruptcy announcement.... Like, where have you guys been?" he said in a media report.[13]

After the breaches were discovered Nortel changed compromised passwords of employees but key cyber security recommendations by Shields were not implemented. Nortel is also reported to have done nothing to investigate if products were compromised. In 2008, when Shields found evidence of hackers breaching the CEO's own computer, Nortel's IT security manager refused to give permission for the computer to be thoroughly examined, on the grounds that the CEO was too busy. After the breaches were publicly disclosed in 2012, Neil Roiter, research director for Corero Network Security, noted: "perhaps the danger was less clear eight years ago than it is now, but the continued failure of what was viewed as an innovative and sophisticated IT company to appreciate and address the risk is puzzling."[14] Even more puzzling since products similar to Nortel's were being made in China by Huawei, "right down to the instruction manuals."[15]

Whether from fear of the effects on legal liability, consumer confidence, or the impact on share prices, or because executives were preoccupied with the company's rapidly declining performance, Nortel did not disclose the infiltration to shareholders, or even to creditors or purchasers of its potentially compromised technologies. Inexplicably, the breach of Nortel's networks did not become public knowledge until after the company had been divested. In other words, the systematic IP theft was not reported until after Nortel's patents had been sold—with a corresponding, possible loss of integrity in those patents.

About 6,000 patents and patent applications for wireless, 4G, networking, optical, voice, social networking, and semiconductor technologies were sold to a consortium of technology companies for US$4.5 billion.[16] Nortel's remaining business units were sold off to buyers including Ericsson, Avaya, Genband, and Ciena for US$3.2 billion,[17] again without the company disclosing the breach. In addition, former Nortel employees were hired by Huawei's North American R&D facilities, including the former CTO, John Roese, in 2010.[18] Overall, it is hard to place a value on the risk.

Technology loss through a joint venture—and old-fashioned, human intelligence

Further risk must be examined here: Nortel's simultaneous engagement with US government agencies and the Chinese party-state, in the 1990s. This story also remains underexplored.

Telecommunications equipment are the only information systems effectively designed with backdoors built in. The Communications Assistance for Law Enforcement Act (CALEA)[19] in the US, and parallel legislation in other jurisdictions, mandates the architecture of global digital networks be open to government-ordered wiretapping as necessary.[20] As early as 1988, in a program known internally to the FBI as "Operation Root Canal," US law enforcement officials mandated that telephone companies alter their equipment to facilitate the interception of messages.[21] All but one of the major global telecom companies refused to contemplate altering their equipment; the exception was Nortel, which agreed to work closely with the FBI. At the time, more than 75 percent of North American Internet backbone traffic traveled across Nortel equipment, and the company derived a significant proportion of its sales revenue from the US telecom market.[22] Given Nortel's early involvement in the development of standards in support of the CALEA legislation, it is unsurprising that the first digital switch to reach market, and give service providers and vendors the ability to meet basic CALEA compliance, should have been developed by Nortel.[23]

In 1993 Nortel signed a Memorandum of Understanding with China's State Planning Commission (today known as the National Development and Reform Commission, NDRC, 国家发展和改革委员会), for a joint venture: Guangdong–Nortel Telecommunication Equipment Co. Ltd., (广东北电通信设备有限公司), which began work in 1995.[24] Importantly, Nortel's sophisticated DMS★ Supernode family of switching technology (essentially, wiretapping-compliant digital switches) was manufactured in China through this joint venture with the Chinese government. At the time, Nortel said of this technology transfer that it would "contribute immeasurably to the development of the Chinese telecommunications industry."

Nortel invested an extra US$37 million in Guangdong–Nortel (GDNT) in 1998, after the US government announced it would compensate for the implementation of CALEA.[25] Nortel also agreed to an "expert exchange program" with China and a joint research laboratory at Tsinghua University.[26]

The creation of GDNT was facilitated by Merry Glory Ltd, a Hong Kong consulting company founded by a Los Angeles-based businesswoman, Katrina Leung (陈文英). Ms. Leung was hired by Nortel in October 1990, for US$1.2 million.[27] She was subsequently alleged to have been a spy for China's security agency, the Ministry of State Security (MSS, 国家安全部), while simultaneously acting as an informant for the FBI.[28]

According to allegations made in 2003, Ms. Leung was involved in an "intimate romantic relationship" with one FBI agent, and "a sporadic affair" with another over the nearly two decades the two agents recruited and handled her—and was paid US$1.7 million by the FBI to spy on senior Chinese politicians.[29] Court documents allege she stole classified documents from US federal agents which she passed to the MSS in Beijing. These circumstances surrounding the incorporation of GDNT—the vehicle through which the first wiretapping-compliant digital switches were transferred to the PRC—remain a puzzling footnote in accounts of Nortel's technology transfer China, and its engagement with the US and PRC governments in the 1990s.

The Nortel case study uniquely highlights what can occur in the absence of management awareness of risk. It occurred prior to adequate government or corporate attention to the consequences of PRC-backed cyberespionage through APTs. The consequences—dramatic decline of a national icon, ultimately corporate extinction—yield rich lessons for corporate boards and governments engaging with China, and Chinese technology companies, today. Canada lost global leadership in telecommunications equipment manufacturing as well as its largest corporation. At its peak, Nortel had a market capitalization of US$250 billion. Its IP passed to PRC competitors, who remain implicated in the breach. PRC manufacturers also benefited by hiring Nortel's world-class engineers in the US and Canada, who are today helping Huawei establish market leadership in epoch-defining telecommunication technologies, especially in the Artificial Intelligence of Things (AIoT) and 5G.

The NucTech case: the monkey king's piercing eyes

This section examines how an early act of copying a particular piece of European technology has resulted, two decades later, in a PRC state-owned company with close ties to China's military and public security systems cornering a substantial portion of the European and global market. The area, "intelligent," border and in-country scanning and surveying technologies, has national security implications for the countries where the equipment is in use.

In May 2018, in the Estonian town of Narva, on the border with Russia, Chinese diplomats delivered a large piece of X-ray scanning equipment to Estonian customs authorities.[30] Made by the Chinese company NucTech (同方威视) in its factory in Poland, the machine was destined to scrutinize cargo crossing between Narva and the town of Ivangorod in Russia. The Narva river separates Estonia and Russia here, at the outer border of the European Union and the North Atlantic Treaty Organization (NATO).[31]

It was the first "first full-automatic railway scanner (sic)" in Estonia, according to the Xinhua news agency, and the last of five recent deliveries of NucTech-made equipment (motto: "Creating a safer world") to the Baltic nation.[32] Other radiation-based imaging equipment was already operating at the Estonian customs points in Luhamaa and Koidula and elsewhere in the Baltic republics.[33] The new system would "crack down on smuggling and maintain national security," promised the Chinese ambassador to Estonia, Li Chao (李超), at the ceremony at Narva's railway crossing point.

Nuctech won the project due to its "favorable price and the provision of full maintenance and guarantee for ten years,"[34] according to a report by Estonian customs.[35] The company's bid of 10.1 million euros was one-third less than two other bids: Rapiscan Systems' 14.9 million euros bid (plus a five-year, ten-month guarantee), and L3Harris's bid of 15.9 million euros (three-year, four-month guarantee).[36] Estonia paid 75 percent of the cost, the European Union the rest.

Yet there was a twist, or rather two. NucTech's beginnings arose from an act of copying completed exactly two decades earlier. More on that below.

Second, despite the low bid, NucTech's parent company, Tsinghua Tongfang (THTF, 同方股份, hereafter Tongfang), was experiencing growing, apparently insoluble, financial difficulties that would lead to a drop in revenue of 5 percent in 2018, including an 18 percent loss in its international business alone.[37] The financial situation was so severe that in January 2020, Tongfang was taken over by China National Nuclear Corporation (CNNC, 中国核工业集团), a defense industry-linked conglomerate.[38] The ownership switch makes Tongfang and its subsidiary, NucTech, part of the very top line of state-owned industry in China, directly under the State-owned Assets Supervision and Administration Commission of the State Council (SASAC, 国务院国有资产监督管理委员会).[39] The switch undoubtedly reflects Tongfang's importance to the party-state. For SASAC's problems are the Politburo's problems—and strengths.

Tongfang develops, manufactures, and sells multiple hi-tech products, receiving state subsidies via reduced taxation, for public and national security, including for the PLA. In its 2018 company report, Tongfang said its companies specialized, among other things, in "constructing super large-scale Chinese and foreign knowledge resource databases," and "actively carry out the national strategy of military–civilian fusion, encircling both the military and civilian markets." These databases support the flow of power in China including "party-building" (党建)

and state prosecution work, thus "continuously forging a great security production chain," (不断打造"大安全"产业链).[40]

There is software, and hardware: Tongfang's network of companies make RFID (radio-frequency identification devices) for person and object tracking, and data collection; major aspects of business focus on "smart," networked, cloud-based and intelligent information, "informatization" (信息化), and "seize the serious, international anti-terrorist situation in order to develop opportunities for the security and protection industry."[41] Terrorism is a global concern but notably it's the CPC's definition for a range of Uyghur activities in China's Western province of Xinjiang, and has been used to justify the construction of a giant camp system there as well other ways of targeting and controlling individuals.[42]

NucTech, one of the companies belonging to Tongfang that does apparently make a profit,[43] is today one of the biggest manufacturers in the world of X-ray-based, cargo, vehicle, and people security screening equipment on land, sea, and air. These technologies can gather and "intelligentize" personal and logistics information, feeding data banks such as those described above.

Set up by Tsinghua University in Beijing in 1997 as part of the CPC's push to commercialize technologies, today NucTech has overseas factories in Brazil and Poland as well as China. One of its early executives was Hu Haifeng (胡海峰), the son of the former CPC general secretary Hu Jintao. Hu Jr. today is the party secretary of Lishui (丽水) in Zhejiang province, according to official sources.[44] After its "coming out" party supplying equipment for the 2008 Beijing Summer Olympics, NucTech supplied the Rio Games in 2016, just one of many high-profile, international events it has supplied.[45]

In Europe, the company whose name derives from an earlier one, "Nuclear Technology," manufactures in Kobyłka, Northeast of Warsaw, a location it describes as "a transportation hub between Asia and Europe." Customers include Poland, Germany, Sweden, and Hungary, as well as the Baltics, Balkans, and other European locations.[46] One report assessed that NucTech had signed 58 public procurement contracts, such as the Narva one, with border and customs authorities, ministries, police departments, and other government organizations, in 22 of the 28 (now 27) EU member countries, in the six years to 2020. Overall, the market in Europe alone is worth billions of euros, or dollars, annually.[47] And yet, 23 years ago, the company didn't even exist. How—where—did it all begin?

Scroll back to the end of the 1980s, when European companies were developing radiation-based, large cargo container screening technologies to better manage the security needs of fast-growing global trade. Driving this development were concerns over smuggling of goods and humans, and terrorism. Notably, China itself had significant problems with smuggling in the 1990s.[48]

A first machine, developed in France, was installed at a Paris airport in early 1991. China was taking note. "In the face of this trend," in late 1991, the State Science and Technology Commission (precursor to MOST) directed that a research project should be set up to develop the new technology. The machines had to be "better and cheaper" than the foreign ones, Li Lanqing (李岚清), the deputy premier responsible for foreign trade and education, said.[49] The project was designated as "strategic" within China's 8th Five-Year Plan. Officials, and scientists from Tsinghua University's nuclear institute, and engineering physics department, were ordered onto the job, according to a book published in 2003 by Tsinghua University Press,[50] in events also described in Chinese-language media reports.[51]

A remarkable, painstaking act of copying followed. The Tsinghua scientists procured and pored over descriptions of machines, issued by their European manufacturers, "re-inventing," though the word was not yet in use back then, building a machine piece by piece by trial and error:

> "At the time, the only information we had were a few commercial advertising samples from foreign companies, so the problems we ran into were enormous," wrote An Jigang (安继刚), the author of "Cobalt-60 Digital Radiation Imaging Container Detection System."[52]
>
> The problems "first showed up mainly in the overall design and the detector array," An wrote. "In analyzing technical problems for the overall design such as the technical plan, determination of the correct indicators, and breaking down each of the subsystems, we had to grope our way forward, simultaneously designing, experimenting and improving," he wrote.
>
> "As a result of moving in logical steps—formulating the correct technical path, choosing to move from small to big, building a prototype of the system section-by-section—and by relying on hard work by everyone, in the end we worked out the system's parameters and produced a rational, overall design," he wrote.

In 1995, the government bought two cargo scanning machines, made by British Aerospace and Heimann AG, and installed them in Shenzhen. NucTech was rushed onto the Shanghai stock exchange in the summer of 1997, with the machine passing final state approval in 1998. The Tsinghua research team was "transplanted" (带土移植) into NucTech, in line with the commercialization-of-research policies of the Chinese state.[53]

The cost: about one-third of the European machines, according to a 2003 report by *People's Daily Overseas*.[54] NucTech still sells equipment significantly more cheaply, about two-thirds of the price of its competitors, going by the Narva example. The first international sale was to Australia in 2001, according to the company. Innovation followed, and indeed was said also to be part of the re-invention process.[55] Notably, one innovation that took off was for mobile screening equipment, to suit sometimes crowded conditions at Chinese ports.[56]

This act of copying produced not only a flourishing, global, state-run business for the PRC that is challenging European competitors that produced the first machines, such as Heimann AG, but also raising surveillance and data privacy issues. As one European media put it in an article entitled, "Meet the Huawei of Airport Security," "The growing dominance of a Chinese vendor of scanning equipment at airports and other ports of entry has European lawmakers and analysts worried about Beijing's influence in the sensitive border and aviation security sectors."[57]

"We make national requirements our own responsibility" ("以国家需求为己任") said Fu Qiyuan (付祁远), the general manager of NucTech business headquarters in The Netherlands, in an interview in 2017.[58] "NucTech takes serving the national security, social security, economic security, environmental security, human security and products security as its strategic mission and direction," according to the company website.[59] Notably, China's National Security Law of 2015 states that national security is maintained "by promoting international security," enabling China to "walk a path of national security with Chinese characteristics."[60]

More recent NucTech products include cloud-integrated body, baggage and vehicle inspection systems, positioning, and biometric devices tailored to "specific regions, buildings and organizations," and AI-supported, multi-information security platforms that "tap the potential value of data."[61] The company also specializes in fingerprint acquisition and identification, facial recognition, risk assessment, and strategic decision-making via networked big data, "law enforcement, critical infrastructure, terrorism prevention and prison [sic]." It provides "big data of BRI regions based on the information collected by smart logistics equipment."[62] Other companies in the Tongfang portfolio include Tongfang Industrial (同方工业) that equips and supports command and control systems (C2C) for the People's Liberation Army.[63] The chairman of Tongfang, Zhou Liye (周立业), is secretary of the company's party committee.[64]

A Xinhua report, titled, "How the globalization of 'piercing eyes' was accomplished," drew on a vivid literary allusion to Monkey King, from the novel "Journey to the West," to illustrate the importance of NucTech in China today: "Once upon a time, people dreamed of having the 'piercing eyes' (火眼金睛) of Sun Wukong (孙悟空) to see past surfaces into the true nature of things. Today, Tongfang Weishi's high-tech 'piercing eye' upholds security in 160 countries around the world," using the Chinese name for the company (同方威视).[65] (The figure for how many countries NucTech sells to vary in the company's own literature).

NucTech has supplied security equipment in Southeastern Europe. In Serbia, where Chinese police today patrol with their Serbian counterparts,[66] a range of equipment was put into use in 2011 at "ports, wharfs, airports and other places of significance."[67] In 2014, the company donated scanners to Bosnia–Herzegovina, according to that country's Ministry of Security website.[68] It also offered equipment to the Republika Srpska, a part of the state of Bosnia–Herzegovina. Fu, the head of NucTech Europe, met with officials from that territory's interior ministry, according to a report on an official Republika Srpska website.[69] They expressed "gratitude for interest expressed by NucTech company, and emphasized the significance of such a donation for the activities of the Republic of Srpska Police in countering smuggling of goods, organized crime and terrorism more efficiently," according to the report. The ministry would be "open and ready to cooperate in similar initiatives in future with the Government of the People's Republic of China."

Chinese companies are deepening their "international development" profile, especially along the Belt and Road. On an inspection tour of the company, a Ministry of Commerce (商务部) official in Beijing noted NucTech supports the state's "overseas aid" (援外) work; Xiao Fenghuai (肖凤怀), deputy head of the China International Center for Economic and Technical Exchanges,[70] visited the company in Beijing in August 2019, to listen to company officials report on "party-building, business development, science and technology results transformation [sic], and the implementation of overseas aid projects."[71]

Russia too is a partner. In December 2019, NucTech deputy general manager, Miao Qitian (苗齐田) and Russian officials agreed at the launch of a new Russia Institute at Tsinghua University (part of Putin and Xi's "New Era China-Russia Strategic Collaboration")[72] that NucTech would collaborate with St. Petersburg State University on projects including "high energy X-ray imaging technology, security screening and anti-terrorism equipment," using the new institute as a "platform."[73] The plan circles NucTech almost all the way back to Narva; St. Petersburg lies just 85 miles (135 kilometers) Northeast of the Estonian town on the EU, and NATO, border with Russia.

Vignettes of future capabilities: biotech and medical research

Genetically modified grain

Throughout its history, food security has been a major factor in regime stability. Accordingly, China has made developing genetically modified crops a key part of its development strategy, highlighted not only in the general "biotechnology" area of the MLP and Five-Year Plans, but also in specific mega-projects.[74] The US Department of Agriculture (USDA) estimates China's corn consumption will increase to 22 million metric tons by 2023,[75] a clear demand signal—and driver for technology transfer.

In 2011, Mo Hailong (莫海龙) and his co-conspirators were caught digging up test seed in an Iowa cornfield.[76] Mo was employed by Kings Nower Seed (金色农华种业科技有限公司), a corn seed subsidiary of the Chinese conglomerate Dabeinong Technology Group Co., Ltd (大北农), itself a "national agricultural industrialization leading enterprise, state-level high-tech enterprise, state validated enterprise technical center, [and] *national innovation enterprise*" (our italics).[77] From a US Department of Justice press release:

> According to the plea agreement entered on January 27, Mo Hailong admitted to participating in a long-term conspiracy to steal trade secrets from DuPont Pioneer and Monsanto. Mo Hailong participated in the

theft of inbred corn seeds from fields in the Southern District of Iowa and elsewhere for the purpose of transporting the seeds to DBN in China. The stolen inbred, or parent, seeds were the valuable trade secrets of DuPont Pioneer and Monsanto.[78]

In a rare instance of successful prosecution of a Chinese commercial espionage case, Mo was awarded 36 months incarceration for conspiracy to steal trade secrets. That aside, the seeds represent the most time and resource intensive part of the agriculture development cycle, and China eventually obtained (re-innovated) the technology through other means.

Medical research and pharmaceuticals

China has made dominating biotech and the global pharmaceutical industry a priority and has adopted supporting policies such as Made in China 2025[79] and the Precision Medicine Initiative[80] to reach this goal. If past actions are a guide, this aim will be achieved by targeting the early stages of cutting-edge research, buying companies with key technology, and becoming a chokepoint for pharmaceutical ingredients or generic medicines.

An example of early targeting is the MD Anderson Cancer Center. In this instance, grant proposals sent for peer review were passed to China, where "shadow labs" were set up to mimic research meant to be done in the US. What is at stake, according to the president of the center, is "the integrity of the peer review system" and the "intellectual property being created by US-based investigators."[81]

The CPC also targets key products on which the world is dependent. The last US manufacturer of penicillin went out of business after China dumped chemicals at low prices for 4 years. The Chinese government in this case actually filed a brief saying the companies had to set prices low because of Chinese law.[82] Examples from the pharmaceutical industry could be multiplied, including PLA infiltration of foreign regulatory agencies, which test the limit of what the present authors are able to disclose. Suffice it to say that not all foreign participants in irregular transfers are unwitting dupes, that blame in some cases is shared by both sides.[83]

Conclusion

While China's goal is technological self-sufficiency, it is pragmatic in its efforts and views "self-sufficiency" in ways that confound most "Western" interpretations. Sustained use of legal and extralegal transfer methods to obtain foreign technologies, and the ability to mobilize domestic infrastructure to adapt them for commercial use is, has been, and will remain part of the equation. Even where transfer is not an issue, companies and researchers outside China are up against the market strategies of a nation-state with the political will to see its efforts through over time. We sum up this chapter by pointing to four key challenges, illustrated in these examples, that mitigation policies must address:

- a decentralized response to demand that utilizes all aspects of China's S&T infrastructure;
- detailed technical requirements that come straight from the end-user;
- support from Beijing that is not focused on private wealth generation or efficiency, or even commercial goals, in the short term;
- deliberate extraction activities that include official support for a "two bases" formula, "short-term visits" and "serving in place."[84]

Given the scope and scale of these activities, a re-evaluation of our underlying assumptions and how we evaluate risk is essential to countering China's whole-of-nation assault on the world's liberal market principles.

Notes

1 The Canadian Encyclopedia, "Nortel," www.thecanadianencyclopedia.ca/en/article/nortel. The Globe and Mail, "Nortel's History with BCE," updated March 23, 2018.
2 "Timeline, Key Dates in the History of Nortel," Reuters, January 15, 2009. www.reuters.com/article/us-nortel-timeline-sb/timeline-key-dates-in-the-history-of-nortel-idUSTRE50D3N120090115.
3 Ibid.
4 Many media reports contain pieces of the truth; it is uncertain if the whole will ever be revealed, as this would depend also on information from China.
5 "Cisco Drops Huawei Lawsuit," *The Register*, July 29, 2004.
6 Michael Chase and James Mulvenon, "Government Counterstrategies," in *You've Got Dissent! Chinese Dissident Use of the Internet and Beijing's Counter-Strategies*, Santa Monica, CA; Arlington, VA; Pittsburgh, PA: RAND Corporation, 2002, pp. 45–92. www.jstor.org/stable/10.7249/mr1543.9.
7 FireEye Annual Report, M-Trends 2019, p. 29. https://content.fireeye.com/m-trends/rpt-m-trends-2019.
8 Ibid.
9 www.yumpu.com/en/document/read/34648582/targeted-trojan-email-attacks-briefing-08-2005-cpni.
10 For media reports on the hacking, see, "Chinese Hackers Suspected in Long-term Nortel Breach," *WSJ*, February 14, 2012; "Did Huawei Bring Down Nortel? Corporate Espionage, Theft, and the Parallel Rise and Fall of Two Telecom Giants," *National Post*, February 24, 2020; "The Mystery of the Listening Devices at DND's Nortel Campus," *Ottawa Citizen*, October 18, 2016.
11 "Julian Assange, the Man Who Exposed the World," Maclean's, December 13, 2010. www.macleans.ca/society/technology/a-man-of-many-secrets/.
12 "Nortel Turned to RCMP about Hacking in 2004, Ex-employee Says," *The Globe and Mail*, May 3, 2018.
13 Ibid.
14 "Nortel Did Nothing About Data Breach, Report Alleges," *ITWorld Canada*, February 15, 2012.
15 Terry Dawes, "Nortel Syndrome: Why Large Companies Will Continue to be Hacked," *CanTech Letters*, February 21, 2013.

16 "Nortel Sells Remaining Patents for US$4.5B," *Design Engineering*, July 4, 2011.
17 See, Bankrupt.com, March 23, 2010, Vol. 14 No. 81. www.bankrupt.com/TCR_ Public/100323.mbx.
18 Terry Dawes, "Huawei Names ex-Nortel CTO to North America R&D Post," *PCWorld*, November 24, 2010.
19 Federal Communications Agency website. www.fcc.gov/public-safety-and-homeland-security/policy-and-licensing-division/general/communications-assistance.
20 Mike McLeod, "A Risk Analysis of Huawei," *Lawfare*, April 17, 2019. "US Officials Say Huawei Can Covertly Access Telecom Networks," *WSJ*, February 12, 2020.
21 European Parliament, Scientific and Technical Options Assessment (STOA), "Development of Surveillance Technology and Risk of Abuse of Economic Information," European Parliament, Directorate General for Research, Vol. 1/5, December 1999. www.europarl.europa.eu/RegData/etudes/etudes/join/1999/168184/DG-4-JOIN_ ET%281999%29168184_EN.pdf.
22 Greg Walton and International Centre for Human Rights and Democratic Development, "China's Golden Shield: Corporations and the Development of Surveillance Technology in the People's Republic of China," *Rights & Democracy*, 2001.
23 Ibid.
24 "Nortel Networks Signs Contract Valued at over US$120 Million," November 25, 1998, Response Source Press Release Wire. https://pressreleases.responsesource.com/news/1834/ nortel-networks-signs-contracts-valued-at-over-us-120-million/?export=pdf.
25 Greg Walton, op. cit.
26 "Nortel Networks Signs Contract Valued at over US$120 Million," op. cit.
27 "Spy Case Shakes Up Nortel," *The Globe and Mail*, originally published April 12, 2003, updated April 18, 2018.
28 Ibid.
29 US Dept. of Justice, Office of the Inspector General, "A Review of the FBI's Handling and Oversight of FBI Asset Katrina Leung," May 2006, Office of the Inspector General. https://oig.justice.gov/special/s0605/final.pdf.
30 I thank Frank Jüris of the Estonian Foreign Policy Institute for his contribution to this chapter.
31 NucTech website, accessed February 27, 2020. www.nuctech.com/SitePages/ SeNormalPage.aspx?nk=ABOUT&k=HAFICG.
32 "Narva Railway Border Crossing Point Got a New X-ray Equipment," May 31, 2018, Estonian Tax and Customs Board. www.emta.ee/eng/narva-railway-border-crossing-point-got-new-x-ray-equipment. Xinhua report of the same event, June 1, 2018. www. xinhuanet.com/english/2018-06/01/c_137222780_2.htm.
33 ERR News (English-language service of Estonian Public Broadcasting), November 23, 2017. https://news.err.ee/644479/estonia-employs-x-ray-inspection-equipment-at-luhamaa-border-checkpoint.
34 Ibid.
35 See Estonian Tax and Customs Board report, op. cit.
36 Email communication with Estonian Tax and Customs Board, January 2, 2020. NucTech dumping investigation: www.wto.org/english/tratop_e/dispu_e/cases_e/ds425_e.htm.
37 For details of the mounting debt problems and exhausted credit lines at Tongfang, see annual company report, 2018: http://pdf.dfcfw.com/pdf/H2_AN201904251322616010_1.pdf.
38 www.wxnmh.com/thread-6432651.htm and www.bjnews.com.cn/finance/2020/01/ 03/669494.html.
39 SASAC, http://en.sasac.gov.cn/.
40 Tongfang 2018 report, http://pdf.dfcfw.com/pdf/H2_AN201904251322616010_1.pdf.
41 Ibid.
42 "Uyghurs for sale," Australian Strategic Policy Institute, March 1, 2020.
43 Tongfang 2018 report, http://pdf.dfcfw.com/pdf/H2_AN201904251322616010_1.pdf.

44 Few Chinese-language reports about Hu Jr. remain online. See, www.caixinglobal.com/ 2018-07-03/hu-haifeng-moves-up-the-party-ranks-101291149.html. See also http:// ldzl.people.com.cn/dfzlk/front/personPage15556.htm.

45 www.nuctech.com/SitePages/HomePage.aspx.

46 "NucTech Warsaw to Build a New Workshop," October 18, 2018. http://en.thholding. com.cn/2017-10/18/c_107229.htm.

47 *Politico*, February 11, 2020, www.politico.eu/article/beijing-scanners-europe-nuctech/.

48 Lai Changxing smuggling case, www.chinadaily.com.cn/china/2007-03/14/content_ 827211.htm.

49 *Xinhua Silk Road*, April 16, 2019. www.imsilkroad.com/news/p/355500.html.

50 An Jigang (安继刚), "Cobalt-60 Digital Radiation Imaging Container Detection System" (钴-60 数字辐射成像集装箱检测系统), Beijing: Tsinghua University Press, 2003.

51 *People's Daily Overseas edition* (人民日报海外版), January 10, 2003. www.people.com. cn/GB/paper39/8214/774990.html.

52 Literally, "product advertising samples," (产品广告样本), i.e., illustrated brochures or booklets with some technical specifications, generally drawn up by specialists, to give potential buyers a good idea of the product.

53 "带土移植" (lit. "bring soil and transplant"), http://news.tsinghua.edu.cn/publish/thu news/10303/2016/20160926142538455723530/20160926142538455723530_.html.

54 www.people.com.cn/GB/paper39/8214/774990.html.

55 See An Jigang (安继刚), 2003, op. cit.

56 Google patents, Patent no. CN1401995A. https://patents.google.com/patent/ CN1401995A/zh.

57 "Meet the Huawei of Airport Security," *Politico*, February 14, 2020.

58 NucTech, 实现欧洲制造 在荷兰建立首个海外研发中心 ("Report on the website of "Invest in Holland"), a government international investment initiative. https://china. investinholland.com/success-stories/同方威视/.

59 www.nuctech.com/en/SitePages/ThNormalPage.aspx?nk=GAH&k=GIBGAA.

60 "National Security Law of the People's Republic of China (2015)." http://eng.mod. gov.cn/publications/2017-03/03/content_4774229.htm. We wish to thank Samantha Hoffman for her research, and for private conversations, on the issue of company activity and national security in China.

61 www.nuctech.com/SitePages/ThDetailPage.aspx?nk=PAS&k=IDFBCF.

62 Chongqing Liangjiang New Area, Liangjiang government website, english.liangjiang. gov.cn via *China Daily*, "Chongqing to establish BRI platform," March 26, 2019.

63 Tongfang Industrial (同方工业) says it "provides technical support for command-control equipment's civil–military integration for the whole army of PRC." http:// en.thholding.com.cn/2016-08/17/c_55953.htm.

64 www.thtf.com.cn/en/about/executive.html.

65 *Xinhua Silk Road*, April 16, 2019. The figure of how many countries NucTech exports to varies, with its own website offering either 160 or 130. For the former figure, see the 'About Us' section on the company website, for the latter figure, see the 'Contact Us' section.

66 Security partnership: https://chinaobservers.eu/securing-the-sino-serbian-partnership/. Police patrols: www.xinhuanet.com/english/2019-09/18/c_138402282.htm.

67 Press release on the website of "Airport Suppliers," United Kingdom, an "airport procurement portal," part of RBS Global Media Ltd., "Nuctech Serve the State Visit President Xi Jinping Pays to Serbia," July 12, 2016. www.airport-suppliers.com/ supplier-press-release/nuctech-serve-state-visit-president-xi-jinping-pays-serbia/.

68 Ministry of Security of Bosnia–Herzegovina, "Deputy Čavar Met with Representatives of the Company Nuctech," August 26, 2014. http://msb.gov.ba/vijesti/saopstenja/ default.aspx?id=11421&langTag=en-US.

69 Ministry of the Interior of the Republic of Srpska. Not to be confused with the neighboring country of Serbia (www.mup.vladars.net/eng/index.php?vijest=12495& vrsta=novosti). For more on NucTech's global progress, see its octolingual homepage: www.nuctech.com/SitePages/HomePage.aspx. See also, "China's 'Silicon Valley' applies tech prowess to Belt and Road," Zhongguancun Science Park (Z-Park), *China Daily*, May 15, 2017.

70 www.cicete.org.cn/.

71 MofCom account, http://zxw.mofcom.gov.cn/article/shangwubangzhu/201908/2019 0802890212.shtml.

72 NucTech and St. Petersburg State University cooperation. www.nuctech.com/SitePages/SeNormalPage.aspx?d=888&nk=ABOUT&k=NewsCenter.

73 Ibid.

74 Wübbeke, Jost, Mirjam Meissner, Max J. Zenglein, Jaqueline Ives, and Björn Conrad. "Made in China 2025: The Making of a High-Tech Superpower and Consequences for Industrial Countries," *MERICS*, December 2016.

75 Hansen, James and Fred Gale, "China in the Next Decade; Rising Meat Demand and Growing Imports of Feed," United States Department of Agriculture, Economic Research Service, April 7, 2014. www.ers.usda.gov/amber-waves/2014/april/china-in-the-next-decade-rising-meat-demand-and-growing-imports-of-feed/.

76 "The Saga of the Chinese Spies and the Stolen Corn Seeds: Will it Discourage Economic Espionage?" *LA Times*, October 31, 2016; Farm Journal Ag Web, "Mo Hailong Pleads Guilty to Seed Theft Conspiracy," January 28, 2016.

77 DBN Group Profile. http://gabif.dbn.cn/en/index.shtml.

78 US Department of Justice, "Chinese National Sentenced to Prison for Conspiracy to Steal Trade Secrets," DOJ Office of Public Affairs, October 5, 2016.

79 国务院关于印发《中国制造2025》的通知国发 ("Notice on Issuing 'Made in China 2025'"), State Council (28), May 8, 2015.

80 A Chinese Academy of Sciences US $9.2 billion, 15-year project announced in March 2016 to manufacture medicines for specific patients based on the genomic data.

81 "MD Anderson Researchers Ousted as NIH and FBI Target Diversion of Intellectual Property," The Cancer Letter, 26 April 2019, https://cancerletter.com/articles/2019 0426_1/.

82 *Animal Science Products, Inc. v. Hebei Welcome Pharmaceutical Co. Ltd.*, 585 U.S. ___, 138 S. Ct. 1865 (2018). www.supremecourt.gov/opinions/17pdf/16-1220_3e04.pdf.

83 There has been complicity among those affected: entrepreneurs and researchers, universities and corporations, and—in some cases—the bureaucrats and elected officials who represent us. It is a situation beyond the scope of the present study.

84 Hannas, William C. James Mulvenon, and Anna B. Puglisi, *Chinese Industrial Espionage*. Routledge (New York and London, 2013).

Bibliography

An Jigang (安继刚). 钴-60 数字辐射成像集装箱检测系统 (*Cobalt-60 Digital Radiation Imaging Container Detection System*), Beijing: Tsinghua University Press, 2003.

Becker, Peggy, Duncan Campbell, Frank Leprevost, Chris Elliot, and Niko Bogolikos. "Development of Surveillance Technology and Risk of Abuse of Economic Information— Appraisal of Technologies of Political Control" (Volume 1 to 5), *Panel for the Future of Science and Technology (STOA)*, European Parliament, March 28, 1999.

Cao, Cong, Richard Suttmeier, and Denis Fred Simon. "China's 15-year Science and Technology Plan," *Physics Today*, December (2006), pp. 38–43.

Center for the Protection of National Infrastructure. Targeted Trojan Email Attacks, Briefing 8/25, June 16, 2005.

Dawes, Terry, Nick Waddell, Jayson MacLean and Staff. "Nortel Syndrome: Why Large Companies Will Continue to be Hacked," *Cantech Letter*, February 21, 2013.

Heracleous, Loizos and Katrin Werres. "On the Road to Disaster: Strategic Misalignments and Corporate Failure." *Long Range Planning*, 49, no. 4 (2016), pp. 491–506. https://doi.org/10.1016/j.lrp.2015.08.006.

Hoffman, Samantha. "Engineering Global Consent: The Chinese Communist Party's Data-Driven Power Expansion," Australian Strategic Policy Institute, October 14, 2019.

Lee, Kai-Fu. *AI Superpowers: China, Silicon Valley and the New World Order*, Boston, MA: Houghton Mifflin Harcourt, 2018.

Lessambo, F.I. *Corporate Governance, Accounting and Auditing Scandals*, The International Corporate Governance System. Global Financial Markets series. London: Palgrave Macmillan, 2014.

Lewis, James. "How Much Have the Chinese Actually Taken?" *CSIS*, March 22, 2018. www.csis.org/analysis/how-much-have-chinese-actually-taken.

Libby, T. and L. Thorne. "The Development of a Measure of Auditors' Virtue," *Journal of Business Ethics*, 71 (2006), pp. 89–99.

M-Trends, FireEye Annual Report p. 29, 2019. https://content.fireeye.com/m-trends/rpt-m-trends-2019.

Magnan, Michel, Timothy J. Fogarty, Garen Markarian, and Serge Bohdjalian. "Inside Agency: The Rise and Fall of Nortel," February 1, 2008. https://ssrn.com/abstract=1092288.

Mazzucato, Mariana. "The Entrepreneurial State: Debunking Public vs. Private Sector Myths," *Public Affairs*, 2015.

McLeod, Mike. "Nortel Sells Remaining Patents for US\$4.5B," *Design Engineering*, July 4, 2011.

同方股份同方股份有限公司2018年年度报告, Tsinghua Tongfang Co., Ltd., 2018 annual report, published 2019. http://pdf.dfcfw.com/pdf/H2_AN201904251322616010_1.pdf.

US Dept. of Justice, Office of the Inspector General. "A Review of the FBI's Handling and Oversight of FBI Asset Katrina Leung," 2006. https://oig.justice.gov/special/s0605/final.pdf.

Walton, Greg, and International Centre for Human Rights and Democratic Development. "China's Golden Shield: Corporations and the Development of Surveillance Technology in the People's Republic of China," *Rights & Democracy*, 2001.

Weaver, Nicholas. "A Risk Analysis of Huawei 5G," *Lawfare*, April 17, 2019.

PART V

Technology in the shadows

13

THE PEOPLE'S LIBERATION ARMY AND FOREIGN TECHNOLOGY

Elsa Kania and Peter Wood

Throughout its history, the modernization and technological development of China's military has benefited significantly from the transfer and acquisition of foreign technologies. Once relatively backwards as a force, the People's Liberation Army (PLA) has found itself at the center of global concern and attention due to its recent deployment of advanced fighters, missiles, and ships, and other advanced capabilities. Although initially heavily reliant upon procurement and reverse engineering of foreign weapons systems and defense technologies, the PLA today appears to be in the process of transforming into a force capable of truly indigenous innovation.

For the Chinese military, technology transfer and innovation are not contradictory. The very process of indigenizing foreign technologies, including their reverse engineering, requires skill and some amount of innovation to be successful. Theft to achieve technological development can also co-exist with further investment in indigenous innovation capabilities, both to successfully re-innovate acquired technologies as well as to create truly original innovations in related fields.

But as one Chinese expert noted in 2018, China still has major issues with "key core technologies" (关键的核心技术),[1] and this deficit will continue to plague the PLA in its efforts to become a truly world-class military, while also ensuring its continued efforts to exploit foreign transfer venues.

This chapter traces the primary phases China has passed through as it works to become a "world-class military" (世界一流军队). While Chapter 6 provided some background on the logic and direction of China's military modernization, this chapter attempts to characterize the arc and role of foreign technology in the industrial development of China's military and defense over the last several decades.

If the 1950s were characterized by direct transfers from the Soviet Union, then China's subsequent phases in the 1970s through to the early 1990s saw the PLA's first real steps toward indigenizing foreign technologies and expertise. Following China's rapid economic growth, growing rapprochement with the Soviet Union (and then Russia), and instigated further by post-Tiananmen restrictions on access to foreign technology, China entered into its current phase of technological development: targeted attempts to acquire and integrate foreign technologies combined with high levels of domestic investment, and a major focus on military modernization. This latest era has its starting point in the mid-1990s.

The degree of reliance on foreign technologies, and assessing China's progress in absorbing them, remains difficult to assess. As several scholars have noted, the sheer complexity of modern military systems often means that even wholesale purchase or stealing of plans is not enough to replicate them.[2] China's defense industries have relied upon and continue to leverage the "absorption" and "re-innovation" of foreign technologies, to a degree that remains striking to this day.[3] Often, weapons systems and capabilities that are characterized as indigenous are, in fact, partly or even primarily the result of the foreign components. Over time, the sophistication of these efforts has increased, involving a complex interplay of skills including mastering particular purchased or stolen technologies, and further indigenizing them.

The era of direct transfers (1950s–1980s)

As mentioned above, direct transfers from the Soviet Union enabled and shaped Chinese military capabilities throughout the early years of the PRC. During this time, China's ballistic missile, aeroengine, and air-to-air missile programs all owed (and to varying degrees continue to owe) major debts to the Soviet Union.

For instance, China's progress in developing main battle tanks, a priority investment for land powers, largely appears to be traceable to technologies from Russia and Ukraine, particularly their engines.[4] Early drone technology, specifically the La-17, was acquired from the USSR and later reverse engineered, acting as a starting point for China's future drone development.[5]

Through such early Soviet assistance, China was able to make significant progress in basic aeronautics, with some notable milestones including successful test flights of training aircraft (1954), multi-use civilian aircraft (1957) and helicopters (1958).[6] But after this promising start, the Sino-Soviet split abruptly interrupted the dynamic, forcing the Chinese military and defense industry to explore alternative avenues for their continued modernization, including seeking other foreign sources of technologies and deepening the drive for indigenous innovation.

For aeronautics, this split was fatal. After the initial surge of new capabilities, including the establishment of R&D centers in the 1950s, progress faltered. In one notable example, true Chinese innovation in avionics seemingly failed to emerge until after the 1990s. Over this time, most claimed breakthroughs in the 1970s, 1980s, and 1990s could be traced to licensing or purchases of foreign technology from the UK and Israel. For example, acquisition of aircraft fire control radars from these countries enabled the PLA to take its first real steps toward all-weather fighter aircraft.[7] The J-8 fighter, for example, was essentially toothless without requisite radars or air-to-air missiles, until the intervention of the United States in the early 1980s to help China build a credible fighter aircraft. While China has made significant progress in building its own defense aviation, electronics, and ballistic missile capabilities, the degree to which the PLA continues to rely on foreign-derived technologies is noteworthy.

The era of foreign military sales (1980s–1990s)

The Chinese military's access to foreign technology at various moments in its history has been largely determined by the geopolitical situation then confronting it. Along the way, thaws in relations with the Soviet Union and Western powers provided key opportunities for China to purchase technologies that it had been unable to successfully indigenize after the Sino-Soviet split and in the midst of the turmoil of the Great Leap Forward (大跃进) and the Cultural Revolution (文化大革命). In typically oblique language, official mentions of R&D efforts then observe that progress was "complicated."[8]

In one example, China's helicopter industry owes a huge debt not only to aforementioned Soviet support in the 1950s, but also to significant military sales from France beginning in the 1970s. In 1977, China purchased at least two Alouette IIIs (YC-II) scout helicopters from France, beginning an important relationship that later led to its acquisition of Dauphin and Super Frelon helicopters.[9] Domestically produced versions of these helicopters (the Z-9 and Z-8) today form the mainstay of China's rotary wing force.[10] Successful production of the Z-8 beginning in 1985 gave China its first indigenous heavy military helicopter transport. Development of the WZ-9 turboshaft engine helped China overcome a dangerous reliance on imported engines and set up the production of Z-10 and Z-19 attack helicopters in the 2000s, both of which use the domestically produced engine.

American antecedents

It is undoubtedly an irony of history that the United States once sought to strengthen the Chinese military in the triangular dynamics of Cold War rivalry, as a bulwark against the Soviet Union, yet today fears the results of that rise. During the Reagan Administration, the United States engaged in a relatively extensive program of foreign military sales to China, starting in 1981.[11] The composition of the arms sales, which included avionics packages, anti-submarine warfare (ASW) torpedoes, and gas turbine engines that were used by the PLA Navy, was initially decided through a Chinese military delegation headed by Admiral Liu Huaqing (刘华清), which visited Washington in August 1981.[12] This earlier epoch of Sino-American friendship extended to cooperation between American defense contractors and their counterparts in the Chinese industry, such as support by McDonnell-Douglas to the skills and industrial foundations of Chinese aviation through large-scale collaboration and co-production.[13]

As Sino-US relations became increasingly fraught, the Cox Report, released in 1999, condemned the impact of tech transfer and the lapse in export control regulations.[14] In particular, the report alleged that Chinese intelligence stole information on advanced thermonuclear weapons systems, claiming "PRC penetration of our national nuclear weapons laboratories spans at least the past several decades and almost certainly continues today."[15] At the time, the report was criticized for "exhibit[ing] too many examples of sloppy research, factual errors, and weakly justified inferences" in its research and analysis.[16] Irrefutably, it highlighted urgent issues and concerns that persist to this day. From a contemporary perspective it is worth reviewing this history to note these issues are not new or unique to the current moment in US–China relations.

In the pursuit of opportunities for foreign military sales, China's military modernization leveraged its acquisitions broadly, including of "dual-use" (or "military–civilian fusion") technologies. Less studied but important was the transfer of key design and manufacturing techniques, many of which were purchased commercially. Notable is the acquisition of foreign design, forging, CNC, and 3D manufacturing technologies, particularly laser additive manufacturing (LAM), which while ostensibly civilian, play an important role in underpinning China's growing defense–industrial capability. Development of the J-10 multi-role fighter in the 1990s reportedly benefited dramatically from foreign computer design software, despite the Chengdu Aircraft Design Institute only having a few computer terminals and needing to run usage on them in shifts.[17]

In the aftermath of the fall of the Soviet Union, post-Soviet states were a valuable source of foreign military technology for China. In particular, China-Ukraine cooperation in aviation has been extensive and continues to the present-day.[18,19] Subsequent military aircraft developed during the 2000s, such as the Y-20, saw years shaved off development times due to large-scale absorption of these foreign technologies.[20] The ASN-306 anti-radiation missile displayed during the PLA's 2017 parade is believed to be a reverse-engineered Harpy, acquired from Israel during the 1990s.[21]

The era of acquisitions and talent cultivation (2000s–2010s)

As China's military and defense industry has become more capable its targeting has evolved and matured, shifting from the outright theft and reverse engineering of IP to subtler tactics that can be more challenging to constrain. Yet bottlenecks remain, in particular talent and expertise, including the tacit knowledge that informs the engineering of complex systems. Sometimes IP theft alone is not enough.[22] While egregious examples of such IP theft remain prevalent, particularly in sectors in which Chinese technological developments is at a relative disadvantage, PRC efforts have increasingly concentrated on building up a more robust skills ecosystem, as well as leveraging cooperation with overseas knowledge sources.

Such patterns play out in parallel across a number of sectors. In effect, the latest directions in PRC policies and practices, which will be discussed toward the end of this section, have evolved in recognition of core features of the current information environment and characteristics of contemporary technologies, which diffuse rapidly because of their relative openness, yet have military and strategic implications because of their dual-purpose potential. China's tech transfer tactics have adapted as its priorities in defense innovation and military modernization have progressed.

Avionics

In recent years, access to foreign avionics technologies may have enabled advances in Chinese systems. In 2009, General Electric Co. and China's Aviation Industry Corporation created a joint venture in avionics that focused on the development of new equipment for the C919 passenger jet.[23] In the GE–AVIC joint venture, GE provided its cutting-edge capability in avionics, including the system that operates Boeing's 787 Dreamliner, unique in apparently involving the sharing of highly confidential technology and construction of a new laboratory for research and development,[24] in a joint venture known as Aviage Systems.[25] Although there were attempts at the time to firewall this partnership relative to AVIC's military projects, it is unclear how effective these measures were, particularly considering AVIC's institutional commitment to military–civil fusion which takes leveraging dual-use synergies as a core direction of its development.[26] In October 2018, PRC national Xu Yanjun was charged with targeting a number of aerospace companies, including GE Aviation, at the behest of the Ministry of State Security (MSS), through techniques that included inviting experts to travel to China for exchanges as an initial vector of recruitment.[27]

Given the promise and potential of the Chinese aviation industry as a market it is hardly surprising that a growing number of foreign players have engaged with Chinese counterparts, including prominent stakeholders in the Chinese defense industry. For instance, Rockwell Collins has a long-established partnership with CETC Avionics Company (CETCA),[28] and also established a joint venture with AVIC LETRI.[29] The creation of the "AVIC Leihua Rockwell Collins Avionics Company" concentrated on "bringing the latest surveillance products to the Commercial Aircraft Corporation of China Ltd. (COMAC) C919 aircraft."[30] In addition, Thales has also established a joint venture with CETC, which supported the C919 systems, providing advances in avionics.[31] This access to and potential repurposing of foreign avionics has also contributed to the Chinese defense industry's competitiveness in foreign military sales.[32]

Aeroengines

China's knowledge and capabilities in developing aircraft engines is largely based on Western technology acquired through partnerships or technology transfer agreements with Western manufacturers, or through the direct acquisition of foreign assets. Analysis of China's WS-10 [涡扇-10] Turbofan engine (meant to reduce China's reliance on imports of Russian engines like the AL-31F) reveals that even its domestically produced engines are in fact copies of foreign imports.[33] In 1974, GE and the French company Safran initially created a joint venture called CFM International (CFMI). CFMI used GE's F101 engine, used to power the USAF B-1 Lancer, to design the CFM56, which would go on to power McDonnell Douglas, Boeing, Airbus, and the KC aerial refueling aircraft.[34] A 1982 article in *Aviation Week* and *Space Technology* claimed that China was seeking to procure two CFM56-2 turbofan engines to upgrade their Trident airliners. In 1985, Chinese airlines China Southwest Airlines and China Eastern Yunnan purchased two Boeing 737s, which were powered by CFM56-3s, the 3rd-generation of that engine.[35] These procurements allowed Shenyang Liming-Aero Engine to examine the CFM56 turbofan technology, which heavily influenced the WS-10A turbofan's core.[36]

The Cox Report asserted that PRC access to aeroengines made by the company Garrett, that were co-produced in China, may have provided significant support to various dual-use efforts, including development of a Full Authority Digital Engine Control (全权数字发动机控制, FADEC), a key computer system that monitors and adjusts the engine to temperature and pressure changes.[37] An unspecified indigenous FADEC type was approved for use by the PLA Air Forice (PLAAF) in 2003.[38] China claims to have developed its own "completely indigenous" (self-developed IP) in the mid-2000s.[39]

A key challenge the WS-10 project faced was material sciences, as it was difficult to replicate fan blade material that was heat resistant, flexible, and precise enough for turbofan technology. Images taken by Chinese military enthusiasts and posted on forums appear to show the WS-10 being tested on a J-20 prototype. The WS-10 was meant for the J-10, but was not ready at the time of production, thus they used the Russian AL-31F. A follow-on engine meant for the J-20, the WS-15, has continued to have production problems. Reportedly, issues with the WS-15's single-crystal turbine blades prevented J-20s equipped with the new powerplant from appearing at the 2018 Zhuhai Air Expo.[40] These deficiencies continue to manifest in the targeting and attempts to transfer foreign sources of expertise, including an incident in which an engineer stole GE turbine technology and components.[41]

Semiconductors

China has struggled to catch up in semiconductors. The reliance upon foreign technologies has been recognized as a critical weakness and vulnerability that Xi Jinping has personally emphasized must be redressed.[42] Chinese companies have continued to take advantage of access to foreign sources through chips purchases, such as from Intel and NVIDIA. This sector has also been the subject of repeated attempts at highly targeted corporate acquisitions, notably succeeding in the case of Dynex Semiconductors, a purchase which later appears to have enabled advances in Chinese railguns and electromagnetic launch.[43] In another prominent incident, after several failed Chinese attempts at acquisitions, American semiconductor company Atop, a cutting-edge automated designer capable of high-end microchips, was acquired in bankruptcy proceedings by Avatar, for which the board chairman is a prominent Chinese steel magnate.[44] This targeting through legal and extralegal mechanisms is likely to continue.

China has also benefited from access to foreign technologies through partnerships. One example is the effort by Sugon Information Industry Service Co, established in 1996 by the Chinese Academy of Sciences (CAS),[45] to support advances in high-performance computing.[46] In June 2015, CAS Sugon (中科曙光), NVIDIA, and the CAS Institute of Computing Technologies jointly established a strategic partnership focused on deep learning.[47] The strategic partnership sought to take advantage of NVIDIA's advanced graphics processing unit (GPU) technology, CUDA parallel performing platform, GPU math library, and other forms of support to advance deep learning in China.[48]

In April 2015, the US government had banned NVIDIA and Intel from selling GPUs to China's four supercomputer centers.[49] However, the ban does not appear to have curtailed NVIDIA's partnership with Sugon, which has continued, and through which Sugon was able to release the XSystem deep learning platform for commercial use, comprised of the XSharp deep learning software and XMachine system, making use of NVIDIA's Deep Learning GPU Training System (DIGITS) development.[50] The "ICT-SUGON-NVIDIA Deep Learning Joint Laboratory" has remained a mechanism for continued engagement.

Although this partnership has focused on commercial applications of deep learning, such as biomedical data,[51] Sugon's engagement with Nvidia, including access to GPUs, likely contributed to China's indigenous ability in artificial intelligence. Given Sugon's parallel support to the PLA, this engagement may have supported military applications, inasmuch as Sugon was actively participating in "military–civil fusion" (军民融合). Remarks by Sugon's vice president highlighted "deep applications" of its products in the domain of national defense.[52]

At present, Sugon is involved in research and development of Chinese military command information systems. In January 2016, the China Institute for Command and Control (CICC, 中国指挥与控制学会), which supports Chinese military initiatives in next-generation C4ISR capabilities, signed a strategic cooperation agreement with the company.[53] This "comprehensive, in-depth" partnership was expected to promote autonomous, controllable technologies in national defense construction and national security applications. Dai Hao (戴浩), chairman of CICC, noted that this partnership would enable advances in "cloud-ization" (云化) and intelligentization (智能化) of China's military command information systems.[54]

Sugon has been at the center of other ventures and partnerships leveraged for tech transfer. In June 2019, the company went on the US Entity List, along with related and subsidiary entities, including Higon, Chengdu Haiguang Integrated Circuit, Chengdu Haiguang Microelectronics Technology, and Wuxi Jiangnan Institute of Computing Technology, which is the PLA Strategic Support Force's 56th Research Institute.[55] Their partnerships with foreign firms, including the prominent American semiconductor manufacturer AMD, have involved a strong nexus with defense research from the start.

China's targeting of semiconductor technology has involved traditional (human) espionage as well. In July 2019, a UCLA professor faced 219 years in prison for conspiring to export military-grade chips to China. According to the Department of Justice, the defendant posed as a customer in order to target "monolithic microwave integrated circuits, or MMICs, that are used in missiles, fighter jets, electronic warfare, and radar applications."[56] These efforts enabled the transfer of chips to a company known as Chengdu GaStone Technology Co., which was building a MMIC manufacturing facility in China.[57]

The dual-use dilemma in technological engagement

The PLA aspires to emerge as a leader in new military technologies, including robotics, artificial intelligence, and biotechnology. Tech transfer and talent acquisition, particularly the cultivation and recruitment of foreign talent, are also important accelerators in these fields. In certain incidents, the targeting of foreign technology has been explicit, involving, for example, the theft and smuggling of components of underwater robotics.[58] In emerging technologies that are dual-use in their applications, including robotics and advanced materials, the PLA has leveraged research partnerships and pursued opportunities for overseas collaborations to support definite advances. Such developments, bolstered by significant investments, contrast with parts of the Chinese defense industry that are less innovative.

Yet in some cases, supposed developments in indigenous innovations have turned out to be less so than initially characterized, which was particularly prominent in the case of the "Redcore" (Hongxin 红芯) webbrowser and "Mulan" (木兰) programming language. Initially, these reported advances were heralded as examples of China's "indigenous innovation" and advancement in computer science. Later, after their developers were revealed to have copied heavily from foreign sources, there were embarrassing retractions and forced resignations. In 2018, start-up Redcore had to issue retractions after developers noticed it borrowed heavily from the Chromium source code, the open-source code at the heart of Google's Chrome browser.[59]

Similarly, in January 2020, the China Academy of Science (CAS) suspended Liu Lei, a researcher at its Institute of Computing Technology, who claimed to have developed the "Mulan" programming language, later revealed to be primarily the Python language.[60] Although this "indigenization" of open-source technology might be characterized as a failure of innovation, the capacity to leverage open-source tools and platforms does indicate China's capacity and inclination to make use of off-the-shelf technology that is readily available, which increasingly defines success.

This applies to mature technologies for which uses have been defined. At the other end of the spectrum, the boundary between beneficial and problematic collaboration is especially hard to determine for dual-use/dual-purpose technologies that remain at a more nascent stage in their operationalization. Scientists at leading US universities, including those engaged in basic research with no clear commercial or military applications, are, accordingly, targeted by China's talent plans and companies, in recognition of this blurring distinction between abstract and practically oriented research.

A case in point is that of Liu Ruopeng (刘若鹏), a Duke Ph.D. student who allegedly appropriated research on meta-materials, and returned to China to fund a multibillion dollar research institute that supports Chinese defense technology development,[61] while actively exploring partnerships with foreign companies and institutions.[62]

In other cases, Chinese quantum scientists have been recruited from leading international institutions to China's National University of Defense Technology (国防科技大学) (NUDT). NUDT has also sent abroad, by some estimates, several thousand students and researchers to leading universities.[63] One prominent researcher returned to NUDT's Center for Interdisciplinary Quantum Information Science to "devote all his energy to the military" after post-doctoral research at Stanford.[64] In January 2020, the Department of Justice indicted an active duty PLA lieutenant conducting research on US military robotics and computer science projects at Boston University, while working at NUDT's direction.[65]

Although scientific collaboration in basic research is important, these connections can become problematic or have the potential for negative externalities when the research and institutions in question blur the boundaries between defense and commercial applications. In January 2020, Harvard University professor Charles Lieber, a pioneer and global leader in nanotechnology, was charged with obscuring his involvement in China's "Thousand Talents" program, through which he was recruited by the Wuhan University of Technology (武汉理工大学, WUT) as a "strategic scientist."[66] WUT is known for its defense research in materials science, which is among the priority fields in China's national strategy and initiatives for military–civil fusion.[67] Given WUT's pursuit of advances in materials science and nanotechnology that have dual-use potential, it is worth asking if Harvard University or Dr. Lieber took measures to evaluate and mitigate the potential for risk in collaboration.

Among Chinese military researchers in computer science and artificial intelligence, a significant proportion have overseas experience and/or ongoing collaborations. A number of joint laboratories have been set up involving military-relevant universities. For instance, the Harbin Institute of Technology has pursued research through a joint laboratory with Microsoft that has concentrated on natural language processing, which is a general-purpose technique but has relevance to military intelligence. As Chinese technological collaboration with the US comes under pressure, these efforts to access foreign expertise and technology, whether through acquisitions or research partnerships, are being diverted and diversified, including to Europe, Israel, and Australia.[68]

Meanwhile, China's Belt and Road Initiative (BRI) is expanding into scientific collaboration, including plans to establish 50 joint laboratories; aspects of this will involve military–civil fusion. The "Belt and Road Science, Technology and Innovation Cooperation Action Plan" in particular includes initiatives that concentrate on technology transfers and joint laboratories.[69] This is a fast-developing area that requires more, multilingual scrutiny.[70]

Notes

1 Guo Kaizhou (郭开周),"如何提高我国核心技术创新力," *China Science Daily* (中国科学报), October 22, 2018. www.qstheory.cn/science/2018-10/22/c_1123593527.htm.

2 See, for instance: Andrea Gilli and Mauro Gilli, "Why China Has Not Caught Up Yet: Military-technological Superiority and the Limits of Imitation, Reverse Engineering, and Cyber Espionage." *International Security* 43, no. 3, 2019, pp. 141–189.

3 Tai Ming Cheung, "The Chinese Defense Economy's Long March from Imitation to Innovation," *The Journal of Strategic Studies* 34, no. 3 (2011): 325–354. Tai Ming Cheung, "Innovation in China's Defense Technology Base: Foreign Technology and Military Capabilities." The *Journal of Strategic Studies* 39, no. 5–6, 2016, pp. 728–761.

4 Michael Kofman, "An Uneasy Ménage à Trois," *Foreign Affairs*, December 4, 2014.

5 Elsa Kania, "The PLA's Unmanned Aerial Systems: New Capabilities for a 'New Era' of Chinese Military Power," China Aerospace Studies Institute, August 8, 2018.

6 中国航空工业大事记 (1951–2011) (The Chronicle of the Chinese Aerospace Industry (1951–2011)), 航空工业出版社, 2011.

7 Work on a US upgrade for the J-8 was canceled, but China was later able to acquire improved airborne radars from Israel. See Yefim Gordon and Dmitriy Komissarov, *Chinese Aircraft: China's Aviation Industry Since 1951*, Crowborough, UK: Hikoki Publications, 2008, p. 83.

8 For instance, see this reference by AVIC. "The First Successful Test of a Z-5 Was Held in December 1958."发展历程,"AVIC. www.avic.com.cn/cn/gxwm/jqgk/fzlc/index.shtml.

9 CIA Crest, "Helicopter Deployment in China," October 1973, p. 1. https://www.cia.gov/library/readingroom/docs/CIA-RDP78T05162A000300010062-0.pdf.

10 IISS, The Military Balance, February 2017. https://www.iiss.org/publications/the-military-balance/the-military-balance-2017.

11 Bernard Gwertzman, "US Decides to Sell Weapons to China in Policy Reversal," *New York Times*, June 17, 1981.

12 Ibid.
13 Jonathan D. Pollack, "The Cox Report's Dirty Little Secret," April 1999. www. armscontrol.org/act/1999-04/cox-reports-dirty-little-secret.
14 "Report of the Select Committee on US National Security and Military/Commercial Concerns with the People's Republic of China," submitted by Mr. Cox of California, Chairman. www.govinfo.gov/content/pkg/GPO-CRPT-105hrpt851/pdf/GPO-CRPT-105hrpt851.pdf.
15 Ibid.
16 Alastair Iain Johnston, W. K. H. Panofsky, Marco Di Capua, and Lewis R. Franklin, "The Cox Committee Report: An Assessment," Carnegie Endowment, December 1999.
17 "揭秘歼-10研制全过程:6.7万多张图纸一年时间出手," *Chengdu Evening News* (成都晚报), October 17, 2014. www.81.cn/hkht/2014-10/17/content_6184104_4.htm.
18 Brett Forrest, "US Aims to Block Chinese Acquisition of Ukrainian Aerospace Company," *Wall Street Journal*, August 23, 2019.
19 Anton Troianovski, "At a Ukrainian Aircraft Engine Factory, China's Military Finds a Cash-Hungry Partner," *Washington Post*, May 20, 2019.
20 3D打印助军事变革: 研制新战机从20年缩短到3年("3D Printing Supports Military Transformation: Research and Development of New Fighter Jets from 20 Years Shortened to 3 Years"), *China Aviation News*, January 29, 2015. Technology Supports the Y-20; 技术助力运20 3D打印迎重磅利好 ("3D Printing Lightens a Heavy Load"), *Beijing Times*, March 22, 2013.
21 For a more detailed accounting, see; Elsa Kania, "China's Threat to American Government and Private Sector Research and Innovation Leadership," Testimony before the House Permanent Select Committee on Intelligence, July 19, 2018.
22 Andrea Gilli and Mauro Gilli, "Why China Has Not Caught Up Yet: Military–Technological Superiority and the Limits of Imitation, Reverse Engineering, and Cyber Espionage." *International Security* 43, no. 3, 2019, pp. 141–189. Cavusgil, S. Tamer, Roger J. Calantone, and Yushan Zhao. "Tacit Knowledge Transfer and Firm Innovation Capability," *Journal of Business & Industrial Marketing*, 18, no. 1, 2003, pp. 6–21.
23 "GE and China's AVIC to form avionics joint venture," *Reuters*, November 14, 2009.
24 David Barboza, Christopher Drew, and Steve Lohr, "G.E. to Share Jet Technology With China in New Joint Venture," *New York Times*, January 11, 2017.
25 www.aviagesystems.com/en/company.
26 两大航空工业央企印发军民融合相关决定 实现深度发展 ("Two Major Aviation Industry Central Enterprises Release and Issue Military–Civil Fusion Decisions, Achieving In-Depth Development), *Securities Times Network* (证券时报网), June 22, 2017.
27 "Chinese Spy Charged with Trying to Steal US Aviation Trade Secrets," *Reuters*, October 10, 2018.
28 "Rockwell Collins and CETCA celebrate their joint venture and its contributions to the COMAC C919's successful first flight." www.rockwellcollins.com/Data/Success-Stories/Our-Story/2017-Cal-Yr/CETCA.asp.
29 "Rockwell Collins Establishing Joint Venture with AVIC LETRI in China," April 2, 2012. www.businesswire.com/news/home/20120401005035/en/Rockwell-Collins-Establishing-Joint-Venture-AVIC-LETRI.
30 Ibid.
31 "Thales and China Electronics Technology Avionics Sign Joint Venture Agreement for the New C919 Aircraft," July 9, 2012. http://onboard.thalesgroup.com/thales-and-china-electronics-technology-avionics-sign-joint-venture-agreement-for-the-new-c919-aircraft/.
32 Richard Bitzinger, "Chinese Fighter Jets Struggle to Target Buyers," *Asia Times*, July 17, 2019.
33 30 年不断改进，推出至少7个型号，涡扇-10"太行"发动机已堪大用! ("30 Years of Continuous Improvement, Launching at Least 7 Models, Turbofan-10 "Taihang"

Engine Has Been Very Useful!"), December 2019. https://new.qq.com/omn/20191221/20191221A0KHOP00.html.

34 Tomas Kellner, "Up in the Air: the World's Hardest-Working Jet Engine Has Logged 91,000 Years in Flight," *GE Reports*, June 7, 2016.

35 "CFM Celebrates 30 Years in China," CFM, April 30 2015. www.cfmaeroengines.com/press-articles/cfm-celebrates-30-years-in-china/.

36 Richard Fisher, "Analysis: Can China Break the Military Aircraft Engine Bottleneck?" *Flight International*, June 2, 2015.

37 "Cox Report: Manufacturing Processes," *CNN*, 1999. www.cnn.com/ALLPOLITICS/resources/1999/cox.report/manufacturing/pg7.html.

38 "中国发动机全权限数字电子控制系统通过验收," AVIC Website, August 15, 2003. http://mil.news.sina.com.cn/2003-08-15/143715.html.

39 "航空报国心志坚 创新超越谱华章," *AVIC News*, May 6, 2010. www.cannews.com. cn/zghkb/html/2010-05/06/content_7120.htm.

40 China's New J-20 Stealth Fighter Engine a No-Show at Zhuhai Air Show after it Fails Reliability Tests," *South China Morning Post*, November 7, 2018.

41 Ellen Nakashima, "US Charges American Engineer, Chinese Businessman with Stealing GE's Trade Secrets," *Washington Post*, April 24, 2019.

42 For context, see: Kinling Lo, "Xi Jinping Urges China to Go All in on Scientific Self-Reliance after ZTE Case Exposes Hi-tech Gaps," *South China Morning Post*, May 28, 2018.

43 Gareth Corfield, "Has China Used British Technology to Build a Railgun?," *The Times*, March 4, 2018.

44 Cory Bennet and Bryan Bender, "How China Acquires 'the Crown Jewels' of US Technology," May 22, 2018. www.politico.com/story/2018/05/22/china-us-tech-companies-cfius-572413.

45 It received support through the National High Technology Research and Development Program (国家高技术研究发展计划, "863 Program"). "Shuguang—Company Profile." www.sugon.com/about/intro.html.

46 Ibid.

47 强强联合，曙光布局人工智能领域 ("With Powerful Partnership, Sugon Opens the Domain of Artificial Intelligence"), June 29, 2015. www.sugon.com/about/detail/id/391.html.

48 Ibid.

49 Joseph Pagliery, "Nuclear Worries Stop Intel From Selling Chips to Chinese Supercomputers," *CNN*, April 10, 2015.

50 Ibid.

51 中科曙光在美发布LAMBDA平台 ("CAS Sugon Releases the LAMBDA Platform in the U.S"), *China Science Times* (中国科学报), May 11, 2017.

52 Ibid.

53 中国指挥与控制学会联手中科曙光 ("China Command and Control Society Joins Hands with CAS Sugon"), *China News Network*, January 15, 2016.

54 推进军事指挥信息系统"云"化和智能化 ("Accelerate the "Cloud-ization" and Intelligentization of Military Command Information Systems"), *Global Times*, January 17, 2017.

55 "The US Blacklists Five Chinese Supercomputer Firms, Including AMD Joint Venture THATIC," June 21, 2019. www.pcworld.com/article/3404464/the-us-blacklists-five-chinese-supercomputer-firms-including-amd-joint-venture-thatic.html.

56 Colleen Shably, "UCLA Professor Faces 219 Years in Prison for Conspiring to Send US Missile Chips to China," *LA Times*, July 11, 2019. See also DOJ, 2 July 2019, www.justice.gov/opa/pr/electrical-engineer-convicted-conspiring-illegally-export-china-semiconductor-chips-missile.

57 It was added to the entity list in July 2018: "Addition of Certain Entities; and Modification of Entry on the Entity List: A Rule by the Industry and Security Bureau," August 1, 2018.

www.federalregister.gov/documents/2018/08/01/2018-16474/addition-of-certain-entities-and-modification-of-entry-on-the-entity-list.

58 Josh Saul, "Chinese Spy in Florida Sent Drone Parts to China for Military," *Newsweek*, April 22, 2016.

59 Sarah Dai, "Redcore CEO Admits '100pc China-developed Browser' is Built on Google's Chrome, Says Writing Code from Scratch Would 'Take Many Years'," *South China Morning Post*, August 17, 2018.

60 "红芯浏览器曝"自主创新"尴尬' -" ("Red Core Browser Exposed, an 'Independent Innovation' Embarrassment"), *Beijing Daily* (北京日报), August 20, 2018.

61 Ana Swanson and Keith Bradsher, "White House Considers Restricting Chinese Researchers Over Espionage Fears," *New York Times*, April 30, 2018.

62 "KuangChi's Technology Lift With Martin Aircraft's ASX Listing," February 24, 2015. www.globenewswire.com/news-release/2015/02/24/1236616/0/en/KuangChi-s-Technology-Lift-With-Martin-Aircraft-s-ASX-Listing.html.

63 Alex Joske, *Picking Flowers, Making Honey: The Chinese Military's Collaboration with Foreign Universities*. Australian Strategic Policy Institute, International Cyber Policy Centre, 2018.

64 张超凡：把平凡的基础研究做超凡 ("Zhang Chaofan: Making Ordinary Basic Research Extraordinary"), *China Military Online*, July 7, 2017.

65 "Harvard University Professor and Two Chinese Nationals Charged in Three Separate China Related Cases," Department of Justice, January 28, 2020. www.justice.gov/opa/pr/harvard-university-professor-and-two-chinese-nationals-charged-three-separate-china-related.

66 Ibid.

67 See this detailed profile in the "China Defense Universities Tracker" created by the Australian Strategic Policy Institute. https://unitracker.aspi.org.au/universities/wuhan-university-of-technology/.

68 Danit Gal, "The US-China-Israel Technology Triangle," *Net Politics*, July 30, 2019.

69 "China to Set Up 50 Joint Laboratories along B&R," *Xinhua*, May 14, 2017.

70 For an encyclopedic assessment and analysis of BRI collaboration and influence activities with specific university and science components, see Nadege Rolland, "Mapping the Footprint of Belt and Road influence operations," Sinopsis, August 12, 2019. https://sinopsis.cz/en/rolland-bri-influence-operations/.

Bibliography

"30 年不断改进，推出至少7个型号，涡扇-10'太行'发动机已堪大用！" ("30 Years of Continuous Improvement, Launching At Least 7 Models, Turbofan-10 'Taihang' Engine Has Been Very Useful!"), December 2019. https://new.qq.com/omn/20191221/2019 1221A0KHOP00.html.

"3D 打印助军事变革: 研制新战机从20年缩短到3年" ("3D Printing Supports Military Transformation: Research and Development of New Fighter Jets from 20 Years Shortened to 3 Years"), *China Aviation News*, January 29, 2015.

"推进军事指挥信息系统'云化'和智能化" ("Accelerate the 'Cloud-ization' and Intelligentization of Military Command Information Systems"), *Global Times*, January 17, 2017.

"中国指挥与控制学会联手中科曙光" ("China Command and Control Society Joins Hands with CAS Sugon"), China News Network, January 15, 2016.

"国防科大海外留学生同步学习党的十九大报告" ("NUDT Overseas Students Study in Step the 19th Party Congress Report"), October 20, 2017.

"技术助力运 20 3D 打印迎重磅利好" ("Technology Supports the Y-20; 3D Printing Lightens a Heavy Load"), 京华时报 (*Beijing Times*), March 22, 2013.

"中国航空工业大事记 1951–2011" ("The Chronicle of the Chinese Aerospace Industry 1951–2011"), 航空工业出版社, 2011.

"两大航空工业央企印发军民融合相关决定 实现深度发展" ("Two Major Aviation Industry Central Enterprises Release and Issue Military–Civil Fusion Decisions, Achieving In-Depth Development"), 证券时报网 (Securities Times Network), June 22, 2017.

"强强联合，曙光布局人工智能领域" ("With Powerful Partnership, Sugon Opens the Domain of Artificial Intelligence"), June 29, 2015. www.sugon.com/about/detail/id/391.html.

AVIC. "The First Successful Test of a Z-5 Was Held in December 1958," 发展历程, AVIC. www.avic.com.cn/cn/gxwm/jqgk/fzlc/index.shtml.

Barboza, David, Christopher Drew, and Steve Lohr. "G.E. to Share Jet Technology With China in New Joint Venture," *New York Times,* January 11, 2017.

Bennet, Cory and Bryan Bender. "How China Acquires 'the Crown Jewels' of US Technology," *Politico,* May 22, 2018.

Bitzinger, Richard. "Chinese Fighter Jets Struggle to Target Buyers," *Asia Times,* July 17, 2019.

Cavusgil, S. Tamer, Roger J. Calantone, and Yushan Zhao. "Tacit Knowledge Transfer and Firm Innovation Capability." *Journal of Business & Industrial Marketing,* 18, no. 1 (2003), pp. 6–21.

Chan, Tara Francis. "Pentagon to End Language Funding for Universities that Host Chinese Communist Party-funded Confucius Institutes," *Newsweek,* April 30, 2019.

Cheng, Yangyang. "Don't Close the Door on Chinese Scientists Like Me," *Foreign Policy,* June 4, 2018.

Corfield, Gareth. "Has China Used British Technology to Build a Railgun?," *The Times,* March 4, 2018.

"China to Set up 50 Joint Laboratories along B&R," *Xinhua,* May 14, 2017.

"Chinese Spy Charged with Trying to Steal US Aviation Trade Secrets," *Reuters,* October 10, 2018.

CIA CREST. "Helicopter Deployment in China," p. 1, October 1973. www.cia.gov/library/readingroom/docs/CIA-RDP78T05162A000300010062-0.pdf.

Cheung, Tai Ming. "The Chinese Defense Economy's Long March from Imitation to Innovation," *The Journal of Strategic Studies* 34, no. 3, 2011, pp. 325–354.

Cheung, Tai Ming. "Innovation in China's Defense Technology Base: Foreign technology and Military Capabilities." *The Journal of Strategic Studies* 39, no. 5–6, 2016, pp. 728–761.

"China's New J-20 Stealth Fighter Engine a No-Show at Zhuhai Air Show after it Fails Reliability Tests," *South China Morning Post,* November 7, 2018.

Dai, Sarah. "Redcore CEO Admits '100pc China-Developed Browser' is Built on Google's Chrome, Says Writing Code from Scratch Would 'Take Many Years'," *South China Morning Post,* August 17, 2018.

Federal Register. "Addition of Certain Entities; and Modification of Entry on the Entity List: A Rule by the Industry and Security Bureau," August 1, 2018.

Fisher, Richard. "Analysis: Can China Break the Military Aircraft Engine Bottleneck?" *Flight International,* June 2, 2015.

Forrest, Brett. "US Aims to Block Chinese Acquisition of Ukrainian Aerospace Company," *Wall Street Journal,* August 23, 2019.

Gal, Danit. "The US-China-Israel Technology Triangle," *Net Politics,* July 30, 2019. www.cfr.org/blog/us-china-israel-technology-triangle.

"GE and China's AVIC to Form Avionics Joint Venture," *Reuters,* November 14, 2009.

Gilli, Andrea and Mauro Gilli. "Why China Has Not Caught Up Yet: Military–Technological Superiority and the Limits of Imitation, Reverse Engineering, and Cyber Espionage." *International Security* 43, no. 3, 2019, pp. 141–189.

Gwertzman, Bernard. "US Decides to Sell Weapons to China in Policy Reversal," *New York Times*, June 17, 1981.

Guo Kaizhou (郭开周). "如何提高我国核心技术创新力" ("How to Improve Chinese Innovation in Core Technologies"), 中国科学报 (*China Science Daily*), October 22, 2018.

Hruska, Joel. "AMD's Chinese Joint Venture Now Shipping 'Homegrown' x86 CPUs," *Extreme Tech*, July 9, 2018.

Johnston, Alastair Iain, W. K. H. Panofsky, Marco Di Capua, and Lewis R. Franklin. "The Cox Committee Report: An Assessment," *Carnegie Endowment*, December 1999.

Joske, Alex. *Picking Flowers, Making Honey: The Chinese Military's Collaboration with Foreign Universities*. Australian Strategic Policy Institute, International Cyber Policy Centre, 2018.

Kania, Elsa. "China's Threat to American Government and Private Sector Research and Innovation Leadership," Testimony before the House Permanent Select Committee on Intelligence, July 19, 2018.

Kania, Elsa. "The PLA's Unmanned Aerial Systems: New Capabilities for a 'New Era' of Chinese Military Power," China Aerospace Studies Institute, August 8, 2018.

Kellner, Tomas. "Up in the Air: the World's Hardest-Working Jet Engine has Logged 91,000 years in flight," *GE Reports*, 7 June, 2016.

Kofman, Michael. "An Uneasy Ménage à Trois," *Foreign Affairs*, December 4, 2014.

Levesque, Greg and Mark Stokes. "Blurred Lines: Military–Civil Fusion and the 'Going Out' of China's Defense Industry," Pointe Bello, December 2016.

Lo, Kinling. "Xi Jinping Urges China to Go All in on Scientific Self-Reliance after ZTE Case Exposes Hi-tech Gaps," *South China Morning Post*, May 28, 2018.

Lubold, Gordon and Dustin Volz. "Chinese Hackers Breach US Navy Contractors," *Wall Street Journal*, December 14, 2018.

Nakashima, Ellen. "US Charges American Engineer, Chinese Businessman with Stealing GE's Trade Secrets," *Washington Post*, April 24, 2019.

Pagliery, Joseph. "Nuclear Worries Stop Intel from Selling Chips to Chinese Supercomputers," *CNN*, April 10, 2015.

Pollack, Jonathan D. "The Cox Report's 'Dirty Little Secret'," April 1999. www.armscontrol. org/act/1999-04/cox-reports-dirty-little-secret.

"Rockwell Collins Establishing Joint Venture with AVIC LETRI in China," April 2, 2012. www.businesswire.com/news/home/20120401005035/en/Rockwell-Collins-Establishing-Joint-Venture-AVIC-LETRI.

Saul, Josh. "Chinese Spy in Florida Sent Drone Parts to China for Military," *Newsweek*, April 22, 2016.

Shably, Colleen. "UCLA Professor Faces 219 Years in Prison for Conspiring to Send US Missile Chips to China," *LA Times*, July 11, 2019.

Swanson, Ana and Keith Bradsher. "White House Considers Restricting Chinese Researchers over Espionage Fears," *New York Times*, April 30, 2018.

"Thales and China Electronics Technology Avionics Sign Joint Venture Agreement for the New C919 Aircraft," July 9, 2012. http://onboard.thalesgroup.com/thales-and-china-electronics-technology-avionics-sign-joint-venture-agreement-for-the-new-c919-aircraft/.

"The US Blacklists Five Chinese Supercomputer Firms, Including AMD Joint Venture THATIC," June 21, 2019. www.pcworld.com/article/3404464/the-us-blacklists-five-chinese-supercomputer-firms-including-amd-joint-venture-thatic.html.

Troianovski, Anton. "At a Ukrainian Aircraft Engine Factory, China's Military Finds a Cash-Hungry Partner," *Washington Post*, May 20, 2019.

US Department of Justice. "Harvard University Professor and Two Chinese Nationals Charged in Three Separate China Related Cases," January 28, 2020.

Zhang Chaofan (张超凡). "把平凡的基础研究做超凡" ("Making Ordinary Basic Research Extraordinary"), *China Military Online*, July 7, 2017.

14

FOREIGN TECHNOLOGY AND THE SURVEILLANCE STATE

Dahlia Peterson

The Chinese party-state has long practiced mass surveillance. Since 1949, it has relied on information gathering and social control tools, such as *danwei* (单位) work units, the *hukou* (户口) residency registration system, and *dang'an* (档案) secret political files, to monitor people and maintain tight social control.[1] But mass migration and privatization as a result of economic reforms after 1978 have undermined the efficacy of these older practices.[2] The 1989 democracy protests and the following bloody crackdown jolted the party-state leadership into realizing that it must strengthen surveillance over an increasingly mobile and demanding society. The fast rise of the Internet, and people's growing digital footprint associated with a range of online activity, contributed significantly to the authorities' greater interest in developing new technologies for social control. The 2008 Beijing Olympics along with major meetings such as the 2016 Hangzhou G20 became opportunities for the authorities to acquire and run new surveillance systems.[3]

Against this backdrop, the Ministry of Public Security (MPS, 公安部) significantly overhauled its intelligence-gathering infrastructure in the early 2000s to achieve "information dominance" for the purpose of social control and crime-fighting.[4] It launched the Golden Shield Project (金盾工程) around 2000, which aimed to put in place a nationwide and intelligent system that can monitor society and identify individuals through multi-sensory networks, smart cards, social credit, and databases of personal information. Western companies, notably Canada's biggest company Nortel Networks, played a major role in the Project.[5]

The construction of this massive surveillance infrastructure went largely unnoticed by the broad public both in and outside China until mid-2017, when human rights and media organizations began to report on the ever-tightening net these systems have woven across the country. Many people inside China remain unaware of the true scope of surveillance, or welcome it as a source of "security." This chapter first gives an overview of these systems, then discusses how Western companies and academia have aided the growth of China's surveillance state.

How does China's surveillance state work?

The government issues every citizen a national identification card which is essential to access many public and private services. This "real name registration" (实名登记) requirement enables authorities to collect and compile vast databases of personal profiles linked to an individual's ID. At the same time, the government has blanketed the country with closed-circuit surveillance cameras (监控摄像头, CCTV).[6] The police have used artificial intelligence technologies to automatically scan people from surveillance footage streams, telephone calls, and media access control (MAC) addresses, and international mobile equipment identity (IMEI) numbers emitting from phones.[7] The police compel ordinary individuals—neither convicted nor suspected of a crime—to have their DNA taken and inputted into a national, searchable database with over 60 million entries.[8] They also use big data systems to identify individuals whom they consider "problematic," including those who "undermine stability," those involved with drugs, and other broad categories known as "focus personnel."[9] The collection of these biometrics is part of the government's drive to form a "multi-modal" biometric portrait of individuals and to gather ever more data about its citizens.

In Xinjiang, Northwestern China, where 22 million people live, the authorities have gone the furthest in "innovating" for social control. Under the "Strike Hard Campaign against Violent Extremism" (严打暴恐专项行动) the government has subjected 13 million ethnic Uyghurs and other Turkic Muslims there to mass arbitrary detention, forced political indoctrination, restrictions on movement, and religious oppression.[10] Credible estimates indicate that under this heightened repression, at least 1 million people are being held in "political education" camps.[11]

In addition to collecting biometrics—including DNA samples, voice samples, fingerprints, iris scans, and blood types of residents in the region—the Xinjiang police has also used a big data program called the "Integrated Joint Operations Platform" (IJOP, 一体化联合作战平台) to track everyone in the region.[12] The IJOP monitors people and their relationships by tracing their phones, vehicles, and ID cards, and keeps tabs on their use of electricity and gas stations. It treats many ordinary and lawful activities, such as using WhatsApp or VPNs, driving a car that is not one's own, or using "too much" electricity, as indicators of suspicious behavior. It automatically alerts officers of these individuals who are then further interrogated; some are detained or imprisoned. In this way, the IJOP works to form a series of invisible or virtual fences. Freedom of movement is restricted to varying degrees, depending on programmed factors that codify the threat authorities perceive they pose.

The depth, breadth, and intrusiveness of the Chinese government's mass surveillance of citizens may be unprecedented in modern history. These systems remain unchallenged in China because there are few meaningful checks on government powers. The MPS is accountable only to the Chinese Communist Party (CCP) top leadership—it is not required to report surveillance activities to any other government agency, or to publicly disclose this information. While the Chinese Constitution guarantees people's "privacy of correspondence" (通信秘密), China does not have a unified privacy or data protection law. It is all but impossible for people to know what personal information the government collects, and how the government uses, shares, or stores their data. Although the government shows growing interest in regulating private companies' collection of consumer data, such regulations are limited to the commercial sphere.[13]

The party-state's ever-burgeoning demand for mass surveillance has greatly benefited Chinese AI companies that supply the police with such systems. Major AI companies that supply the MPS and its provincial and local counterparts include iFlytek (for voice recognition), Sensetime, Yitu, Cloudwalk and Megvii (for facial recognition) and major state defense contractor China Electronics Technology Group Corporation (CETC), for both big data and extraction of MAC addresses and IMEI numbers. There are, however, many more Chinese surveillance companies that sell to the police. In 2018, China's surveillance market expanded by 13.5 percent, versus 5 percent for the rest of the world.[14] That same year, in facial recognition alone, China accounted for nearly half the planet's business.[15] By 2020, China's "AI + security" software and hardware market is projected to reach 45.3 billion yuan, or about 6.5 billion US$.[16]

As these companies search for export opportunities, and as the Chinese government expands its political, economic, and technological influence globally via its Belt and Road Initiative, the Chinese "model" of surveillance is set to continue spreading.[17] From Kyrgyzstan to the Philippines, video surveillance systems equipped with facial recognition capabilities and connected to police command centers are provided by Chinese companies to governments that have a track record of abusing human rights with few privacy protections.[18] However, we are yet to see these governments adopt the kind of multi-layered and multi-dimensional mass surveillance systems that the Chinese government is developing. It remains a question whether these governments can or are willing to implement such systems, as they require massive human and financial resources. This also calls for a highly centralized state able to make administrative requirements, such as the "real name registration" system, hard to circumvent.

China's dependence on Western hardware companies

Amid this, Western companies provide core support to buttress China's surveillance state. Multiple paths of involvement exist, including investment and/or financing ties and, importantly, academic and research partnerships that provide technology.

This chapter will focus on Western-provided hardware solutions, as this is where Chinese companies still largely cannot provide their own substitutes and are thus heavily reliant on the West.[19] These hardware solutions include items that form parts of a class of 'AI chips' that make up the physical infrastructure of deep learning and storage hard drives optimized for surveillance applications, such as graphics processing units (GPUs) and field-programmable gate arrays (FPGAs).

GPUs, traditionally used for faster rendering in gaming applications, have been instrumental to the acceleration of machine learning applications. For tasks that can be broken down into parts and parallelized in execution, GPUs can greatly speed up these processes.[20] For AI and machine learning (ML) algorithms, particularly the deep neural network (DNN) algorithm, which requires a high number of calculations to be parallelized, GPUs' ability to execute many operations at once means they are suitable for the 'training' process, when algorithms' development is iterated.[21]

GPUs from Intel and NVIDIA have brought direct benefits to Chinese companies operating in the surveillance space. The China Security Industry Network (中国安防行业网) states:

> Many chipmakers—with NVIDIA as the representative example—have seen the intelligentized development of the security industry and seized the opportunity to inseparably cooperate with Chinese security manufacturing companies. In the era of big data, this cooperation has upgraded these companies' data mining and computing capabilities.[22]

One example of this is California-based Amax—which specializes in high-performance computing for deep-learning applications—partnering with state-owned Hikvision (海康威视).[23] Newer GPUs from NVIDIA and Intel's Movidius provide the deep learning infrastructure to cameras and recorders.[24] Deep learning algorithm developers can then create video surveillance-dedicated training models either on an unsupervised or semi-supervised basis for face recognition, vehicle recognition, or other video analysis based on deep learning infrastructure.[25] In 2018, Dahua (大华科技) launched a series of DNN-equipped network video recorders (NVRs) with built-in real-time face detection and facial recognition. The NVRs take pictures rather than continuous video for reduced bandwidth requirements, and the built-in AI automatically discards blurry or angled images.[26]

According to video-surveillance trade magazine *IPVM*, Dahua's Deep Sense server uses NVIDIA's Tesla 4 GPUs, while Hikvision uses NVIDIA's Jetson GPU platform for its smart-city applications, with servers powered by NVIDIA's Tesla P4 GPUs, and NVIDIA's DGX-1 AI supercomputer.[27] *IPVM* also found that, in 2016, Hikvision partnered with Intel Movidius to add DNN capabilities to their AI cameras via its Myriad 2 vision processing unit (VPU).[28] Hikvision's NVRs and "open-source smart cameras" use Intel processors, while Dahua NVRs use Intel processors and its people-counting cameras use Movidius chips.[29]

By providing hardware to Chinese surveillance companies, NVIDIA and Intel are also directly contributing to an increasingly prevalent aspect of facial recognition in China: Uyghur detection and analytics. *IPVM* revealed that Uyghur analytics are present in at least 12 different government projects across China, and required by the Ministry of Public Security's draft facial recognition guidelines from December 2017.[30] To place Western reliance in even more stark relief, at least eight Chinese Ministry of Public Security police projects across China call for NVIDIA and Intel chips for use in Uyghur detection and analytics systems.[31] Hikvision is a notable example of a company that actively marketed its Uyghur detection and analytics capabilities—only to cover them up later.[32] Intel responded to *IPVM* condemning the use of their products to abuse human rights, claiming it was unaware of this, and could not fully control the final destination of its chips. NVIDIA did not respond.[33]

Once algorithms have been sufficiently trained, they undergo "deployment" by being tested on unseen data in the "inference" stage—here FPGAs are mostly used.[34] FPGAs are reconfigurable to each application.[35] In facial recognition, FPGAs can be used to implement algorithms such as the Viola-Jones face detection algorithm, which is key to video surveillance and tracking applications.[36] Hikvision uses leading US company Xilinx's FPGAs via purchasing through resellers.[37] Xilinx says it does not control how customers use or sell products, and complies with government requests in the places it does business.[38]

In the global GPU market, US companies NVIDIA and AMD reign, while Xilinx and Intel dominate in FPGAs. In both GPUs and FPGAs, China does not have competitive, well-functioning alternatives.[39]

China is avidly seeking to meet its own chip ambitions and play catch-up to large semiconductor companies with widely used GPU and FPGA designs.[40] Chinese AI chip start-ups like Cambricon (寒武纪) and Horizon Robotics (地平线机器人), as well as Huawei Hisilicon (华为海思) and Hikvision (海康威视), have developed application-specific integrated circuit (ASIC) chips, also classified as "AI chips."[41] However, these chips are used more for the "inference" stage than the "training" stage, leaving Chinese developers still highly dependent on the West for components that it can use to train its image recognition algorithms.[42]

These AI chips power deep learning's physical infrastructure, and therefore its accompanying deep learning algorithms for pattern analysis. This means deep learning technologies are increasingly enabling onboard, adaptive analytical capabilities that can shift processing from the cloud to the edge—in other words, onto the devices themselves in real-time—and ultimately require less calibration of algorithms.[43] This has unlocked many opportunities for the video surveillance industry, which traditionally relied on analyzing surveillance feeds after the fact.[44] This growth in including analytics sensors on network video recorders (NVRs) continues to soar.[45]

Chinese AI surveillance companies have also acknowledged their reliance on leading American companies such as Seagate and Western Digital, which provide surveillance hard drives, and a newer class of drives with AI-enabled surveillance. Western Digital's AI-surveillance enabled WD Purple surveillance hard drives—released in June 2018—are heavily used by Hikvision and Dahua.[46] According to employees from Chinese surveillance companies Hikvision, Dahua, and Uniview (宇视科技), Seagate has lent a significant hand to their operations and products—one Dahua employee calls Seagate a "strategic partner."[47] Chengdu Xiwu Xinan, a contractor in Tacheng, Xinjiang, stated that they only use Western Digital and Seagate's products, adding that "sometimes [Chengdu's] buyers themselves requests their [Western Digital and Seagate] products."[48]

Seagate has worked with Hikvision since 2005 to develop the world's first surveillance hard drive.[49] In a Seagate website post that was reportedly deleted in May 2019, Seagate claimed it had dispatched a dedicated engineering team to China to help tailor-make a drive that could handle large amounts of footage around the clock.[50] In October 2017, following what Seagate lauded as a ten-year track record in delivering surveillance-optimized storage solutions, Seagate released its first storage drive for "AI-enabled surveillance"—the SkyHawk™ AI hard disk drive (HDD).[51] It claims to provide "unprecedented bandwidth and processing power to manage always-on, data-intensive workloads while simultaneously analyzing and recording footage," supporting up to 64 HD cameras and 16 additional 'AI channels'.[52]

Pu Shiliang (浦世亮), dean of Hikvision Research Institute, said: "The outstanding performance of NVIDIA's GPU and its end-to-end AI and deep learning platform can be used for video streaming to create smarter applications for multiple industries."[53] Indeed, papers authored or co-authored by Hikvision demonstrate their involvement in traffic management, on customer identification in banking, and on enforcing blacklists and safety through facial analysis in rail transit.[54] These aims fall into Chinese smart cities' goal of increasing cities' efficient operations and reaping large benefits for public security, yet this has demonstrably been to the detriment of individual liberties.[55]

Hikvision has also published papers in areas that have clear human rights implications. Along with authors from the University of the Chinese Academy of Sciences (UCAS, 中国科学院大学), Hikvision received funding in 2018 from the Xinjiang Public Security Department's 2018 Big Data Application Project 2018GA026 for a paper on assessment processes for 'high-risk personnel'.[56]

Western government-funded surveillance research moves to China

In 2012, a group of scientists at Duke University founded a company called Aqueti, when their developing gigapixel technology was being funded by a US Department of Defense Advanced Research Projects Agency (DARPA) grant with the intention of being used by the US Navy for long-range surveillance.[57] Aqueti claims to use "parallel supercamera technology" to form images by digitally combining data from many micro-cameras. These images become interactive digital streams allowing multiple users to manipulate and control feeds to meet their application needs.[58]

The US government did not ultimately adopt the technology.[59] Instead, different Aqueti cameras started being manufactured with a partnership in China after its lead researcher, David Brady, moved to China in 2016 to become co-chair of Aqueti China Technology.[60] In response to criticism that his "supercameras" could be used in applications that harm human rights, he claimed: "China is a major technological center, and to work in technology you really have to work with China in some way or another. In the same way, our cameras can be used in good or bad ways." He went on to say, "That's true of computers [and] all information technology products. It's not possible, or really appropriate, for companies to control how their things are used."[61]

Aqueti China has caught the eye of AI and innovation focused Chinese funds. In February 2018, two funds—the Shanghai Chuanghehui Fund (上海创合汇), along with CAS Star (中科创星)—made a cumulative 6.3 million USD (40 million RMB) investment into Aqueti China.[62]

In Australia, academic and funding ties from the Australian Research Council and the University of Queensland unwittingly helped the rise of Chinese surveillance company Koala AI, which aims to become Western China's first AI unicorn.[63] Koala AI was created and staffed by individuals who either taught or studied in Australia before being recruited by China's Thousand Talents Program, placing a spotlight on human rights concerns raised by a recruitment program traditionally scrutinized more for its risk as a vector of economic espionage.[64]

Aqueti and Koala AI serve as a warning tale for educational and research efforts funded by Western governments where the intended recipients are either Western or Chinese nationals that later are drawn in by the allure of China's burgeoning surveillance market. While universities and governments must take care to not adopt overly broad policy responses in the face of such case studies, it merits more careful study to determine how to safeguard against Western government-funded research later contributing to programs that harm human rights.

Western academics and universities provide support to Chinese entities

Western academia and companies also play a role in tacitly supporting China's advancing surveillance state capabilities. A notable example is one the world's largest defense companies—state-run Chinese military-surveillance giant China Electronics Technology Group Corporation (CETC, 中国电子科技集团公司). It is responsible for the creation of the Integrated Joint Operations Platform (IJOP) police surveillance app in Xinjiang through a wholly owned subsidiary.[65] At least 28 CETC research institutes or subordinate institutions were placed on the US Department of Commerce Bureau of Industry and Security's Entity List in August 2018 due to high risk or illicit procurement of US technology for Chinese military end-use activities.[66] Western companies have not shied away from supporting CETC: in 2017, Microsoft announced its joint venture with CETC had completed developing "Windows 10 China Government Edition."[67]

CETC is actively expanding its international reach. After partnering with Austria's Technical University Graz (TU Graz) in 2015, CETC launched its first European R&D center in Graz in 2016.[68] CETC has also had funding ties to the University of Technology Sydney (UTS) since 2015, and subsequently established research centers and a public security video retrieval project with them between 2017 and 2018.[69] Facing public scrutiny, UTS subsequently launched an internal review into its partnership with CETC, ultimately recommending to agree with CETC to cease working on its surveillance-relevant project "given the nature of the work and current concerns about potential future use."[70]

Continued lack of ethical publication standards

In the publication space, publishers such as the US journal Wiley provide high-profile platforms for Chinese academics to analyze how to harness computer vision to perform ethnicity recognition.[71] One such example is a 2018 paper published on Wiley Interdisciplinary Reviews (WIREs) Data Mining and Knowledge Discovery—the paper received a grant from China's National Natural Science Foundation of China (NSFC, 国家自然科学基金委员会) to explore facial feature discovery on groups such as Uyghurs and Tibetans.[72] Despite facing intense backlash for the publication, Wiley did not take down the paper; instead, the editor-in-chief of the Data Mining and Knowledge Discovery section argued that the paper "underwent a stringent editorial process," and stated that the editors and Wiley did not agree with or support the harnessing of these technologies for "possible unexpected malicious purposes."[73] While no direct evidence exists to show that the paper directly contributed to repression of Uyghurs and other ethnic minorities in China, James Leibold of Australia's La Trobe University responded that "there is a significant possibility that this research will adversely affect minority communities in China due to the widespread use of pre-emptive racial profiling, which violates the presumption of innocence and other rights of the individual."[74]

Countermeasures

The growing press scrutiny over the role Western companies and academia play in fostering the Chinese surveillance state has led to attempts to address these issues. In June 2019, Brad Sherman, a member of the US House of Representatives, introduced the Uyghur Human Rights Act. If passed, this would allow the US president to impose sanctions under the Global Magnitsky Act against senior Xinjiang regional officials responsible for abuses. Implementation of the Global Magnitsky Act freezes the assets of those targeted in the US—and consequently, international—financial system.[75] However, no Chinese officials or companies has yet been subjected to these sanctions.

In October 2019, the US government placed eight Chinese companies on its Entity List for their role in human rights violations in Xinjiang. These companies included video surveillance firms Dahua and Hikvision, facial recognition unicorns Yitu (依图), Megvii (旷视), and Sensetime (商汤), voice recognition giant iFlytek (科大讯飞), digital forensics company Meiya Pico (美亚柏科信息) and nanotechnology Yixin Technology Company (溢鑫科创), effectively blocking them from accessing US components.[76] Some academic institutions are reconsidering or severing their ties with these companies. For example, Rutgers University ended its links with iFlytek in early 2019 while the Massachusetts Institute of Technology and University of Technology Sydney (UTS) are reviewing their partnerships and funding from Sensetime and iFlytek, as well as CETC, respectively.[77] However, there is little evidence to suggest that universities are developing guidelines to ensure their research partnership and funders are not tied to human rights abuses, which is a better way of ensuring ethical partnerships than evaluating each on a case-by-case basis.

Moreover, the Entity List's impact on the Chinese tech companies may be limited. Evidence suggests that Hikvision and Dahua had stockpiled important components since June 2019 in anticipation of the sanctions.[78] In investor calls following the decision, Hikvision and Dahua claimed they had successfully sourced alternative components and new design solutions, and would continue to increase research and development processes; however, US-made CPUs, GPUs, and FPGAs could be difficult to replace.[79] It remains to be seen what will happen once Hikvision and Dahua stockpiles run out. Other analysts suggest that the sanctions will spur Chinese companies to accelerate the development of key components to wean dependency from the West.[80] It is yet unclear if the sanctions may have slowed China's ambitions to increase AI-powered CCTV coverage across the country, or Chinese companies' expansion internationally.

Going forward, it is of crucial importance that more scrutiny be placed closer to home: Western technology companies and universities—wittingly or unwittingly—are undoubtedly contributing to the advancement of China's surveillance state. Yet the phenomenon continues to escape widespread public attention. More research is needed to document in greater detail the role of Western companies in the Chinese surveillance state, including Intel, NVIDIA, Seagate, and Western Digital. Other Western companies may also be contributing, that richly deserve the same sort of scrutiny their products and technology enable China to exercise.

Notes

1 Priyanka Juneja, "China's Hukou System," *The Diplomat*, July 14, 2017; (https://thediplomat.com/2017/07/chinas-hukousystem/); Andrew Jacobs, "A Rare Look Into

One's Life on File in China," *New York Times*, March 15, 2015; Xiaobo Lu and Elizabeth J. Perry, ed., *Danwei: The Changing Chinese Workplace in Historical and Comparative Perspective*, London: Routledge, 1997.

2 Maya Wang (Human Rights Watch), "China's Dystopian Push to Revolutionize Surveillance," *Washington Post*, August 18, 2017. See also Zhou Yongkang, "加强和改进社会管理促进社会稳定和谐" *People's Daily*, October 25, 2006.

3 Zhejiang Radio and TV Group. "浙江创客：人脸识别系统'黑'科技服务G20峰会 ("Zhejiang Maker: Facial Recognition Used at G20 Summit"), August 17, 2016. http://n. cztv.com/news/12183147.html.

4 Edward Schwarck, "Intelligence and Informatization: the Rise of the Ministry of Public Security in Intelligence Work in China," *The China Journal*, vol. 80, March 28, 2018.

5 Greg Walton, "China's Golden Shield: Corporations and the Development of Surveillance Technology in the People's Republic of China," Montreal: International Centre for Human Rights and Development, 2001.

6 Efforts to increase CCTV coverage in China's urban areas are generally known as Project Skynet (天网工程). Equivalent efforts to expand surveillance camera coverage in the rural areas, known as Project Sharp Eyes (雪亮工程), started around 2016. See Chen Shixian and Li Zhen, "天网网什么" (What is Project Skynet"), *People's Weekly*, Issue 20, 2017. China had 176 million surveillance cameras in public and private spaces in operation in 2016, and is expected to more than triple to reach 626 million by 2020, according to IHS Markit. See "Q Daily, "中国安装了 1.76 亿个监控摄像头，这市场还在增长" ("China Has Installed 176 Million Surveillance Cameras and the Market Is Still Expanding"), November 21, 2017.

7 Major AI companies that supply the MPS and its provincial and local counterparts include iFlytek (for voice recognition), Sensetime, Yitu, Cloudwalk, and Megvii (for visual-related recognition) and major state defense contractor CETC (for both big data and extraction of MAC addresses and IMEI numbers) but there are many more Chinese surveillance companies that sell to the police. See: Human Rights Watch, "Voice Biometric Collection Threatens Privacy," October 22, 2017. www.hrw.org/news/2017/10/22/china-voice-biometric-collection-threatens-privacy; Josh Horwitz, "The Billion-dollar, Alibaba-backed AI Company That's Quietly Watching People in China," April 16, 2018. https://qz.com/1248493/sensetime-the-billion-dollar-alibaba-backed-ai-company-thats-quietly-watching-everyone-in-china.; Tom Simonite, "Behind the Rise of China's Facial-Recognition Giants," *Wired*, September 3. www. wired.com/story/behind-rise-chinas-facial-recognition-giants/; Paul Mozur, "One Month, 500,000 Face Scans: How China Is Using A.I. to Profile a Minority, *New York Times*, April 14, 2019; Human Rights Watch, "China's Algorithms of Repression: Reverse Engineering a Xinjiang Police Mass Surveillance App," May 1, 2019. www. hrw.org/video-photos/interactive/2019/05/02/china-how-mass-surveillance-works-xinjiang.

8 Human Rights Watch, "Police DNA Database Threatens Privacy," May 15, 2017. www. hrw.org/news/2017/05/15/china-police-dna-database-threatens-privacy. See also, Human Rights Watch, "Minority Region Collects DNA from Millions," December 13, 2017. www.hrw.org/news/2017/12/13/china-minority-region-collects-dna-millions.

9 Human Rights Watch, "Police 'Big Data' Systems Violate Privacy, Target Dissidents," November 19, 2017. www.hrw.org/news/2017/11/19/china-police-big-data-systems-violate-privacy-target-dissent.

10 Maya Wang, "'Eradicating Ideological Viruses'—China's Campaign of Repression Against Xinjiang's Muslims," Human Rights Watch, September 9, 2018. www.hrw. org/report/2018/09/09/eradicating-ideological-viruses/chinas-campaign-repression-against-xinjiangs.

11 United Nations Office of the High Commissioner for Human Rights, "Committee on the Elimination of Racial Discrimination Reviews the Report of China," August 13,

2018. www.ohchr.org/EN/NewsEvents/Pages/DisplayNews.aspx?NewsID=23452&
LangID=E. Estimates also range to 1.8 million or more, see Associated Press, "Secret Documents Reveal How China Mass Detention Camps Work," November 25, 2019. https://apnews.com/4ab0b341a4ec4e648423f2ec47ea5c47.

12 Human Rights Watch, "China's Algorithms of Repression: Reverse Engineering a Xinjiang Police Mass Surveillance App," May 1, 2019. www.hrw.org/video-photos/interactive/2019/05/02/china-how-mass-surveillance-works-xinjiang.

13 This is in part due to public outcry and push back against commercial practices, which have been reported by the media. See, for example, AFP, "China Facial-Recognition Case Puts Big Brother on Trial," January 12, 2020. www.hongkongfp.com/2020/01/12/china-facial-recognition-case-puts-big-brother-trial.

14 Yuan Yang and Madhumita Murgi, "How China Cornered the Facial Recognition Surveillance Narket," *Financial Times*, December 9, 2019.

15 Ibid. While it is worth noting that the US actually has a slightly higher surveillance camera per capita figure than China, the US—unlike China—does not appear to be aiming to mass upgrade its surveillance cameras with facial recognition technology, nor does it have multiple unicorns (each valued over $1 billion) dedicated solely to facial recognition. See Coco Feng, "China the Most Surveilled Nation? The US Has the Largest Number of CCTV Cameras Per Capita," *South China Morning Post*, December 9, 2019. The US has 15.28 surveillance cameras per 100 citizens, compared to China's figure of 14.36.

16 Security Exhibition Network. "2019年中国AI+安防行业发展研究报告" ("2019 China AI + Security Industry Development Research Report"), May 10, 2019. www.afzhan.com/news/detail/74994.html.

17 By certain estimates, Chinese filtering or surveillance technology has diffused to at least 73 countries. See Valentin Weber, "The Worldwide Web of Chinese and Russian Information Controls," *Centre for Technology and Global Affairs*, September 2019.

18 Laura Mills and Maya Wang, "Facial Recognition Deal in Kyrgyzstan Poses Risks to Rights," November 15, 2019. www.hrw.org/news/2019/11/15/facial-recognition-deal-kyrgyzstan-poses-risks-rights; CNN Philippines. "DILG Launches Chinese CCTV Surveillance System in Metro Manila," November 22, 2019. https://cnnphilippines.com/news/2019/11/22/DILG-Chinese-CCTV-Manila-Safe-Philippines.html.

19 Lorand Laskai and Helen Toner, "Can China Grow Its Own AI Tech Base?," *New America*, November 4, 2019.

20 George Anadiotis, "GPU Databases Are Coming of Age," *ZDNet*, March 26, 2018.

21 Faizan Shaikh, "Why Are GPUs Necessary for Training Deep Learning Models?," *Analytics Vidhya*, May 18, 2017.

22 China Security Industry Network. "AI芯片厂商与传统安防制造企业紧密合作拓展安防业务" ("AI Chip Manufacturers Work Closely with Traditional Security Manufacturing Companies to Expand Security Business"), December 28, 2017. http://news.21csp.com.cn/c34/201712/11365694.html. The China Security Industry Network is sponsored by the MPS's Bureau of Science and Technology Informatization (公安部科技信息化局).

23 Lindsay Gorman and Matt Schrader, "US Firms Are Helping Build China's Orwellian State," *Foreign Policy*, March 19, 2019. See also John Honovich, "Hikvision And The Chinese Government," *IPVM*, December 7, 2015. https://ipvm.com/reports/heres-what-really-sets-hikvision-apart.

24 IHS Markit, "Top Video Surveillance Trends for 2017." https://cdn.ihs.com/www/pdf/TEC-Video-Surveillance-Trends.pdf.

25 Ibid.

26 Stephen Mayhew, "Dahua Launches Efficient IP Camera Series with Built-in AI Facial Recognition," *Biometric Update*, July 16, 2018.

27 IPVM. "Congressional Letter Calls Out US companies Supporting Dahua and Hikvision," March 11, 2019. https://ipvm.com/reports/letter-support.

28 IPVM. "Hikvision Partners with Intel Movidius for Artificial Intelligence Cameras," October 25, 2016. https://ipvm.com/reports/movidius-hikvision.

29 IPVM. "Congressional Letter Calls Out US companies Supporting Dahua and Hikvision," March 11, 2019. https://ipvm.com/reports/letter-support.

30 Charles Rollet, "China Government Spreads Uyghur Analytics Across China," *IPVM*, November 25, 2019.

31 The eight projects requiring Uyghur analytics in 2018–2019 are from Public Security Bureaus in Chongqing megacity, and Zhejiang, Henan, Gansu, Fujian, Jiangsu, Shanxi, Shaanxi, Anhui provinces. See *IPVM*, "China Uyghur Analytic Projects Require Intel and NVIDIA, Intel Condemns, NVIDIA Silent," December 2, 2019.

32 Charles Rollet, "Hikvision Markets Uyghur Ethnicity Analytics, Now Covers Up," *IPVM*, November 11, 2019.

33 *IPVM*, "China Uyghur Analytic Projects Require Intel and NVIDIA, Intel Condemns, op. cit.

34 Xilinx, "FPGAs in the Emerging DNN Inference Landscape," Xilinx, October 28, 2019. www.xilinx.com/support/documentation/white_papers/wp514-emerging-dnn.pdf.

35 George Anadiotis, "AI Chips for Big Data and Machine Learning: GPUs, FPGAs, and Hard Choices in the Cloud and On-premise," *ZDNet*, August 20, 2018.

36 See, e.g., Peter Irgens, Curtis Bader, Theresa Le, Devansh Saxena, Cristinel Ababei. "An Efficient and Cost-effective FPGA Based Implementation of the Viola-Jones Face Detection Algorithm," HardwareX, vol. 1, April 2017. https://doi.org/10.1016/j.ohx.2017.03.002.

37 Liza Lin and Josh Chin, "US Tech Companies Prop Up China's Vast Surveillance Network," *Wall Street Journal*, November 26, 2019.

38 Ibid.

39 China's top GPU company is Jingjia Microelectronics, a military–civilian integrated company that made China's first domestic GPU, the JM5400, and in 2019 released its latest GPU, the JM7200. See Zhiye Liu, "Chinese Vendor Developing PCIe 4.0 GPU With 16GB HBM and GTX 1080-Like Performance," *Tom's Hardware*, August 22, 2019. However, the JM7200 is still 25x slower compared to a leading US GPU. See Jia Xiaobian, "The Successful Generation of Domestic Next-Generation GPU JM7200 Is Still Far from the World's Leading Level (国产下一代GPU JM7200成功流片 与世界领先水平仍有较大差距)," *PCOnline*, September 5, 2018. Likewise, Chinese FPGA companies Efinix, Gowin Semiconductor, and Shenzhen Pango Microsystem have not developed advanced FPGAs. See He Huifeng, "'Made in China 2025': The Guangzhou Start-up Aiming Big in Semiconductors," *SCMP*, September 24, 2018. See also Paul Triolo and Jimmy Goodrich, "From Riding a Wave to Full Steam Ahead," February 28, 2018. www.newamerica.org/cybersecurity-initiative/digichina/blog/riding-wave-full-steam-ahead.

40 Synced Review, "A Look at China's Growing Semiconductor Industry," April 20, 2019, https://syncedreview.com/2019/04/20/a-look-at-chinas-growing-semiconductor-industry.

41 Ibid.

42 Lorand Laskai and Helen Toner, "Can China Grow Its Own AI Tech Base?" *New America*, November 4, 2019.

43 IHS Markit, "Top Video Surveillance Trends for 2017," (https://cdn.ihs.com/www/pdf/TEC-Video-Surveillance-Trends.pdf). See also: Jessica Burton, "How the New SkyHawk AI Enables Video To Serve Us Better," Seagate Blog. https://blog.seagate.com/business/new-skyhawk-ai-enables-video-serve-us-better.

44 Ibid.

45 IHS Markit, "Top Video Surveillance Trends for 2017," op. cit.

46 IPVM. "Congressional Letter Calls Out US companies Supporting Dahua and Hikvision," March 11, 2019. https://ipvm.com/reports/letter-support.

47 Seagate, "Seagate Launches First Drive For AI-Enabled Surveillance," October 28, 2017. www.seagate.com/news/news-archive/seagate-launches-first-drive-for-ai-enabled-surveillance-master-pr/.

48 Liza Lin and Josh Chin, "US Tech Companies Prop Up China's Vast Surveillance Network," *Wall Street Journal*, November 26, 2019.

49 Ibid.

50 Seagate, "Seagate Launches First Drive For AI-Enabled Surveillance," op. cit.

51 Ibid.

52 The specs of the Skyhawk AI surveillance drive are described here: www.seagate.com/internal-hard-drives/hdd/skyhawk.

53 NVIDIA 成为 GPU 成为人工智能计算平台的领导者 ("NVIDIA becomes GPU leader in artificial intelligence computing platforms"), *China Security Industry Network* (中国安防行业网), February 21, 2019.

54 See Li Chenyu et al., 数据驱动下的交通治理核心技术 ("Core Technology for Data-driven Traffic Governance"), *China Public Security* (中国公共安全), July 2019; Jin Hong et al., 银行营业网点客户识别架构探讨 ("Discussion on Customer Identification Structure of Banking Business Outlets"), *China Public Security* (中国公共安全), June 2019; and Chen Yongzheng, 视频智能分析在轨道交通的运用 ("Application of Intelligent Video Analysis in Rail Transit"), Intelligent Building (智能建筑), November 2014.

55 Jamil Anderlini, "How China's Smart-City Tech Focuses on Its Own Citizens," *Financial Times*, June 4, 2019.

56 Zhang Wei et al., 大数据背景下基于过滤式-包裹式方法的高危人员风险预警 ("Risk Assessment of High-Risk Personnel Based on the Filter-Wrapper Method in the Context of Big Data"), *Science & Technology for Development* (科技促进发展), August 2018.

57 Wenxin Fan, "How a Powerful Spy Camera Invented at Duke Ended Up in China's Hands," *Wall Street Journal*, June 11, 2018.

58 For more information on Aqueti, see www.aqueti.com/.

59 Wenxin Fan, "How a Powerful Spy Camera Invented at Duke Ended Up in China's Hands," op. cit.

60 Ibid. See also Bre Bradham, "Duke Professor Takes His 'Supercamera' Manufacturing to China, Sparking Questions about the Technology's Use," www.dukechronicle.com/article/2018/09/supercameras-duke-research-goes-to-china-david-brady-dku.

61 Bre Bradham, op. cit.

62 For details on the investment, see https://zdb.pedaily.cn/inv/show17985. For more information on CAS Star, one of the few Chinese funds to disclose information publicly, see www.cbinsights.com/investor/cas-star and http://casstar.com.cn/.

63 Alex Joske, "The company with Aussie roots that's helping build China's surveillance state," Australian Strategic Policy Institute, August 26, 2019.

64 Ibid.

65 Human Rights Watch, "China's Algorithms of Repression: Reverse Engineering a Xinjiang Police Mass Surveillance App," May 1, 2019.

66 Federal Register, "Addition of Certain Entities; and Modification of Entry on the Entity List," August 1, 2018. www.federalregister.gov/documents/2018/08/01/2018-16474/addition-of-certain-entities-and-modification-of-entry-on-the-entity-list.

67 "Announcing Windows 10 China Government Edition and the New Surface Pro," Microsoft Corporate Blogs, May 23, 2017.

68 "China Electronics Technology Group Corporation," Australian Strategic Policy Institute, updated October 29, 2019. https://unitracker.aspi.org.au/universities/china-electronics-technology-group-corporation.

69 Ibid.

70 "UTS CETC Review," University of Technology Sydney. www.uts.edu.au/news/media-contacts/uts-cetc-review.

71 Charles Rollet, "Western Academia Helps Build China's Automated Racism," *Coda Story*, August 6, 2019.

72 https://onlinelibrary.wiley.com/doi/full/10.1002/widm.1278.

73 See message response posted by Wiley on Twitter: https://twitter.com/wileyinresearch/status/1136676684135116800/photo/1.

74 Charles Rollet, "Western Academia Helps Build China's Automated Racism," op. cit.

75 See www.state.gov/global-magnitsky-act.

76 Catherine Shu, "Eight Chinese Tech Firms Placed on US Entity List for Their Role in Human Rights Violations against Muslim Minority Groups," *TechCrunch*, October 8, 2019.

77 "MIT Reviews Partnerships with Blacklisted Chinese Tech Firms," Associated Press, October 12, 2019; Madhumita Murgia and Christian Shepherd, "US Universities Reconsider Research Links with Chinese AI Company." www.ft.com/content/2f112da0-8e19-11e9-a1c1-51bf8f989972; Sophie McNeill, Jeanavive McGregor, Meredith Griffiths, Michael Walsh, and Echo Hui, "UTS, Curtin Unis Announce Reviews over Links to Surveillance Tech Used by Chinese Government," *ABC*, July 16, 2019.

78 Sarah Dai, "Chinese Surveillance Giant Hikvision Stockpiles Crucial Parts to Guard against Potential US Ban," *South China Morning Post*, July 22, 2019.

79 无惧"被列实体清单" 海康、大华称已有替代方案 ("Fear Not: Hikvision and Dahua Already Have Alternate Solutions Following their Placement on the Entity List"), Sina Finance, October 10, 2019.

80 Scott Tong, "Chinese Surveillance Companies on US Blacklist Still Using Silicon Valley Components," *Marketplace Public Radio*, December 20, 2019.

Bibliography

Anadiotis, George. "GPU Databases Are Coming of Age," *ZDNet*, March 26, 2018.

Anderlini, Jamil. "How China's Smart-City Tech Focuses on Its Own Citizens," *Financial Times*, June 4, 2019.

Associated Press. "MIT Reviews Partnerships with Blacklisted Chinese Tech Firms," October 12, 2019.

Australian Strategic Policy Institute. "China Electronics Technology Group Corporation," updated October 29, 2019. https://unitracker.aspi.org.au/universities/china-electronics-technology-group-corporation.

Baltrusitis, Justinas. "Top 10 Countries and Cities by Number of CCTV Cameras," PreciseSecurity.com, December 4, 2019. www.precisesecurity.com/articles/Top-10-Countries-by-Number-of-CCTV-Cameras.

Bradham, Bre. "Duke Professor Takes His 'Supercamera' Manufacturing to China, Sparking Questions about the Technology's Use," September 4, 2018. www.dukechronicle.com/article/2018/09/supercameras-duke-research-goes-to-china-david-brady-dku.

Burton, Jessica. "How the New SkyHawk AI Enables Video to Serve Us Better," Seagate Blog, https://blog.seagate.com/business/new-skyhawk-ai-enables-video-serve-us-better.

Chen, Shixian and Zhen Li. "'天网'网什么," (What is Project Skynet), *People's Weekly*, Issue 20, 2017.

Chen, Yongzheng. "视频智能分析在轨道交通的运用" ("Application of Intelligent Video Analysis in Rail Transit"), 智能建筑 (*Intelligent Building*), November 2014.

"China Facial-Recognition Case Puts Big Brother on Trial," *AFP*, January 12, 2020.

China Security Industry Network. "AI芯片厂商与传统安防制造企业紧密合作 拓展安防业务" ("AI Chip Manufacturers Work Closely with Traditional Security

Manufacturing Companies to Expand Security Business"), December 28, 2017. http://news.21csp.com.cn/c34/201712/11365694.html.

China Security Industry Network. "NVIDIA 成为 GPU 成为人工智能计算平台的领导者" ("NVIDIA Becomes GPU Leader in Artificial Intelligence Computing Platforms"), February 21, 2019.

CNN Philippines. "DILG Launches Chinese CCTV Surveillance System in Metro Manila," November 22, 2019. https://cnnphilippines.com/news/2019/11/22/DILG-Chinese-CCTV-Manila-Safe-Philippines.html.

Dai, Sarah. "Chinese Surveillance Giant Hikvision Stockpiles Crucial Parts to Guard against Potential US Ban," *South China Morning Post*, July 22, 2019.

Fan, Wenxin. "How a Powerful Spy Camera Invented at Duke Ended up in China's Hands," *Wall Street Journal*, June 11, 2018.

Federal Register. "Addition of Certain Entities; and Modification of Entry on the Entity List," August 1, 2018. www.federalregister.gov/documents/2018/08/01/2018-16474/addition-of-certain-entities-and-modification-of-entry-on-the-entity-list.

Gorman, Lindsay and Matt Schrader. "US Firms Are Helping Build China's Orwellian State," *Foreign Policy*, March 19, 2019.

Honovich, John. "Hikvision and the Chinese Government," *IPVM*, December 7, 2015.

Horwitz, Josh. "The Billion-Dollar, Alibaba-Backed AI Company That's Quietly Watching People in China," *Quartz*, April 16, 2018.

Human Rights Watch. "China's Algorithms of Repression: Reverse Engineering a Xinjiang Police Mass Surveillance App," May 1, 2019. www.hrw.org/video-photos/interactive/2019/05/02/china-how-mass-surveillance-works-xinjiang.

Human Rights Watch. "Minority Region Collects DNA from Millions, December 13, 2017. www.hrw.org/news/2017/12/13/china-minority-region-collects-dna-millions.

Human Rights Watch. "Police 'Big Data' Systems Violate Privacy, Target Dissidents," November 19, 2017. www.hrw.org/news/2017/11/19/china-police-big-data-systems-violate-privacy-target-dissent.

Human Rights Watch. "Police DNA Database Threatens Privacy," May 15, 2017. www.hrw.org/news/2017/05/15/china-police-dna-database-threatens-privacy.

Human Rights Watch. "Voice Biometric Collection Threatens Privacy," October 22, 2017. www.hrw.org/news/2017/10/22/china-voice-biometric-collection-threatens-privacy.

IHS Markit. "Top Video Surveillance Trends for 2017." https://cdn.ihs.com/www/pdf/TEC-Video-Surveillance-Trends.pdf.

IPVM. "China Uyghur Analytic Projects Require Intel and NVIDIA, Intel Condemns, NVIDIA Silent," December 2, 2019. https://ipvm.com/reports/uyghur-intel-nvidia.

IPVM. "Congressional Letter Calls Out US companies Supporting Dahua and Hikvision," March 11, 2019. https://ipvm.com/reports/letter-support.

IPVM. "Hikvision Partners with Intel Movidius for Artificial Intelligence Cameras," October 25, 2016. https://ipvm.com/reports/movidius-hikvision.

Irgens, Peter et al. "An Efficient and Cost Effective FPGA Based Implementation of the Viola-Jones Face Detection Algorithm," *HardwareX*, Vol. 1, April 2017.

Jacobs, Andrew. "A Rare Look into One's Life on File in China," *New York Times*, March 15, 2015.

Jin, Hong et al. "银行营业网点客户识别架构探讨" ("Discussion on Customer Identification Structure of Banking Business Outlets"), 中国公共安全 (China Public Security), June 2019.

Joske, Alex. "The Company with Aussie Roots That's Helping Build China's Surveillance State," *Australian Strategic Policy Institute*, August 26, 2019. www.aspistrategist.org.au/ the-company-with-aussie-roots-thats-helping-build-chinas-surveillance-state.

Juneja, Priyanka. "China's Hukou System," *The Diplomat*, July 14, 2017.

Laskai, Lorand and Helen Toner. "Can China Grow Its Own AI Tech Base?," *New America*, November 4, 2019.

Li, Chenyu et al. "数据驱动下的交通治理核心技术" ("Core Technology for Data-Driven Traffic Governance"), 中国公共安全, (China Public Security), July 2019.

Lin, Liza and Josh Chin. "US Tech Companies Prop up China's Vast Surveillance Network," *Wall Street Journal*, November 26, 2019.

Liu, Zhiye. "Chinese Vendor Developing PCIe 4.0 GPU with 16GB HBM and GTX 1080-like Performance," *Tom's Hardware*, August 22, 2019.

Lu, Xiaobo and Elizabeth J. Perry, eds. *Danwei: The Changing Chinese Workplace in Historical and Comparative Perspective*, London: Routledge, 1997.

Mayhew, Stephen. "Dahua Launches Efficient IP Camera Series with Built-in AI Facial Recognition," *Biometric Update*, July 16, 2018.

McNeill, Sophie et al. "UTS, Curtin Unis Announce Reviews over Links to Surveillance Tech Used by Chinese Government," *Australian Broadcasting Corporation*, July 16, 2019.

Microsoft Corporate Blogs. "Announcing Windows 10 China Government Edition and the New Surface Pro," May 23, 2017.

Mills, Laura and Maya Wang. "Facial Recognition Deal in Kyrgyzstan Poses Risks to Rights," *Human Rights Watch*, November 15, 2019.

Mozur, Paul. "One Month, 500,000 Face Scans: How China is Using AI to Profile a Minority," *New York Times*, April 14, 2019.

Murgia, Madhumita and Christian Shepherd. "US Universities Reconsider Research Links with Chinese AI Company," June 13, 2019. www.ft.com/content/2f112da0-8e19-11e9-a1c1-51bf8f989972.

Q Daily. "中国安装了 1.76 亿个监控摄像头，这市场还在增长" ("China Has Installed 176 Million Surveillance Cameras and the Market Is Still Expanding"), November 21, 2017.

Rollet, Charles. "China Government Spreads Uyghur Analytics across China," *IPVM*, November 25, 2019.

Rollet, Charles. "Hikvision Markets Uyghur Ethnicity Analytics, Now Covers Up," *IPVM*, November 11, 2019.

Rollet, Charles. "Western Academia Helps Build China's Automated Racism," *Coda Story*, August 6, 2019.

Schwarck, Edward. "Intelligence and Informatization: The Rise of the Ministry of Public Security in Intelligence Work in China," *The China Journal*, Vol. 80, March 28, 2018.

Seagate. "Seagate Launches First Drive for AI-Enabled Surveillance," October 28, 2017. www.seagate.com/news/news-archive/seagate-launches-first-drive-for-ai-enabled-surveillance-master-pr.

Security Exhibition Network. "2019年中国AI+安防行业发展研究报告" ("2019 China AI + Security Industry Development Research Report"), May 10, 2019. www.afzhan.com/news/detail/74994.html.

Shaikh, Faizan. "Why Are GPUs Necessary for Training Deep Learning Models?," *Analytics Vidhya*, May 18, 2017.

Shu, Catherine. "Eight Chinese Tech Firms Placed on US Entity List for Their Role in Human Rights Violations against Muslim Minority Groups," *TechCrunch*, October 8, 2019.

Simonite, Tom. "Behind the Rise of China's Facial-Recognition Giants," *Wired*, September 3, 2019.

Sina Finance. "'无惧'被列实体清单'海康、大华称已有替代方案" ("Fear Not: Hikvision and Dahua Already Have Alternate Solutions Following Their Placement on the Entity List"), October 10, 2019. https://finance.sina.cn/stock/ssgs/2019-10-10/detail-iicezuev1116708.d.html.

Synced Review. "A Look at China's Growing Semiconductor Industry," April 20, 2019. https://syncedreview.com/2019/04/20/a-look-at-chinas-growing-semiconductor-industry.

Tong, Scott. "Chinese Surveillance Companies on US Blacklist Still using Silicon Valley Components," *Marketplace Public Radio*, December 20, 2019.

Triolo, Paul and Jimmy Goodrich. "From Riding a Wave to Full Steam Ahead," *New America*, February 28, 2018.

United Nations Office of the High Commissioner for Human Rights. "Committee on the Elimination of Racial Discrimination Reviews the Report of China," August 13, 2018.

University of Technology Sydney. "UTS CETC Review." www.uts.edu.au/news/media-contacts/uts-cetc-review.

US Department of State. "Global Magnitsky Act." www.state.gov/global-magnitsky-act.

Walton, Greg. "China's Golden Shield: Corporations and the Development of Surveillance Technology in the People's Republic of China," International Centre for Human Rights and Democratic Development, 2001.

Wang, Cunrui et al. "Facial Feature Discovery for Ethnicity Recognition," *Wiley Data Mining and Knowledge Discovery* 9, no. 1, 2019.

Wang, Maya. "China's Dystopian Push to Revolutionize Surveillance," *Washington Post*, August 18, 2017.

Wang, Maya. "'Eradicating Ideological Viruses'—China's Campaign of Repression against Xinjiang's Muslims," *Human Rights Watch*, September 9, 2018.

Weber, Valentin. "The Worldwide Web of Chinese and Russian Information Controls," *Centre for Technology and Global Affairs*, September 2019.

Xilinx. "FPGAs in the Emerging DNN Inference Landscape," October 28, 2019. www.xilinx.com/support/documentation/white_papers/wp514-emerging-dnn.pdf.

Yang, Yuan and Madhumita Murgia. "How China Cornered the Facial Recognition Surveillance Market," *Financial Times*, December 9, 2019.

Zhang, Wei et al. "大数据背景下基于过滤式-包裹式方法的高危人员风险预警" ("Risk Assessment of High-Risk Personnel Based on the Filter-Wrapper Method in the Context of Big Data"), 科技促进发展 (Science & Technology for Development), August 2018.

Zhejiang Radio and TV Group. "浙江创客：人脸识别系统'黑'科技服务G20峰会 ("Zhejiang Maker: Facial Recognition Used at G20 Summit"), August 17, 2016. http://n.cztv.com/news/12183147.html.

Zhou, Yongkang. "加强促进社会稳定和谐" ("Strengthen and Facilitate Social Stability and Harmony"), *People's Daily*, October 25, 2006.

15

THE UNITED FRONT AND TECHNOLOGY TRANSFER

Alex Joske and Jeffrey Stoff

Attention is growing around the world on the activities of the CPC's united front system (统战系统), which is a grouping of party and state agencies that oversee and carry out the party's efforts to consolidate an alliance of co-opted individuals and groups. These efforts are known as united front work, and the alliance it builds is known as the United Front. United front work draws on Leninist tactics that began their life in Soviet Russia and were fine-tuned in Germany in the 1920s, as communists battled independents and social democrats for dominance on the left. The CPC credits its use of the United Front during the Chinese Civil War, when it undermined and infiltrated the Chinese Nationalist Party at the same time as it co-opted other sympathetic parties, to its emergence as the ruling party of mainland China.

In the words of the director of the CPC Central Committee's United Front Work Department (UFWD, 中共中央统一战线工作部), "The United Front has long been an important component of the party's greater direction and greater policies, and an important magic weapon for the party to lead the people to achieve victory in the endeavors of revolution, development and reform."[1] The UFWD coordinates the CPC's efforts to strengthen its influence and co-option of representatives of different parts of society, both domestically and internationally. Groups targeted by united front work range from ethnic minorities, religious groups, and business leaders to Chinese diaspora communities and intellectuals.[2] More than two dozen central agencies are involved in united front work, and a member of China's Politburo Standing Committee is responsible for overall leadership of this system.[3] Co-opted individuals and groups can be mobilized as needed for specific ends. Those ends include technology transfer.

More recently the growing attention on united front work is due of course to China's growing international presence, of which united front work is a key part. The "friendship-building," network-cultivating influence work that is a prominent aspect of united front work grows more visible to researchers and scholars overseas, who are now familiarizing themselves with concepts and tactics that have been overlooked since the fall of the Berlin Wall in 1989.

Although the united front system's political influence activities have come under increased scrutiny in the West,[4] there is still insufficient understanding of their role in China's state-directed technology transfer, including talent recruitment programs and entrepreneurial contests. This chapter offers such a survey, demonstrating the key role united front work plays in forming overseas organizations, and managing "overseas scholars" and other foreign experts, in pursuit of technology transfer objectives.

We begin with a brief background, followed by two case studies illustrating how the United Front achieves technology transfer through a diverse group of actors. For more on this activity, and many examples, see Chapters 7 and 8, on Europe and Germany. We then examine a key facilitator: the Western Returned Scholars Association (WRSA, 欧美同学会).[5] A further case study shows how a city in China, Dalian (大连), is pioneering the use of the united front system to access and acquire global technology.

United front work as a vector for tech transfer

Since the early days of the PRC, the united front system has been central to the CPC's efforts to gain technology and expertise from abroad. Among 12 categories of people formally targeted by united front work, at least four are associated with technology transfer efforts: non-party intellectuals, "new social strata personages" (新的社会阶层人士) such as employees of foreign enterprises, personnel that have studied abroad and returned to China, and overseas Chinese students and scholars.[6]

The overlap between the united front system and technology transfer is best exemplified in the person of Wan Gang (万钢), an individual who, for more than a decade, sat at the very nexus of China's S&T development and talent recruitment efforts.

Between 2007 and 2018, Wan was China's Minister of Science and Technology at MOST, the central government ministry now charged with "implementing the CPC Central Committee's policies and decisions on scientific and technological innovation."[7] Since 2007, Wan has also served as chair of the Zhigong Party (致公党, or "Public Interest Party"), one of the United Front's constituent minor parties tucked under the CPC's leadership (see Chapter 7 for more on the Zhigong Party and Wan).

The Zhigong Party represents "middle and upper-class" overseas Chinese who have returned to China, family members of nationals residing abroad, as well as certain PRC individuals with extensive overseas ties.[8] At least one of its provincial branches runs its own talent recruitment scheme—the "Attracting Phoenixes

Project" (引凤工程)—for enticing overseas talent to return to China and "serve the country."[9] In addition to his work with the Zhigong Party, Wan also served as a vice chairperson of the United Front's main forum, the Chinese People's Political Consultative Conference (CPPCC, 中国人民政治协商会议).

Wan's overlapping positions within the united front system, MOST, and the Zhigong Party are likely no accident. The united front system's relationships with overseas communities and professional associations positions it well to facilitate the type of talent recruitment and technology transfer sought by China.

Since 2015, the united front system's involvement in overseas talent recruitment appears to have expanded.[10] That year, Xi Jinping underscored that "overseas students and scholars are an important component of talent and a new focus of united front work,"[11] thereby signaling an emphasis on the system's talent work aimed at augmenting its role in technology transfer. The following year, the CPC General Office, which implements the Central Committee's day-to-day work, issued recommendations on strengthening the Western Returned Scholars Association, a key component of China's tech transfer enterprise, profiled later in this chapter.[12]

Case study: Yang Chunlai

The case of Yang Chunlai (杨春来) offers a window into the overlap of political influence and technology transfer in united front work. Yang was a computer programmer at CME Group, which manages derivatives and futures exchanges such as the Chicago Mercantile Exchange. Employed at CME Group since 2000, Yang was arrested by the FBI in July 2011 for theft of trade secrets[13] and convicted in 2015 of stealing CME Group source code to set up an exchange company in the city of Zhangjiagang, China. Before his arrest, Yang played a senior role in an organization promoting talent recruitment and technology transfer to China, which led to his contact with the Zhangjiagang municipal government and ultimately to steal CME's source code. Yang's prolific involvement in united front work also led him to develop friendships with US politicians and bureaucrats during his time in the US.

Yang Chunlai was president of the Association of Chinese–American Scientists and Engineers (ACSE, 旅美中国科学家工程师专业人士协会) from 2005–2007 and chairman of the group from 2007–2009.[14] ACSE is one of several dozen groups for ethnic Chinese scientists closely linked to the PRC government. ACSE and its leaders (including Yang) frequently met with PRC government officials and diplomats, particularly those from the State Council Overseas Chinese Affairs Office (OCAO, 国务院侨务办公室),[15] the CPPCC, and the All-Chinese Federation of Returned Overseas Chinese (ACFROC, 中华全国归国华侨联合会 or 中国侨联), which are all key components of the united front system.

In May 2006, Yang visited Beijing for a training course for "young overseas Chinese leaders" run by the OCAO. Speaking to the *People's Daily* (人民日报) during the course, Yang said, "It's not that those who stay abroad don't love China; it's the opposite. The longer one stays in foreign lands, the greater one's understanding of the depth of homesickness."[16]

In the same interview, Yang hinted at his later decision to steal technology and move to China. Asked about work in the software industry being outsourced to China, India and Russia, Yang said, "From the perspective of a company's leadership, [work on] core software cannot be outsourced to a foreign company. Using CME Group where I work as an example, when this issue was raised my supervisor clearly said, 'we'll do whatever we can do ourselves.'" Qualifying his previous statement, however, Yang continued, "Of course, even with things the way they are, everyone is still looking for suitable *entrepreneurial opportunities to return to China*" (our emphasis in italics).[17]

In 2009, an "entrepreneurial opportunity" may have presented itself when ACSE hosted a talent recruitment session run by a delegation from the city of Zhangjiagang (张家港).[18] At the event, ACSE signed a cooperation agreement with Zhangjiagang to "jointly build a Sino-US exchange platform, and to contribute to the development of the homeland and the leap in science and technology."[19] Yang participated in this event in his role as chair of the ACSE council (理事长). The heads of the PRC Consulate's science and technology and overseas Chinese affairs sections were also present.

In March 2010, ACSE held a banquet for Xu Yousheng (许又声), deputy chief of the OCAO, at which he encouraged talented individuals to return to China. Xu Yousheng is now both head of the OCAO and deputy head of the UFWD. At the banquet, Xu reportedly stated, "There are many ways to serve the nation; you don't have to return to China and start an enterprise. You can also return to China to teach or introduce advanced foreign technology and experience—this is a very good way to serve China."[20] These remarks echo the policies and mechanisms for overseas Chinese to serve China previously described in Chapters 2 and 3. Xu's comments and engagement with ACSE suggest PRC government and CPC officials (especially those from the united front system) work to influence, guide, or task overseas organizations like ACSE to further China's interests.

In 2008, Yang was appointed to the OCAO's expert advisory committee.[21] Also in 2010, Yang spoke about ACSE's close relationship with the Western Returned Scholars Association,[22] a UFWD subdivision profiled later in this chapter. Yang was also a standing committee member of the Chinese American Association of Greater Chicago (大芝加哥地区华侨华人联合会), which appears to be another united front organization.[23]

The criminal complaint in Yang's case states that he wrote a letter addressed to the director of the OCAO's Department of Economics, Science and Technology asking for a referral letter to Zhangjiagang in support of Yang's company. Thus, Yang's relationship with OCAO likely facilitated his starting a company in China using technology and intellectual property he illegally obtained from his US employer.

ACSE and Yang's activities appeared to go beyond promoting technology transfer and talent recruitment; there are indications they were also involved in building political influence. At a 2007 OCAO-organized conference in Beijing for overseas Chinese groups, Yang said,

> China has gone through three stages regarding its approach to overseas Chinese making contributions to China. The earliest stage was emphasizing that overseas scholars should return home to serve China. Later, we realized that serving China doesn't necessarily require returning to China. Now, China is placing an emphasis on our development in foreign countries, paying close attention to whether or not we can enter local mainstream society and play an active role in the politics and debate of our host countries.

Yang also said, "Next year is a big election year in America; voting is hard logic. ACSE hopes to take advantage of this opportunity to further expand our influence on American mainstream society."[24]

Yang also noted in his speech that Luo Haocai (罗豪才), chairman of the Zhigong Party and vice chairman of the United Front's CPPCC, met with ACSE on a trip to the United States and strongly encouraged the organization to participate in politics and integrate itself into mainstream society. Yang described Luo's words as a "whip" encouraging groups like his to play a role in mainstream society.[25]

Yang's conviction of stealing CME Groups source code resulted in a four-year probation sentence, avoiding prison time. The judge received 95 character letters supporting Yang. The court also heard that Yang was among a group of Chinese engineers who met with then PRC President Hu Jintao when he visited Chicago in 2011, apparently to demonstrate his good character.[26]

Case study: Cao Guangzhi

Cao Guangzhi (曹光植) is another example of how the united front system intersects with China's technology transfer objectives. In March 2019, electric car manufacturer Tesla sued Cao, a former employee, alleging that he stole its autopilot source code and took it to a rival start-up, China's Xiaopeng Motors.[27] The lawsuit is pending as of this writing.

The origins of Cao's involvement with PRC state and CPC entities began when he was submitting his doctoral thesis to Purdue University in 2009. He and three friends established the "Association of Wenzhou Ph.D.s USA" (全美温州博士协会). All four of the founders hail from Wenzhou, a city South of Shanghai known for its hard-to-grasp dialect and the hundreds of mathematicians who were born there.[28] From its inception, the Association of Wenzhou Ph.D.s USA has worked closely with the PRC government. A report from Wenzhou's local newspaper claims that the Wenzhou Science and Technology Bureau, OCAO, and

Overseas Chinese Federation gave the group a list of US-based Ph.D. students and graduates from the town, whom they later recruited as members.[29] The head of the Wenzhou UFWD praised the association during a 2010 trip to America as "the first of its kind and highly significant."[30]

The Association of Wenzhou Ph.D.s USA carries out talent recruitment activities on behalf of the PRC government. The year after its establishment (2010), it signed an agreement with the UFWD of a county in Wenzhou to run a talent recruitment workstation, through which it gathers information on overseas scientists and carries out recruitment work to meet China's technological needs.[31] That year, it also arranged for 13 members to visit Wenzhou for meetings with talent recruitment officials from organizations like the local foreign experts affairs bureau[32] as well as representatives of local companies. Several of the members also brought their research with them, presenting technologies such as a multispectral imaging tool.[33]

Within a few years of its founding, the association had built up a small but skilled group of over 100 members. By 2017 its members reportedly included the Wenzhou-born secretary-general of the International Monetary Fund, engineers from Google, Apple, Amazon, Motorola and IBM, scholars at Harvard and Yale, and six US government employees.[34] At least one of its members became a Zhejiang Province Thousand Talents Programme scholar through the group's recommendation.[35] It also arranged for a member working on materials science at the US Department of Energy's Argonne National Laboratory to join Wenzhou University under a talent recruitment program.[36]

One of the associations founders, now its lifetime honorary president, is a professor at Northwestern University's Feinberg School of Medicine.[37] He is also affiliated with Wenzhou Medical University, serving as the American director of a Sino-American joint research institute on brain scans that was established with Northwestern University through the group's work.[38]

The Western Returned Scholars Association

The Western Returned Scholars Association or Overseas-Educated Scholars Association of China (欧美同学会·中国留学人员联谊会), hereafter abbreviated as WRSA, is a China-based organization "under the leadership of the CPC Central Committee Secretariat and administered by the CPC Central Committee United Front Work Department" (由中共中央书记处领导，中央统战部代管).[39] It illustrates some characteristics of the united front system's talent recruitment and technology transfer efforts, including the overlap in overseas political influence and technology transfer as exemplified by one of its senior members, Wang Huiyao (王辉耀, See Box 15.1). WRSA has a global presence and claims to have over 220,000 individual members, over 50 local and national chapters or subcomponents, while keeping "close contact with more than 100 associations of Chinese scholars overseas."[40]

The WRSA was established in Beijing in 1913. As its name indicates, its original leaders were prominent scholars who had returned from overseas, and who hoped to encourage China's development and self-strengthening through acquisition and dissemination of Western science and foreign ideas. After the PRC's founding in 1949, however, the CPC took control of the WRSA and its focus narrowed, with a mission to "become a bridge between the Party and overseas students and scholars, and assist in the work of the Party and government towards them."[41]

PRC leadership have highlighted the importance of the WRSA, with keynote speeches delivered by serving PRC presidents at WRSA's 80th, 90th, and 100th anniversaries. The WRSA's role appears to have been elevated after President Xi Jinping's speech at the 100th anniversary, which also serves as guidance for the WRSA's future work.[42] In 2016, its mission was further defined in a CPC General Office document, "Opinions on Strengthening WRSA Construction," which instructs the WRSA to become a

> talent pool of overseas scholars serving the nation, a think tank offering advice and suggestions, a new force in civil [people-to-people] diplomacy, and to promote comprehensively the strategy of rejuvenating the country through science and education and the talent superpower strategy (人才强国战略).[43]

The WRSA has long supported technology transfer through its involvement in talent plans, start-up contests and other organizations. For example, the Thousand Talents Expert Association is a branch of the WRSA. So is the Beijing-based "Entrepreneur Alliance" (欧美同学会企业家联谊会), founded in 1994, whose members include about 1,000 entrepreneurs, financiers, and managers with overseas academic experience who have returned to China. The alliance has its own "experts think tank" (专家智库), for which members are provided consulting, information sharing, training and related resources to return to China, and/or support to expand businesses internationally.[44]

The WRSA is active across the globe. In March 2017, the WRSA announced the inaugural round of its Overseas Scholars Innovation and Entrepreneurship Competition (首届海外留学人员创新创业大赛). Initial rounds were held in London, Paris, San Francisco, and Sydney. Contestants were from elite universities, companies, or research organizations identified by WRSA's "overseas liaison stations" (欧美同学会海外联络站) and various associations of overseas scholars. Projects were evaluated by the Thousand Talents Expert Association. Winners were to be provided investment support and "landing platforms" (对接落地平台) to settle in China.[45]

The competition sought projects both for S&T innovation and entrepreneurship and for "cultural and creative entrepreneurship." The S&T category included electronic information technologies (IC design, big data, cloud computing, mobile Internet, smart devices, etc.), as well as biopharmaceuticals, new materials, new energy, environmental protection, and high-end equipment manufacturing. The cultural and creative category included creative design, cultural software, video games, new media, digital publishing, etc. Cooperating entities included the Sino-European Innovation Institute based in Milan (中欧创新中心), the Chinese Students and Scholars Association UK (全英中国学生学者联谊会), US–China Association of High-Level Professionals (美中高层次人才交流协会, UCAHP) and KH Innovation Institute (鲲海创新研究院).[46]

The UCAHP is a Silicon Valley-based organization that runs its own start-up contests and is involved in angel investment and venture capital activities.[47] It appears to serve as a WRSA "overseas liaison workstation."[48] KH Innovation Institute is a Beijing-based "non-profit" organization focused on "frontier and high-technology innovative research" meant to address "national strategic needs, national defense needs, and industrial development needs" founded by ten Thousand Talents Plan selectees. Two founders are vice chairpersons of the WRSA, four others help chair the Thousand Talents Expert Association. The institute's home page shows the banner: "putting DARPA mechanisms into practice in China," in reference to the USG's Defense Advanced Research Projects Agency.[49] Its site claims that many members have experience working on DARPA projects and seek to replicate DARPA innovation concepts and successes.[50]

BOX 15.1 WRSA'S WANG HUIYAO (王辉耀)[1]

WRSA deputy chairman Wang Huiyao, who helped draft China's ten-year Talent Development Plan (see Chapter 3), figures prominently in technology transfer. His posts have included:

- member of the Central Committee of the Jiusan Society (a UF political party for intellectuals) and Deputy Director of its Central Economics Committee
- member of the OCAO's expert advisory committee
- member of the All-China Federation of Returned Overseas Chinese's expert advisory group
- Vice President of the Overseas Chinese History Society of China (run by the UFWD)
- member of the United Front Work Department's expert advisory group
- Senior director of the China Overseas Friendship Association (also run by the UFWD)

Wang, in addition, is founder and chair of the Center for China and Globalization (中国与全球化智库, CCG). Information on the center's website indicates it was created by a WRSA committee. The CCG describes itself as an "all-China talent theory research base" for the CPC Organization

Department's Talent Work Coordination Group. It houses the MOHRSS's China-International Talent Expert Committee (人社部中国国际人才专业委员会所在地), is a member of an alliance of think tanks supporting the CPC International Liaison Department's "One Belt, One Road" strategy, and is part of the Ministry of Finance's "Alliance of U.S. Research Think Tanks" (财政部美国研究智库联盟). CCG also collaborates closely with the WRSA as both organizations jointly hosted "2019 Overseas Scholars Innovation and Entrepreneurship Forum and 14th WRSA Beijing Forum" (2019 中国留学人员创新创 业论坛暨第 14 届欧美同学会北京论坛).

Note

1 Following media scrutiny of Wang's United Front ties, references to several of these appointments were removed from his biography on the CCG website. The information here is from a cached version.

WRSA overseas liaison "workstations"

The WRSA has recently expanded its overseas presence through talent recruitment "workstations" or "liaison stations." WRSA Chair Chen Zhu (陈竺) noted in early 2015 that in 2014, the WRSA began "entrusting the influence and strength of overseas scholar organizations" to establish "overseas liaison workstations." Initial locations, according to Chen, were Japan, Singapore, Sweden, England, Ireland, the United States, and Canada.[51]

Besides the US–China Association of High-Level Professionals (see above), the Seattle Chinese Biomedical Association (SCBA, 西雅图华人生物医学协会) also earned the WRSA's "liaison workstation" (联络工作站) title in May of 2016, at a ceremony attended by Chen Zhu[52] and representatives from the University of Washington Chinese Students and Scholars Association (a "CSSA," its full Chinese name is 华盛顿大学中国学生学者联谊会), the Chinese Institute of Engineers, USA (美洲中国工程师学会), Society of Chinese–American Aerospace Engineers (美华航太工程师协会), and the Chinese Microsoft Employees Association (微软华人协会).[53] Its mission is the usual one:

> The Seattle liaison workstation will rejuvenate the motherland through S&T education; [pursue the] talent superpower strategy; implement Thousand Talents Plan recommendations; organize overseas scholars for suggestions and advice on China's economic construction and social development; and build a platform for overseas scholars to return to China to work and/or serve the country.[54]

SCBA itself is a University of Washington-based nonprofit organization established in 1993 by Seattle area biomedical professionals.[55] In 2017 it served as a "coordinating organization" (协办单位) for the aforementioned WRSA-sponsored entrepreneurship competition.[56]

These examples demonstrate the CPC's use of the UFWD and its subordinate WRSA to co-opt and leverage "non-profits" overseas to further national interests, while providing plausible deniability to participants, i.e., without revealing PRC state and party sponsorship. Its objectives are clear: facilitate talent recruitment and support other tech transfer efforts such as start-up contests and platforms for overseas scholars to "serve" China, either by returning to China to work or start a business, or by "serving the country" while overseas.[57]

Overseas talent recruitment workstations

Overseas United Front groups play an important role in identifying and recruiting talent. The WRSA's overseas stations are one of hundreds set up by Chinese government organs abroad. Dalian city alone has contracted organizations in 22 countries outside China to run 30 "talent recruitment workstations" that serve as "promoters and contact points for talent recruitment and introducing expertise."[58] These stations, centred in areas with large communities of overseas Chinese professionals, were set up under a 2012 initiative by the city's UFWD, but have also been established by other elements of the municipal government.

The CPC's first "overseas talent workstation" (海外人才工作站) was established by Shanxi province in 2006.[59] Since then, the model has proliferated and been adopted by national agencies as well as county-level governments. More than 500 of these workstations have been identified and the actual number is probably higher.[60]

Organizations hosting the stations are paid to facilitate talent recruitment work and receive bonuses when they recruit senior scientists.[61] They have been known to maintain databases of potential recruits. For example, one city government's regulations for overseas workstations states that they "should get hold of information on 50 or more professors, researchers, senior managers, and others high-level talent of the same level or higher and update it every year."[62]

Some organizations host multiple recruiting stations while serving as umbrella groups for CPC-aligned expert associations. The Federation of Chinese Professional Associations in Europe, profiled by this volume's co-editor in *The Atlantic*, counts at least 60 European associations among its member organizations.[63] Its 2019 annual forum for Chinese scientists in Europe was attended by the vice chairperson of the United Front's All-China Federation of Returned Overseas Chinese, the Zhigong Party's vice chairperson, and over 300 ethnic-Chinese professionals (this is further documented in Chapter 7).[64] A German association for Chinese computer scientists, the Gesellschaft Chinesischer Informatiker (GCI), founder of the aforementioned federation, hosts ten talent recruitment workstations.[65] The

State Council's Overseas Chinese Affairs Office first set up overseas workstations in 2014.[66] Absorbed into the UFWD in 2018, the OCAO was of the CPC's most active talent recruitment organs. Since 2005, major meetings have been held every two years for heads of overseas Chinese professional associations attended by senior UF officials.[67]

The 'Dalian Model': United Front technology transfer in action

Dalian, a coastal city in China's Northeast, showcases the integration of united front work and technology transfer. The "Dalian model" is a cross-border system of organizations, funds, events, and people-to-people networks that links overseas talent to companies, universities and research organizations in Dalian.[68]

Domestically, Dalian's UF worked with the WRSA to establish the country's first "Study Abroad, Serve the Country Base" (留学报国基地) in 2009 to "recruit, cultivate, and recommend talent and incubate enterprises" by relying on the "WRSA's advantages in resourcing and the UFWD's advantages in liaising."[69]

The "base" is located in Dalian's High-tech Industrial Zone and is said to include 6,500 m^2 of incubation space for companies. By 2013, it had attracted 53 high-level "talents," 48 projects, and had recruited another five highly skilled personnel for universities in Dalian.[70] In 2016, the base was expanded to accommodate the WRSA's "Overseas Returnees Entrepreneurial College." The "college" is not a traditional institution of higher education, but an overseas talent training program in entrepreneurship that links with the base to attract investment.[71]

Scientists recruited through the base have "brought back" valuable expertise and technology, including some with defense applications. In 2009, a Chinese–Canadian Ph.D. graduate founded a cybersecurity company there after having lived overseas for a decade.[72] He was recruited at an annual talent recruitment event in Liaoning Province, and quickly established his company at the base using technology he "brought back to China."[73] Doubling down on his service to the ancestral country, he then joined the provincial overseas Chinese entrepreneurs association and became an advisor to the province's overseas Chinese federation—both United Front appointments. A *People's Daily* article said the company's encryption tools are used in government agencies and the defense industry.[74]

Another recruit who returned to China in 2011 after working and studying in Japan gained an appointment at Dalian Maritime University and established a company specializing in environmental sensing technology.[75] In 2015, the company reportedly occupied 60 percent of the market for pollution control technology used in China's ports.[76] In 2016, he was selected as a Thousand Talents Plan scholar.[77] He also received a stipend from China's State Council.[78]

As is the case with other forms of transfer venues, Dalian's "model" of overseas scholar bases and entrepreneurial colleges is being replicated across China. Bases have subsequently been established in Zhongshan, Jiashan, Harbin, Xixian, Daqing, Shenzhen, Chengdu, Nanjing, Wuxi, Xi'an, Inner Mongolia, and Tianjin.[79] A further one is planned in Guangzhou.[80]

Domestic United Front groups are mobilized to "broadly discover talent" and this feature is exemplified in the "Dalian model." A 2018 Dalian UFWD document specifies that local units in subordinate counties, universities and research institutes, in nominal political parties (the Zhigong Party), and overseas Chinese federations and business associations work to identify and organize "talent."[81] The Dalian UFWD explains how it also established United Front associations involved in talent recruitment work, such as the Dalian Overseas Friendship Association, not just at the municipal level, but also in counties and universities that have attracted over 4,500 members.[82]

Overseas networks feed talent into Dalian's domestic technology transfer and innovation infrastructure, a pattern found across the country. These overseas associations organize delegations to visit universities and talent recruitment events around Dalian. Liaoning Province, where Dalian is located, runs an annual "China Overseas Scholars Entrepreneurship Week" event (中国海外学子创业周 or 海创周). In 2010, the Dalian UFWD and its "Study Abroad, Serve the Country Base" invited representatives of overseas United Front-linked associations to attend. They included over 60 scholars affiliated with groups in Australia, the United States, the United Kingdom, Japan, Singapore and other countries. At the event, 15 scientists finalized agreements to set up projects at the Dalian base through talent recruitment initiatives.[83] What happens in Dalian is typical of other major cities throughout the country.

Conclusion

Xi Jinping has bolstered the importance of the party's united front system and its overseas presence. The system leverages vast overseas networks to expand its footprint, and the organizations and activities surveyed here indicate technology transfer is an important goal. While this chapter focused on entities in the United States, similar structures can be found across the developed world. More scrutiny is needed to expose their partnerships with PRC state and party organs and roles in facilitating technology transfer. The lack of awareness in the international community of this aspect of united front work, combined with their successes and party's growing emphasis on it, guarantees these efforts will continue.

Notes

1 http://theory.people.com.cn/n1/2019/1126/c40531-31474052.html.
2 http://cpc.people.com.cn/n/2015/0923/c64107-27622040.html.
3 https://sinopsis.cz/en/joske-united-front-work-lsg/.
4 See, for example, Gerry Groot, "The CCP's Grand United Front Abroad," Sinopsis, September 24, 2019; Clive Hamilton, *Silent Invasion: China's Influence in Australia*,

Melbourne: Hardie Grant, March 2018; and Anne-Marie Brady, "Magic Weapons: China's Political Influence Activities under Xi Jinping," Wilson Center, September 18, 2017. See also work by Jichang Lulu and Didi Kirsten Tatlow on the topic on the Sinopsis site.

5 Chapter 3 discussed how the WRSA supports China's flagship talent recruitment program the Thousand Talents Plan. Here we examine more broadly the Association's leadership, activities, and overseas operations.

6 http://cpc.people.com.cn/n/2015/0923/c64107-27622040.html.

7 MOST website, Introduction: www.most.gov.cn/zzjg/.

8 Introduction to the Zhigong Party: www.zg.org.cn/zgdjj/zgjj/201504/t20150418_20276.htm.

9 http://web.archive.org/web/20190707140047/www.hzzg.gov.cn/ http://blog.sina.com.cn/s/blog_ba677ee80101ax0q.html.

10 https://web.archive.org/web/20191219094527/http:/www.xinhuanet.com/politics/2015-05/20/c_1115351358.htm.

11 Ibid.

12 www.wrsa.net/content_40128737.htm.

13 https://archives.fbi.gov/archives/chicago/press-releases/2011/libertyville-man-arrested-for-theft-of-trade-secrets-from-cme-group.

14 www.acse.org/index.php?sub=about.

15 The OCAO was an administrative office under the PRC State Council (central government) until March of 2018, when the government announced OCAO was to be absorbed under the CPC Central Committee United Front Work Department (www.gov.cn/zhengce/2018-03/21/content_5276191.htm#1). The OCAO still exists in name; however, it is synonymous with the UFWD's overseas Chinese affairs bureaus while many of its responsibilities have been taken up by ACFROC.

16 http://paper.people.com.cn/rmrbhwb/html/2006-06/13/content_7040836.htm.

17 Ibid.

18 www.chinaqw.com/lxs/ycjc/200903/16/155125.shtml.

19 Ibid.

20 www.acse.org/news/20100316newsletter.pdf.

21 www.acse.org/news/ACSE17thBrochure.pdf and www.usachinanews.com/archives/20575.

22 www.fudan-chicago.org/articles/SoCAPSReturnedScholar.htm.

23 www.caagc.us/page3.html; http://web.archive.org/web/20160516171626/http:/caagc.org:80/home/zh-hans/node/6.

24 www.thedailybeast.com/how-china-built-an-army-of-influence-agents-in-the-us and http://news.163.com/07/0621/14/3HH3RC6A000120GU.html.

25 https://web.archive.org/web/20200130044752/www.chinaqw.com/zgqj/qjdt/2007 06/21/76830.shtml.

26 www.lexology.com/library/detail.aspx?g=24bf72f8-2edd-4fe6-a897-fb35a0ae3666.

27 www.reuters.com/article/us-tesla-lawsuit/tesla-sues-former-employees-for-allegedly-stealing-data-autopilot-source-code-idUSKCN1R21P9.

28 https://web.archive.org/web/20040925233643/http://tech.sina.com.cn/o/2002-08-23/0832134267.shtml.

29 https://web.archive.org/web/20190726040703/ and www.wzrb.com.cn/article774631 show.html.

30 https://web.archive.org/web/20190726045212/www.wztz.org.cn/dzsj/wzr20120102.pdf (p. 35).

31 https://web.archive.org/web/20190726052853/www.wztz.org.cn/system/2011/12/30/102940694.shtml.

32 This office is a local affiliate of the State Administration of Foreign Expert Affairs, a State Council organ that was absorbed into MOST and described in previous chapters.

33 https://web.archive.org/web/20190726052853/www.wztz.org.cn/system/2011/12/30/102940694.shtml.

34 https://web.archive.org/web/20190726040703/www.wzrb.com.cn/article774631show.html.

35 https://web.archive.org/web/20200130060436/www.xinouzhou.com/detail/109392.

36 https://web.archive.org/web/20190726040703/www.wzrb.com.cn/article774631show.html.

37 https://web.archive.org/web/20190708023554/www.feinberg.northwestern.edu/faculty-profiles/az/profile.html?xid=35124.

38 https://web.archive.org/web/20200130060449/https://news.wmu.edu.cn/show/45/15940.html; https://web.archive.org/web/20200130060553/www.sohu.com/a/245528240_467543; https://web.archive.org/web/20190726040703/www.wzrb.com.cn/article774631show.html.

39 "Introduction to the WRSA," www.wrsa.net/content_40128737.htm, January 2, 2018.

40 Ibid.

41 Ibid.

42 Ibid.

43 中共中央办公厅印发《关于加强欧美同学会（留学人员联谊会）建设的意见》("CPC Central Committee General Office Issues Opinions on Strengthening Western Returned Scholars Association—Overseas Educated Scholars Association of China Construction") xinhuanet.com, August 3, 2016.

44 www.wrsaea.com/detail.php?sort=595&id=587 and www.wrsaea.com/detail.php?sort=629&id=587.

45 cn.chinadaily.com.cn/2017-03/31/content_28757556.htm.

46 Ibid, www.wrsa.net/content_40124056.htm.

47 http://ucahp.com/zh.

48 www.zytzb.gov.cn/tzb2010/S2012/201702/580f7e3c64dc43ed91a0c5afa9d6687d.shtml.

49 Defense Advanced Research Projects Agency (DARPA).

50 www.khii.org/.

51 陈竺:欧美同学会将"立足国内、开拓海外 ("Chen Zhu:WRSA 'Be Based Domestically, Open Up Overseas'"), January 14, 2015. http://people.china.com.cn/2015-01/14/content_7591399.htm.

52 www.uschinapress.com/2016/0522/1065039.shtml; scbahome.org/欧美同学会与西雅图华人生物医学协会共建联络工.

53 Ibid; https://cssauw.org/; www.scaae.org; www.microsoftchime.org/ on May 8, 2018.

54 The Chinese phrase is: "西雅图联络工作站将为祖国科教兴国、人才强国战略和实施"千人计划"举荐人才，组织留学人员为祖国经济建设和社会发展建言献策，为留学人员回国工作、为国服务搭建平台," www.uschinapress.com/2016/0522/1065039.shtml. The references to "return to China" and "serve the country" are the same terms used for buckets one and three of the "three-in-one" policy system discussed in Chapter 2.

55 http://scbahome.org.

56 www.ausinan.org/cms/news/2017-03-31/首届欧美同学会海外留学人员创新创业大赛.

57 This "three-in-one" policy system is outlined in Chapter 2.

58 https://web.archive.org/web/20190412024115/www.dltzb.gov.cn/v-1-22683.aspx.

59 http://archive.ph/2019.07.07-070612/http://paper.people.com.cn/rmrbhwb/html/2013-07/04/content_1263586.htm.

60 Forthcoming ASPI ICPC report.

61 https://web.archive.org/web/20191217035741/http://www.xinhuanet.com/politics/2016-06/24/c_129087171.htm.

62 http://hrss.qingdao.gov.cn/n28356070/n32563349/n32563364/180606140419216075.html.

63 www.theatlantic.com/international/archive/2019/07/chinas-influence-efforts-germany-students/593689/.

64 http://web.archive.org/web/20200130062842/www.fcpae.com/?p=2231.

65 http://web.archive.org/web/20190420122218/www.gci-online.de/index.php?option=com_content&view=article&id=124&Itemid=410.

66 http://web.archive.org/web/20181211104043/www.aicf.fr/重庆市海外引才联络站-中国旅法工程师协会/.

67 www.gqb.gov.cn/news/2009/0112/1/12059.shtml.

68 www.wrsa.net/content_40008875.htm.

69 Ibid.

70 https://web.archive.org/web/20200128002204/http:/dl.sina.com.cn/news/s/2013-06-27/08207130.html. Also, https://web.archive.org/web/20200128013120/http:/www.dlxww.com/news/content/2013-06/27/content_985046.htm.

71 http://media.tibet.cn/special/c/tyzxzwn/wgwn/sbkjc/1504256066413.shtml.

72 https://web.archive.org/web/20200128002204/http:/dl.sina.com.cn/news/s/2013-06-27/08207130.html.

73 https://web.archive.org/web/20200128032100/http:/msn.finance.sina.com.cn/gdxw/20110824/0758252380.html.

74 https://web.archive.org/web/20200128031647/http:/paper.people.com.cn/rmrbhwb/html/2011-07/09/content_867000.htm.

75 https://web.archive.org/web/20200128044604/http:/roll.sohu.com/20160629/n456817569.shtml.

76 Ibid.

77 https://web.archive.org/web/20200128043611/http://ln.sina.com.cn/edu/news/2016-08-15/1006472399.html.

78 https://web.archive.org/web/20200128044008/www.wdspharma.com/news_detail/id/38.html.

79 For an overall discussion of the program, www.zytzb.gov.cn/tzb2010/S1813/201505/fe8697ea81e74f549fc271dccbae4ae1.shtml For individual sites.

> Zhongshan: http://archive.fo/u0dy6.
> Jiashan: http://zjnews.zjol.com.cn/system/2014/12/14/020410842.shtml.
> Harbin: www.songbei.gov.cn/art/2018/11/9/art_20343_694234.html.
> Xixian: www.xjorsa.net/?fnew/i801.
> Daqing: http://hlj.people.com.cn/n2/2017/0508/c220027-30148857.html.
> Shenzhen: http://world.people.com.cn/n/2015/1123/c1002-27846363.html.
> Chengdu: www.sohu.com/a/347681729_116237?_f=index_pagerecom_17.
> Nanjing: www.chinaqw.com/jjkj/2014/07-31/12230.shtml.
> Wuxi: http://cpc.people.com.cn/n/2014/0717/c87228-25291132.html.
> Xi'an: www.xjorsa.net/?fnew/i1423.

80 http://archive.fo/vrqq5.

81 https://web.archive.org/web/20190412024115/www.dltzb.gov.cn/v-1-22683.aspx.

82 Ibid.

83 https://web.archive.org/web/20100705102612/http://politics.people.com.cn/GB/14562/11989835.html.

Bibliography

Allen-Ebrahimian, Bethany. "Rubio Questions DC Panel on China Influence," *Foreign Policy*, May 7, 2018.

Allen-Ebrahimian, Bethany. "China Built an Army of Influence Agents in the US," *Daily Beast*, July 18, 2018.

Brady, Anne-Marie. "Magic Weapons: China's Political Influence Activities under Xi Jinping," Wilson Center, September 18, 2017. www.wilsoncenter.org/article/magic-weapons-chinas-political-influence-activities-under-xi-jinping.

Communist Party of China Central Committee. 中共中央办公厅印发《关于加强欧美同学会（留学人员联谊会）建设的意见》("CPC Central Committee General Office Issues Opinions on Strengthening Western Returned Scholars Association—Overseas Educated Scholars Association of China Construction," CPC, August 3, 2016.

Communist Party of China Central Committee. 中共中央印发《深化党和国家机构改革方案》("Communist Party Central Committee Issues 'Plan for Deepening Party and National Organizational Reforms'"), CPC, March 21, 2018.

Communist Party of China (CPC). 中国共产党统一战线工作条例（试行）("CPC United Front Work Regulations (Proposed)", *People's Daily Online*, September 23, 2015.

Editorial. "留学报国大连基地创大连模式被中央统战部推广" ("Dalian Study Abroad—Serve the Country Base Creates a Dalian Model for the CPC United Front Work Department to Popularize"), *Dalian Daily*, June 27, 2013.

Hamilton, Clive. *Silent Invasion: China's Influence in Australia*, Melbourne: Hardie Grant, 2018.

Lu, Chunyan (陆春艳). "杨春来: 海外侨胞要落地生根　积极融入主流社会" ("Yang Chunlai: Overseas Chinese Should Put Down Roots and Vigorously Integrate with Mainstream Society"), *Overseas Chinese Network*, June 21, 2007.

Mukherjee, Supantha and Stephen Nellis. "Tesla Sues Former Employees for Allegedly Stealing Data, Autopilot Source Code," *Reuters*, March 21, 2019.

Qingdao Municipal Bureau of Human Resources & Social Security. 关于组织开展2018年度青岛市海外引才引智工作站认定工作的通知 ("Notice Regarding Determination Work for Organizing and Developing 2018 Qingdao Municipal Overseas Talent Introduction Workstation"), Qingdao HRSS, June 6, 2018.

Ren, Yilin (任一林) and Wan Peng (万鹏) eds. "尤权: 坚持大统战工作格局" ("You Quan: Adhering to Great United Front Work Structures"), *People's Daily*, November 26, 2019.

Tatlow, Didi Kirsten. "The Chinese Influence Effort Hiding in Plain Sight," *The Atlantic*, July 12, 2019.

Tian, Tong (田彤), Zhang Siqing (张四清), and Zhang Yangqi (张洋齐). "大连设立首个海外人才工作站 搭建'筑巢引才'平台" ("Dalian Established the First Overseas Talent Workstation—Builds 'Nest for Attracting Talent' Platform"), *Xinhua Online*, June 24, 2016.

Wang, Chunyan (王春燕). "留学报国大连基地共　引进53个高端人才项目" ("Dalian Study Abroad—Serve the Country Base Has Attracted 53 High-End Talent Projects"), *Dalian News Online*, June 27, 2013.

Wang, Jinhai (王金海) and Zhang Shi-an (张世安). "留学报国大连基地引进15个高科技人才项目" ("Dalian Study Abroad—Serve the Country Base Has Attracted 15 High-Tech Talent Projects"), *People's Daily Online*, June 28, 2010.

Wang, Zhao (王昭). "杨春来: '月是故乡明' (专访)," *People's Daily Overseas Edition*, June 13, 2006.

Xinhua. "习近平: 巩固发展最广泛的爱国统一战线" ("Xi Jinping: Consolidating and Developing the Most Extensive Patriotic United Front"), *Xinhua News Agency Online*, May 20, 2015.

Yang, Kaiqi (杨凯淇). "陈竺: 欧美同学会将 '立足国内、开拓海外'," ("Chen Zhu: WRSA 'Be Based Domestically, Open Up Overseas'"), *Zhongguorenwu Online*, January 14, 2015.

Ye, Feng (叶锋). "全美温州博士协会 '藏龙卧虎,' 有古根海姆奖得主, 苹果谷歌工程师" ("Association of Wenzhou Ph.D.s USA Are 'Hidden Dragons, Crouching Tigers,' Guggenheim Award Winners, Apple, Google Engineers"), *Wenzhou City Daily*, April 14, 2017.

Zhang, Qizhi (张奇志). "学者研究温州何以成为 '数学家之乡'," (Scholars Study How Wenzhou Became the 'Hometown of Mathematicians'"), *Xinhua Online*, August 23, 2002.

Zhou, Dazheng (周大正). "做好温美合作的 '摆渡人'" (Being good "Ferrymen" of Wenzhou-US Cooperation), *Wenzhou Broadcasting*, November 1, 2017.

PART VI

Managing the transfer problem

16

CHINESE STUDENTS, SCHOLARSHIP, AND US INNOVATION

Anna B. Puglisi

Perhaps no other issue in this book elicits a more visceral response than the role of foreign talent in US society. We are a country of immigrants and the contributions of those who have chosen to come here, or have sought refuge from war, persecution or poverty, have shaped what the US is today. Welcoming the "best and brightest" is of central importance to our future. A recent report by the JASON group[1] "reconfirms the value of and need for" foreign talent in the US—a position we easily support. There is no place in the US for hostility, xenophobia, or ethnic profiling.

Still the Chinese government's explicit efforts to exploit its diaspora—and our innovation base—must be addressed and countered.[2] The rights of persons of Chinese ethnicity in the US must be protected despite this deliberate exploitation which is damaging to those rights by exposing such persons to criticism which may be unjustified. This makes for a difficult balance. Our response must be two-handed: protect the rights of the people targeted by the CPC while dealing with transgressions. Notable here is the fact that increasingly, the CPC targets non-ethnic Chinese, too, showing how this issue is not, in essence, one of ethnicity. Thus, the US must continue to encourage academic exchange and an influx of scientific "talent" while at the same time find nuanced policy solutions not only to stop the hemorrhaging of critical military and industrial technologies, but also, crucially, to "play offense" and continue to grow our national innovation base. While this chapter is directed at the United States, the comments apply equally to liberal states worldwide.

Scholars point to how the US World War II effort and space program benefited from immigrant scientists and—by extrapolation—how any restrictions now will disadvantage US innovation. Yet it is also true—in contrast to some cases we see today—that those scientists did not also work for a "non like-minded" state.

Einstein, Szilard, and Fermi were not taking research from the Manhattan Project and funneling it to German weapons programs.[3] They were not using US funds and resources to train students and researchers that would form the technical and commercial foundation of a strategic competitor.

In addition, our institutions were not designed to counter the threat to academic freedom and manipulation of public opinion that China's policies pose. Beijing in many ways understands our societal tensions, which include race issues, and its statecraft is directed at them, exploiting identity politics by promoting any changes in US policy as ethnic profiling (whether deserved or not), offering a narrative about being merely a proponent of "development" and science, in order to divert attention from its own questionable behavior.[4]

The story of foreign talent: assumptions, benefits, and challenges

In our agreements[5] and collaborations with China—government-to-government, institution-to-institution, lab-to-lab, even scientist-to-scientist—which are rooted in the ideal of open exchange, we overlook the control China has, or can have if it chooses, over its citizens.[6] Students sent overseas can be put under technical surveillance, while their statements and behavior are monitored by peer informants.[7] We ignore this, preferring to believe they are neutral emissaries, who while contributing to US prosperity and innovation (they do) will return home bearing the seeds of democracy and serving as agents of change.

We accept, and in many cases fund, foreign students on the premise that cooperation benefits both parties, yet the Chinese party and government view Western education pragmatically as an entry point into the US innovation base. President Xi Jinping has called talent the "first resource" (第一资源)[8] and China's policies reflect this (see Chapter 1 for a sampling).

BOX 16.1 QIAN NING (钱宁). 留学美国 (*STUDYING IN AMERICA*)[1]

"Sending out the students to foreign countries was never for China a matter of cultural exchange. The goal is to make China a strong country—a fact which the overseas students must face."

Note

1 Qian Ning (钱宁). 留学美国 (*Studying in America*). Nanjing: Jiangsu Wenyi Chubanshe, 1996.

Given these policies, no discussion of innovation or the role of foreign talent in the US can be complete without addressing how Beijing leverages the expertise they gain from overseas trained students, whether they return to China or stay in the US.[9] The short of it is: Beijing has made talent development and the exploitation of overseas students, universities, and government labs a central part of its technology acquisition strategy since the country's "opening" around 1978.[10]

In the post-Mao era, foreign knowhow was seen as a catalyst to jump-start China's quest for capable military systems and industries and to build capacity for the future. The first wave of post-Cultural Revolution (1965–1975) students to go abroad tended to reflect this approach. Nearly all were government-funded and more mid-career. Beginning in the early 1990s, students tended to be self-funded, reducing Beijing's leverage over their career choices, and leading to a doubling down of policies aimed at inducing support from the students "by various means."[11] The central tenet of these policies—to exploit the openness of the academic culture for China's strategic gain—while no doubt reasonable from the party's perspective, challenges global research norms. These policies have not let up. Even as China has become more capable and developed, its approach continues to view foreign-trained talent as a commodity to be leveraged by the CPC.

A glimpse into how the past and future merge is afforded by China's *Medium-and Long-Term Plan for S&T Development, 2006–2020* (中长期科技发展规划, 2006–2020).[12] This S&T blueprint lays out a development strategy that still relies on returnees and foreign collaboration. While the ultimate goal is self-sufficiency and domination, China continues to look to overseas training as a way to build capacity it does not have. This attitude extends to training at home, which also depends on foreigners onsite to help expand and perfect its university system.

The human cost of China's policies accrues in both directions, as Beijing disadvantages and tarnishes its own scientists, trying honestly to work within global norms, because its domestic laws compel the disclosure of data/information. In this sense, the US and Western countries are also culpable, because by treating China as a neutral actor, and pretending that we operate within the same kind of system, we undercut those scientists and institutions in China trying to follow international norms. By not holding the Chinese government accountable, we give credence to a system that deprives China's educated elite from the dignity they aspire to and deserve.

"Picking flowers in foreign lands to make honey in China"[13]

China says it will use any knowledge or technology it acquires for its military. This is not conjecture, profiling, or analysis, but China's stated position for decades. From early military–civilian integration (军民结合) policies to the more recent military–civilian fusion (军民融合), China takes a holistic approach to development, blurring what is civilian, what is military, what is private and what is public.[14] This impacts the basis for entry of Chinese students and post-docs into US labs because of China's ability to compel citizens to share information. It also challenges existing export and visa policies that build their restrictions around affiliations with a military end-user but make exceptions for civilian uses.

Beijing's policies are dynamic and tailored to the changing landscape of technology development. This is best illustrated by the *"13th Five-year Plan for S&T Military and Civil Fusion"* ("十三五" 科技军民融合发展专项规划") established in 2017 and focused on emerging technologies. The plan specifically calls for a "cross-pollination of military and civilian technology in areas not traditionally seen as 'national security issues,' such as quantum telecommunication and computing, neuroscience and brain-inspired research," and states that such projects will be supported by foreign outreach initiatives. In addition to these overarching projects, there are programs to develop specific high-tech areas such as biotechnology,[15] integrated circuits,[16] and "next-generation" artificial intelligence.[17] Each such program highlights the role foreign "talent" is expected to play, in part because Beijing has relied on this venue for decades, in part because the country's former policies have not produced a spontaneous outpouring of indigenous talent and creativity.

Impact on US innovation system and values

This determined push from China has been matched by a retreat by the US over the last several decades: both federal and state funding for scientific and engineering research has decreased.[18] According to recent Organization of Economic Cooperation and Development (OECD) data, the United States has slid to 28th of 39 nations in government funding for university research as a share of GDP, with the 12 leading governments investing more than double the US investment.[19] Between 2011 and 2017, US government funding for university research as a share of GDP fell by nearly one-quarter. States collectively cut spending to colleges and universities by 16 percent in real terms between 2008 and 2017, according to the Center on Budget and Policy Priorities.[20] Meanwhile, per-student funding in Alabama, Arizona, Illinois, Louisiana, New Mexico, Oklahoma, Pennsylvania and South Carolina fell by more than 30 percent. From 2000–2017, R&D spending in the US grew at 4.3 percent a year; during that same time spending in China grew 17 percent per year. According to the National Science Foundation (NSF), preliminary data from 2019 indicates China has passed the US in total R&D spending.[21,22,23]

As a result, the US STEM graduate pipeline is no longer self-sustaining. The decline of government-sponsored research has led to more short-term thinking—and focus—that ignores the foundational research and institutions that build and sustain industries of the future. The early stages of development of many emerging technologies will be the most critical for government support and policies. These "first-mover" advantages—especially in artificial intelligence (AI), aspects of biotechnology, and advanced communications—may be so critical that those nations that fail to make similar investments may have difficulty catching up. Will the US, essentially, become the Qing dynasty of the twenty-first century, self-defeating, apparently unable to change, increasingly vulnerable? This slippage has an impact on day-to-day business too: a survey by Manpower Group found that 46 percent of American employers cannot find the workers they need, and the US Chamber of Commerce says this is keeping 40 percent of businesses from taking on more work. According to the OECD, the US ranked 13th in the world in the number of 25- to 34-year-olds who have college or university credentials.[24]

According to the National Science Foundation statistics:

- In 1995 there were nearly equal numbers of US and international full-time graduate students in computer science. Between 1995 and 2015, the number of U.S students increased by 45 percent (8,627 to 12,539), while the number of international students soared by 480 percent (7,883 to 45,970).[25]
- During the same period, the number of US graduate students in electrical engineering (EE) actually *decreased* by 17 percent, while the number of foreign students rose 270 percent.[26]
- As of 2017, foreign students represented 35 percent of graduate students throughout the science, health, and engineering fields. In the physical sciences, over 30 percent of masters and over 40 percent of Ph.D. students were foreign.[27]

Regardless of how one feels about whether China is innovative or not, even with the influx of foreign talent, if we cut funding and aren't doing the research, and if we do not have a workforce that is technically proficient, we cannot innovate and will lose our ability to attract the best and brightest. It is a slippery slope. So, while discussing the pros and cons of foreign students keeping our labs going, we should also rethink our funding levels, ponder why US students are not going into STEM areas, and contemplate what is needed to change this trend.

Universities have increased the number of faculty positions that are funded through "soft money." This decline in federal and state funding puts additional pressure on faculty to seek funds from other sources, making them more vulnerable to malign attempts to exploit their knowledge and/or position through financial incentives, including the placement of students and post-docs into certain laboratories, a situation that pertains in all developed countries. This is not only at universities, but at federally funded research and development centers (FFRDCs), Department of Energy (DOE) National Labs and Department of Defense (DOD) labs.

We have witnessed this influence play out over the past several years in the form of self-censorship in the classroom, universities canceling speakers that would "offend" China, and the demonstrations and threats of violence that mainland students fomented in response to the democracy protests in Hong Kong.[28] Nor by any means is it limited to the US. In Germany, a contract signed by the Free

University of Berlin for a chair of China studies paid by the Confucius Institute headquarters in Beijing agreed to follow Chinese law for those programs.[29]

Reciprocity has not grown over the last decades. Comparing the policies of Department of Energy Labs—American's nuclear R&D facilities—regarding visitors with the number of US scientists with access to China's equivalents, e.g., the Chinese Academy of Engineering Physics institutes in Mianyang, China, makes the one-way nature of these exchanges clear.[30]

Worryingly, university charters in China have begun replacing token expressions of freedom of enquiry and thought with language that emphasizes loyalty to the CPC.[31] Stories are also re-emerging about "student informants" (学生信息员)— similar to the Red Guards (红卫兵) during China's Cultural Revolution (文化大革命, 1966–1976)—who keep an eye on their professors and fellow students.[32] Are international universities willing to implement a two-tier system that adheres to openness and academic freedom at home, but acquiesces to standards set by the CPC in their campuses in China?

Does it matter?

Public discussion of the benefit of foreign students to the US economy often focuses on how much each student spends in the local economy or, for undergraduate and master's students, that they pay full price of their tuition and expenses. This assessment does not consider the opportunity costs of funding foreign Ph.D. students associated with tuition, stipends, access to high-end equipment and supplies, faculty time, and grant support. The roles and concerns related to undergraduates, graduate students, and post-doctoral visitors are not the same and the benefits and cost of those different groups of students to our institutions is also not the same, so more study is needed here.

Arguments favoring broad support for foreign talent raise the following points: the average quality of those who go back is not as good as those who remain in the US; students who do return to China are disadvantaged by loss of their "guanxi" (关系) network of personal connections; the number of students involved is too small to matter; and any restrictions the US government may put in place would hurt the US more than China. There are many assumptions baked into these perspectives. We review them one by one:

Issue of quality

Faculty in China's top universities and research institutes reveals a wide range of US Ivy league graduates, alumni of the top European and Japanese institutions, as well as former members of the US DOE, DOD, and government labs. Many are recipients of prestigious awards from the National Science Foundation (NSF), the Defense Advanced Research Projects Agency (DARPA), and Oppenheimer Fellowships awarded only once a year. Others sit on the editorial boards of leading scientific journals, and are co-authors with faculty throughout the world. Rather than debate the "average" quality level of returnees vis-à-vis those who stay abroad, it is sufficient to note that among those who do return are many of China's movers-and-shakers. The impact of these elite returnees is magnified by how they how train their students.[33] A smaller group of "high-flyers" with state-of the art lab facilities, research money, and a technically competent workforce can have a huge impact. Qian Xuesen (钱学森), father of China's missile program, is the storybook example but many more can be cited.[34]

Issue of numbers

The question of numbers of foreign students often seems to center on the importance of self-funded undergraduates and Master's degree students, because we have stopped funding our own programs and our institutions depend on foreign students' tuition. Again, this is an area where distinctions between undergraduates, self-funded master's students, and Ph.D. students are important. Zwetsloot et al. make the important point that in sheer size, the fact that the US was able to compete with the former Soviet Union using mostly indigenous talent does not transfer to the challenge we face with China.[35] However, it is unclear that there is enough excess capacity—and access to world-class facilities—outside the US at present to host the number of China's graduate students, even if they should decide to go elsewhere, although that situation, if true, would not persist long.

System issues

There is no question that China's innovation system has challenges[36] in how it is run, what gets funded, and the issue of *guanxi*. However, many editorials in our scientific journals written by Western-trained Chinese scientists who returned to China overplay these negative aspects of doing research in China, in some cases as an artifact of inter-ministry bureaucratic infighting or, it would seem, as a platform for the CPC science establishment to tell overseas audiences what they expect to hear about how defective the Chinese system is. Overlooked are the following facts:

- Many newer institutes have personnel policies similar to Western institutions. In these facilities *guanxi* networks are still important, but it is more of a meritocracy.
- People self-select—there are many factors that go into decisions to return to China including family situations and professional opportunities, but ultimately most returnees understand and/or accept the political system they are returning to.
- Funding has become hard to come by in the US, in contrast to China where money is more readily available and scientists have the opportunity to build their research cadre and infrastructure from the ground up.

How do we protect research integrity without becoming China?

The problems we outline call for realistic solutions. Extreme propositions, such as closing our eyes (*laissez faire*) or closing our doors, only benefit China, the latter by discrediting en masse all efforts to address the problem and by depriving ourselves of the contributions of foreign-born scientists.

In considering our policy options, it will help to keep a few points in mind. First, we enter the contest from a position of strength. Despite the rhetoric that China has many options, access to US institutions is still a lever of influence because of the level of academic excellence here and in other Western countries. Second, we must remind ourselves that China is extraordinarily adept at what is now known as "influence operations," namely, sustained efforts through media and other venues of persuasion to play on our divisions through accusations of xenophobia and profiling in ways that paralyze us from addressing the problem. Beijing will try to control the narrative and promote the fiction that it champions global scientific "exchange" at the same time it entices our academics and researchers with budgets and salaries that the US cannot or is unwilling to match. At the end of the day, this last issue is what matters. The United States must promote S&T development and STEM education in a tangible manner—with funding and support—to protect the national innovation base from exploitation by China or any other nation.

Our future competitiveness will rely on our ability to find nuanced and dynamic ways to protect what is important, accepting foreign talent that abides by the rules and encouraging them to stay, while at the same time calling out those nations that exploit their diaspora. The US needs to play offense and remember what went into building our national innovation base prior to the last two decades,[37] and do more, including greater educational support and opportunity across the board. The National Science Foundation (NSF) warns that "many groups of Americans continue to be underrepresented in STEM."[38] Industrial policy is not a dirty word. The US needs to resume its investing in the future. This should not be a partisan issue. Private wealth generation is not synonymous with innovation and innovation is more than making apps or the next smart phone.

Therefore, we recommend the following:

- *Improve ourselves:* The US and other liberal democracies must invest in their futures. Not all discovery has immediate commercial applications—it took 30 years from discovery to development of the lithium-ion battery. We must accept that everything is not about the lowest cost but the highest value for the nation. We have to get past the perception that the US is "anti-science."
- The US must encourage STEM education and create support networks for under-represented populations in the STEM fields. Many students leave STEM fields in the first year.[39] If you are working your way through college

you may not have time for lab work or research experiences. Funding should be provided for this as we are leaving whole segments of our population behind.

- *Face the facts*: Acknowledge that Beijing is not a neutral actor and that it does not share the political values of openness that the US, Europe and other "like-minded" countries have long shared. This complicates mitigation, because we are not negotiating on individual policies but against a different system, and the people who come here, however well-meaning they are personally, are to a greater or lesser extent beholden to a system.
- Acknowledge that existing policies and laws are insufficient to address the level of influence the CPC exerts in our society—especially in academia. The CPC exploits identity politics through United Front influence campaigns, as described in Chapter 15—this must be addressed and called out. By the same token, we must increase reporting requirements for foreign money at our academic and research institutes to better identify these avenues of influence.
- *Reciprocity:* Connecting China's reciprocity and sharing of scientific data to its access to US institutions and big science facilities is a leverage point.
- Greater cooperation and integration with like-minded countries such as the EU and Japan will not only foster the development of emerging tech industries, but also create alternative innovation hubs that mitigate China's unfair practices and continue to foster the global norms of science.

Notes

1 JASON Study on protecting research integrity, December 2019.
2 E.g., "The IP Commission Report." The Commission on the Theft of American Intellectual Property, May 2013. William C. Hannas, James Mulvenon and Anna Puglisi, *Chinese Industrial Espionage*, London and New York: Routledge, 2013 hereafter "*CIE*." Michael Brown and Pavneet Singh, "China's Technology Transfer Strategy" (DIUX, February 2017). Section 301 *Report into China's Acts, Policies, and Practices Related to Technology Transfer, Intellectual Property, and Innovation.* Office of the United States Trade Representative, 27 March 2018. US–China Economic and Security Review Commission, "2019 Annual Report to Congress," November 2019.
3 We acknowledge allegations that the Manhattan Project was penetrated by Soviet Russia.
4 See a more robust description of China's influence in Chapter 15.
5 In this context and throughout this Chapter the "agreements" we refer to are agreements the US government has made with China since 1979 including the "US–China Agreement on Cooperation in Science and Technology (S&T)" which has periodically been updated, as well as separate agreements other universities and government labs have made with Chinese entities. These often fall below the level of "Treaties."
6 See Chapter 5 for how China's laws compel its citizens and businesses to cooperate with the government, military and intelligence services. Yet even without these laws, the CPC demands this allegiance. China's constitution states that China is led by the party. Its "United Front" system of "democratic parties" was "formed under the leadership of the Communist Party of China … The system of the multi-party cooperation and political consultation *led by the Communist Party of China* will exist and develop

for a long time to come (author's italics)" See, www.npc.gov.cn/zgrdw/englishnpc/ Constitution/node_2825.htm and https://npcobserver.files.wordpress.com/2018/12/ PRC-Constitution-2018.pdf.

7 For example:"It doesn't matter where I am, or what passport I hold [Chinese authorities] will terrorize me anywhere, and I have no way to fight that." Kenneth Roth, *China's Global Threat to Human Rights*, Global Report, 2020.

8 习近平眼里的"第一资源"为何如此重要 ("Why is Xi Jinping's 'First Resource' So Important?"), *People* (人民网).

9 Chapter 1 describes China's policies aimed at students who stay overseas to "serve in place."

10 Hannas et al., *CIE.*

11 Ibid.

12 Cong Cao, Dennis Fred Simon, and Richard P. Suttimeier, "China's 15-year Science and Technology Plan," *Physics Today*, December 2006; James McGregor, China's Drive for "Indigenous Innovation" A Web of Industrial Policies, Global Regulatory Cooperation Project," US Chamber of Commerce, APCO, July 23, 2010.

13 异国采花，中华酿蜜.

14 We acknowledge that China's MCF programs are not unique to China. What is different about China is the ability to coerce involuntary participation to some extent.

15 "十三五" 生物技术创新专项规划 ("13th Five-year Plan for Biotechnology Innovation"). MOST, 2017.

16 国家集成电路产业发展推进纲要 ("National Integrated Circuit Industry Development Plan"). SC, 2014.

17 新一代人工智能发展规划. ("Next-Generation Artificial Intelligence Development Plan"). SC, 2017.

18 Federal and State funding apply to different things in the university system. For an in-depth description see "Two Decades of Changes in Federal and State Higher Education Funding" *Pew Charitable Trust*, Issue Brief, October 2019.

19 OECD (2017), *Benchmarking Higher Education System Performance: Conceptual Framework and Data, Enhancing Higher Education System Performance*, Paris: OECD.

20 Ibid.

21 www.nsf.gov.

22 A history of China's investment programs and policies can be found in the following: Simon, Dennis Fred and Cong Cao, *China's Emerging Technological Edge*, Cambridge: Cambridge University Press, 2009; Richard Applebaum, Cong Cao, Xueying Han, Rachel Parker, and Denis Simon, *Innovation in China*, Cambridge, UK: Polity, 2018; and Hannas et al., *CIE*, Routledge, 2013.

23 By 2013, China had surpassed the United States in the number of scientific publications in physics and astronomy, considered as fraction of world production. China also took the publication lead in many other S&T fields, including chemistry, renewable energy, computer science, quantum computation, artificial intelligence, electrical engineering, nanotechnology, nuclear engineering, materials science, and biotechnology, among others. https://nsf.gov/news/special_reports/jasonsecurity/JSR-19-2IFundamentalResearchSecurity_12062019FINAL.pdf.

24 OECD, *Benchmarking higher education system performance.* op. cit.

25 National Science Board, National Science Foundation. "Higher Education in Science and Engineering. Science and Engineering Indicators 2020." Available at https://ncses.nsf.gov/pubs/nsb20197/. National Foundation for American Policy, "The Importance of International Students to American Science and Engineering." NFAP Policy Brief, available at https://nfap.com/wp-content/uploads/2017/10/The-Importance-ofInternational-Students.NFAP-Policy-Brief.October-20171.pdf. See also National Science Board, National Science Foundation, "International Science and Engineering Partnerships: A Priority for US Foreign Policy and Our Nation's Innovation Enterprise"; "2012 Global R&D Funding Forecast"; Battelle, "2018 Global R&D Funding Forecast";

"SCImago Journal & Country Rank." "Battelle-R&D Magazine Release Newest Global Research Funding Forecast," Press Release, December 18, 2012. www.battelle.org/newsroom/press-releases/press-releases-detail/battelle-r-d-magazine-release-newest-globalresearch-funding-forecast.

26 Ibid.

27 Ibid.

28 Larry Diamond and Orville Schell, *China's Influence and America's Interests: Promoting Constructive Vigilance*, Stanford, CA: Hoover Institute Press, 2019.

29 The original article that broke the story, in German, by a co-author of this book: www.tagesspiegel.de/wissen/umstrittene-konfuzius-institut-senat-will-von-china-finanzierte-professur-an-der-fu-ueberpruefen/25444134.html.

30 An examination of the rosters of these institutions—where available—illustrate this disparity. Many of the CAEP institutions do not list their faculty/researchers. Additionally, discussions by the author with US faculty highlight that they are not given the same amount of unfettered access to facilities in China including freedom of movement and access to the computer systems.

31 Emily Feng and Amy Chang, "Chinese Universities are enshrining Communist party control in their charters," *All Things Considered*, 20 January 2020. www.npr.org/2020/01/20/796377204/chinese-universities-are-enshrining-communist-party-control-in-their-charters.

32 Ibid.

33 The present author observed first hand faculty members, who had trained in the West and Japan, running their labs differently than those who had not. Many new institutes are staffed entirely by returnees, which is changing the culture at these places.

34 Qian returned to China and built China's missile program, described in Iris Chang's *Thread of the Silkworm*, New York: Basic Books, 1996. He is also an example of short-sighted US policies that fail to keep the best and brightest.

35 Remco Zwetsloot and Dahlia Peterson, "The US-China Tech Wars: China's Immigration Disadvantage: How the US Can Retain Technological Leadership Despite its Demographic Deficit," *The Diplomat*, December 31, 2019.

36 Cong Cao, Richard Suttmeier, and Denis Fred Simon. "China's 15-year Science and Technology Plan," *Physics Today*, December, 2006, pp. 38–43; National Academy of Sciences, *Fostering Integrity in Research*, Washington, DC: National Acadamies Press, 2017; Simon and Cao, *China's Emerging Technological Edge: Assessing the Role of High-End Talent*, Cambridge, UK: Cambridge University Press, 2009.

37 Mariana Mazzucato, "The Entrepreneurial State: Debunking Public vs. Private Sector Myths," *Public Affairs*, 2015.

38 National Academy of Engineering and National Research Council, *Community Colleges in the Evolving STEM Education Landscape: Summary of a Summit*. Washington, DC: The National Academies Press, 2012. https://doi.org/10.17226/13399.

39 Ibid.

Bibliography

Alderman, Daniel. "An Introduction to China's Strategic Military–Civilian Fusion," in *China's Evolving Military Strategy*, Joe McReynolds, ed., Washington, DC: Brookings Institution Press, 2016.

Alderman, Daniel, Lisa Crawford, Brian Lafferty, and Aaron Straberg. "The Rise of Chinese Civil–Military Integration," in Tai Ming Cheung, ed., *Forging China's Military Might: A New Framework for Assessing Innovation*, Baltimore, MD: Johns Hopkins Press, 2014.

American Association of University Professors. *Recommended Principles to Guide Academy-Industry Relationships*. Champaign, IL: University of Illinois Press, 2014.

American Association of University Professors and American Council on Education. "On Preventing Conflicts of Interest in Government-Sponsored Research at Universities; a Joint Statement of the Council of the American Association of University Professors and The American Council on Education," *American Association of University Professors Bulletin*, 1965, vol. 51, pp. 42–43.

American Physical Society. "19.1 Guidelines on Ethics (Full Statement)." American Physical Society Office of Government Affairs, April 10, 2019.

Applebaum, Richard P., Cong Cao, Xueying Han, Rachel Parker, and Denis Simon. "Innovation in China: Challenging the Global Science and Technology System," *Polity*, 2018.

Battelle. "2012 Global R&D Funding Forecast," Advantage Business Media, December 2011. www.battelle.org/docs/default-source/misc/battelle-2012-misc-rd-funding-forecast.

Battelle. "Battelle-R&D Magazine Release Newest Global Research Funding Forecast," Press Release, December 18, 2012. www.battelle.org/newsroom/press-releases/press-releases-detail/battelle-r-dmagazine-release-newest-global-research-funding-forecast.

Berger, Suzanne. "Why Manufacturing Matters," *MIT Technology Review*, July 1, 2011.

Bush, Vannevar. "Science, the Endless Frontier: A Report to the President on a Program for Postwar Research." National Science Foundation. United States Government Printing Office, July 1945.

Cao, Cong, Richard Suttmeier, and Denis Fred Simon. "China's 15-Year Science and Technology Plan," *Physics Today*, pp. 38–43, December 2006.

Carter, Ashton B. "Memorandum from Under Secretary of Defense, Ashton B. Carter to the Secretaries of the Military Departments Regarding Fundamental Research," *US Department of Defense, Acquisitions, Technology, and Logistics*, May 24, 2010.

Cervantes, Mario and Dominique Guellec. "The Brain Drain: Old Myths, New Realities," *Organization for Economic Co-operation and Development Observer*, 230, January 2002.

Chen, Stephen. "China's Brain Drain to the US is Ending, Thanks to Higher Salaries and Donald Trump," *South China Morning Post*, August 6, 2018.

Cheung, Tai Ming. "The Chinese Defense Economy's Long March from Imitation to Innovation," *Journal of Strategic Studies* 34, no. 3, June 2011.

Cheung, Tai Ming. ed. *Forging China's Military Might: A New Framework for Assessing Innovation*, Baltimore, MD: Johns Hopkins Press, 2014.

Cheung, Tai Ming. *Fortifying China: The Struggle to Build a Modern Defense Economy*, Ithaca, NY: Cornell University Press, 2009.

Collins, Francis. "Statement on Protecting the Integrity of US Biomedical Research," US Department of Health and Human Services, National Institutes of Health, August 23, 2018.

Diamond, Larry and Orville Schell, editors. *China's Influence & American Interests: Promoting Constructive Vigilance*, Stanford, CA: Hoover Institution Press, 2019.

Dong, Hongliang and Chen Baosheng. "'New Ideas' Should Enter Academic Courses," *People's Daily*, January 25, 2018.

Erickson, Stephen and Karen Muskavitch. "Administrators and the Responsible Conduct of Research: Conflicts of Commitment," US Department of Health and Human Services. https://ori.hhs.gov/education/products/rcradmin/.

Feigenbaum, Evan. *China's Techno-Warriors: National Security and Strategic Competition from the Nuclear to the Information Age*, Stanford, CA: Stanford University Press, 2003.

"Framework Document on Managing Financial Conflicts of Interest," *Association of American Universities*, May 1993.

Gu, Mini. "The Economy of Fraud in Academic Publishing in China," *World Education News and Reviews*, World Education Services, April 3, 2018.

Hamilton, Clive. *The Silent Invasion*, Melbourne, Australia: Hardie Grant, March 20, 2018.

Hannas, William et al. *Chinese Industrial Espionage: Technology Acquisition and Military Modernization*, London and New York: Routledge, 2013.

Jiang, Hua and Xiaobin Li. "Party Secretaries in Chinese Higher Education Institutions: What Roles Do They Play?" *Journal of International Education and Leadership* 6, no. 2, Summer 2018.

Joske, Alex. "Picking Flowers, Making Honey—The Chinese Military's Collaboration with Foreign Universities." *Australian Strategic Policy Institute*, International Cyber Policy Centre, October 30, 2018.

Lamberth, Megan. "America Desperately Needs AI Talent, Immigrants Included," *Breaking Defense*, December 23, 2019.

Lauer, Michael. "Responding to Undue Foreign Influence and Security Concerns: Perspectives of the National Institutes of Health," JASON Summer Study 2019, National Institutes of Health, La Jolla, CA briefing, July 10, 2019.

Lauer, Michael and Sally Amero. "Breaches of Peer Review Integrity." National Institutes of Health, Office of Extramural Research, June 25, 2019.

Lee, Kai-Fu. *AI Superpowers: China, Silicon Valley and the New World Order*," New York: Houghton Mifflin Harcourt, 2018.

Lloyd-Damnjanovic, Anastasya. *A Preliminary Study of PRC Political Influence and Interference Activities in American Higher Education*, Wilson Center, Washington, DC, 2018.

Mann, James. *The China Fantasy: How Our Leaders Explain Away Chinese Repression*, New York: Viking, 2007.

National Academies of Sciences, Engineering, and Medicine. *Fostering Integrity in Research*, Washington, DC: The National Academies Press, 2017.

National Academies of Sciences, National Academy of Engineering, and Institute of Medicine. *Responsible Science: Ensuring the Integrity of the Research Process: Volume I*, Washington, DC: The National Academies Press, 1992.

National Archives and Records Administration. "CUI Category: Export Controlled Research," *CUI*, August 9, 2018. www.archives.gov/cui/registry/category-detail/export-controlled-research.

National Archives and Records Administration. "CUI Registry," *CUI*, October 7, 2019. www.archives.gov/cui.

National Foundation for American Policy. "The Importance of International Students to American Science and Engineering," NFAP Policy Brief, October 2017.

National Research Council. *Beyond 'Fortress America': National Security Controls on Science and Technology in a Globalized World*, Washington, DC: The National Academies Press, 2009.

National Research Council. *Science and Security in the Post 9/11 World: A Report Based on Regional Discussions Between Science and Security Communities*, Washington, DC: National Academies Press, 2007.

National Science Board, National Science Foundation. "Higher Education in Science and Engineering. Science and Engineering Indicators 2020," NSB-2019-7, Alexandria VA: National Science Foundation, 2019.

National Science Board, National Science Foundation. "International Science and Engineering Partnerships: A Priority for US Foreign Policy and our Nation's Innovation Enterprise," NSB-08-4, National Science Foundation, February 14, 2008.

National Science Foundation. *National Science Foundation Act of 1950*. Pub. L. 81–507. 64 Stat. 149, May 20, 1950. https://legcounsel.house.gov/Comps/81-507.pdf.

National Science Foundation. "Proposal and Award Policies and Procedures Guide (PAPPG)," NSF 19-1, February 25, 2019.

National Science Foundation. "Research Misconduct." Title 45 Code of Federal Regulations, pt. 689, 2012. www.nsf.gov/oig/_pdf/cfr/45CFR-689.pdf.

National Science Foundation, National Center for Science and Engineering Statistics. "Survey of Doctorate Recipients, 2015," February 18, 2017.

National Science Foundation, National Center for Science and Engineering Statistics. "Doctorate Recipients from US Universities: 2017," NSF 19-301, Alexandria VA, 2018.

National Security Decision Directive (NSDD) 189. "National Policy on Transfer of Scientific, Technical, and Engineering Information," September 21, 1985.

Portman, Rob. *Threats to the US Research Enterprise: China's Talent Recruitment Plans*, Committee on Homeland Security and Governmental Affairs, Permanent Subcommittee on Investigations, United States Senate, 2019.

PRC National Development and Reform Commission. *13th Five-Year Plan for Economic and Social Development of the People's Republic of China (2016–2020)*, Beijing: Central Compilation and Translation Press, January 2016.

R&D Magazine. "2018 Global R&D Funding Forecast," WTWH Media LLC, December 2017.

Redden, Elizabeth. "Ready to Go Expat?" *Inside Higher Ed*, July 26, 2017.

Reisch, Marc. "Scientist Gets 10 Years for Theft of Gene-Modified Rice," *Chemical and Engineering News*, April 6, 2018.

Roth, Kenneth. *China's Global Threat to Human Rights*, Global Report, 2020.

Saxenian, Annalee. *Regional Advantage: Culture and Competition in Silicon Valley and Route 128*, Harvard University Press, 1996.

Simon, Denis and Cong Cao. *China's Emerging Technological Edge: Assessing the Role of High-End Talent*, Cambridge, UK: Cambridge University Press, 2009.

Taber, Nick. "How Xi Jinping is Shaping China's Universities," *The Diplomat*, August 10, 2018.

Tanner, Murray Scot. "Beijing's New National Intelligence Law: From Defense to Offense." *Lawfare*, July 20, 2017.

The University of Texas at Austin, Office of the Executive Vice President and Provost. "Conflict of Interest, Conflict of Commitment, & Outside Activities," The University of Texas at Austin, 2019.

Truex, Rory. "Colleges Should All Stand Up to China," *The Atlantic*, December 28, 2019.

US Department of Health and Human Services, National Institutes of Health, Office of Budget. "Appropriations History by Institute/Center (1938 to Present)." National Institutes of Health, 2019.

US Department of Justice. *United States of America ex. Rel. Daniel Feldman v. Wilfred van Gorp and Cornell University Medical College. 697 F.3d 78*, United States Court of Appeals, Second Circuit, 2012.

US Executive Office of the President [Barak Obama]. Executive Order 13556: *Controlled Unclassified Information*, November 4, 2010.

US General Services Administration. *Federal Acquisition Regulation*, 2019. www.acquisition.gov/sites/default/files/current/far/pdf/FAR.pdf.

US National Archives and Records Administration. "Public Health Service Policies on Research Misconduct: Final Rule." 70 Federal Register 94, May 17, 2005.

US Office of Science and Technology Policy. *Federal Policy on Research Misconduct: Preamble for Research Misconduct Policy*, White House Office of Science and Technology Policy, 2000.

Wilhelm, Ian. "Falsified Applications Are Common among Chinese Students Seeking to Go Abroad, Consultant Says," *The Chronicle of Higher Education,* June 14, 2010.

Zhou, Youyou. "Chinese Students Increasingly Return Home after Studying Abroad," *Quartz,* July 29, 2018.

Zweig, David, Chen Changgui, and Rosen Stanley, "Globalization and Returnee Scholars to China," *China Quarterly* 179, September 2004.

17

ECONOMIC ESPIONAGE AND TRADE SECRET THEFT CASES IN THE US

James Mulvenon

Chapter 17 summarizes and analyzes US government investigations and prosecutions of economic espionage and trade secrets thefts. It directly confronts the issue of racial bias in investigation and prosecution, first by systematically dissecting the methodological and empirical flaws of the Andrew Kim/Committee of 100 (百人会) study, "Prosecuting Chinese 'Spies'." The chapter then offers an alternative line of analysis, concluding that nationality, not ethnicity, is the key variable in understanding China-related technology espionage and theft of trade secrets. Finally, the chapter analyzes key commonalities in tradecraft in all cases of economic espionage or theft of trade secrets involving China or Chinese entities since 2004, highlighting trends and indicators.

Assessment of racial bias: Andrew Kim's "Prosecuting Chinese 'Spies'"

The most common criticism of the US government's legal efforts against technology theft from China is that the program is driven by racial bias. The oft-cited example is the May 2017 study by Andrew Kim, whose statistical analysis is presented by the Committee of 100 as counter-evidence of the pervasiveness of Chinese economic espionage and as proof of ethnic bias in the prosecution system.[1] Yet Kim's study contains methodological flaws, and is undermined by the absence of key data.[2]

Methodologically, the authors say they are using "a random sample of cases charged under the Economic Espionage Act (EEA) from 1997 to 2015 (136 cases involving 187 individual defendants), using publicly available court documents drawn from the Public Access to Court Electronic Records system (PACER)."[3] First, this statement reflects a lack of understanding of the statistical meaning of a "random sample," which does not mean "publicly available court documents drawn from the Public Access to Court Electronic Records system (PACER)" *that we found in our searches.* Moreover, given this small N, analyses of percentages within a given year are statistically unstable, averaging only ten per year over the period in question. It is therefore not surprising that one of the study's reviewers, Dr. David Harris, advises the reader to "recognize the limitations of these data."[4] Harris argues that from the data, "we cannot tell how many investigations under the EEA (as opposed to cases charged) took place during the study period, what ethnic groups the targets of those investigations came from (Chinese or Asian or other), and the rate at which those investigations actually blossomed into charged cases." This leads Harris to conclude that "the data presented in the study do not prove the existence of 'researching while Asian'," which is the core argument of the entire document. Kim actually asks the right question later in the conclusion, but his findings depend on knowing the answer.[5]

These methodological problems undermine the study's main conclusions. For example, the author begins with an initial caveat that the findings are "not conclusive," which immediately gives the reader pause.[6] They continue with the very first summary statement that "the percentage of people of Chinese heritage charged under the Economic Espionage Act (EEA) has tripled since 2009, to 52%," but the reader is not given the corresponding increase in charges for the same crime against non-Chinese for comparison purposes. This error is common in analyses of racial bias. The gold standard test for discrimination would be similar to the question of the proportion of whites charged with the same crime as blacks for selling the same kind of cocaine. If blacks disproportionately are charged with more serious offenses for the same action, then there is evidence of some kind of discrimination. If the *probability* of being arrested for espionage is higher for Chinese than non-Chinese in the same conditions, then discrimination exists. But the author does not provide the necessary data to evaluate the situation.

Second, Kim expands the aperture of his analysis by asserting that "62% of EEA defendants charged since 2009 have been people of Asian heritage." By including the undefined category of "people of Asian heritage," the author dilutes the strength of his conclusions, since he does not provide data about the relative percentage of non-Chinese Asians arrested each year since 2009 and therefore cannot refute the supposition that Chinese themselves are not disproportionately being arrested. Moreover, the author does not provide a rationale for choosing 2009 as the starting point. Data provided later in the study show that if you use 2007, the percentage drops to 42 percent and over the entire period since 1996 it is 25 percent. This is a classic statistical manipulation involving adjusting the numbers on the Y or X axis to exaggerate the seeming conclusion. In addition, the author asserts that "22% of people of Asian heritage charged with economic espionage were never convicted of espionage," but fails to provide the non-conviction rate for non-Asians.

Additionally, the data cannot tell you if Chinese are disproportionately charged if you do not also know the underlying pool, e.g., percentage of people working on sensitive technology. In the tech secrets cases under discussion, the author needs to show the relative differential in the prosecution rates for Chinese and non-Chinese, adjusting for the percentages of each group in the overall pool of people engaged in similar work on sensitive technologies. One cannot use population of the US as a metric since the relevant pool is people working in domains where the EEA could apply. According to the authors' data, for example, the "Western:Chinese" ratio of those accused of economic espionage is roughly 1.8 : 1, but we do not know the overall ratio of those two groups in the population of personnel working in EEA-relevant domains and therefore cannot really conclude disproportionate discrimination.

Third, the author asserts that in almost half "(48%) of cases of economic espionage in the dataset, the alleged beneficiary of espionage was an American entity while [only] a third (34%) of cases involved a Chinese beneficiary."[7] But this statistical sleight-of-hand is meant to confuse the reader. The data clearly show that Chinese perpetrators overwhelmingly were seeking data for a Chinese beneficiary, and in 57% of cases the beneficiary was a "foreign instrumentality" of the Chinese government.[8]

Fourth, the author insists that "the average sentence for Chinese and all Asian defendants convicted of espionage was 25 months and 22 months respectively, twice as long as the 11-month average sentence for defendants with Western names."[9] The problem with this analysis takes us back to the examples of whites and blacks charged with cocaine-related crimes. If blacks disproportionately receive more severe punishments for the same crime than whites, then there's evidence of discrimination. But the author of this study does not break down the EEA violations by any measure of scope or scale, such as numbers of transfers or the financial value of the transfers, making it impossible to judge the relative differences. Also, a name alone may tell us little about a person.

Finally, the author claims as evidence of discrimination that "as many as 1 in 5 Asian people prosecuted as spies may be innocent, a rate twice as large as for other races."[10] Rather than point to discrimination, the data actually implies that Asians are twice as likely to be charged but ultimately not convicted, which might point to discrimination in charging thresholds but also could mean that the cases are weaker OR that the evidence of espionage is more sensitive and they are convicted of other things (e.g., mishandling classified materials). While there is surely reputational and financial damage from these aborted prosecutions, they also perversely validate the independence and fairness of the American judicial system.

To summarize, the Kim study contains several methodological and empirical flaws. To make the study more methodologically sound, its author should answer four empirical questions:

- Were the crimes for which "Western"-named people and Chinese-named people were charged the same in terms of degree?

• What is the pool of people working in sensitive tech, and what is their distribution by ethnicity?
• What was the rationale behind the timeframe of the evidence offered?
• What is the nationality of Chinese charged? Does the percent of PRC citizens go up after 2009, while the percent of US Chinese–Americans charged remain the same? If so, does this suggest nationality not ethnicity is driving the data?

The Kim study does not answer these key questions, which undermines its— admittedly cautious—conclusions that current DoJ prosecutions are motivated by racial bias. There is another interpretation: that *nationality*, not ethnicity, is the critical factor.

Another way to look at the issue of racial bias in economic espionage cases: nationality vs. ethnicity

This section analyzes the complete set of indictments and/or prosecutions of thefts of trade secrets and economic espionage by individuals in the United States seeking to transfer technologies to Chinese entities, either to companies owned by themselves, or their co-conspirators, or "foreign instrumentalities" of the Chinese government or military since 2004.[11] It does not include espionage cases related to the theft of classified US government secrets or technology espionage carried out by Chinese government or military hackers or spies. The major findings:

• Between 2004 and 2019, 147 individuals were indicted or convicted for economic espionage or trade secret theft involving China, which breaks down to 33 indictments (many of which are still pending) and 114 convictions.
• As can be seen in Figure 17.1, the number of indictments or convictions for economic espionage or trade secret theft between 2004 and 2019 averaged over 9 per year, rising to more than 11 if you start in 2008. The spikes in cases in 2009 and 2013 during the Obama Administration certainly belie the popular argument that the dramatic growth in these prosecutions started with the 2017 Department of Justice China Initiative under President Trump, though certainly 2019 eclipsed all previous years and 2020 is projected (judging by the number of 2019 indictments) to be comparable.
• As shown in Figure 17.2, PRC nationals or naturalized US citizens of PRC origin make up the majority of those indicted or convicted of economic espionage or trade secret theft from 2004 to 2019. Excluding Taiwanese or ethnic Chinese from other countries (e.g., Singapore, Malaysia), Figure 17.2 shows the percentages of PRC nationals or naturalized US citizens of PRC

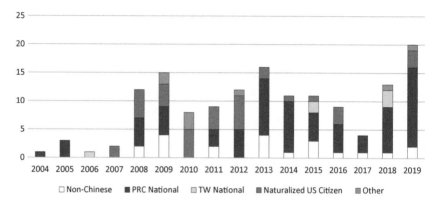

FIGURE 17.1   Indictments and prosecutions of individuals for China-related economic espionage and theft of trade secrets, 2004–2019.

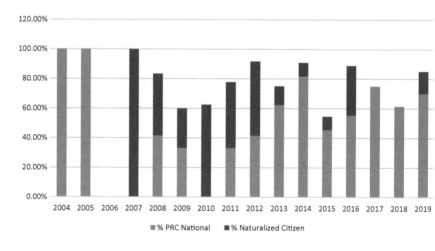

FIGURE 17.2   Percentages of indictments and convictions associated with PRC nationals or naturalized US citizens of PRC origin.

origin indicted or convicted in each year since 2004. *With the exception of 2006, the percentage of China-related technology theft cases involving individuals of PRC origin never drops below 50 percent.*

• The percentage of non-ethnic Chinese US citizens indicted or convicted has always been a relatively minority of cases, *in sharp contrast to the recent spike in non-ethnic Chinese individuals (e.g., Greg Bergerson, James Fondren, Benjamin Bishop, Glenn Duffie Schriver, Kevin Patrick Mallory) indicted or convicted of non-technology espionage on behalf of the Chinese intelligence services.*

BOX 17.1 CAST-IRON TECHNOLOGY TO CHINA

Cast-Iron Technology to China[1]—In October 2019, Robert O'Rourke was sentenced to a year and a day in prison, and was also fined $100,000, according to the US Attorney's Office of the Northern District of Illinois. He was convicted in March 2019 on seven counts of theft of trade secrets. In September 2015, O'Rourke downloaded company documents without authorization two days before leaving Dura-Bar, a Woodstock-based cast-iron manufacturer, prosecutors said. Two days later, he resigned from Dura-Bar, where worked since 1987 as a plant metallurgist, quality assurance manager, and salesperson, prosecutors said. The next week, O'Rourke went to O'Hare International Airport to catch a flight to China, but federal authorities arrested him and seized the stolen trade secrets, prosecutors said. He helped Dura-Bar develop business in China and other locations, and in 2013 began to negotiate to take a similar job with a rival firm in Jiangsu, China.

Note
1 https://chicago.suntimes.com/crime/2019/10/10/20908255/china-trade-secrets-robert-orouke-dura-bar-lake-geneva-woodstock-sentence

BOX 17.2 MILITARY NIGHT VISION TECHNOLOGY TO CHINA

Military Night Vision Technology to China[1]—On December 3, 2007, Philip Cheng, a Taiwanese–American residing in Cupertino, California, was sentenced in the Northern District of California to two years in prison and ordered to pay a $50,000 fine for his role in brokering the illegal export of a night vision camera and its accompanying technology to China in violation of federal laws and regulations. Mr. Cheng, who operated a San Jose company called SPCTEK, pleaded guilty in October 2006 to brokering the sale of a thermal-imaging infrared camera called Panther I without the approval of the State Department. Cheng established a separate technology transfer company with the intention of producing the camera in China. Cheng tried to avoid detection by the US government, meeting in Asia to discuss the export of the technology and establishing a camera factory in China. He created shipping documents stating that Taiwan was the final destination for the cameras, when in fact the cameras were to be diverted to China.

Note
1 www.sfgate.com/bayarea/article/Cupertino-man-gets-2-years-for-exporting-military-3235173.php

- The percentage of Taiwanese citizens indicted or convicted has almost been an outlier, which is notable because ethnic and linguistic compatibility as well as high levels of economic intercourse between China and Taiwan theoretically lowers the barriers to economic espionage or theft of trade secrets on behalf of the mainland.

Overall, the data confirms some of the conventional wisdom about economic espionage and theft of trade secrets bound for China, especially the prevalence of PRC nationals and naturalized US citizens of PRC origin in the cases, but also punctures some key narratives: that the increase comes with the Trump Administration or the Obama Department of Justice China Initiative. The data also show similarly large spikes in previous administrations.

An analysis of commonalities in theft/espionage tradecraft

Breaking down the data along different lines offers interesting findings with respect to patterns of tradecraft across the 93 cases:

- As shown in Figure 17.3, more than 57 percent of economic espionage or trade secrets theft cases between 2004 and 2019 benefited a "foreign instrumentality," which will be defined in more detail later in the chapter but can simply be summarized as an "entity controlled by the government of a foreign country that performs a function the controlling government treats as its own."
- Over 20 percent of economic espionage or trade secrets theft cases between 2004 and 2019 benefited a private PRC commercial company, often a competitor of the US victim, though the incidence of non-government, commercial-focused espionage has increased dramatically in 2018–2019, *surpassing foreign instrumentality cases for the first time.*

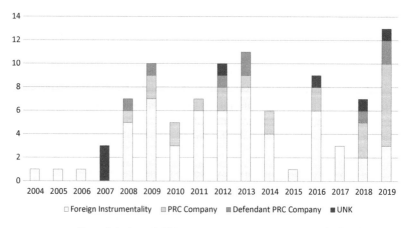

FIGURE 17.3   Beneficiaries of Chinese economic espionage or theft of trade secrets, 2004–2019.

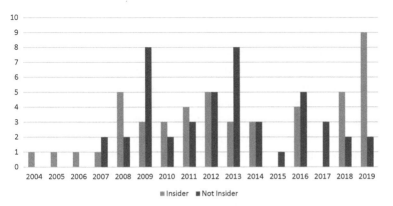

FIGURE 17.4 Insider vs. outsider threats in economic espionage and theft of trade secrets to China, 2004–2019.

- Only 6 percent of economic espionage or trade secrets theft cases between 2004 and 2019 benefited a company established in the PRC by the defendant for private commercial purposes.

BOX 17.3 NEXT-GENERATION BATTERY TECHNOLOGY TO CHINA

Next-Generation Battery Technology to China[1]—In November 2019, Hongjin Tan, a Chinese national and US legal permanent resident, pleaded guilty in federal court to theft of a trade secret, unauthorized transmission of a trade secret, and unauthorized possession of a trade secret. The defendant stole the information from US-based Philips 66 regarding the manufacture of next-generation battery technologies for stationary energy storage, specifically flow batteries, with estimated value of more than $1 billion. Tan was employed as an associate scientist for the US petroleum company starting in June 2017 until his arrest in December 2018. In his plea agreement, Tan admitted to intentionally copying and downloading research and development materials without authorization from his employer. A company laptop computer issued to Tan contained a letter written in Chinese that was a job offer from a Chinese battery company, located in Xiamen, China, promising Tan $58,000 for "introducing the talent" and a salary equal to about $116,000 annually.

Note

1 www.justice.gov/usao-ndok/pr/chinese-national-pleads-guilty-committing-theft-trade-secrets; and DoJ Public Affairs, "Chinese National Pleads Guilty to Committing Theft of Trade Secrets," 12 November 2019, accessed at: www.justice.gov/opa/pr/chinese-national-pleads-guilty-committing-theft-trade-secrets

---

BOX 17.4 THEFT OF MEDICAL DEVICE TECHNOLOGY

Theft of Medical Device Technology[1]—In January 2019, Wenfeng Lu, 46, was sentenced after pleading guilty in May 2018 to six counts of unauthorized possession and attempted possession of trade secrets related to medical devices used to treat cardiac and vascular ailments. Lu admitted that he stole confidential and proprietary trade secrets from two different medical device companies with research facilities in Irvine, where Lu worked from January 2009 until he was arrested in this case in 2012. Lu first worked at ev3 (which later became part of Covidien, and then Medtronic), and later at Edwards Lifesciences Corporation. Lu copied numerous documents belonging to both of his employers that contained technical information and trade secrets. While he was working for the companies, Lu traveled multiple times to the People's Republic of China (PRC), where he had obtained approximately $2 million RMB (about 328,000 US$) in financing and free rent for a period of three years in a laboratory in a technology park located in Nanjing Province in the PRC and was preparing to open a company in the PRC that would manufacture devices used to treat vascular problems.

Note

1 www.justice.gov/usao-cdca/pr/chinese-national-who-stole-trade-secrets-while-working-medical-device-companies

---

The data also offer tradecraft insights about the relative prevalence of "insider" activity by company employees or "outsider" attempts to acquire and illegally export another company's products.

- The data reveal that both insider and outsider approaches to economic espionage and trade secret theft have been used over the time period, almost evenly divided between 48 insider cases and 46 outsider cases.
- While insiders have been working since the beginning of the time period, they appear to be an increasing majority of cases, particularly since 2018, making up 71.4 percent and 81.8 percent of the cases in 2018 and 2019 respectively.
- Outsider cases, particularly those involving corporate platforms seemingly designed to acquire and illegally export electronics components (see the Fushine, Chitron cases, etc.), had their heyday between 2009 and 2016 and appear to be on the decline as a tradecraft of choice.

Overall, the data confirms the central role of foreign instrumentalities, in other words, elements of the Chinese government, as the primary beneficiaries of China-related economic espionage and theft of trade secrets in the United States,

BOX 17.5 SODIUM CYANIDE SECRETS TO CHINA

Sodium Cyanide Secrets to China[1]—In June 2018, Jerry Jindong Xu pleaded guilty to a US charge that he conspired to steal trade secrets related to its lucrative sodium cyanide business and sell them to Chinese investors. Jerry Jindong Xu had worked for DuPont since 2004 and was involved in marketing sodium cyanide-based products. His employment was terminated by Chemours in 2016, prosecutors said. The indictment accused Xu of using his position with Chemours to obtain trade secrets and confidential information, including reports and spreadsheets regarding three different company projects related to cyanide plants and facilities. Prosecutors said his main goal was to either help investors build a competing sodium cyanide plant or become an import competitor. He told one potential investor that he wanted to do the project "for himself and not to slave away at this only to benefit someone else," prosecutors said.

Note

1 https://news.yahoo.com/ex-chemours-employee-pleads-guilty-u-trade-secrets-162445545-finance.html

and validates the counterintelligence concerns about "insiders" in US industry and government as a vector for threats.

Economic espionage prosecutions and "foreign instrumentality"

Investigators and prosecutors need a clearer definition of "foreign instrumentality," since the concept describes the beneficiaries of much of the illegal activity under discussion, and especially within the complex political, economic, and ideological milieu of China. The 11th Circuit in 2014 defined "instrumentality" as an "entity controlled by the government of a foreign country that performs a function the controlling government treats as its own."[11] According to the court, there are two elements in deciding whether an entity is an instrumentality: whether the foreign government controls the entity and whether the entity performs a function that the government treats as its own. The court listed factors relevant to the first element: whether the government has a majority interest in the entity; the government's ability to hire and fire the entity's principals; the extent to which the entity's profits go directly into the government coffers; the extent to which the government funds the entity if it fails to break even; and the length of time these factors have existed. Factors of the second element, also from the Organization for Economic Cooperation and Development (OECD) Convention language, include whether the entity has a monopoly over the function it carries out; whether the government subsidizes the costs associated with the entity providing services; whether the entity provides services to the public at large in the foreign country; and whether the public and the government of that foreign country generally perceive the entity to be performing a governmental function.

But what does that mean in China? Some elements of the system are easy to define. Active-duty People's Liberation Army units, PRC government ministries, intelligence organizations like the Ministry of State Security, and Communist Party of China organizations are all clearly foreign instrumentalities of the Chinese "government" broadly defined. If any of those organizations appear as the requirements provider, logistics or financial facilitator, or end-user beneficiary of the transaction, then the path is clear.

The next layer of complexity arises from state-owned enterprises (国有企业), such as Sinopec or Sinochem. These are not private companies in the Chinese system, even though they engage in commerce in the global system and interact with foreign companies as counterparts. Moreover, the Chinese system itself does not treat them as private companies, but rather as state assets. They are formally subordinate to the State-owned Assets Supervision and Administration Commission (SASAC), which is a special commission directly subordinate to the PRC State Council. SASAC appoints the leaderships of these companies, and those leaders regularly rotate back to the government ministry to serve as regulatory officials. SASAC approves the budgets of these companies, and also oversees any mergers, acquisitions, and investments. Because of this state direction and control, China's state-owned enterprises are clearly foreign instrumentalities of the Chinese government.

One subset of state-owned enterprises are China's ten defense–industrial corporations, which grew out of government defense–industrial ministries. After another recent round of consolidation, the current structure of those corporations is as follows:

- China Aviation Industry Corporation (formerly AVIC 1 and AVIC 2)
- Aero Engine Corporation of China (AECC)
- China Electronics Technology Group Corporation (CETC)
- China Electronics Corporation (CEC)
- China South Industries Group Corporation
- China North Industries Group Corporation
- China State Shipbuilding Corporation (includes former China Shipbuilding Industry Corporation)
- China Aerospace Science and Technology Corporation (CASC)
- China Aerospace Science and Industry Corporation (CASIC)
- China National Nuclear Corporation (CNNC)

Subordinate to each of the corporations are dozens of numbered research institutes and factories, as well as large numbers of publicly acknowledged

BOX 17.6 FOUR OWNERS AND OPERATORS OF NJ COMPANY
ADMIT TO ILLEGALLY EXPORTING PRODUCTS TO CHINA

**Four Owners and Operators of NJ Company Admit to Illegally
Exporting Products to China**[1]—On September 13, 2005, four owner and
operators of Manten Electronics, Inc. of Mount Laurel, NJ pleaded guilty to
charges that they used their business to illegally transfer sensitive national
security controlled items to state-sponsored research institutes in China. All
four defendants, including Manten Electronics, Inc.'s president Xu Weibo,
Chen Xiuling, Chen Haoli, and Chan Kwan-Chun, are naturalized US citizens.
The defendants pleaded guilty to illegally exporting items, including monlithic
microwave integrated circuits, that are used in a wide variety of defense
weapons systems, including radar, smart weapons, electronic warfare and
communications. The illegal exports were destined for numbered institutes
under the China Electronics Technology Group Corporation (CETC). At their
plea hearings, the defendants admitted that they used various techniques
to conceal their export activities, such as providing false written and verbal
statements that purported that the recipient of the restricted items was a
United States corporation rather than a government entity of the People's
Republic of China, and falsifying shipping documents to conceal the true
contents of their shipments to China.

Note
1 https://tradelawnews.blogspot.com/2005/09/four-owners-and-operators-of-nj.html

corporate subsidiaries and a smaller number of front companies. Because they
are state-owned enterprises AND because of their defense–industrial mission for
the military, they are clearly foreign instrumentalities of the Chinese government.

At the research level are China's universities and research institutes, and their
corresponding commercial entities. Within China is a type of university unknown
in the West that might be termed a "defense–industrial university," with close
ties to the defense industry and military. These universities, which are directly
subordinate to the State Administration for Science, Technology and Industry for
National Defense (SASTIND) under the Ministry of Industry and Information
Technology, include (but are not limited to):

- Beijing Institute of Technology
- Beijing University of Aeronautics and Astronautics (BUAA)
- Changchun University of Science and Technology
- Chongqing University of Technology

- Harbin Engineering University
- Harbin Institute of Technology
- Nanjing University of Aeronautics and Astronautics (NUAA)
- Nanjing University of Science and Technology
- North University of China
- Northwest Polytechnical University
- Shenyang Ligong University
- Xi'an Technological University

Because of their direct subordination to China's Ministry of Industry and Information Technology (MIIT) and their defense industry relationships, these universities are clearly foreign instrumentalities of the Chinese government.

Next are defense research laboratories. ASPI's "China Defence Universities Tracker" has identified more than 160 defense-focused laboratories in civilian universities, divided into three groups:[12]

- National defense science and technology key laboratories (国防科技重点实验室).
- National defense key discipline laboratories (国防重点学科实验室).
- Ministry of Education national defense key laboratories (教育部国防重点实验室).

BOX 17.7 SYSTEMS AND COMPONENTS FOR MARINE SUBMERSIBLE VEHICLES TO CHINA

Systems and Components for Marine Submersible Vehicles to China[1]—On September 26, 2016, in the Middle District of Florida, Amin Yu was sentenced to 21 months in federal prison for acting in the US as an illegal agent of a foreign government without prior notification to the Attorney General and for conspiring to commit international money laundering. According to the plea agreement dated June 10, 2016, from at least 2002 until February 2014, at the direction of co-conspirators working for Harbin Engineering University (HEU), a state-owned entity in the People's Republic of China, Yu obtained systems and components for marine submersible vehicles from companies in the United States. She then illegally exported those items to the PRC for use by her co-conspirators in the development of marine submersible vehicles— unmanned underwater vehicles, remotely operated vehicles and autonomous underwater vehicles—for HEU and other state-controlled entities.

Note
1 www.justice.gov/nsd/page/file/1044446/download

There are 74 national defense science and technology key laboratories, which like the defense–industrial universities are subordinate to SASTIND and guided by Chinese military requirements. An additional 39 of these labs can be found in civilian universities. Because of their direct subordination to MIIT and their defense industry and military relationships, these universities are clearly foreign instrumentalities of the Chinese government.

The last and most contested category of organizations are Chinese civilian universities, which in many public and superficial ways resemble their foreign counterparts. However, Chinese universities are directly subordinated to the government and the Party in ways very different from the relationship of US universities to the Department of Education, for example. The Ministry of Education in China appoints university leaders and approves their budgets, which are often the two most important indicators of power and authority. Moreover, the Communist Party of China is dominantly present in universities; the university party secretary,

---

BOX 17.8 SOPHISTICATED WIRELESS TECHNOLOGY TO CHINA

Sophisticated Wireless Technology to China[1]—In October 2019, Hao Zhang was convicted in San Jose. In May 2015, he and five other Chinese nationals were charged by the Justice Department with conspiracy to commit economic espionage on behalf of a foreign instrumentality, conspiracy to steal trade secrets, economic espionage, and theft of trade secrets as part of a 32-count indictment. In 2005, Wei Pang, a Tianjin University professor, accepted a position as a thin-film bulk acoustic resonator (FBAR) engineer with Avago Technologies, in Fort Collins, Colorado. FBARs are radio frequency filters used in cellphones and other wireless devices. In 2006 and 2007, Pang prepared an FBAR business plan with Hao Zhang, another Tianjin University professor and former FBAR engineer with Skyworks Solutions Inc. in Massachusetts. According to the indictment, Pang, Zhang and four other co-conspirators stole confidential and proprietary information from Avago and Skyworks, and used the information as the basis of a joint venture with Tianjin University called ROFS Microsystems. Using the stolen information, Tianjin University was able to build a state-of-the-art FBAR fabrication facility.

Note

1 www.justice.gov/opa/pr/chinese-professors-among-six-defendants-charged-economic-espionage-and-theft-trade-secrets; www.justice.gov/file/439936/download; and Adrian Garcia, "Prof Charged with Espionage," *Fort Collins Coloradoan*, May 20, 2015; Ellen Nakashima, "Six Indicted in Plot to Steal Technology," *Washington Post*, May 20, 2015.

for instance, is more powerful that the university president, and the party committees throughout the schools and departments are the true source of decision-making power. Because of these institutional realities, even civilian universities in China should be seen as foreign instrumentalities of the Chinese government.

Conclusion

This chapter has illustrated key empirical and tradecraft trends in China-related economic espionage and trade secrets theft in the United States. While similar data are not available for other technologically advanced countries, it would not be surprising to see similar phenomena, given commonalities in academic and commercial structures. The chapter also outlined one of the most important issues in China-related cases, precisely defining "foreign instrumentalities" for the purpose of 18 USC 1831 economic espionage prosecutions.

Notes

1 Andrew Kim, "Prosecuting Chinese 'Spies': An Empirical Analysis of the Economic Espionage Act," New York: Committee of 100, May 2017. https://committee100. org/wp-content/uploads/2017/05/2017-Kim-White-Paper-online.pdf?mc_cid=4a0392728d&mc_eid=3d797e54a9.
2 In the following analysis I am indebted to comments from Harvard's Iain Johnston, the "dean" of methodological rigor in the China field.
3 Kim, p. 7.
4 Kim, p. 12.
5 Kim, p. 11.
6 Kim, p. 6.
7 Kim, p. 6.
8 Author review of DoJ technology theft cases 2004 through 2019, available on request.
9 Kim, p. 10.
10 Kim, p. 6.
11 US Court of Appeals for the Eleventh Circuit (Eleventh Circuit), United States v. Esquenazi, May 16, 2014.
12 See ASPI's China Defense Universities Tracker at: www.aspi.org.au/report/china-defence-universities-tracker.

Bibliography

Kim, Andrew. "Prosecuting Chinese 'Spies': An Empirical Analysis of the Economic Espionage Act," New York: Committee of 100, May 2017. https://committee100. org/wp-content/uploads/2017/05/2017-Kim-White-Paper-online.pdf?mc_cid=4a0392728d&mc_eid=3d797e54a9.
US Court of Appeals for the Eleventh Circuit (Eleventh Circuit), United States v. Esquenazi, May 16, 2014. https://caselaw.findlaw.com/us-11th-circuit/1666851.html.

18

MITIGATION EFFORTS TO DATE

James Mulvenon, Didi Kirsten
Tatlow, and Alex Joske

What have governments done to combat unwanted technology transfer to China? The answer rests to some extent on whether one adopts a "narrow" (though pertinent) definition of actions, for example, scrutinizing Chinese investments in overseas companies and technologies that form part of critical national infrastructure; or a broader definition that includes pushing back against political influencing and the social and professional networks aimed at effecting extraction.

Some challenges, such as buying sensitive technology or dual-use companies, are of course more concrete than others, and responses, such as export control systems, are naturally examined in this chapter. Other challenges, such as political influencing, are more indirect and are also examined. Responses are the most advanced, and have the most longevity, in the United States. Australia has made a push in recent years with several new laws. Awareness is growing in Europe where the European Union has introduced an investment screening mechanism, and is revising regulations on the export of dual-use goods.[1] However, while the European Union offers an opportunity for coordinated action, there are definite gaps due to its mosaic of national and supranational competencies.

United States

From the Cold War to the present, the United States has pursued a range of technology controls, with variable levels of effectiveness, and supported those with different types of intelligence and law enforcement exploitation programs. This section summarizes and assesses the current relevant programs, with the goal of extracting lessons for the current challenge.

Arms Export Control Act (AECA) and the International Trafficking in Arms Regulation (ITAR)

Enacted in 1976, the Arms Export Control Act (AECA) provides the authority to control the export of defense articles and services. Executive Order 13637 delegates this statutory authority to the Secretary of State, who administers the law through the Directorate of Defense Trade Controls (DDTC).[2] Within the text of the statute, the International Traffic in Arms Regulations (ITAR) implement the AECA.[3] It includes the United States Munitions List (USML), which defines and lists specific defense articles requiring license for export. The USML is divided into 21 categories of items, ranging from firearms to submersible vehicles. It is updated on an annual basis, and contains a special annex for the Missile Technology Control Regime. More broadly, ITAR also covers technical data and "defense services" that may not be provided to foreign persons without license. A recent example of the importance of AECA and ITAR in technology dealings with China is the case of Wei Sun, who was arrested in January 2020 for transporting a Raytheon Missile Systems laptop to China containing five files covered under ITAR restrictions.[4]

Export Administration Regulations (EAR)

In parallel to the State Department system, the Department of Commerce regulates the export, reexport, and in-country transfer of items on the Commerce Control List (CCL) and other items subject to its jurisdiction, as well as the provision of certain proliferation activities, under the Export Administration Regulations (EAR).[5] Administered under the Bureau of Industry and Security, the EAR primarily covers items that are considered "dual-use," in other words possessing both commercial and military proliferation applications, and therefore requiring a license for export.[6] The determination that an item belongs on the CCL usually derives from an assessment that its transfer involves "national security, foreign policy, short supply, nuclear nonproliferation, missile technology, chemical and biological weapons, regional stability, crime control, or anti-terrorism."[7] Items that fall under the jurisdiction of the Commerce Department but are not listed the CCL are considered "EAR99" and therefore not subject to export licensing. While judged to be generally effective, the EAR system has generated criticism over the years, outlined below in the discussion of the Obama Administration's Export Control Reform Initiative.

The "Farewell Dossier": a model for effective counter-operations?

After a Soviet KGB "Line X"[8] science and technology officer walked in and offered himself to the French service in the early Reagan Administration, the

Western alliance used the "Farewell Dossier" to conduct a national-level program of technology espionage interdiction, double agent operations, and technology insertion operations that caused tremendous damage in the Soviet Union, including a pipeline detonation that is one of the largest recorded explosions on Earth.[9] Key to the success of the program was the establishment of a clearing house for intelligence and law enforcement intelligence, centered in the CIA, and decision-making for the program at the highest possible level, centered in the White House, which allowed for deconfliction and prioritization of operations.

Wassenaar Arrangement

The Wassenaar Arrangement was established on 19 December 1995, after a lengthy negotiation among the previous CoCom countries,[10] CoCom "cooperating countries" (Austria, Finland, Ireland, New Zealand, Sweden and Switzerland), and an initial group of former Comecon members (Russian Federation, Czech Republic, Hungary, Poland, and the Slovak Republic).[11] Like its CoCom predecessor, Wassenaar is an "informal arrangement lacking a legal basis in a formal treaty."[12] The organization's charter covers "transfers of conventional arms and dual-use goods and technologies," which are detailed in the evolving Wassenaar "List of Dual-Use Goods and Technologies and the Munitions List."[13] The Munition List contains 22 main entries with approximately 300 items specially designed for military use;[14] while the Dual-Use List contains nine categories (with approximately 1,000 items) and two annexes: (1) Sensitive List and (2) Very Sensitive List. The Lists are reviewed annually.

Like CoCom, Wassenaar is based on coordination of national controls, rather than international management of international trade in controlled items."[15] Each of the "Participating States" are required to "report their arms transfers and transfers/denials of certain dual-use goods and technologies to destinations outside the Arrangement on a six-monthly basis" and synchronize their domestic export munitions and technology control lists to conform to the Wassenaar list. As Ambassador Philip Griffiths, head of the Wassenaar Secretariat put it in a 2017 interview, the organization's "work is characterized by a balance between collective agreement on key principles and the preservation of national discretion in implementing them."[16] Unlike CoCom, the Wassenaar Arrangement is not restricted in its membership, and has subsequently grown to 41 countries.[17] China is not a member of the Wassenaar Group, but the latter regularly conducts outreach to Beijing and provides briefings on the results of plenary meetings and changes to the control lists.[18] China's military export control list is generally judged to be similar to that of the Wassenaar Group, but there are still important differences in the way Beijing manages dual-use controls.

Deliberations among Wassenaar members are not public, and all decisions are taken by consensus, which is both the greatest strength and weakness of the organization. Other criticisms arise from advocates of strong nonproliferation controls, who argue that Wassanaar, "conceived as a forum for instituting arms export restraint, merely provides a forum for exchanging information on arms shipments."[19] Another critic claimed that "the failure of Wassenaar served to increase US reliance on unilateral controls."[20] At the same time, Wassenaar has placed significant priority on "dual-use" items, which are increasingly as important to monitor as traditional munitions. The Wassenaar Dual-Use List contains more than 1,000 entries, ranging from special materials, to electronics, computers, lasers and navigation, marine and aerospace equipment.[21] Wassenaar discussions have also waded into some of the most controversial dual-use areas, including computer network attack tools, encryption, drones, 3-D printing, communications intercept equipment, and artificial intelligence and machine learning systems.[22] While China has not been a source of disputes among the Wassenaar Arrangement members, Dieter Bohn makes a compelling argument that China's push for indigenous innovation is driven by what he calls a "Wassenaar effect," since Western controls on core dual-use technologies have forced Beijing to emphasize domestic R&D and innovation.[23]

The Obama Administration

The Obama Administration undertook extensive export control reforms, began more aggressively confronting illicit Chinese technology transfer, and began systematically "naming and shaming" Chinese cyber intrusion sets.

In August 2009, the Obama Administration launched the Export Control Reform Initiative (ECRI), which sought to modernize and streamline the US export control system and make it more flexible and nimble in dealing with the rapidly changing technology landscape.[24] In the view of the reformers, the "outdated" Cold War system:

- did not prioritize controls, resulting in a disproportionate focus on the least sensitive items instead of the most sensitive items;
- strained government resources by attempting to protect all items in a control category equally, and harmed interoperability with US allies and partners by causing delays in exports of items that support allies and partners operating alongside US forces; and
- harmed the US defense–industrial base, because foreign manufacturers have increasingly sourced non-sensitive parts and components from outside the United States to avoid the licensing requirements of the US munitions export control system.[25]

Other identified weaknesses of the export control system included:

- slow pace of obtaining an export license;
- overregulation of small parts;

- the failure of the government to standardize and interconnect information technology systems;
- inefficiencies and redundancies in export law enforcement efforts.[26]

On October 2013, the White House announced the first set of changes to the CCL and USML, summarizing the fundamental shift in control strategies:

> The controls effective today are no longer overly broad generic controls that capture everything, but instead are detailed, enumerated lists that impose controls based on the sensitivity of the item and the destination. For example, our most sensitive items—such as bombers, fighters, unmanned aerial vehicles, and their key subsystems, parts, and components—remain on the USML, while less sensitive items, mostly parts and components like cockpit gauges, steel brake wear pads and fuel filters, are now subject to the more flexible authorities of the CCL.[27]

In addition, an Export Enforcement Coordination Center (E2C2) was established under the Department of Homeland Security's Immigration and Customs Enforcement organization to serve as "the primary forum within the federal government for executive departments and agencies to coordinate and enhance their export control enforcement efforts."[28] In retrospect, the reforms were a mixed bag, and more work is certainly needed. The program met its goal of downgrading of thousands of items from the stricter USML to the more flexible CCL, though the associated assessment process took most of the 6 years of the reform program and has been criticized for being too aggressive and not improving the enforcement process for either system.[29] The administration succeeded in publishing a Consolidated Screening List (CSL) in 2010 of entities and individuals so that exporters and the government no longer needed to consult up to six separate lists for denied parties. The new "strategic trade authorization," which is a mechanism that allows for unlicensed exports within a certain set of criteria to a specified group of trusted countries, still risks that "proliferation may occur outside the awareness or scrutiny of the United States."[30] The designation "specially designed," which covered specific components and was introduced to "narrow the scope of the controls over smaller parts and items that are used in larger military equipment," has encountered significant challenges in judicial proceedings. Moreover, the goal of the "four singles" (single export licensing agency, merge commodity control lists into a single list, adopt a common IT system, and move most export enforcement efforts under the purview of a single agency) were not achieved "due to a shortage of time and a lack of Congressional support for carrying out a bureaucratic restructuring of this scale."[31]

Naming and shaming

Another notable feature of the Obama Administration's response to Chinese technology espionage and non-traditional collection was a greater willingness to "name and shame" the perpetrators, even when identified to be Chinese government or military personnel. The most prominent example was the published indictment of five Chinese military intelligence officers associated with Unit 61398,[32] which had been exposed in a Mandiant report as performing cyber espionage against US companies for the benefit of Chinese state-owned enterprises.[33] Specifically, the officers were charged with (1) conspiring to commit computer fraud and abuse; (2) accessing (or attempting to access) a protected computer without authorization to obtain information for the purpose of commercial advantage and private financial gain; (3) transmitting a program, information, code, or command with the intent to cause damage to protected computers; (4) aggravated identity theft; (5) economic espionage; and (6) theft of trade secrets. In another unprecedented move, the Justice Department identified victim companies, including Westinghouse, SolarWorld, US Steel, Allegheny Technologies Inc. (ATI), the United Steel, Paper and Forestry, Rubber, Manufacturing, Energy, Allied Industrial and Service Workers International Union (USW), and Alcoa. Previously, companies had been unwilling to be named for fear of threatening their business interests in China, but the scale and the brazenness of Chinese intelligence activity had finally crossed an unacceptable threshold. The Trump Administration followed suit in 2017 with an indictment of three Chinese hackers (Wu Yingzhuo, Dong Hao, and Xia Lei) employed by a Chinese government contractor company (Boyusec, 广州博宇信息技术有限公司), charging them with "computer hacking, theft of trade secrets, conspiracy and identity theft directed at US and foreign employees and computers of three corporate victims in the financial, engineering, and technology industries between 2011 and May 2017."[34] The specific named victim companies were Moody's Analytics, Siemens AG, and Trimble.

The Obama Administration escalated its "name and shame" strategy in April 2015 with the promulgation of Executive Order (EO) 13694, "Blocking the Property of Certain Persons Engaging in Significant Malicious Cyber-Enabled Activities."[35] The EO declared that "increasing prevalence and severity of malicious cyber-enabled activities originating from, or directed by persons located, in whole or in substantial part, outside the United States constitute an unusual and extraordinary threat to the national security, foreign policy, and economy of the United States." For our purposes, the EO targeted two key categories of person, including those:

- "causing a significant misappropriation of funds or economic resources, trade secrets, personal identifiers, or financial information for commercial or competitive advantage or private financial gain;"

- "responsible for or complicit in, or to have engaged in, the receipt or use for commercial or competitive advantage or private financial gain, or by a commercial entity, outside the United States of trade secrets misappropriated through cyber-enabled means, knowing they have been misappropriated, where the misappropriation of such trade secrets is reasonably likely to result in, or has materially contributed to, a significant threat to the national security, foreign policy, or economic health or financial stability of the United States."

The proscribed penalty was sanctions against persons and property, with the concrete result of seizure of assets and the restrictions of international financial transfers and travel associated with being placed on the Interpol "red notice" list. The Chinese reaction to this EO was swift and intense, though not surprising given that it potentially implicated senior government officials serving as the heads of large state-owned enterprises. Beijing dispatched CPC Central Political and Legal Affairs Commission (中央政法委员会) Secretary Meng Jianzhu (孟建柱) to Washington in September 2015 for consultations ahead of Xi Jinping's state visit later that month, reportedly giving him unusually wide latitude to negotiate an arrangement that would preclude a set of public sanctions for commercial cyber espionage.[36] Chinese state media reported after the meeting that Meng reached an "important consensus" with the US, and said China will punish domestic hackers, including cyber thieves that steal corporate secrets.[37] This commitment was then consummated with an "understanding" between Xi and Obama in a joint press conference, agreeing that neither government would knowingly support cyber theft of corporate secrets or business information.[38]

Foreign Investment Risk Review Modernization Act (FIRRMA)

Led by Senator John Cornyn, the Trump Administration and its Congressional allies reformed the law of the Committee for Foreign Investment in the United States (CFIUS) in 2019 to better track and interdict creative Chinese efforts to acquire US technology. The previous CFIUS law was perceived by its critics and supporters alike to have some structural weaknesses, and was badly in need of updating because of these new challenges. Specific problems with CFIUS included:

- lack of scrutiny of certain types of joint ventures, minority position investments, and real estate transactions near military bases or other sensitive national security facilities;[39]
- lack of ability for CFIUS to initiate investigations, especially those transactions involving "critical technologies" to include emerging technologies that could be essential for maintaining the US technological advantage over countries that pose threats, such as China.

To remedy these shortcomings, Senator Cornyn and others proposed the Foreign Investment Risk Review Modernization Act (FIRRMA). After significant negotiations, the signed version of the law included the following new features:

- **Expands the scope of covered transactions:** FIRRMA broadens the purview of CFIUS by explicitly adding four new types of covered transactions: (1) a purchase, lease, or concession by or to a foreign person of real estate located in proximity to sensitive government facilities; (2) "other investments" in certain US businesses that afford a foreign person access to material nonpublic technical information in the possession of the US business, membership on the board of directors, or other decision-making rights, other than through voting of shares; (3) any change in a foreign investor's rights resulting in foreign control of a US business or an "other investment" in certain US businesses; and (4) any other transaction, transfer, agreement, or arrangement designed to circumvent CFIUS jurisdiction.
- **Declarations:** Provides for an abbreviated filing or "light filing" process through a new "declarations" procedure that could result in shorter review timelines. It also allows CFIUS some discretion to require parties to file with CFIUS before closing a transaction.
- **Expands CFIUS's timelines:** Expands CFIUS's review period from 30 to 45 days and allows an investigation to be extended for an additional 15-day period under extraordinary circumstances.
- **Mitigation:** Strengthens requirements on the use of mitigation agreements, including the addition of compliance plans to inform the use of such agreements.
- **Special hiring authority and funding:** Grants special hiring authority for CFIUS and establishes a fund for collection of new CFIUS filing fees.[40]

In exchange for the broadening of the scope of reviews, the US government offered businesses greater clarity, speed, and opportunities to present mitigating information. Future modifications of the law could include the ability to examine any joint venture, including ones based in China, and the authority to initiate investigations based on the involvement of specific critical technologies, defined by an updated version of the 1996 Militarily Critical Technology List.[41]

2019 John S. McCain National Defense Authorization Act (NDAA)

In 2019, the National Defense Authorization Act established new programs to prevent technology subversion by Chinese companies and protect critical military technology from Chinese exploitation.[42] Section 889 of the NDAA specifically barred the Department of Defense from procuring "telecommunications equipment produced by Huawei Technologies Company or ZTE Corporation (or any subsidiary or affiliate of such entities)," as well as "video surveillance and telecommunications equipment" produced by Hytera Communications Corporation (海能达), Hangzhou Hikvision Digital Technology Company (海康威视), or Dahua Technology Company (大华科技) (or any subsidiary or affiliate of such entities). Section 1286 of the NDAA, titled "Initiative to support protection of national security academic researchers from undue influence and other security threats," called for information exchange, training, and assistance to academic institutions in understanding the technology threat from foreign intelligence services and their non-traditional collection programs.[43] The teeth of the section instructed the government to "limit or prohibit funding provided by the Department of Defense for institutions or individual researchers who knowingly violate regulations developed under the initiative, including regulations relating to foreign talent programs," such as China's Thousand Talents Program.[44] The many law enforcement prosecutions for Thousand Talents Program-related violations described throughout this book are an early indicator of the success of this initiative.

DOJ China Initiative

The Department of Justice initiated its own China Initiative in 2018 designed to increase the investigation and prosecution of Chinese economic espionage-related crimes in the United States. According to official DOJ sources, the key goals of the Initiative are as follows:

- Identify priority trade secret theft cases, ensure that investigations are adequately resourced; and work to bring them to fruition in a timely manner and according to the facts and applicable law; Develop an enforcement strategy concerning non-traditional collectors (e.g., researchers in labs, universities, and the defense–industrial base) that are being co-opted into transferring technology contrary to US interests.
- Educate colleges and universities about potential threats to academic freedom and open discourse from influence efforts on campus.
- Apply the Foreign Agents Registration Act to unregistered agents seeking to advance China's political agenda, bringing enforcement actions when appropriate.
- Equip the nation's US Attorneys with intelligence and materials they can use to raise awareness of these threats within their Districts and support their outreach efforts.
- Implement the Foreign Investment Risk Review Modernization Act (FIRRMA) for DOJ (including by working with Treasury to develop regulations under the statute and prepare for increased workflow).
- Identify opportunities to better address supply chain threats, especially ones impacting the telecommunications sector, prior to the transition to 5G networks.

- Identify Foreign Corrupt Practices Act (FCPA) cases involving Chinese companies that compete with American businesses.
- Increase efforts to improve Chinese responses to requests under the Mutual Legal Assistance Agreement (MLAA) with the United States.
- Evaluate whether additional legislative and administrative authorities are required to protect our national assets from foreign economic aggression.[45]

At the time of writing, it is still too early to assess the success of many of the DOJ China Initiatives, but the increase in the number of arrests and prosecutions for China-related technology transfer violations likely reflects the increased prioritization.

Australia

Technology transfer and research collaboration are emerging as major issues in Australia, which experiences high levels of interference from the CPC. To date, however, concerns about CPC interference have mostly focused on political influence efforts. Australia is sometimes described as a global leader in its responses to foreign political interference, particularly for having begun significant remedial action in recent years in the face of pressure from China to desist. The media has played an active role in exposing these activities. In response to growing interference by the CPC, the government took several key steps in 2018 that included passing three pieces of legislation:

- The *National Security Legislation Amendment (Espionage and Foreign Interference) Act 2018* (EFI).[46] This introduced foreign interference as a crime for the first time.
- The *Foreign Influence Transparency Scheme Act 2018*[47] established a public register of entities engaging in political influence activities.
- The *Electoral Legislation Amendment (Electoral Funding and Disclosure Reform) Act 2018* restricted political donations from foreign entities.

In addition, the government barred Huawei and other "high-risk" companies from 5G networks.

However, industrial espionage was an early concern in Australia, especially in the mining sector—unsurprisingly perhaps since Australia's raw material export industries are heavily reliant on PRC demand. In 2010, the mining company Rio Tinto (and two other mining companies) was targeted by cyberattacks from China, after the arrest of an executive in Shanghai as part of a diplomatically and economically sensitive bribery case.[48] The intrusions, it emerged, may have been designed to give Chinese companies an edge in iron ore price negotiations.[49]

Since then, cyberattacks targeting government and research institutions have been identified, including Australia's Bureau of Meteorology, the Australian Parliament, the Lowy Institute, a contractor building the headquarters of the Australian Security Intelligence Organisation, and the Australian National University.[50] In each case, Chinese state-linked actors are believed to be the probable culprits. While these incidents are likely to have been politically motivated, it is difficult to rule out economic or technological motivations behind some.

Australian research institutions have pursued close engagement with the PRC and are coming under increasing pressure to ensure these activities align with the national interest and improve security. Some examples of recent high-profile cases of concerning research activities and breaches are:

- In 2013, a nanotechnology scientist at the Commonwealth Scientific and Industrial Research Organisation (CSIRO), a government agency, unexpectedly disappeared from his job to return to China, prompting an industrial espionage probe and an overhaul of the organization's data security.[51]
- In November 2019, it emerged that an alleged PLA intelligence operative sought to purchase office space in a facility run by CSIRO.[52] In another case, a Department of Defence scientist was found to have an undisclosed business relationship with a subsidiary of a Chinese missile manufacturer.[53]
- One professor worked with a Chinese university in an area that raised human rights concerns: facial recognition of Uyghurs.[54]
- Another professor at an Australian university joined the Thousand Talents Plan and set up a company in China that supplied surveillance technology to authorities in Xinjiang, which may not have been disclosed to his university.[55]
- Australian universities are also working with the PLA and have trained as many as 300 PLA scientists.[56] In one case, a university professor trained or worked with nearly a dozen members of China's military supercomputer program, which is used to develop nuclear weapons.[57]

Formulating a pushback, in 2017, the government completed a classified study of CPC interference led by former China correspondent and advisor to the prime minister John Garnaut.[58] In April that year, the government appointed the first national counter-foreign interference coordinator to integrate efforts across government.[59] The next month, the director-general of the Australian Security Intelligence Organisation warned that foreign interference against Australia was occurring "at unprecedented scale."[60] In addition, in December 2019, the government announced AU$88 million (US$60 million) in funding for a new, interagency counter-foreign interference task force.[61]

The new laws cover some forms of technology transfer activity, though they primarily respond to political interference. For example, someone seeking to covertly influence a government funding decision or government agency's research partnership with a Chinese institution, on behalf of the CPC, would be committing an illegal act of foreign interference. Lobbying for greater scientific collaboration between Australia and China as part of an undisclosed arrangement with the Chinese government could also be illegal.[62]

Australia's Foreign Investment Review Board also has the power to scrutinize foreign investment. After a Chinese company announced plans to buy an Australian healthcare company, potentially giving it access to medical records of defense personnel, the government indicated it would review any attempted acquisition.[63]

However, in contrast to the United States, the Australian government has primarily pursued a consultative approach to dealing with concerns about university sector engagement with China. In August 2019, the Minister for Education announced the creation of a University Foreign Interference Taskforce. Composed of university, Department of Education, and national security representatives, the task force soon released guidelines on areas including research collaboration, cybersecurity, and intellectual property.[64] While the guidelines were officially non-prescriptive, due to an unwillingness by universities to commit to fully implementing counter-foreign interference measures, they include helpful recommendations.[65]

The Minister for Education also indicated that the taskforce would participate in ongoing examinations of the *Defence Trade Controls Act 2012*, which regulates the export of dual-use or military-use technologies,[66] saying: "This taskforce will … develop practical, risk-based legislative proposals to address identified gaps in the Defence Trade Controls Act."[67]

The Act, unlike comparable legislation in the United States, does not regulate the transfer of technology to foreign nationals within Australian borders. This has allowed PLA scientists to study and work on sensitive technologies that could not normally be exported to them. So while Australia is, in some ways, at the forefront of formulating policies to push back against foreign interference and an example for countries facing similar challenges, in the area of technology transfer and talent recruitment there remains an incomplete policy response.

Australia's Department of Defence has an "Online DSGL Tool" to help businesses, including academics and researchers (people dealing in intellectual property) to self-assess whether or not their work or products require an export permit.[68] The tool has been singled out by the "League of European Research Universities" (LERU) as something urgently needed in Europe, where there are many vexing, unresolved questions about the legality of dual-use goods, as LERU makes clear below.

Europe

Greater attention is being paid than before at the European Union to the growing "systemic" competition with China.[69] As a senior EU official put it in early 2020, the EU and its 27 member states need to be "clear-eyed, not blue-eyed."[70] Practical responses remain few, however, especially in knowledge outflow and CPC influencing.

A comprehensive overview of the situation in 27 EU nations would be a book in its own right, thus this section will restrict itself to the umbrella, or coordinating, function of the EU. Member states broadly follow overall principles and guidelines established by Brussels, however, the reader should keep in mind that national governments also operate their own systems, for example in export control. One such is Germany's export regime run by the Federal Office for Economy Affairs and Export Control (BAFA).[71] Particularly since the United Kingdom left the EU in January 2020 the situation is in flux.

A mosaic of competencies, a relatively low level of security awareness and strategic thinking and, increasingly, the cultivation by the CPC of a special bloc of "17 + 1" nations in Eastern and Southern Europe work against easy mitigation of technology transfer and political influencing activities.[72] Member states are responsible for their own national security; the EU has some functions in this area, mostly drawn from member state inputs.

Perhaps the best-known of the EU's tools designed to deal with technology loss to China entered into force in April 2019: the "Investment Screening Regulation."[73] This was designed to "safeguard Europe's security, public order and strategic interests when it comes to foreign investments into our Union."[74] "(W)hen it comes to defending Europe's interests we will always walk the talk (sic)" said the former EU Commissioner, Jean-Claude Juncker.

Overall, the regulation aims to set up a new EU-wide mechanism, "enabling Member States and the Commission to exchange information and raise concerns related to specific foreign investments."When fully applied in October 2020, it will allow the Commission "to issue opinions when an investment poses a threat to the security or public order of more than one Member State, or when an investment could undermine a project or programme of interest to the whole EU, such as Horizon 2020 or Galileo," the EU's research funding mechanism and satellite system respectively. The move came in response to growing acquisitions, often from China, of critical infrastructure and technology.[75] However, the framework remains voluntary for member states; currently, 14 of 27 have a mechanism in place.[76]

Another, older, measure is an arms embargo, in place since the PLA's suppression of the Tiananmen Square democracy demonstrations of 1989. Though under incessant pressure from Beijing to drop the embargo,[77] the EU "continues to uphold the arms embargo vis-à-vis China, which was established by the European Council Conclusions in 1989, as well as the eight criteria established under the Council Common Position on exports of military technology and equipment."[78]

That may be broadly true, but a report on the implementation of the "Council Common Position" above, which tracked "licences and exports of conventional arms from EU Member States" (these are on a "EU Common Military List"), recorded 190 such exports to China in 2018 from just over half a dozen EU nations (including the United Kingdom, still a member that year).[79] The UK in fact made up the bulk with 81 exports, pipping France (80) by one. Other countries included Czech Republic (11) and Germany (9). Twenty-seven requests from China were refused, the report says (31 when multiple categories or items outside the military list are included).[80] Curiously, perhaps, 21 of the 190 exports are labeled simply as "Technology" (*sic*), one of 22 categories of weapons identified by the list. Here too the UK led, with 16 out of 21.[81]

Weapons trade between European nations and China is also recorded by the Stockholm International Peace Research Institute (SIPRI). SIPRI's 2018 trade register of "transfers of major weapons" shows that Germany and France both exported diesel engines and diesel engine technologies for use by the PLAN, with France additionally exporting helicopters.[82]

With regard to dual-use items, most European nations are members of the Wassenaar Arrangement.[83] The EU updates its "Dual-Use Regulation" of 2009 (which is anyway undergoing revision), to match that,[84] with additional input from the Missile Technology Control Regime (MTCR), Nuclear Suppliers Group, and the Australia Group (AG).[85]

Still, "It is difficult to obtain reliable information on overall dual-use exports (including non-listed dual-use items) as there is no correspondingly defined economic sector," according to a 2019 report on the control of exports, transfer, brokering and transit of dual-use items.[86] The report also indicated that China was the recipient of about 12 percent of the value of the EU's (extra-EU) dual-use exports which totaled EUR 36.6 billion in 2017.[87] It adds: "With respect to enforcement, 120 breaches of export control regulations were recorded in 2017, while 130 administrative penalties and 2 criminal penalties were applied by national law enforcement authorities."[88] Some loopholes may be due to understaffing and a lack of definitions—though a common complaint about Brussels is excessive bureaucracy, not too little. The EU's control export network, made up of people working at the member state level and the Commission in Brussels, consisted of "over 300 staff" in 2018, perhaps not much for more than two dozen countries plus a central bureaucracy.

The technology outflow situation at European universities is impossibly heterogeneous to demonstrate here but overall poorly controlled (see Chapter 8 on Germany for individual examples). One organization of 23 research-intensive institutions is the Belgium-based "League of European Research Universities" (LERU).[89] LERU has called for far greater guidance on how to work on dual-use research with partners outside the EU.[90] In a 2018 statement, referring to the Dual-Use Regulation, LERU asked the institutions of the EU, above all the Commission, to:

- Formulate the Regulation in an unambiguous way and do not leave open areas of legal uncertainty as a consequence of clauses that need a lot of interpretation.
- Provide the necessary tools for universities to be able to comply with the Regulation with legal certainty and without too many burdens being imposed.

• Improve access to, and guidance from, regulatory bodies so that research projects are not unduly delayed.[91]

In an email sent in February 2020, 19 months after the publication of the above statement in July 2018, LERU's secretary-general, Kurt Deketelaere, said its position was "unmodified and still valid."[92] Key factors requiring far greater assistance for researchers included:

• large documents, typically of the order of hundreds of pages;
• lists updated on an annual basis;
• interpretation and integration with local regulations in each EU jurisdiction;
• increasingly wide reach into other regulations (e.g., human rights).

Among the tools needed are a well-staffed helpline and an easy-to-use self-assessment tool, such as Australia's DOD checker (DSGL).

> A user-friendly interface, backed up by an accurate, easy to use and up to date database could significantly aid correct identification by scientists on whether their research falls under the scope of the dual-use controls or not.… Such tools are used in other regions, for example in Australia and the USA, and LERU believes that the European Commission would be best placed to develop and maintain such a database for use across Europe.[93]

Discussions were beginning in Brussels in 2020 on the desirability of a mechanism to scrutinize political influence and interference by the CPC, but expectations were the EU would not, at least initially, match in scale or ambition those in the US or Australia.[94]

Notes

1 www.europarl.europa.eu/thinktank/en/document.html?reference=EPRS_BRI(2016) 589832.
2 www.pmddtc.state.gov/ddtc_public?id=ddtc_public_portal_itar_landing#tab-aeca.
3 www.pmddtc.state.gov/ddtc_public?id=ddtc_kb_article_page&sys_id=24d528fddbfc9 30044f9ff621f961987.
4 For a copy of the indictment, see www.scribd.com/document/445173882/Wei-Sun-Superseding-Indictment.
5 www.ecfr.gov/cgi-bin/text-idx?SID=70e390c181ea17f847fa696c47e3140a&mc=true &node=pt22.1.120&rgn=div5#se22.1.120_15.
6 www.export.gov/article?id=Export-Administration-Regulations.
7 Ibid.
8 "Line X" was a section of the KGB First Chief Directorate assigned to acquire Western technology.
9 Sergei Kostin and Eric Reynaud, *Farewell: The Greatest Spy Story of the Twentieth Century*, Amazon Crossing, 2011.

10 As the Iron Curtain fell across Eastern Europe, the Western Bloc established the Coordinating Committee for Multilateral Export Controls (COCOM) in the first five years after the end of World War II. At its max, COCOM had 17 members, overlapping but not coterminous with NATO membership: Australia, Belgium, Canada, Denmark, France, West Germany, Greece, Italy, Japan, Luxembourg, Netherlands, Norway, Portugal, Spain, Turkey, United Kingdom, and the United States. The goal of COCOM was to embargo the Comecon countries (Bulgaria, Cuba, Czechoslovakia, East Germany, Hungary, Mongolia, Poland, Romania, Soviet Union, Vietnam), maintaining and enforcing a control list of denied technologies. While COCOM achieved some notable successes, it was not without criticism. Critics bemoaned the dominance of the US in the group, the difficulty of achieving unanimous consensus, disputes over what items were to be controlled, and even conflicts over the extent to which an economic embargo was desirable at all. COCOM was disbanded on March 31, 1994, and replaced with the Wassenaar Arrangement.
11 www.wassenaar.org/about-us/.
12 Michael Lipson, "The Reincarnation of Cocom: Explaining Post-Cold War Export Controls," *The Nonproliferation Review/Winter*, 1999, p. 39.
13 www.wassenaar.org/control-lists/.
14 The current comprehensive control lists can be viewed here: www.wassenaar.org/controllists/index.html.
15 Michael Lipson, "The Reincarnation of Cocom: Explaining Post-Cold War Export Controls," *The Nonproliferation Review/Winter*, 1999, p. 39.
16 www.wassenaar.org/app/uploads/2019/consolidated/CD_012017_Interview.pdf.
17 www.wassenaar.org/about-us/.
18 Safeworld, "Strengthening Dialogue between China and the Wassenaar Arrangement," June 2014. www.files.ethz.ch/isn/182707/strengthening-dialogue-between-china-and-the-wassenaar-arrangement.pdf.
19 "Commentary: Wassenaar's Weakness," *Defense News*, January 26, 1997, p. 18.
20 Michael S. Lelyveld, "US, High-Tech Group Synchronize Export Rules; 33 Nations Form Pact, Giving Them Wide Berth to Make High-Tech Deals," *Journal of Commerce*, January 20, 1998, p. 3A.
21 www.wassenaar.org/app/uploads/2019/consolidated/CD_012017_Interview.pdf.
22 Ibid.
23 Dieter Ernst, "Indigenous Innovation and its Effect on China's Semiconductor Industry," East-West Center, 2012. www2.itif.org/2012-semiconductor-ernst.pdf.
24 https://2016.export.gov/ecr/.
25 Office of the Press Secretary, The White House, "Fact Sheet: Announcing the Revised US Export Control System," October 15, 2013. https://obamawhitehouse.archives.gov/the-press-office/2013/10/15/fact-sheet-announcing-revised-us-export-control-system.
26 Andrea Stricker with David Albright, "US Export Control Reform: Impacts and Implications for Controlling the Export of Proliferation-Sensitive Goods and Technologies, A Policy Document for the New President and Congress," Institute for Science and International Security, May 17, 2017. https://isis-online.org/isis-reports/detail/US-export-control-reform-impacts-and-implications/.
27 Office of the Press Secretary, The White House, "Fact Sheet: Announcing the Revised US Export Control System," October 15, 2013, https://obamawhitehouse.archives.gov/the-press-office/2013/10/15/fact-sheet-announcing-revised-us-export-control-system.
28 www.ice.gov/eecc.
29 Stricker and Albright, *US Export Control Reform*, Executive Summary.
30 Ibid.
31 Ibid.

32 Office of Public Affairs, Department of Justice, "US Charges Five Chinese Military Hackers for Cyber Espionage Against US Corporations and a Labor Organization for Commercial Advantage—First Time Criminal Charges Are Filed Against Known State Actors for Hacking," May 19, 2014. www.justice.gov/opa/pr/us-charges-five-chinese-military-hackers-cyber-espionage-against-us-corporations-and-labor.

33 Fireeye, *APT1: Exposing One of China's Cyber Espionage Units*, 2014. www.fireeye.com/content/dam/fireeye-www/services/pdfs/mandiant-apt1-report.pdf.

34 Office of Public Affairs, Department of Justice, "US Charges Three Chinese Hackers Who Work at Internet Security Firm for Hacking Three Corporations for Commercial Advantage," May 19, 2014.

35 Office of the Press Secretary, The White House, "Executive Order—'Blocking the Property of Certain Persons Engaging in Significant Malicious Cyber-Enabled Activities'," April 1, 2015.

36 Office of the Press Secretary, The White House, "Readout of Senior Administration Officials' Meeting with Secretary of the Central Political and Legal Affairs Commission of the Communist Party of China Meng Jianzhu," September 12, 2015.

37 Chen Weihua, "China, US Gradually Move to Manage Cyber Dispute," *China Daily*, September 14, 2015.

38 Matt Spetalnick and Michael Martina, "Obama Announces 'Understanding' with China's Xi on Cyber Theft but Remains Wary," *Reuters*, 25 September 2015.

39 One oft-cited example was the CFIUS blocking of a bid by a Chinese private company to install an offshore wind farm near a US Navy weapons systems training facility in Oregon. See Rachelle Younglai, "Obama Blocks Chinese Wind Farms in Oregon over Security," *Reuters*, September 29, 2012.

40 Office of Public Affairs, Department of Treasury, "Summary of the Foreign Investment Risk Review Modernization Act of 2018." www.treasury.gov/resource-center/international/Documents/Summary-of-FIRRMA.pdf.

41 An archived copy of the MCTL can be found here: https://fas.org/irp/threat/mctl98-2/mctl98-2.pdf?bcsi-ac-1890e3206a556864=2719591600000002F/TsYSvv5/XAezA+SOjI61QQ32zuFQAAAgAAALx+UgCEAwAAEQAAAFSfCAA=. See also: General Accounting Office, "DOD's Critical Technologies Lists Rarely Inform Export Control and Other Policy Decisions," GAO-06-793, July 2006, www.gao.gov/assets/260/250929.pdf.

42 H.R.5515—John S. McCain National Defense Authorization Act for Fiscal Year 2019.

43 Ibid.

44 Ibid.

45 Office of Public Affairs, Department of Justice, "Attorney General Jeff Session's China Initiative Fact Sheet," November 1, 2018. www.justice.gov/opa/speech/file/1107256/download.

46 www.legislation.gov.au/Details/C2018A00067.

47 Ibid.

48 www.news.com.au/breaking-news/chinese-cyber-attacks-on-bhp-billiton-rio-tinto-and-fortescue-metals-group/news-story/05ae5020ff713abf3d1c89abdb270853.

49 www.bloomberg.com/news/features/2018-07-13/did-china-hack-rio-tinto-to-gain-a-billion-dollar-advantage.

50 www.afr.com/companies/the-lowy-institute-hit-by-chinese-hackers-20181203-h18nn3;www.reuters.com/article/us-australia-china-cyber-exclusive/exclusive-australia-concluded-china-was-behind-hack-on-parliament-political-parties-sources-idUSKBN1W00VF; www.abc.net.au/news/2013-05-27/asio-blueprints-stolen-in-major-hacking-operation/4715960?pfmredir=sm; www.smh.com.au/politics/federal/china-behind-huge-anu-hack-amid-fears-government-employees-could-be-compromised-2019 0605-p51uro.html; www.abc.net.au/news/2015-12-02/china-blamed-for-cyber-attack-on-bureau-of-meteorology/6993278.

51 www.afr.com/technology/csiro-spent-millions-after-chinese-data-breach-20180403-h0y9b3; www.smh.com.au/politics/federal/chineses-scientist-absence-exposed-alleged-spying-activities-at-csiro-20131204-2yr3e.html.

52 www.theage.com.au/national/multimillion-dollar-offer-from-alleged-chinese-agent-for-a-prime-spot-in-csiro-20191125-p53dqg.html.

53 www.smh.com.au/politics/federal/defence-department-scientist-had-separate-role-with-china-linked-firm-20180323-p4z5xb.html.

54 www.abc.net.au/news/2019-07-16/australian-unis-to-review-links-to-chinese-surveillance-tech/11309598.

55 www.theaustralian.com.au/nation/politics/uq-researcher-probed-over-ai-uighur-surveil/news-story/33a6ae6b304c6363d2a4be6a22bc4887; www.aspistrategist.org.au/the-company-with-aussie-roots-thats-helping-build-chinas-surveillance-state/.

56 www.aspi.org.au/report/picking-flowers-making-honey.

57 www.theaustralian.com.au/nation/politics/professor-chinese-generals-coauthored-defence-research/news-story/8c7e063b06c0198b7b4ba9e357a8bffd.

58 www.abc.net.au/news/2018-05-29/chinas-been-interfering-in-australian-politics-for-past-decade/9810236.

59 https://web.archive.org/web/20190924035721/www.homeaffairs.gov.au/about-us/who-we-are/our-senior-staff/chris-teal; www.theaustralian.com.au/nation/crack-unit-to-ward-off-threats-from-espionage/news-story/8409b24c8595bee1bc27e9927f05fbd5.

60 www.smh.com.au/politics/federal/asio-chief-duncan-lewis-sounds-fresh-alarm-over-foreign-interference-threat-20180524-p4zhdk.html?js-chunk-not-found-refresh=true.

61 www.sbs.com.au/news/government-announces-88-million-task-force-to-fight-foreign-interference.

62 www.legislation.gov.au/Details/C2018A00067.

63 www.smh.com.au/politics/federal/chinese-firm-s-takeover-plan-raises-concern-in-canberra-over-access-to-adf-medical-records-20190812-p52gd5.html?js-chunk-not-found-refresh=true.

64 https://ministers.education.gov.au/tehan/taskforce-protect-universities-foreign-interference.

65 www.education.gov.au/ufit.

66 www.legislation.gov.au/Details/C2012A00153.

67 https://ministers.education.gov.au/tehan/taskforce-protect-universities-foreign-interference.

68 https://dsgl.defence.gov.au/Pages/Home.aspx.

69 https://ec.europa.eu/commission/sites/beta-political/files/communication-eu-china-a-strategic-outlook.pdf.

70 Author's personal observation and source, Brussels, February 2020.

71 www.bafa.de/EN/Home/home_node.html.

72 www.china-ceec.org/eng/.

73 https://ec.europa.eu/commission/presscorner/detail/en/IP_19_2088.

74 https://eur-lex.europa.eu/eli/reg/2019/452/oj.

75 www.50hertz.com/en/News/FullarticleNewsof50Hertz/id/5815/closing-kfw-replaces-ifm-as-share-holder-in-50hertz-holding-company Kuka: www.kuka.com/en-de/press/news/2018/03/kuka-expands-china-business the now Chinese-owned, Germany-founded company, bought in 2016, says it will produce a total of "up to 100,000 robot units per year" by 2024, in China.

76 https://trade.ec.europa.eu/doclib/docs/2019/june/tradoc_157946.pdf.

77 www.globaltimes.cn/content/1049431.shtml.

78 https://eur-lex.europa.eu/legal-content/EN/TXT/?uri=CELEX%3A32008E0944.

79 https://op.europa.eu/en/publication-detail/-/publication/1e49557d-2ade-11ea-af81-01aa75ed71a1.

30 Ibid.
31 Ibid.
32 http://armstrade.sipri.org/armstrade/page/trade_register.php.
33 www.wassenaar.org/participating-states/.
34 https://ec.europa.eu/transparency/regdoc/rep/1/2019/EN/COM-2019-562-F1-EN-MAIN-PART-1.PDF.
35 http://trade.ec.europa.eu/doclib/docs/2018/october/tradoc_157452.pdf.
36 https://ec.europa.eu/transparency/regdoc/rep/1/2019/EN/COM-2019-562-F1-EN-MAIN-PART-1.PDF.
37 Ibid, Figure 3.
38 Ibid.
39 www.leru.org/.
40 www.leru.org/news/leru-welcomes-the-recast-of-the-dual-use-regulation-but-requests-increased-clarity-over-its-scope.
41 www.leru.org/files/Publications/LERU-Dual-Use-Note-July-2018.pdf.
42 Email communication with the author, Feb. 13, 2020.
43 www.leru.org/files/Publications/LERU-Dual-Use-Note-July-2018.pdf.
44 Author's personal source in the EU, Nov. 2019.

Bibliography

Baker, Richard, and Nick McKenzie. "Chinese's Scientist Absence Exposed Alleged Spying Activities at CSIRO," *Sydney Morning Herald*, December 4, 2013.

Benson, Simon. "Crack Unit to Ward Off Threats from Espionage," *The Australian*, April 25, 2018.

Borys, Stephanie. "China's 'Brazen', Decade-Long Interference Outlined in Top-Secret Report," *ABC News*, May 29, 2018.

Bundesamt für Wirtschaft und Ausfuhrkontrolle (BAFA). *Homepage*. www.bafa.de/EN/Federal_Office/federal_office_node.html.

Chellel, Kit, Franz Wild, and David Stringer. "When Rio Tinto Met China's Iron Hand," *Bloomberg*, July 13, 2018.

Chen Weihua. "China, US Gradually Move to Manage Cyber Dispute," *China Daily*, September 14, 2015.

"Commentary: Wassenaar's Weakness," *Defense News*, January 26, 1997, p. 18.

Ernst, Dieter, "Indigenous Innovation and Its Effect on China's Semiconductor Industry," "East-West Center, 2012. www2.itif.org/2012-semiconductor-ernst.pdf.

European Union. *EU–China—A strategic outlook*, March 12, 2019. https://ec.europa.eu/commission/sites/beta-political/files/communication-eu-china-a-strategic-outlook.pdf.

European Union. *Regulation (EU) 2019/452 of the European Parliament and of the Council of 19 March 2019 Establishing a Framework for the Screening of Foreign Direct Investments into the Union*. https://eur-lex.europa.eu/eli/reg/2019/452/oj.

European Union. *Report from the Commission to the European Parliament and the Council on the Implementation of Regulation (EC) No 428/2009 Setting Up a Community Regime for the Control of Exports, Transfer, Brokering and Transit of Dual-Use Items*, November 4, 2019. https://ec.europa.eu/transparency/regdoc/rep/1/2019/EN/COM-2019-562-F1-EN-MAIN-PART-1.PDF.

European Union. *Twenty-First Annual Report of Council Common Position 2008, Defining Common Rules Governing the Control of Exports of Military Technology and Equipment*, December 30, 2019. https://eur-lex.europa.eu/legal-content/EN/TXT/?qid=15780600 03872&uri=OJ:JOC_2019_437_R_0001.

Fireeye. "APT1: Exposing One of China's Cyber Espionage Units," 2014, www.fireeye. com/content/dam/fireeye-www/services/pdfs/mandiant-apt1-report.pdf.

Grigg, Angus, et al. "CSIRO Spent Millions after Chinese Data Breach," *Australian Financial Review*, April 3, 2018.

Grigg, Angus and McKenzie, Nick. "Lowy Institute Hit by Chinese Hackers," *The Australian Financial Review*, December 3, 2018.

General Accounting Office. "DOD's Critical Technologies Lists Rarely Inform Export Control and Other Policy Decisions," GAO-06-793, July 2006.

Hamilton, Clive, with Alex Joske. *Silent Invasion: China's Influence in Australia*, Melbourne: Hardie Grant Books, March, 2018.

H.R.5515—John S. McCain National Defense Authorization Act for Fiscal Year 2019, www.congress.gov/bill/115th-congress/house-bill/5515/text.

Joske, Alex. *Picking Flowers, Making Honey*, Australian Strategic Policy Institute International Cyber Policy Centre, October 30, 2018.

Joske, Alex. "The Company with Aussie Roots That's Helping Build China's Surveillance State," *The Strategist*, August 25, 2019.

Kostin, Sergei, and Eric Reynaud. *Farewell: The Greatest Spy Story of the Twentieth Century*, Amazon Crossing, 2011.

League of European Research Universities. "LERU Welcomes the Recast of the Dual Use Regulation, But Requests Increased Clarity over Its Scope," July 4, 2018. www.leru.org/ news/leru-welcomes-the-recast-of-the-dual-use-regulation-but-requests-increased-clarity-over-its-scope.

League of European Research Universities. "The Dual Use Regulation—Specific Concerns from the Academic Sector, Full paper," July 2018. www.leru.org/files/Publications/ LERU-Dual-Use-Note-July-2018.pdf.

Lelyveld, Michael S. "US, High-Tech Group Synchronize Export Rules; 33 Nations Form Pact, Giving Them Wide Berth to Make High-Tech Deals," *Journal of Commerce*, January 20, 1998, p. 3A.

Lipson, Michael. "The Reincarnation of Cocom: Explaining Post-Cold War Export Controls," *The Nonproliferation Review/Winter*, 1999, p. 39.

McKenzie, Nick, et al. "Multimillion-Dollar Offer from Alleged Chinese Agent for a Prime Spot in CSIRO," *The Age*, November 25, 2019.

McNeill, Sophie, et al. "Australian Unis Linked to Surveillance and 'Racial Profiling' Tech Used by China," *ABC News*, July 16, 2019.

Ministers' Media Centre. Australian Government. "Taskforce to Protect Universities from Foreign Interference," Ministers' Media Centre, August 28, 2019.

Office of the Press Secretary, The White House. "Executive Order—'Blocking the Property of Certain Persons Engaging in Significant Malicious Cyber-Enabled Activities'," April 1, 2015. https://obamawhitehouse.archives.gov/the-press-office/2015/04/01/ executive-order-blocking-property-certain-persons-engaging-significant-m.

Office of the Press Secretary, The White House. "Fact Sheet: Announcing the Revised US Export Control System," October 15, 2013. https://obamawhitehouse.archives. gov/the-press-office/2013/10/15/fact-sheet-announcing-revised-us-export-control-system.

Office of the Press Secretary, The White House. "Readout of Senior Administration Officials' Meeting with Secretary of the Central Political and Legal Affairs Commission of the Communist Party of China Meng Jianzhu," September 12, 2015. https://obamawhitehouse. archives.gov/the-press-office/2015/09/12/readout-senior-administration-officials-meeting-secretary-central.

Office of Public Affairs, Department of Justice. "Attorney General Jeff Session's China Initiative Fact Sheet," November 1, 2018. www.justice.gov/opa/speech/file/1107256/download.

Office of Public Affairs, Department of Justice. "US Charges Five Chinese Military Hackers for Cyber Espionage Against US Corporations and a Labor Organization for Commercial Advantage First Time Criminal Charges Are Filed Against Known State Actors for Hacking," May 19, 2014. www.justice.gov/opa/pr/us-charges-five-chinese-military-hackers-cyber-espionage-against-us-corporations-and-labor.

Office of Public Affairs, Department of Treasury. "Summary of the Foreign Investment Risk Review Modernization Act of 2018." www.treasury.gov/resource-center/international/Documents/Summary-of-FIRRMA.pdf.

Packham, Ben. "Professor, Chinese Generals Co-Authored Defence Research," *The Australian*, July 31, 2019.

Packham, Ben. "UQ Researcher Probed over AI Uighur Surveil," *The Australian*, August 26, 2019.

Packham, Colin. "Exclusive: Australia Concluded China Was Behind Hack on Parliament, Political Parties—Sources," *Reuters*, September 16, 2019.

Safeworld. "Strengthening Dialogue between China and the Wassenaar Arrangement," June 2014. www.files.ethz.ch/isn/182707/strengthening-dialogue-between-china-and-the-wassenaar-arrangement.pdf.

Shields, Bevan. "ASIO Chief Duncan Lewis Sounds Fresh Alarm over Foreign Interference Threat," *The Sydney Morning Herald*, May 24, 2018.

Spetalnick, Matt and Martina, Michael. "Obama Announces 'Understanding' with China's Xi on Cyber Theft but Remains Wary," *Reuters*, September 25, 2015.

Stockholm International Peace Research Institute, SIPRI. *Arms Transfers Database.* www.sipri.org/databases/armstransfers.

Stricker, Andrea with Albright, David. "US Export Control Reform: Impacts and Implications for Controlling the Export of Proliferation-Sensitive Goods and Technologies, A Policy Document for the New President and Congress," Institute for Science and International Security, May 17, 2017.

Uhlmann, Chris. "China Blamed for 'Massive' Cyber Attack on BoM Computer," *ABC News*, December 2, 2015.

Uhlmann, Chris. "Chinese Firm's Takeover Plan Raises Concern in Canberra over Access to ADF Medical Records," *The Sydney Morning Herald*, August 12, 2019.

Wroe, David. "China 'Behind' Huge ANU Hack Amid Fears Government Employees Could Be Compromised," *The Sydney Morning Herald*, June 5, 2019.

Younglai, Rachelle. "Obama Blocks Chinese Wind Farms in Oregon over Security," *Reuters*, September 29, 2012.

CONCLUSION

William C. Hannas and Didi Kirsten Tatlow

As we have shown, foreign technology—transferred licitly, illicitly, and "by various means" (以多种方式)—fuels much of China's development, reducing the cost of research and shielding its Communist Party and government from the openness that democracies rely on to fuel innovation. Thanks to these transfer programs and to its own efforts, China can maintain parity or near-parity with advanced countries without the burdens of intellectual diversity. While anathema to widely accepted notions of creativity and research propriety, this mixed system of borrowing, theft, and indigenous development has been remarkably effective.

The fact that many of these transfers are legal, or cannot be easily traced or prevented, does not lessen their impact on the security and interests of donor nations. It was possible for decades to ignore these predations from a "developing" country, but China's emergence as a power on its own terms challenges the rest of the world in ways that are unfair, and dangerous to fundamental rights and protections. We see no signs of abatement. Given its success, why should there be?

The authors believe urgent policy measures are needed to reduce the hemorrhaging of national technology assets. We also wish to ensure—to the extent possible—that the positive aspects of engagement with China can flourish. These goals are hard to realize simultaneously, given the CPC's penchant for exploiting collaboration (a "zero-sum" mentality), then defusing the backlash with claims of victimhood. That said, we must also acknowledge that China's transfer programs could not operate without the complicity of foreign enablers—that is, ourselves.

Accordingly, we offer a collection of remedies suggested to us by academics, corporate leaders, think tank scholars, and officials in democratic nations over the past few years. These proposals are presented below in eight categories to support further discussion. Please refer to the chapters for more specific recommendations.

Standards

Standards should be created, and shared, to determine which technologies are critical to national and democratic interests. Normative criteria are needed to evaluate the impacts of restricting this or that transaction. Most such standards, often expressed as "critical technologies lists," are time dependent and need continuous updating. A few are likely to become permanent features, for example, inhibitions on research collaboration that bolsters China's domestic surveillance or its military industrial base.

Policy

Effective measures to manage China's technology predations presuppose a realignment in national policies toward China in general, reflecting that country's status as a technologically advanced nation and strategic competitor, not a "developing" country in need of a boost and certainly not a cooperating partner in a global order of liberal nations. While new laws and policies are needed, a theme we hear from people at the sharp end of mitigation is that real enforcement of existing laws would counter a lot of the problematic behavior.

Another policy goal should be incentivizing multinational companies to take account of the interests of their home country. Corporate advantage—and the whole area of "legal" transfers that has mostly been ignored in this study—need to be interpreted in a broader context, while hedging against the negative impact of overly restrictive measures on free exchange.

Scrutiny

No one entity in the US government, or anywhere in the world, is chartered continuously to monitor foreign technology transactions, despite their importance, and despite the fact that the problem can be studied almost entirely through open sources. The exception is China itself, which keeps close watch on technologies and transfer opportunities worldwide.[1]

We have discussed this matter with hundreds of civilian and military officials. Their informal view is that a permanent organization is needed within government—but outside the intelligence community—to monitor technology transfers, that is staffed with enough linguists, analysts, data scientists, and subject experts to identify problems and report them *before they occur.*

Although the practicality of this proposal has been demonstrated, the difficulty lies in mobilizing top-level support. Counterintelligence shops traditionally focus on PRC intelligence services, yet they play only a minor role in technology transfer based on the public record. Other US agencies are invested in collection paradigms that emphasize a particular method, not a particular problem. Budgets, when provided at all, are quickly dispersed to traditional targets.

Coordination

A centralized body, multi-agency "task force," or even a simple coalition of the willing needs support. In the United States, this falls on the intelligence agencies, departments of State and Defense, law enforcement, and non-Title 50 organizations (federal agencies not charged with intelligence missions, such as Commerce and Treasury). Coordinating their support is largely the provenance of the Director of National Intelligence (DNI) and, within that office, the National Counterintelligence and Security Center,[2] since the mission is too broad for any one agency.

Accordingly, our vote is to augment the DNI's authority and mission brief to cover this area adequately. That addresses half the problem. The other half involves the need to coordinate with like-minded nations grappling with China's unfair transfer practices, to avoid a whack-a-mole situation whereby mitigation in one country provokes more exploitation of another.

In Europe, we recommend creating a network of specialists at the member state and European Union level to raise analytic capabilities. These must be embedded in language and ethnographic knowledge, and a sound grasp of CPC politics. By sharing methodologies within Europe, and liaising internationally (see above), such a network would significantly support efforts to strengthen democracies and the international order. Funding could be drawn from, or connected to, augmented resources to protect democratic values and transparency in the EU.

Outreach

The US DNI, its associated agencies, and Western governments in general should step up current programs to alert public and private sectors to the risks of technology transactions with China by providing formal criteria on problematic interactions, creating tools to guide transacting parties,[3] and communicating "the scale and scope of problems caused by foreign influence in basic research."[4] Private firms not resourced to navigate China's political economy should be offered knowledge or information to help them make better risk assessments.

Penalties

We have three specific recommendations here, namely:

- Replace the indiscriminate tariffs currently proposed by the US government with targeted sanctions on foreign entities directly involved in technology misappropriation. Blacklist entities seeking critical host country technologies.
- Identify United Front-linked organizations and personnel engaged in talent co-option or foreign influence operations, monitor their activities, expose

their links publicly and, if necessary, criminalize the behavior as state-sponsored adversarial acts.

• Broaden the scope of the Foreign Agents Registration Act to include technical guilds, "talent" co-optees, and foreign transfer intermediaries serving foreign states. Bring in screening and identification mechanisms where they do not exist, such as in Europe.

Academic

Assuming a semblance of continuity in higher education after the coronavirus crisis of 2020, we should go on welcoming foreign students and researchers through positive immigration reforms, and by providing clear and reasonable criteria on acceptable behavior. After graduating, they should be encouraged to stay in the host country, assimilate, and help their new country prosper. At the same time, we support measures to minimize the transfer of critical technologies through national STEM programs and revising existing safeguards to focus on areas of real concern.[5]

Growth

Technology protection measures are useless without increased government and private investment in research and innovation. We must recognize, as has China, that S&T are national assets to be encouraged and protected, and fund it accordingly. At the same time, the S&T base must be grown to avoid a zero-sum struggle. Neither mitigation nor immigration can substitute for positive efforts to expand a country's S&T infrastructure and the skills of the citizens who comprise it. National and local governments should consider broad measures to facilitate access to STEM programs for people marginalized by geography, poverty, and ethnicity.

And finally, we offer a suggestion that may be helpful especially within a global context: researchers who, out of naivety, are "double-dipping," but are prepared to change their behavior, should be allowed a chance to declare their activity, abandon it, and continue to live normally in the host countries which are their homes. While the details need to be carefully managed, we believe this clemency-based approach deserves consideration for humane reasons. Yet generosity must be met with sincerity; action must be worked out within individual legal jurisdictions; and backsliding must be fairly prosecuted. Needless to say, our proposal does not extend to people who deliberately break existing rules or laws, or engage in espionage.

We offer these recommendations in good faith. Our goal is to draw attention to chronic imbalances in China's global S&T relationships, so that concerned people can begin to restore normalcy and work to maintain democratic norms and open society traditions. Technology has always driven human development. If our future is tied to science, the world expects no less.

Notes

1 See Chapter 2, "China's Use of Open Sources," in Hannas, et al., *Chinese Industrial Espionage*, 2013.
2 www.dni.gov/index.php/ncsc-home.
3 Two examples spring instantly to mind: 1. See Chapter 18, a plea by European universities for *a tool to assess research collaboration risk.* 2. The "China Defence Universities Tracker" of ASPI should be continuously updated, expanded, and become a standard reference tool. See www.aspi.org.au/report/china-defence-universities-tracker This model can also be applied to Chinese companies.
4 Gordon Long. "Fundamental Research Security." JASON research paper JSF-19–21, December 2019, p. 2.
5 "(T)he scope of expectations under the umbrella of research integrity should be expanded to include full disclosure of commitments and actual or potential conflicts of interest." Ibid., p. 3.

APPENDIX

Glossary of terms

111 Project　111 计划

863 Program　863 计划

973 Program　973 计划

All-China Youth Federation (ACYF)　中华全国青年联合会（全国青联

All-Chinese Federation of Returned Overseas Chinese (ACFROC)　中华全国归国华侨联合会（中国侨联)

All-Japan Federation of Overseas Chinese Professionals　中国留日同学总会

Association of Chinese-American Scientists and Engineers (ACSE)　旅美中国科学家工程师专业人士协会

Association of Chinese Chemists and Chemical Engineers in Germany (GCCCD　中国旅德学者化学化工学会

Association of Chinese Scientists and Engineers in Japan (ACSEJ)　在日中国科学技术者联盟

Association of Wenzhou Ph.D.s USA　全美温州博士协会

Austria-China International Economic and Trade Promotion Association (OECGIW)　奥中国际经济贸易促进会

Belt and Road Initiative (BRI)　一带一路倡议

CAST-FCPAE European (Belgium) Base for Entrepreneurship and Innovation　中国科协-FCPAE 欧洲 (比利时) 海智创新创业基地

CAST-FCPAE European (Switzerland) Life Sciences Haizhi Double Innovation Base　中国科协-FCPAE欧洲生命科学 (瑞士) 海智创新创业基地

Center for China and Globalization (CCG)　中国与全球化智库

Central Committee of the Communist Party of China 中国共产党中央委员会（中共中央,党中央,中央)

Central Political and Legal Affairs Commission 中央政法委员会

Central Talent Work Coordination Group 中央人才工作协调小组

Changjiang Scholars Award Program 长江学者奖励计划

China Association for Science and Technology (CAST) 中国科学技术协会

China–Britain AI Association 中英人工智能协会

China Council for the Promotion of Peaceful National Reunification 中国和平统一促进会

China Defense Science and Technology Information Center (CDSTIC) 中国国防科技信息中心

China Development Bank (CDB) 国家开发银行

China Electronics Technology Group Corporation (CETC) 中国电子科技集团公司

China Institute for Command and Control (CICC) 中国指挥与控制学会

China International Talent Exchange Association (CAIEP) 中国国际人才交流协会

China International Talent Exchange Centre 中国国际人才交流中心

China International Talent Exchange Foundation 中国国际人才交流基金会

China International Technology Transfer Center 中国国际技术转移中心

China Investment Corporation (CIC) 中国投资公司

China–Italy Technology Transfer Center (CITTC) 中意技术转移中心

China–Japan Association for Artificial Intelligence 中日人工智能协会

China–Japan Large-scale Flagship Projects Joint Research Plan 中日大型旗舰项目的联合研究计划

China–Japan Technology Cooperation Affairs Center 中日技术合作事务中心

China–Japan University Exhibition and Forum 中日大学展暨中日大学论坛

China–Korea Artificial Intelligence Exchange Center 中韩人工智能交流中心

China Manufacturing 2025 (see Made in China 2025) 中国制造 2025

China-Republic of Korea Friendship Association 中国韩国友好协会

China Research and Sakura Science Center 中国研究与樱花科技中心

China Science and Technology Exchange Center 中国科学技术交流中心

China–Sweden Life Science Association 中瑞生命科学协会

China–Switzerland International Technology Transfer Center (CSITTC) 中瑞技术转移中心

Chinese Academy of Engineering (see CAE) 中国工程院

Chinese Academy of Sciences (CAS) 中国科学院

Chinese American Association of Greater Chicago Area　大芝加哥地区华侨华人联合会

Chinese Association for Cross Strait Relations in Austria　奥地利华人海峡两岸关系促进会

Chinese Association for Science and Technology USA　中国留美科技协会

Chinese Association of Professionals in Science and Technology　中国旅美专家协会

Chinese Entrepreneurs Japan　全日本中国留学人员创新创业协会

Chinese Institute of Engineers USA　美洲中国工程师学会

Chinese Microsoft Employees Association　微软华人协会

Chinese People's Political Consultative Conference (CPPCC)　中国人民政治协商会议

Chinese Student and Scholar Associations (CSSAs)　中国学生学者联谊会or中国学生学者联合会

Chunhui Cup　春晖杯

Chunhui Plan (Spring Light/Sunshine Plan)　春晖计划

Commission for Science, Technology and Industry for National Defense (COSTIND)　国防科学技术工业委员会

Committee of 100　百人会

Communist Party of China (CPC)　中国共产党

Department of Foreign Expert Services　外国专家服务司

Department of International Cooperation　国际合作司

Department of Overseas Intellectual Resources Cooperation　引进国外智力管理司

Federation of Associations of Chinese Professionals in Southern USA　美南中国专家协会联合会

Federation of Chinese Professional Associations in Europe (FCPAE)　全欧华人专业协会联合会

Federation of Chinese Student and Scholar Societies in Germany (CASD)　中国留德学者学生团体联合会

Foreign Talent Research Center　国外人才研究中心

French–Chinese Association of Science and Technology　全法中国科技工作者协会

German–Chinese Association of Artificial Intelligence (GCAAI)　德中人工智能协会

Gesellschaft Chinesischer Informatiker in Deutschland　中国留德学者计算机学会

Gesellschaft Chinesischer Physiker in Deutschland　留德中国物理学者学会

Haizhi Plan　海智计划

High-end Foreign Experts Recruitment Plan　高端外国专家引进计划

HOME Program (Help Our Motherland through Elite Intellectual Resources from Overseas Program, see Haizhi Plan)　海外智力为国服务行动计划（海智计划)

Homeland-Serving Action Plan for Overseas Chinese 海外赤子为国服务行动（赤子计划)

Hundred Talents Plan 百人计划

Innovation Service Centers 创业服务中心

Innovation Service Centers for New and High Technology 高新技术创业服务中心

Institute of Scientific and Technical Information of China (ISTIC) 中国科学技术信息研究所

International Cooperation Bureau 国际合作局

Japan–China Innovation Centre 日中创新研究院, 日中イノベーションセンター

Japan–China Science, Technology, and Culture Center 日中科学技术文化中心

Japan Chinese Society of Automotive Engineers (JCSAE) 在日华人汽车工程师协会

Japan Haizhi Innovation and Entrepreneur Base 日本海智创新创业基地建设

Japanese International Cooperation Agency (JICA) 日本国際協力機構

Japanese New Overseas Chinese Association 日本新华侨华人会

Japan Science and Technology Agency (JST) 日本科学技術振興機構

Jiangsu Center of International Technology Transfer 江苏省跨国技术转移中心

KH Innovation Institute 鲲海创新研究院

Korea–China Science & Technology Cooperation Center 韩中科学技术合作中心

Korea Innovation Center in China (KIC) 在华韩国创新中心

Made in China 2025 中国制造 2025

Microsoft Research Asia (MSRA) 微软亚洲学院

Military Science Information Research Center (MSIRC) 军事科学信息研究中心

Ministry of Commerce (MOFCOM) 商务部

Ministry of Education (MOE) 教育部

Ministry of Human Resources and Social Security (MOHRSS) 人力资源社会保障部（人社部)

Ministry of Finance (MOF) 财政部

Ministry of Industry and Information Technology (MIIT) 工业和信息化部

Ministry of Personnel (MOP, see MOHRSS) 人社部

Ministry of Science and Technology (MOST) 科学技术部

Ministry of State Security (MSS) 国家安全部（国安部)

National Basic Research Program (see 973 Program) 国家重点基础研究发展规划

National Defense S&T Industry Technology Research Applications Center 国防科技工业技术研究应用中心

National Development and Reform Commission (NDRC) 国家发展和改革委员会（国家发展改革委)

National Engineering Laboratory for Brain-inspired Intelligence Technology and Application 类脑智能技术及应用国家工程实验室（NEL-BITA(

National High Technology Research and Development Plan (see 863 Program) 国家高技术研究发展计划

National Natural Science Foundation of China (NSFC) 国家自然科学基金委员会

National Technology Transfer Center (NTTC) 国家技术转移中心

New Generation AI Innovation Development Experimental Zones 新一代人工智能创新发展试验区

Next Generation AI Open Research and Education Platform 新一代人工智能开放科研与教育平台

North American Chinese Scholars International Exchange Center 北美洲中国学人国际交流中心

Official Development Assistance (ODA) 政府開発援助

Overseas Chinese Affairs Office (OCAO) 侨务办公室

Overseas Chinese Scholars (OCS) Pioneer Parks 留学人员创业园

Overseas Chinese Science and Technology Organization Federation (OCSTOF) 海外华人科技组织联合会

Overseas-Educated Scholars Association of China 中国留学人员联谊会

Overseas-Educated Scholars Development Foundation 中国留学人才发展基金会

Overseas High-level Talent Introduction Program (see Thousand Talents Plan) 海外高层次人才引进计划 (千人计划)

Overseas Scholar Returnee Service Alliance 留学人员回国服务联盟

Overseas Scholar Returnee Service Workstations 海外留学人员回国服务工作站

People's Bank of China (PBOC) 中国人民银行

Politburo Standing Committee 政治局常委

Project of Introducing Talents of Academic Disciplines to Universities (see 111 Project) 高等学校学科创新引智计划

Promotion Association for Scientific and Technological Cooperation between Austria and China 奥中科技交流协会(PASCO)

Red Boat Cup 红船杯

Sakura Science Plan (Cherry Blossom Plan) 樱花科技计划

Seattle Chinese Biomedical Association (SCBA) 西雅图华人生物医学协会

Service Center for S&T Personnel Exchange and Development 科技人才交流开发服务中心

Silicon Valley Chinese Engineers Association (SCEA) 硅谷华人工程师协会

Silk Road Economic Belt and 21st Century Maritime Silk Road (See BRI) 丝绸之路经济带和 21 世纪海上丝绸之路

Sino-America Biotechnology and Pharmaceutical Professional Association (SABPA) 美中生物技术与制药专业协会

Sino-European Innovation Institute 中欧创新中心

Sino-Japanese Young Scientist Exchange Plan 中日青年科技人员交流计划

Society for German Professors of Chinese Origin (GDPCH) 德国华人教授学会

Society of Chinese–American Aerospace Engineers 美华航太工程师协会

Spring Light Plan 春晖计划

State Administration of Foreign Exchange (SAFE) 国家外汇管理局

State Administration of Foreign Expert Affairs (SAFEA) 国家外国专家局

State Administration of Science & Technology Industry for National Defense (SASTIND) 国家国防科技工业局

State Council (SC) 国务院

Ten Thousand Talents Plan 万人计划

Thousand Talents Plan (TTP) 千人计划

Thousand Talents Venture Capital Center 千人计划创投中心

TTP Expert Association 千人计划专家联谊会

Union of Chinese Residing in Japan 全日本华侨华人联合会

United Front Work Department (UFWD) 统一战线工作部（统战部)

University of Washington Chinese Students and Scholars Association 华盛顿大学中国学生学者联谊会

US–China Association of High-Level Professionals (UCAHP) 美中高层次人才交流协会

US–Zhejiang Innovation Center 美国浙江创新中心

Verein der Chinesischen Wissenschaftler und Studenten in Aachen 亚琛学生学者联合会

Western Returned Scholars Association (WRSA) 欧美同学会

Whampoa Military Academy 黄埔军校

Xi'an Hi-Tech Industries Development Zone 西安高新技术产业开发区

Yellow Crane Cup 黄鹤杯

ZGC Innovation Center @ Silicon Valley 中关村硅谷创新中心

Zhigong Party (Public Interest Party) 致公党

INDEX

Page numbers in **bold** denote tables, those in *italics* denote figures.